THE MASTER BUILDER

WILLIAM BUTTERFIELD

and his times

West Elevation

THE MASTER BUILDER

WILLIAM BUTTERFIELD

and his times

NICHOLAS OLSBERG

Photographs by JAMES MORRIS

LUND
HUMPHRIES

CONTENTS

PROLOGUE   7

I

PAST AND PRESENT

CHAPTER 1
THE CHURCH REVIVAL, 1843–54   12

CHAPTER 2
THE MISSIONARY CATHEDRAL, 1847–53   27

CHAPTER 3
'CHA TILL MI TUILLEADH', 1848–78   35

II

'PAROCHIALIA'

CHAPTER 4
THE NEW PARISH SOCIAL SYSTEM, 1845–51   44

CHAPTER 5
'CHURCH EXTENSION,' 1845–57   55

• Simplification: Five Country Parishes   70

CHAPTER 6
THE FLOWERING OF THE
COUNTRY SCHOOL, 1857–73   82

III

'THE HEARTH, THE ALTAR, AND THE GRAVE'

CHAPTER 7
'SETTING APART', 1854–71   94

• Ideal Village and Minimal Church   108

CHAPTER 8
RECUPERATION OF THE PARISH
CHURCH, 1847–73   120

CHAPTER 9
'ARREARS OF NEGLECT', 1865–84   130

IV

OVERGROWN TOWNS

CHAPTER 10
'THE CLASSES AND THE MASSES':
LONDON, 1850–70   142

• Precincts of London   156

CHAPTER 11
'NORTH AND SOUTH', 1848–65   168

CHAPTER 12
FRESH AIR: RESORT AND COUNTRY
SUBURB, 1845–91   177

V

'THE WAY WE LIVE NOW'

CHAPTER 13
SOCIAL HYGIENE AND CIVIC ORDER, 1857–76   194

• Coal and Cotton, Brick and Stone   208

CHAPTER 14
THE CHURCH AS CIVIC LANDMARK, 1870–96   220

CHAPTER 15
IMPERIAL LONDON AND ITS ORBIT, 1872–92   233

VI

CHARACTER BUILDING

CHAPTER 16
LIBERAL EDUCATION: RUGBY, 1867–85   248

• Modernity and Motion: Rugby School   258

CHAPTER 17
PHYSICAL DISCIPLINE AND MENTAL
CULTIVATION: RUGBY, 1865–85   268

CHAPTER 18
THE EXPANSIVE SCHOOL, 1858–86   276

VII

FELLOWSHIP, DISCIPLINE, DUTY

CHAPTER 19
SELF GOVERNMENT, 1874–92   290

• Common Ground   302

CHAPTER 20
'TO OXFORD': UNIVERSITY EXPANSION
AND REFORM, 1857–64   314

• 'A Community of Feeling': Keble College   322

CHAPTER 21
'PLAIN LIVING AND HIGH THINKING':
KEBLE COLLEGE, 1867–82   334

VIII

REFUGE, REFRESHMENT, REPOSE

CHAPTER 22
COTTAGE, LODGE AND COUNTRY
RETREAT, 1853–90   354

• Art and Craft of Rural Living   364

CHAPTER 23
'FOR THE SOLACE OF HIS SICK POOR':
CHEDDAR HOSPITAL, 1875–84   376

CHAPTER 24
RETREAT AND COMMEMORATION:
HEATH'S COURT, 1878–82   386

• Repose: Ottery St Mary   398

EPILOGUE : REGENERATION, 1884–94   408

Readings   418   Image Credits   421   Index   422

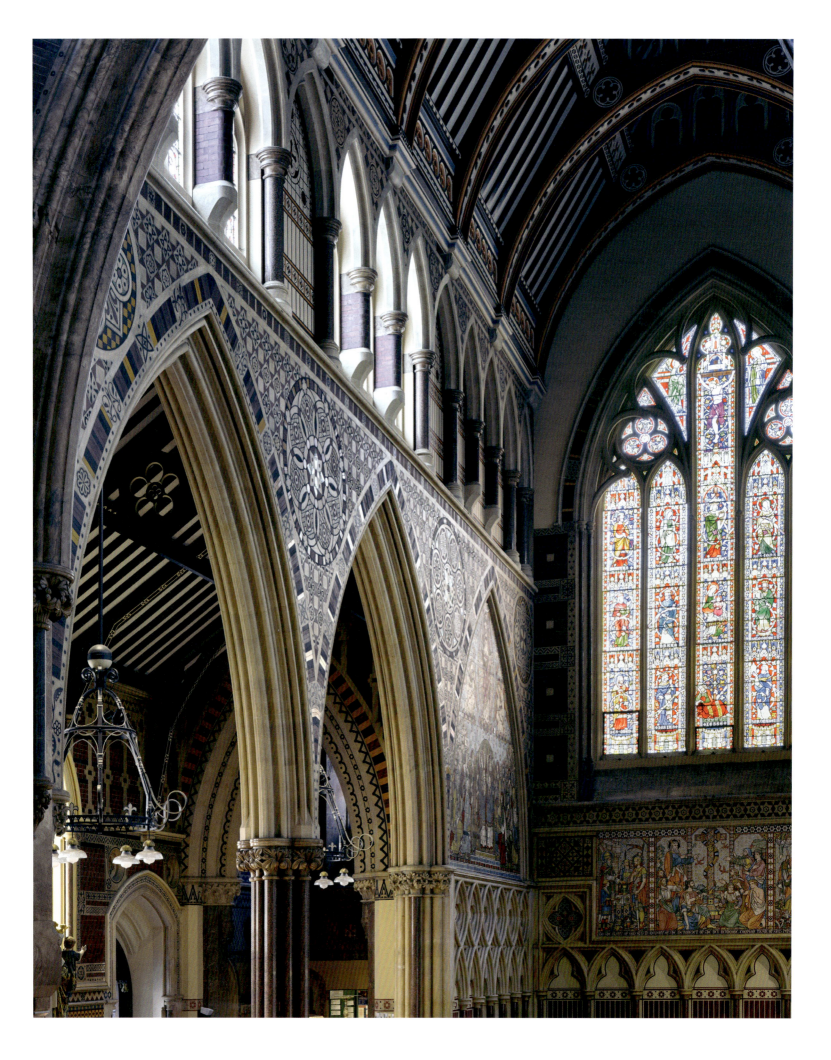

PROLOGUE

ARRIVED AT RUGBY SCHOOL in 1956. It was the summer of the future. Of 'Howl' and 'Heartbreak Hotel'. The first Citroën DS appearing on city streets. 'This Is Tomorrow' and the 'House of the Future'. A child of the Blitz, I was building mad, and when I had days to myself, I would bike to Coventry and watch the promise of a clean and well-lit new life arise in the horizontal layers of the Precincts, the Baths and Belgrade Square, although the first glimmers of a new cathedral that looked suspiciously like Butterfield's brick turned unnaturally to stone left me quite unmoved.

I delighted through my boyhood in looking up at the canyons of brick and terracotta in Manchester. So I warmed only very slowly to the tamer tones of the sturdy past, the demure, provincial, fussy faces of Butterfield's Rugby. But after five years turning through his concrete stairs, lining up in his cloister, playing fives in his courts, jumping in his gym and sitting under the brilliant windows of his chapel, classrooms and library, they achieved their purpose as character-shaping agents. I could finally grasp their endless oddities of conjunction and incident, discern the unity that underlies variety and train my eye to attend with care to the haptic fascinations of their surface. I came secretly (for it would have been shameful to confess) to love them all; would arrive early for Sunday evensong to watch the light come through the claws of the chapel apse; and spared no chance to wander the Temple Reading Room alone and sit with a book beside its great marble heart as the western light faded through the leaded windows.

It was an astonishing library, where I found Engels's *Origin of the Family* and Hegel's *Philosophy of History*, along with a proud treasure trove of Rugby's liberal poets and thinkers, from Arthur Hugh Clough and Matthew Arnold to T.H. Green, R.H. Tawney and R.G. Collingwood. And it was their thinking – especially of the three last, as I understood them – that built the optic through which I have looked at works of art, at states of

society and at the means to read the past: Green's material idealism, so closely akin to Butterfield's intentions, in which there is an absolute truth to be reached through the exercise of concentration that finds the metaphysics of the physical; the insistence of Tawney on recovering the ethical and cooperative health of society from the moral diseases of inequality, property, competition and greed; and Collingwood's plea to see the past first through the hoard of evidence that it has left for us to sort and interpret and then through learning by transference the otherness of a former age, so that we may better make sense of the present. Those were the happy highways where I went, and these the settings that shaped me. So this book in fond homage is an attempt to comprehend Butterfield's works, in their times, as a hoard of our history and an expression of our ever-changing mind.

In the same spirit, I chose to consider and illustrate the works strictly within the visual context of their own times: first as they were conceived and constructed, through examples of the contract drawings that initiated the building process (and, in the rare instances where Butterfield allowed, perspective prints of proposed designs); then as the built works were first recorded, by magazine illustrators and printmakers and by such early souvenir and survey photographers as James Valentine, Henry William Taunt and Francis Frith; and finally as seen, largely unaltered but now in the maturing landscapes and conditions which Butterfield's design anticipated, in the picture postcards that circulated recent architecture to a vast popular audience in the first two decades of the twentieth century. Colour studies by James Morris, taken between 2017 and 2023, show a selection of works as we found them in our own time, looking particularly at colour, texture, incident, vista and the passage of light. By bringing them into dialogue we surprised ourselves by discovering how markedly and differently each work asserts a character of its own.

OPPOSITE:
All Saints'
Margaret Street

7

Jane Fortescue
Coleridge, *William
Butterfield*, black chalk
life-size portrait, 1874

I reference the imaginative literature of the age
only occasionally, but storytellers of Butterfield's
generation like the Trollope of the Barsetshire
Chronicles and the Thackeray of *Pendennis* and
The Newcomes, those of the next, like Charlotte
M. Yonge in her *Daisy Chain*, *Pillars of the House*
and *Mother Carey's Brood*, and writers of the late
Victorian era like W.E. Henley and George Gissing
have all been trusted guides to manners, morals and
mind. To Yonge especially I owe a better sense of
the effectiveness and centrality of the revived parish
in late Victorian society, through her unforgettably
varied portraits of the children and women to
whose use or service so much of this architectural
invention was addressed, and her overriding notion
of individual agency – that 'we are not here to mould
people but to help them mould themselves' – and
of unity achieved from individuality. We hear the
voices – on the state of Church, education and
society and on the qualities of architecture – of three
clerical friends with whom Butterfield worked, John
Sandford, Archibald Tait and Frederick Temple;
and on the metaphorical structure and poetics of
Butterfield's works I turn often to the young Gerard
Manley Hopkins, who analysed them intensely, lived
with them daily at Oxford and admired them for a

time extravagantly, expressing ideas akin to theirs in
his reinventions of a spiritual and lyrical language.
I owe a similar debt to the impossibly eloquent
memorial essay on Butterfield by the architect
Halsey Ricardo, who knew and cared for Butterfield
through his last years, especially in recognising and
conjuring up the sheer excitement of his work. 'I have
reverenced Butterfield's work since I was a schoolboy
at Rugby, and my amazement at his power and the
intensity of his romantic poetry of feeling increases as
the years pass by,' he wrote in a public letter ten years
later: 'The astounding majesty of the narthex at St
Albans, High Holborn, and the inexplicable beauty
of the nave arcades of All Saints, Margaret Street, to
take two London instances, compel one to shout and
to cry at the same moment. How the conviction of the
man burns through all he did.'[1]

A similar sense of intensity is captured in the
words of the intemperate Ian Nairn who, looking as
late as 1966 at All Saints' Margaret Street, concludes
that 'This building can only be understood in terms
of compelling passion. Here is the force of Wuthering
Heights translated into dusky red and black bricks,
put down in a mundane Marylebone street to rivet
you, pluck you into the courtyard with its hard
welcoming wings and quivering steeple.'[2] Nairn was
writing at a time when the view of Butterfield was still
coloured for many by a received opinion that it was
the subject of violent hostility or complete neglect. In
fact, the reputation and status of Butterfield was often
contradictory, but he never quite disappeared. From
the moment of his first departures from orthodoxy
in the 1850s to the time of his death in 1900, he was
held up variously as the leader of a new school or an
eccentric up a creek on his own, and his obituaries
veer drastically between admiration and scorn, and
between those which claim his only good work was
of a long-gone era and those whose admiration
focuses on the work of the 1870s. By the 1920s, he
may have been little regarded, but by the 1930s his
drawings for Rugby parish church were celebrated
in the great anniversary exhibition of the Royal
Institute of British Architects (RIBA).

At about the same time the first demolition of
a Butterfield church took place, in Leeds in August
1938. Between 1957 and 1973, other major works

would fall to the wrecking ball at Edmonton, Portsmouth, Rotherhithe, Regent's Park and Weybridge. Yet discussion of his work was now abundant. The long essay of 1954 by Henry-Russell Hitchcock which concludes his enormous study of early Victorian architecture presents Butterfield and John Ruskin together as the protagonists, by the end of the 1850s, of an entirely new aesthetic (a judgement with which I agree, though by the work of the mid-1860s Butterfield has clearly left Ruskin far behind). He appears in radio talks by Nikolaus Pevsner and John Summerson and on television and film with Reyner Banham and John Betjeman. Above all, an article by Summerson in 1945 on the 'glory of ugliness' introduced Butterfield's severity as a call to arms for a new movement that would form, perhaps unacknowledged, around the Smithsons' concept of Brutalism and, very directly referenced, in Gerhard Kallmann's 'The Action Architecture of a New Generation' of 1959. By the time Peter Collins reviewed the plans for Boston City Hall, in 1963, he could use Butterfield as a readily recognisable point of reference, describing its asymmetry, colliding volumes and shifting heights as 'William Butterfield raised to the terrifying dimensions of the atomic age', and Butterfield rapidly became viewed as the spiritual progenitor of such confrontational works as James Stirling's Florey Building in Oxford and History Faculty Library in Cambridge, and Paul Rudolph's Yale Architecture school.[3]

With Paul Thompson's temperate, wise and comprehensive monograph of 1971 such discussions could finally be informed by the documentary record, and a book like the present one would be unimaginable without Thompson's research. By the 1990s there were historiographical essays relating this quiet and markedly unrebellious architect to the evolution of all manner of radical movements, and a figure like Archigram's Peter Cook could readily and knowledgeably adapt Butterfield's precedents for his Engineering building at Leicester's De Montfort University. It is wonderful to think that a design revolution in one epoch can return to light the flames of other forward adventures more than a century later.

In selecting the works here, from a much larger corpus explored, I have often favoured those with the most illuminating surviving imagery from the time, especially through the core of contract drawings, which, while divided by accidents of descent into different collections, were all conceived, corrected and touched by his hand, true to an eye that envisioned with precision on a single plane at a steady scale the recession, colour, light and texture of space and volume.

I have focused on built works, especially in the British Isles, where he could learn the site and oversee construction and fittings. All of the new town churches have been introduced in some form; while the country schools, parsonages and churches have been addressed by example; and discussion of restorations has been confined to a small number (out of an enormous body) that seemed to best illustrate the social and cultural importance of the parish church and the variety of approaches to reconstruction and repair.

The general trajectory begins with the uses of history and national memory in the formulation of work to answer modern needs; turns to childhood and the countryside to trace the Church revival in rural society; explores the changing world of city and town through the length of the Victorian age; and then addresses the progress of adult life from the quiet revolution in secondary education, training and the construction of community among the middle class to patterns of living in retreat and repose and to the memorialising of the dead.

It has been a lovely voyage, and I hope you enjoy following me as we shadow Butterfield's journey through his times.

NOTES

1. Halsey Ricardo, quoted in a report in *Architect and Contract Reporter*, vol.83, 1910, pp 129–30 and 145–7 on a discussion at the Architectural Association about E. Swinfen Harris's article 'The Life and Work of William Butterfield'.
2. Ian Nairn, revisited by Peter Gasson, *Nairn's London*, Penguin, London, 1988, p.77 (first published 1966).
3. Citations are from Elain Harwood, 'Butterfield and Brutalism', *AAFiles*, Summer 1994, pp 39–46, and Timothy Rohan, 'Instrumentalizing Ugliness: Parallels between High Victorian and Brutalist Architecture', in Wouter Van Acker and Thomas Mical (eds), *Architecture and Ugliness: Anti Aesthetics and the Ugly in Postmodern Architecture*, Bloomsbury, London, 2020, pp 59–76.

I PAST *and* PRESENT

CHAPTER 1

THE CHURCH REVIVAL, 1843–54

THE VIGIL OF ST PETER

EARLY ON 29 June 1848, some 1200 men and women travelled to Canterbury for a signal event in the transformation of Victorian society. They represented the growing movement to revive the Church of England as a corporate instrument for the awakening of conscience; the alleviation of vice, ignorance and poverty; and the restoration of a reverential and inclusive character to a Church grown increasingly careless of its liturgy, its fabric and its duty to the poor. The occasion was the dedication of a new clerical college built within the ruins of England's earliest missionary abbey of St Augustine, in which the aspirations of a revived national Church were seen to be grounded in its ancestral history, and where the scattered, often lonely and sometimes reviled protagonists of this cause were brought together in the light of day.

There was a gasp when the first name called to the chancel of the great cathedral was that of the poet, scholar and priest John Keble, now inhibited by his bishop, whose call to reverse the 'national apostasy' ten years earlier had lit the flame of the Church revival.

As they boarded a special train from the south-eastern terminal at London Bridge, dispatches had been coming in on the Dover trains with reports from the barricades of Paris on the bloody suppression of the workers' uprising that had just taken the life of its archbishop; and some of the joy of the Canterbury occasion derived from the contrast between a continent riven with upheaval and the unexpected quiet that had descended on Britain with the dissipation three months before of the Chartist movement that had threatened revolution in Britain in its attempt to extend the rights and liberties of the working people. 'While other governments were falling, and war and terror raged all over Europe,' wrote the novelist Charlotte Yonge, 'the machinations of the disaffected in Britain were overthrown with scarce the shedding of a drop of blood.'[1] There were many forces at work in the general improvement of national well-being in the half century that followed, but the revival of a corporate Church with a sense of duty to the people was a vital contributor to that general trend, and one of the least expected. As the warden of St Augustine's College, Canterbury, wrote in 1888:

> If fifty years ago anyone had said that from a state of comparative lethargy and torpor the English Church would have been raised to her present position, that her Cathedrals would be restored, her ancient Churches in towns and villages reappear in something of their former beauty, her National and Sunday schools be extended to every hamlet, her Guilds and Sisterhoods be multiplied, her numerous Agencies for relieving the sick and the distressed be seen, who would have credited his prediction?[2]

The story of the college began in September 1843, when the surgeon Robert Brett of Stoke Newington joined a friend on an architectural pilgrimage to Canterbury. Visiting the remains of the great abbey, among the oldest sites in Christendom, they found that the apartments adjoining the gateway were an alehouse, the gateway a brewhouse, the court a bowling green, the chapel a fives court, and the room over the gate a cockpit. Noting that the site might shortly be for sale, a plan emerged that would unite the recovery of the old abbey with an idea long advocated by the Eton tutor Edward Coleridge to create a college for a new generation of Anglican clergy, drawn from many backgrounds and equipped to extend the Church into the outposts of a widening empire and the suddenly overgrown towns of what were called 'our great manufacturing and mining districts'.[3]

Brett was, like Butterfield, an adherent of the high-church Margaret Chapel in London's Fitzrovia, and, with Butterfield, one of thirteen laymen who pledged themselves in June of 1842 to an 'Engagement'. This was a secret confraternity under the spiritual guidance of John Keble, dedicated to self-denial, to the silent use of private wealth to advance public interests, and to advancing moral, physical and religious progress among the people through the instrument of the Church. This vision of a land and people guided by a newly animated national Church, recently enunciated by the future prime minister William Gladstone in a famous essay on Church and state,[4] would provide the impulse for the creation over the next decade of a panoply of social institutions associated – often to the alarm of a populace readily aroused to detect the odour of popery – with the Catholic revival in the Church; and to build the most novel of these endeavours, this movement turned again and again to the earnest and inventive Butterfield. As one after another he brought forth designs for new institutions for which there were no modern precedents, his work was guided by such a firmly established knowledge of medieval art and architecture that we find in all his works, however novel, echoes of past principle that lend them an air of permanence.

The Engagement weakened as decisions of the Church authorities and courts drove many of those leading the Catholic revival to Rome. But for those who stayed within the Anglican fold the associations and deep friendships built around a shared earnestness about moral and spiritual matters endured. That intimacy and sympathy between Butterfield and the progenitors of the Church revival accounts for his sudden appearance on the scene in 1843 at the age of twenty-nine, after twelve obscure years in the building trade. With very little work on the ground or in print, he became architect to both of the two great societies advancing the cause of a new Christian architecture, undertaking on their behalf signal projects of recording and restoring exemplary medieval churches and producing model designs for all manner of church instruments, from communion plate and altar tables to country schools and cemetery chapels.

Well-noticed and pioneering new country buildings by Butterfield appeared as the Canterbury work began – a school at Jedburgh in the Scottish

Borders, a parsonage and school at Wilmcote in Shakespeare's Arden and a model country church and vicarage near Bristol. In the next five years, as his rural interventions extended, came a flood of more ambitious architectural projects for the fledgling Church revival: the first new cathedrals of the industrial age, at Perth in central Scotland and Fredericton in the Canadian province of New Brunswick; a pro-cathedral and ecclesiastical college for the Scottish Isles; experimental colleges for the poor at Harrow Weald, north-west of London; the first convents of the English Church in London and Plymouth; and three extraordinary prototypes for introducing the Church 'among the millions', in Leeds, Huddersfield and the artisan suburbs north of London. Then, when the congregation of the Margaret Chapel decided to advance its Engagement by building a model church to demonstrate a sacred architecture fit for the times, he squeezed into a tiny plot, amid the warren of commerce and common lodgings crowding the borders of the West End, a dumbfoundingly ingenious and impressive precinct of choir school, clergy house and church that became the lasting monument to the spirit of the Oxford movement.

ST AUGUSTINE'S COLLEGE, CANTERBURY

In April 1844, the ruins of St Augustine's Abbey were purchased by the 24-year-old Alexander Hope – son of the great art patron Thomas Hope – who was one of the three undergraduate founders of the Ecclesiological Society in Cambridge and now Member of Parliament for Maidstone. William Hart Coleridge, retired bishop of Barbados, agreed to lead the committee to develop the scope and rules of the college, now devoted strictly to training clergy for overseas missions; fundraising for the restoration, led by Edward Coleridge, was in full swing; and the 30-year-old William Butterfield, then official architect of the Ecclesiological Society, was engaged to design the new institution, with Hope, as proprietor of the property, supervising planning and building.[5] He and Butterfield made their first

site survey together in January 1845, and over a number of further study visits to Canterbury, to tile makers in Staffordshire and to local masons and stone yards, a general scheme of building evolved. It called for accommodation for fifty students, lodgings for five fellows, a warden's residence and a servants' building, with ground reserved for expansion. By October 1845, works were well under way, and at the end of the year, with £39,000 in hand towards building, furnishing and endowment, an opening date of autumn 1846 was projected. After long delays, due to exceptionally bad winters and contractors' difficulties retaining a workforce, the project was finally completed in the spring of 1848, and 'a new life seemed to come out of the old shadows that lay so long over and around the ruins'.

The first popular illustrated weekly, *Illustrated London News*, prepared a number of views for a double-page spread on the college at its opening. One (fig.2) shows the entrance front, with the end wall, steep shed roof and window piercings of the long new dormitory range and cloister. To the right of it are the great gatehouse of 1301–9, now spotlessly restored, with the old porter's lodge; the monastic guest hall, now restored for college dining, with kitchen and staff quarters below it; the small medieval guest oratory, now tripled in size, as Butterfield extended it east to become the college chapel; and last, rising four and then three storeys under a steeply pitched double roof, behind a walled yard, an entirely new warden's house and fellows' lodgings, to which a third, larger and simpler three-storey 'native wing' would be added twelve years later.

Another view (fig.3) stood readers at the corner of the chapel, looking into the quadrangle across the new water 'conduit' to the newly built, hot-water-heated range of student lodgings and cloisters with its stair towers, running 250 feet along a terrace that followed the bare remains of the medieval precinct walls. The terrace is continued along the east side, and the newly built college library seen above it. This was constructed not like the other new and rebuilt buildings, which were all in the economical mix of knapped flint with light stone quoins and dressings, but in carefully cut rag-stone 'for the sake of greater dignity'.

2
St Augustine's College, Canterbury: illustration of gateway from the west, published in *Illustrated London News*, 8 July 1848

3
St Augustine's College, Canterbury: illustration of quadrangle from the south-west, published in *Illustrated London News*, 8 July 1848

PRINCIPAL GATEWAY OF ST. AUGUSTINE'S COLLEGE, CANTERBURY.

THE CLOISTER AND LIBRARY.

St Augustine's
College, Canterbury:
view of the library
from the south-west,
photographed 1864

well had been. This rigorously geometric approach to the topography and character of landscape would characterise Butterfield's precinct designs from village churchyard and country parsonage to the grounds of his Keble College, Oxford, and his Royal Hampshire County Hospital.

The library was the most ambitious of the new constructions on the site and the closest to an historical re-creation. It rises from the foundations of the medieval abbot's hall and follows the six narrow bays with projecting stair tower suggested by this footprint. Butterfield modelled the principal windows on examples from the fourteenth-century great hall of the archbishop's palace at Mayfield in Sussex, and the porch and staircase drew on Howden Minster in Yorkshire. The library is an open-span rectangular hall, 80 feet by 40, with a roof of exposed oak beams and a large stained-glass window at the north end. There was an aisle of floor cabinets down the middle and bays of shelving, forming study alcoves, in each of the windows, with a single table, encouraging students to work together.

Bishop John Medley of New Brunswick, in an address to the college soon after its completion, recognised at once that this was 'no motley collection of ill-assorted plagiarisms', which had become the common approach to the Gothic revival, 'but a positive creation, a *real* thing, which might be said to be like nothing else, and yet like everything else in Christian art'. Together, the ensemble seems at once of the past and in the present, not just in the harmony of shape and surface but in the ruling principle of truthful design, which eschews all the frills and finials of the prevailing neo-Gothic in favour of what the critical language of the time identified as 'realism': forms whose expression derives from the shape and pattern of their structure and materials, rather than from ornament applied for surface incident.

The young designer Charles Locke Eastlake, revisiting it in 1872 for his *History of the Gothic Revival*, would write:

Modesty and economy were the watchwords of Butterfield and Hope's building programme. They looked at a number of arrangements for student lodging, finally settling on rows of monastically tight units: fifty 15-by-9-foot cells, each with a plain table and chair behind a divider. There were two small groups at each end of the great ground-floor cloister, which was fully 150 feet long; and two rows were set above, with a long gallery between them that was described as a solitary ambulatory, a place to 'walk through a problem'. The upper floor was reached from two stair turrets and lit by two constellations of small lancets at either end. The cloister was by contrast a gathering place, visible and conversational, with a vista across what had been the great court of the monastery, now patterned into linear paths and focused on the functional sculpture, like a fountain in a piazza, of Butterfield's water cistern, placed where the ancient

A quarter of a century has elapsed since St Augustine's was begun. Mr. Butterfield's name has since been associated with larger and more important commissions. But though his later works exhibit evidence of mature taste and a wider range of study, no architect of our time has deviated so little from the principles of design which he adopted at the outset of his career.[6]

THE FIRST SISTERHOODS: REGENT'S PARK

The idea of creating an order of sisters in the English Church had been imagined by the poet Robert Southey in the early 1830s as a fellowship of piety, as a sanctuary for women inclined to lives unrestricted by the duties of marriage, and as a service and refuge for the sick, the needy and those at risk.

The movement became urgent as an awakened social conscience among women of the privileged class confronted the tides of distress that washed the shores of Britain and Ireland at mid-century, first among the vast ageing population of the widowed and disabled of the Napoleonic Wars; then from the hunger, revolutionary disorder and violent suppression that surrounded the economic collapse of 1839; and continuing with the fatal famines of the Hungry Forties, the loss of 25,000 young men in Crimea, and the relentless assault of newly virulent diseases, of which the epidemics of cholera and pervasive assaults of typhus and tuberculosis were the most conspicuous but the long-wave pandemic of scarlet fever perhaps the most terrifying, stealing entire families of children overnight.

The idea of the sisterhood was taken up quietly and very personally by another figure closely associated with the Margaret Chapel, the acknowledged leader of the Tractarian movement, the Oxford Professor of Hebrew Edward Bouverie Pusey. The first fruits of his initiative appeared in 1845, when a group of four London women formed a Society of the Holy Cross, organised with his encouragement as a memorial to Southey. Living together in a house close to Regent's Park, and soon governed on a daily basis by a Superior, Emma Langston, they were engaged especially with improving the moral, educational and sanitary lives of the many poor in the parish of Christ Church Albany Street, which counted Butterfield and Sir

John Taylor Coleridge among its members. In 1848, now with eight sisters, the Society came under Pusey's stewardship and a somewhat stricter rule of life modelled on that of Catherine McAuley's Roman Catholic Sisters of Mercy, in the two English convents she sponsored at Bermondsey, south-east London, and Birmingham, both designed by Augustus Welby Northmore Pugin in a domineering manner that Butterfield would not emulate, though he admired and was greatly informed in his conventual work by the gentler domestic buildings of Pugin's Benedictine campus in Margate, Kent.

By early 1850, the sisters' household consisted of a day school for forty children of the very poor, rooms for twenty orphans, whom they boarded and clothed, and accommodation for a growing number of their order, outstripping the capacity of two new houses to which they had moved just north of the church. Land was acquired in Osnaburgh Street, and Pusey invited Butterfield, by now an affectionate and much-respected friend, to draw up plans for a house and chapel, whose social services would be: 'visiting the poor and sick at their own houses; feeding, clothing, and instructing poor and destitute children; giving shelter to distressed women of good character, preparing them for confirmation and training them for servants; feeding strangers whom they could not otherwise relieve; receiving and educating orphans'.[7] To avoid attracting the attention of the 'no Popery' street mob, the foundation stone was laid with great discretion on 14 September 1850 and the house occupied without ceremony in 1852. It was not just a new idea but an idea on a new scale, built 'to provide for . . . thirteen sisters, forty orphans, fifteen poor women, with spare rooms for probationers, a schoolroom for the very poorest children, and an apartment fitted up for homeless wayfarers', together with an 'oratory sufficiently large to admit the whole household'. A rough 1851 ground-floor plan – all that is extant of the designs – shows rooms both for the academic schooling of children and for sewing, cutting and work rooms to train and sustain the orphans; sisters' rooms; a sitting room with fine bay windows looking into the garden; and a modest 'room for family prayers',

5
St Saviour's Home,
Osnaburgh Street,
London: view from
the north-west,
watercolour by
Thomas Hosmer
Shepherd, *c.*1852–4

using a term for the oratory that, like the name of the new institution – 'St Saviour's Home' – reflected the Victorian reformers' ideal of a single 'household' embracing all of its inmates, religious and needy, serving and served, within a single corporate family.

Thomas Hosmer Shepherd's picturesque view (fig.5), with its two black-gowned sisters turning towards their work amongst the distressed community to the north-east of their Home, is one of a large series in which the artist set out to document the rapidly changing shape and scale of modern London. The Home demonstrates the shift towards a more spacious and hygienic urban life to a striking degree. We see its ground floor raised on a platform well above the usual height of the London threshold, clearing the foul surface of waste, dust and debris; three high, well-ventilated floors above ground within an envelope usually fit for five; the whole street front, with its mix of great and narrow windows and huge attic dormers, set well back from the line of its neighbours; and a deep basement yard, wide enough for a full separate entry to kitchen, laundry, supplies and heating services,

and a sanitary means of managing grease, waste and drainage. An open entrance court at the far right leads past a porter's lodge and waiting room to a large garden court that stretches deep into the site, the north side of which is flanked by a long range of school and workshop space with accommodation on two floors above, while a wing to the south serves as a residence for sisters and guests, adjacent to the oratory in which the daily offices were recited.

London was thus introduced to the sight of an entirely new idea of the domestic Gothic, as a geometry of weight and thickness in which shape and texture, space and volume, the roof, the wall, and their openings (with the simplest tracery) constituted all the ornament. It was generous with light, frank about its point of entry, and projected the chimney boldly out to the world. Much changed in the fortunes and purpose of the home even within its first years, and Butterfield returned to it a number of times, until, by the 1880s, when it had become a cancer hospital of uncertain reputation, he had transformed the upper floors into wards and added a small chapel. This itself was utterly transformed in 1888 with a gift of spectacularly ornate Baroque fittings from Bavaria, which Butterfield incorporated into its once plain walls. The chapel promptly entered guidebooks as one of London's 'hidden treasures', and the convent and its daily services then became a city landmark. It was demolished to establish a new traffic systemn in 1961.

. . . AND PLYMOUTH

> Population 5,500, rapidly increasing and will probably be doubled in a few years, owing to the new Steam Dock-yard . . . ; number of children under fourteen years of age 1,807, the great majority unbaptized; houses densely inhabited, as many as forty persons sometimes residing in one house; no school for the poor . . . sadly notorious that the greater part of those who, in these districts, drag out a miserable and hateful existence – loathsome to themselves, closed by an early grave, without a hope beyond that grave – were the orphans of our sailors and soldiers . . . the daughters of those who left them for their country's cause, and in their country's charge, to be trained up in wretchedness and vice.

Such was Lydia Sellon's brilliantly analytical, outraged and compassionate description of the condition entering the new year of 1849 of the Devonport quarter in which she had begun a sisterhood of mercy.[8]

Sellon was the 27-year-old daughter of a naval captain when she decided to answer a call from Bishop Philpotts of Exeter twelve months before for a missionary service to the children of the unsanitary, dangerous and overcrowded districts of Plymouth, in which his thinly spread clergy were overwhelmed. In April 1848 Sellon attached herself – at Pusey's suggestion – to the new parish of St James, Morice Town, and there gathered a small team of sisters into rented quarters, from which they set out to walk the meanest streets of the city, inviting children to their improvised schoolroom. Within the year Sellon's black-robed sisters had extended their work to finding shelter for women at risk, caring for orphans, running an industrial school for girls, and housing probationers to train as nursing and teaching aides. They were challenged and abused on all sides, not just from the customary anti-papist rabble-rousers but by parents refusing to let young women join the community – in at least one case forcing marriage upon a girl to prevent it.

In July 1849 came cholera. Throughout that summer Sellon and her sisters were nursing the sick, consoling the dying and looking after the children left behind, an ordeal from which her own health never fully recovered. Working with a board of health established by the city to address the epidemic, Sellon quickly found a site on the western border of Morice Town for a temporary wooden hospital, serving all of Plymouth, with beds for thirty men and thirty women and a tiny chapel with an altar, so that communion could be served to sisters who could not leave their charges; and she set up quarantine houses for younger sisters in training, orphans and children at risk. As the epidemic ended, with her rented houses overflowing, her credibility established and yet more orphans at the door, Sellon brought in Butterfield, at Pusey's urging, to formulate a more permanent plan of building. The temporary hospital was converted into an orphanage and dispensary, and a large slice of land was acquired just beyond it in the new district of St Peter's Eldad, the domain of an Anglo-Catholic vicar, on the bluff bordering the cemetery of the naval infirmary above the inlet of effluents known to sailors worldwide as 'Shit Creek'.

Ground was broken early in 1850 and the foundation stone laid in a ceremony in October. Sympathetic newspapers reported a procession of 'thousands of children' from schools that the sisters served, wearing blue ribands and singing psalms as they arrived at a tent on the site to feast on cake, while 1000 of the elderly poor were feted with beef, bread and ale. In the evangelical press, quite another picture is painted, in which the event was abandoned after rioters attacked, hurling food from the tents along with sticks and stones as missiles. A sister who was there recalled long after that the procession was indeed mocked by an unruly crowd, and police were called but did not need to

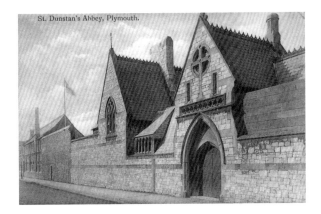

6 (top left)
St Dunstan's Abbey, Plymouth: principal gateway from the south, photographed *c*.1910

7 (bottom left)
St Dunstan's Abbey, Plymouth: the quadrangle, photographed *c*.1905

8 (right)
St Dunstan's Abbey, Plymouth: the quadrangle – rear tower and stair turret, photographed *c*.1900

intervene. The plate designed by Butterfield and inset in the foundation stone described the abbey carefully as 'a house of religion and charity for the Sisters of Mercy'. With walls and foundations in place, progress was impeded by a stream of public controversies, leaving 'the curious looking fabric which is called the Orphans' Home . . . in the same unfinished state' for the next three years.[9] Shortly after, the community began to recover. By July 1853 there were as many as forty-three sisters, beginning again to erect their 'nunnery'; and there was a team of masons back on site in December.

Then came the war in Crimea. A number of the Devonport sisters left to serve with Florence Nightingale at the Scutari Hospital in Constantinople (now Istanbul), and work stalled once more, though temporary buildings were improvised for shelter and schooling of the poor, and a dispensary was built at the abbey gates. Early in 1856, however, with the reputation of the sisters transformed by service among the soldiers, subscriptions and construction began in earnest.

By year's end a full ensemble of living, orphans', refuge and teaching quarters had begun to take shape, and 'St Dunstan's Abbey' was finally on the ground. The plan, shared with the *Plymouth Journal* by Butterfield's builder, Henry Veale, as the new campaign began, involved an E shape – three widely separated arms running south to north towards the bluff, with a long narrow boundary of wall and buildings along the street front. Fusing elements of a collegiate language like that of Winchester and Oxford with medieval manor halls, Cornish round towers and the half-hipped gables of Tudor courtyards, it was quite evidently both a domestic architecture and one with a visible religious character.

When Charles Eastlake described the abbey in 1872, he could observe from a distance 'an admirable group' standing 'on rising ground, with its walls divided into heights of two or three stories as occasion required, breaking out occasionally into an octagonal bay, or sweeping round in an apselike curve, and surmounted by a high-pitched roof of slate'. On closer inspection he noted that 'The cold grey limestone . . . of this district, is generally a dull and formal one . . . ; but Mr. Butterfield, by breaking it up into irregular courses, has given it life and interest.' And, on entering, he found spaces planned with 'the rare quality in modern Gothic of being thoroughly practical and straightforward'.[10] Cutting and laying blocks of stone into a carefully crafted mosaic of varied widths and lines to animate the surface would become a hallmark of Butterfield's masonry, whether as here in a random scheme brought into order by clean-cut courses or in such meticulous later stone works as St Mark's, Dundela, in Belfast, where the layering of different widths establishes a pattern of horizontal lines in the light that visually anchors walls rising to a great height. And the functional frankness of his arrangements would remain the key to his plan and massing.

In the mid-1860s the sisterhood merged with other orders. A number of members moved with the invalid Sellon to a new priory at Ascot, and other arms of charity and the Church were taking up the sisters' challenge to address the dire conditions of life in port and garrison towns. St Dunstan's found a new life at the turn of the century as a boarding school run by the St Mary's sisters of Wantage, preparing young women for universities. Butterfield's site was added to and adapted, but the essential fabric and its history remained, much regarded and visited, as postcards from that era testify.[11]

HOUSES OF REST: LINCOLN BEDEHOUSE CHAPEL

'Watch and pray' was the motto inscribed on the hearths of the St Anne Bedehouses in Lincoln, a gently walled compound of tiny terraced cottages 'where the old might retire to a holy rest and preparation for the grave together'.[12] They had been built to drawings by Pugin on the heath near the east gate of the old cathedral city to house thirteen elderly women of the town, who were admitted on a pension of £18 a year, with an allowance of coal and clothing, including the blue great-cloaks that announced the dignity of a proud community.

The founder and first warden was the erratic but charismatic Richard Waldo Sibthorp, whose clerical path moved back and forth between the English and the Roman Church. His short ministry in a Fenland parish included stewarding an ancient bedehouse, introducing him to the idea of the collegiate refuge for the ageing poor, to which Pugin in *Contrasts* (1836) and Thomas Carlyle in *Past and Present* (1843) had urged the modern world to return, and for which his new community would stand as an example. Butterfield himself would grant a lifetime of honorary service to reviving and modernising the fabric of three ancient almshouses or 'colleges of noble poverty' – for John Mason Neale at Sackville College in Sussex, at St Cross Hospital in Winchester and at St Nicholas's Hospital in Salisbury – and built four entirely new sets of rural almshouses, at Ashwell in Rutland, Heckfield and Emery Down in Hampshire, and Baldersby in Yorkshire. Pugin's dwellings were finished in December 1847, but once his trustees had the funds to move forward on a chapel, Pugin – 'a man rather difficult to work with' – refused to build it 'at the cost and in the way Mr Sibthorp wished: and by his consent that part of the work went into the hands of the very able Mr Butterfield'. Construction commenced early in 1853, using beautifully made, finished and coloured local red brick, and the project was almost complete by April 1854. By the time of its opening in September, the *Lincolnshire Chronicle* could already call it the most impressive modern landmark in the county, not for boasting a lofty tower or displaying great architectural finery, but for its 'quiet and unpretending appearance'.

Though many schemes had run through his head, Sibthorp had settled on the idea of a chapel that would serve as a place of devotion for the community at large as well as a source of comfort for his bedeswomen. Butterfield's plan therefore divided the chapel into two equal parts. To the east was a choir in which thirteen residents were seated on carved oak stalls along the walls, and then a small sacrarium with a raised dais for the altar, with a modest sedilia to the south, and, on the north, a small organ and vestry. The western half housed open pews for 110. A great entry porch, high-gabled in stone, lay at the

9
St Anne Bedehouses,
Lincoln: pencil sketch
by A.E. Garrett, 1874

almost anthropomorphic form like the cloak and hood of the bedeswomen. A stone-framed opening in the gable, strengthened with large bearing blocks and a line of supporting stone, bears a sculpture of the Presentation in the Temple, where the ancient Simeon and the prophet Anna, after whom the bedehouses are named, sing of their readiness to leave the world, having seen their salvation.

A sketch by a local artist some twenty years later (fig.9) looks along the walled courtyard fronting the north range of Pugin's dwellings towards the west window of Butterfield's chapel, as it soars upwards in a steep pitch behind the ivy-covered well-house he had added to close the court. Pugin's buildings, sunk close to the ground, carry an air of 'exaggerated medievalism', delighting in detail and the picturesque. The chapel, in contrast, has a pronounced restraint, built on a massive platform, with tall, even, sharply cut planes. By using similar brick, limiting external decoration, adopting wide windows of a near-domestic character, eschewing a tower and restraining the articulation of the walls, Butterfield manages at once to reconcile the chapel's dramatic height and scale with Pugin's low-lying townscape and to let it attain a powerful character of its own. The chapel appeared at the same time as Butterfield's three church ensembles for East Cowick, Hensall and Pollington in the Humberhead Levels, where the same luscious Lincoln brick and tile were deployed by the same team of master-masons, and the same measure of restraint is applied to almost theatrical effect. With these startlingly fresh brick works we are meeting, all at once and in full flower, the Butterfield who speaks – in an essay written with John Duke Coleridge at this date – of a new 'Realism' that must take hold now that the fundamental lessons of proportion, harmony and structure in the Gothic had been learned. [13]

south-west corner. Nave and choir met at the centre with only the slenderest arch to divide them, making a barely interrupted volume under a continuous bow-beamed dropped ceiling, painted in vermilion, azure and gold. There are two stone-framed windows on either side, four lancets to the west and three to the east, set within wide arched recesses, outlined by projecting cornices in polished brick, and set above sills of large, canted blocks of plain stone. His album of photographs shows a similar irregular order at Santa Maria della Spina in Pisa, and his workbooks carry sketches of the same idea at Wisbech in Cambridgeshire. The blind south wall to the east carried a runic figure in dark brick, perhaps the skeleton of a fish, which Butterfield took from a stone he had found on Great Cumbrae Island. With the delicate octagonal tower and *flèche* – originally in wood – rising more than thirty feet above the steep uninterrupted planes of the roof, the chapel made an assertive statement on the city skyline. The porch is deep, high and wide, shaped into an

THE SCIENCE OF ECCLESIOLOGY

We know little of Butterfield's early life except that he left an apprenticeship with a Pimlico builder in 1833, at eighteen or nineteen, by which time he had already submitted two designs for the

10

Preparatory drawing
in ink and pencil by
Butterfield, 1843, of
the fourteenth-century
church of St John the
Baptist, Shottesbrooke,
for south elevation
(plate V) in *Elevations,
Sections, and Details,
of Saint John Baptist
Church, at Shottesbroke,
Berkshire*, published
for the Oxford
Architectural Society,
1844

competition on the Clifton Bridge, boldly signing
himself as 'Architect, London'. He then studied and
was articled in London, recording and repairing
ancient buildings, before joining Harvey Eginton
in Worcester in about 1836. Eginton's antiquarian
observations and studies were wide-ranging and
adept – he rediscovered and revived the medieval
craft of encaustic tile work and undertook several
pioneering restorations – and in what seems to
have been a rather casual practice, his assistants,
as Butterfield's first sketchbooks show, had many
opportunities to examine examples of ecclesiastical
art in the surrounding landscape. We first know

of him when, late in 1837, a published 'outline
drawing' of the brilliant restoration he and Eginton
undertook in Shakespeare's chancel at Holy Trinity
Church, Stratford-upon-Avon, was issued and
widely advertised, the artist's name given variously
as 'Butterworth' and 'Buttingfield'. About the same
time, he opened his first independent offices in the
capital, first in Norfolk Street, then in chambers
with his solicitor brother James at Lincoln's Inn
Fields, and finally on Adam Street in the Adelphi
buildings below the Strand in 1842, where he
would stay for forty-five years. Although he had
some minor commissions for new work and did the
principal work for Eginton at the pioneering church
of Wilmcote in 1841, he seems to have been most
engaged as an antiquary in the emerging science
of ecclesiology, travelling to church sites with a
little workbook and simple instruments to develop
through measurement and analysis an archaeological
rather than impressionistic understanding of the
methods and instinct for proportion that made
English medieval church architecture of the middle
period so compelling.

Butterfield's field studies cling strictly to the
scientific orthography of the measured elevation or
outline. Perspective and pictorialism are eschewed,
and shading used only where essential to reveal
the plan or profile of a moulding. Elevations are
freed from their context, devoid of staffage, and
he is content to show half of the subject where no
more is needed. Nevertheless, even in the working
notebooks, Butterfield seems incapable of placing
and relating images randomly on the page: every
sheet is a composition, and all elements on the
sheet observe a common scale. As his experience
matures, the same rigour and austerity will apply
to the contract drawings that were the essential
instruments of his practice.

In advancing the reform of church building,
two university associations played the leading
role: the Oxford Architectural Society and the
Cambridge Camden Society, the latter of which
later re-formed outside the university as the
Ecclesiological Society, and whose journal, *The
Ecclesiologist*, edited by Benjamin Webb and
John Mason Neale, was the principal voice of the

11
Design for a ewer,
c.1846

movement. The Oxford society had identified the mid-fourteenth-century Shottesbrooke collegiate church in Berkshire, one of the very rare instances of a medieval church in England built to a single unified scheme, as a model for builders of new churches, commissioning Butterfield early in 1843 to prepare a portfolio of plates. Drawing on almost fanatical field studies, which measure every detail and interval on site to the inch, Butterfield's drawings have an extraordinary precision (fig.10). This radically unromantic, scientific approach to the presentation of antiquities is reflected in the absence of pictorial shadows or hints of the sky or ground. It is concerned not, as were earlier studies of the 'antiquities of England', with recapturing the topography of a site, but with what the mind of the builder might comprehend. His notes on the church stress the absence of anything superfluous to supporting structure, drainage, shelter or the management of light, and the coherence of relative proportion and scale in a work composed to a singular unifying principle.

He was also commissioned by the Ecclesiological Society to provide studies of the thirteenth-to-fourteenth-century church at Teversham in Cambridgeshire as a simple model of a country church for colonial bishops, tracings of which went to New South Wales and New Zealand in November 1844, with full drawings ready by January 1845 for the society to supply on request. Butterfield noted significantly that the prototype could be just as readily adapted for the wants of country parishes at home, where good practical models of unpretending churches suited to a revived liturgy were no more common than they were in New South Wales or New Zealand. As traditional forms of worship were revived, churches also lacked appropriate means for lighting the chancel, chanting the litany, reading the gospel, administering baptism or preparing and distributing the communion, for which only rare examples of plate had survived 200 years of efforts by Commonwealth and crown to melt them down for gain. With few models to follow, the quality of what could be ordered from workaday artisans was questionable. In an early effort to correct this, James Bliss set out to 'rescue our Altars from the shameless neglect and contempt into which they had fallen' by issuing a set of lithographic plates, principally from Butterfield's drawings, of medieval models for church instruments, first appearing in loose sheets about 1842 and gathered as a set in *Specimens of Ancient Church Plate* in 1845.[14]

The Ecclesiological Society followed with two more ambitious projects under Butterfield's superintendence to provide designs for church furnishing and liturgical instruments, first in the form of a series of printed plates, known as *Instrumenta Ecclesiastica*, and then in the manufacture of altar plate, candlesticks and other metal instruments with designated goldsmiths in London and New York (fig.11). They were produced in different metals at different cost but all in conformity with ecclesiological ideas of iconology, form and method, including an insistence that pieces were entirely hammered and not welded. These works spread rapidly through the English-speaking world, took a prominent place in the Great Exhibition of 1851, and together with the *Instrumenta,* established Butterfield's pre-eminence as a designer of church instruments and furnishings,

Church of St Cross,
Winchester: interior
view looking east,
photographed by
James Valentine,
c.1870

sites as they probably looked at the height of their development in the thirteenth and fourteenth centuries, he shocked some from the start with the unfamiliarity and freshness of the result, in which he embraced the vivacity of these early examples. The uncompromising Butterfield was not tamed by these controversies, and his later interventions became ever bolder, most controversially at the church of St Cross Hospital in Winchester (fig.12), where his incremental restoration of the Norman east end, begun in 1859, delighted in unveiling its idiosyncrasy and asymmetry and, in applying vivid colour, based on suggestive stains and fragments he found on the site. This at first raised an outcry from the older generation. But, as time softened the hues, its vivacity – narrowing the distance between the Norman and the Byzantine and using colour to strengthen line and recession – fascinated a younger generation seeking paths forward, like the neo-Romanesque Henry Hobson Richardson, who visited the site and acquired a photograph for studio reference; and then by the advance guard of the Arts and Crafts movement, including William and Evelyn De Morgan and Halsey Ricardo. These adventures, especially in constructional colour, encouraged Butterfield himself to explore a radically geometrical approach to tile decoration that began to mark his churches from that time forward.

from altar plate to seats and screens, that would last the length of his career.

Butterfield in this early period of his work then undertook four pioneering restorations at signal monuments of the Middle Ages: Dorchester Abbey near Oxford, which, starting in 1843 with meagre funds, the Oxford Architectural Society adopted as its principal project; St Davids Cathedral, Pembrokeshire, where he worked for a group of students in the Oxford society, starting in 1846, to restore stone tracery in screen and windows; and converting to clearer devotional purpose the collegiate church of Ottery St Mary in Devon and the chapel of Merton College, Oxford, both starting in 1848–9. Stripping away accretions and replacing decayed matter to recapture the

In this he was emboldened by his knowledge of Venice and Ravenna. It is not clear when Butterfield's journeys to mainland Europe began, but his learned study of continental architecture was already deep enough for Benjamin Webb to have turned to him to draw the outline plans and illustrations to his guide to continental ecclesiology, published early in 1848.[15] There, Butterfield illustrates a number of works that would greatly inform his own, including the Duomo of Torcello, the upper chapel of Saint Francis in Assisi, and the Florentine church of San Miniato, and joins with Webb in validating for the first time sources beyond Brittany and Normandy for the Gothic revival. From at least 1850, the continental tour was fixed in his calendar for the 'dog days' of London's summer, starting late in August, bridging his birthday on 7 September, and closing at the end of the month.

Friends usually joined him, among whom were the essayist and historian Sir Arthur Helps, the Rugby schoolmaster Charles T. Arnold and (until his marriage in 1860) the composer and music educator John Hullah. In an album of photographs are subjects gathered in France, Germany and northern Italy, as well as the abbeys of Kelso, Melrose and Jedburgh in the Scottish Borders and Rievaulx in Yorkshire, in each of whose ruins he could discern more readily the underlying shape, rhythm and proportion, perceiving principles of a medieval spatial geometry upon which he learned to build his own. Theses journeys always involved measuring and sketching details of every variety, acquiring photographs for continued reference and meeting with antiquarian colleagues to guide him – notably his friends the Abbé Cerf in Rheims and Eugène Viollet-le-Duc in Paris.

From such measured contemplation of structure, proportion and detail, Butterfield looked not for replicable patterns and motifs from which 'High Gothic' would emerge, but for principles upon which to ground an entirely new order that could suggest a possible future of architecture. Arthur Beresford Pite, who had once drafted for Butterfield, described how that future was realised in a review of modern architecture presented to the RIBA on 17 December 1900, remembering at the end of the year in which Butterfield had died how, through the stringencies of his antiquarian study, 'He discerned and seized the essential motive of medieval building art, and forthwith strove to think for himself and express his own thought in his material for its modern purpose, with absolutely new art'. The result was that 'in every way all is as freshly modern as theirs was in its day'.[16]

NOTES

1. Charlotte M. Yonge, 'The Years of Revolution', in her jubilee biography of Victoria: *The Victorian Half Century*, Macmillan, London, 1887, p.43.
2. George Frederick Maclear, *St Augustine's, Canterbury: Its Rise, Ruin, and Restoration*, Wells Gardner, Darton & Co., London, 1888, pp 53–4.
3. See Thomas Waugh Belcher, *Robert Brett of Stoke Newington: His Life and Work*, Dutton, London, 1889.
4. W.E. Gladstone, *The State in Its Relations with the Church*, John Murray, London, 1841.
5. The account of the genesis and history of the college is largely drawn from Maclear, *St Augustine's, Canterbury*, op.cit.; Henry Bailey, 'Twenty-five years of St Augustine's college', 1873, in *Occasional Papers from St Augustine's College*, published by the college and assembled in a compendium of 1953; Robert Ewell, *Guide to St Augustine's Monastery and Missionary College*, Cross & Jackman, Canterbury, 1896 and 1902; the annual reports, addresses and occasional papers of the College with other print ephemera, found in the digital library Project Canterbury (http://anglicanhistory.org/england/); and news and journal reports on the inauguration, notably *Illustrated London News*, 8 July 1848. For further references see Paul Thompson, *William Butterfield*, Routledge & Kegan Paul, London, 1971, p.434.
6. Charles Locke Eastlake, *A History of the Gothic Revival: An Attempt to Show How the Taste for Mediaeval Architecture which Lingered in England During the Two Last Centuries Has Since Been Encouraged and Developed*, Longmans, Green & Co., London, 1872, p.228.
7. The account is primarily taken from Henry William Burrows, *The Half-Century of Christ Church, Albany Street*, Skeffington, London, 1887, pp 16–18. The plot plan is in the collections of London Metropolitan Archives.
8. *Liverpool Mail*, 24 February 1849.
9. *Plymouth Gazette*, 5 October 1850.
10. Eastlake, *History of the Gothic Revival*, op.cit., p.256.
11. Sister Margaret Teresa, *The History of St Dunstan's Abbey School, Plymouth*, Underhill, Plymouth, 1928.
12. The account of the St Anne Bedehouses project and its history draws upon *Lincolnshire Chronicle*, 22 September 1854; *The Builder*, 8 April 1854; *Morning Chronicle*, 23 September 1854; Michael John Trott, '"A Simple, Rare, Truly Elect Soul": The Troubled Life of Richard Waldo Sibthorp, 1792–1879', PhD thesis, University of Hull, 2003; and John Fowler, *R.W. Sibthorp: A Biography*, Skeffington, London, 1880, pp 87–122.
13. John Duke Coleridge, 'The Necessity of Modernism in the Arts, Especially When Devoted to the Service of Religion', *Transactions of the Exeter Diocesan Architectural and Archaeological Society*, vol.4, 1854, pp 335–60. A note by Coleridge in this paper, originally presented in 1853, acknowledges that the ideas were developed from his discussions with Butterfield, to whom they should be attributed.
14. James Bliss, Preface to *Specimens of Ancient Church Plate, Sepulchral Crosses, etc.*, Cambridge Camden Society / J.H. Parker, Oxford, 1845.
15. Benjamin Webb, *Sketches of Continental Ecclesiology*, Joseph Masters, London, 1848.
16. Arthur Beresford Pite, 'A Review of the Tendencies of the Modern School of Architecture', *Architects' and Builders' Magazine* (New York), March/April 1901.

CHAPTER 2

THE MISSIONARY CATHEDRAL, 1847–53

CHRIST CHURCH, FREDERICTON

NEW BRUNSWICK was among many vast and distant provinces where the colonial Church, with no state grant to aid it, was severely hampered by the difficulty of training and ordaining clergy, confirming congregants and consecrating new Church missions. In this case, the governing bishop resided in Nova Scotia and was largely absent in England, requiring candidates to travel 300 miles across a wilderness of forest to Quebec for ordination. In 1843 the Anglican missionary societies found funds to endow a new see; and in October of 1844 a bishop was nominated, the rather surprising choice being the 40-year-old high-church Devonshire clergyman John Medley.

Eight years before, Medley had been one of those who founded the Exeter Diocesan Architectural Society, delivering one of its first papers, published in 1841 as *Elementary Remarks on Church Architecture*. The Remarks were directed not at architects but at 'the public mind'. For, as he tells us, 'Our churches are in a course of transformation; and unless the parishioners acquire some better notions of what is due to God's house, our church building zeal will irrecoverably spoil half the old churches in the kingdom, to say nothing of those which are built entirely new.' Medley had studied Gothic churches with great care, and he made an unusually simple and eloquent case for four great fundamentals of the Gothic: 'vertical instead of horizontal lines'; 'the union of the mechanical or actual' with 'the decorative'; 'material truthfulness'; and reliance on 'the extreme flexibility and variety of the arch, with its capability of supporting enormous weights'.[1] Working with the diocesan architect John Hayward, he had demonstrated these principles and his knowledge of

construction in two studiously simplified chapels for distant settlements of his parish.

On his appointment to New Brunswick, a modest testimonial was raised among Medley's friends to initiate the building of a cathedral in the province's capital, Fredericton.[2] By March of 1845, after first considering and then rejecting Butterfield's drawings of Shottesbrooke as a model, he determined, with a young draughtsman in Hayward's office, Frank Wills, on an adaptation of the Norfolk church of St Mary's Snettisham, whose great west window was then in restoration. Instead of a new design, Medley felt that an English cathedral in a distant clime should replicate ancient designs from the home country and chose Snettisham, though it had lost its east end entirely, as a large parish church approaching cathedral proportions and thus a practical model for the limited means at hand. Wills, who would follow the Medleys to Fredericton as diocesan architect, drew a

perspective of a proposed design, adding a short low chancel, and the Medleys crossed the Atlantic late that spring determined to raise the remaining funds for the building among the local people.

When Medley and his family arrived, the population of the province had doubled in twenty years to roughly 170,000 and would rise through massive transatlantic emigration to nearly 250,000 by the time the cathedral was consecrated in 1853. Poverty, isolation and the struggle for a livelihood were everywhere, and with the first flood of emigration from the famine in Ireland that distress became extreme: in March 1847, from one single boat, Medley counted 240 children who had lost their parents to cold, fever or wasting either in the Atlantic passage or the equally arduous river transit from St John's. Since the cathedral was to be used as a parish church, difficulties at once arose with the existing parish of Christ Church, Fredericton. This was an Anglican city congregation composed largely of white Loyalist families, who had settled and once dominated the town and its fertile riverine hinterland some fifty years before. At the same time had come a large number of Black families, some as domestic servants to Loyalist families and others after joining the British forces on the promise of emancipation and resettlement, who, due to prejudice, had built a second, outlying church. There had already been opposition to Medley's cathedral in a city where the spires of Presbyterian, Catholic and Wesleyan churches dominated the landscape and where Anglicans were a small minority identified with a generally unpopular colonial government. More resistance now came from the Anglican Church itself, whose white congregants had no desire to give up their pew rents, admit the poor, welcome Black Anglicans or replace their simple parish worship with a cathedral service.

The dispute came to a head with resistance to Medley's insistence on all races being instructed together in its schools and seated together in its pews. To overcome this, Medley quickly determined on an almost schismatic solution, establishing a new stone chapel of St Anne for the bishop's use with free and open pews, and where the Christ Church congregation might be served when their old wooden church was demolished to complete the new one. The chapel went up rapidly to Wills's design and was completed in 1847 with work on the cathedral under way. But raising local funds for a cathedral in this divisive climate was scarcely viable. As the project

proceeded, other impediments delayed progress. A great fire in 1848 devastated local businesses, leaving Protestant denominations with wooden churches in no position to aid the construction of an Anglican cathedral, and Medley was driven to raise funds in England and the United States.

Work had proceeded in earnest from May to October of 1847, ending the building season with the shell of the nave close to completion. Questions as to whether the stability of the site could sustain a large tower at the crossing had led Wills to develop a new design from the nave eastwards, with twin towers flanking the east end. But the low chancel disappointed those looking for a genuine cathedral, and though Wills modified the design to raise the roof and increase the presence of the east end, by then he had married and moved to New York. Medley returned to England early in 1848 to raise funds to complete the project; he had abandoned the Wills design and invited Butterfield to work with him on an alternative. Since they were virtually completed by this stage, Butterfield left Wills's west front, nave and aisles in place but proposed an entirely new design for the remainder, closing the nave with a wide tower that allowed for a choir at the crossing and a cloister to the south; a broached spire carrying the tower up to a height now twice that of the roof ridge; an attached chapter house with theological library; and a walled precinct. The chancel remained short, but rose to the roofline of the nave and carried a splendid seven-light east window on a fluent model with a version of the rare heart-shaped head tracery found at York Minster and in Lincolnshire at Heckington and Sleaford, to reflect the same aesthetic as the copy of Snettisham's west window that Wills had incorporated at the entry front. This project, now carrying Butterfield's name as architect, was exhibited to architectural societies in England from March 1848 as part of the fundraising campaign, and appeared in the *Ecclesiologist* in June (fig.14).

A number of changes were made before the first working drawings for Butterfield's scheme were completed. He changed the great east window, adapting one of the finest Decorated examples in England, at the fourteenth-century Selby Abbey, Yorkshire; a much more substantial porch was

14

Christ Church Cathedral, Fredericton: perspective outline for Butterfield's revised scheme, lithograph by T. Varty, published in *The Ecclesiologist*, June 1848

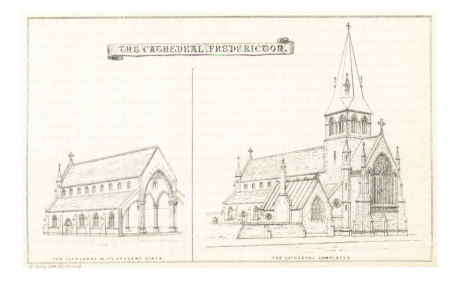

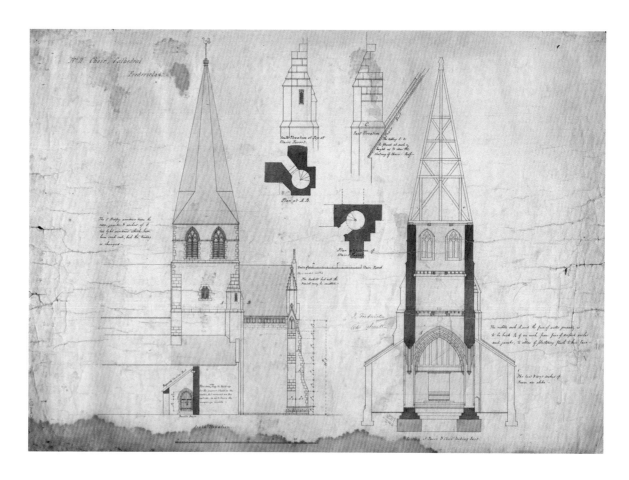

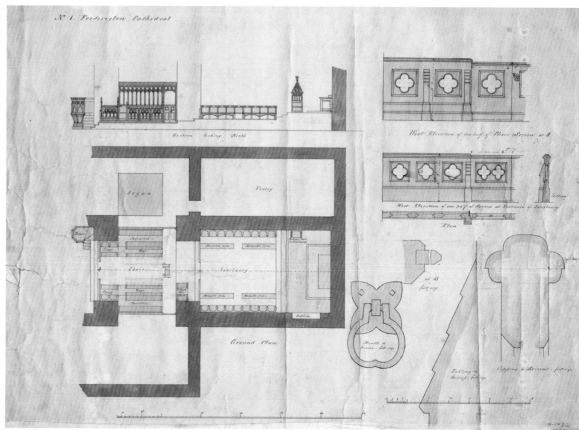

15

Christ Church Cathedral,
Fredericton: choir – south
elevation and section
of choir and sanctuary
looking east, 1848–9

16

Christ Church Cathedral,
Fredericton: plan and
furnishings of choir and
sanctuary, 1850

17
Christ Church
Cathedral,
Fredericton: view
from the south,
albumen print from
pinhole negative
by George Thomas
Taylor, *c.*1865

like the finials that add weight to the towering corner buttresses at the east end. We can actually see him stripping down the detail in the drawing that specifies these pinnacles, where they are peppered with little crockets that he says may be omitted and then happily notes that they have been. And, as his 1850 plan for the furnishing shows (fig.16), he eventually arrived at cathedral and ceremonial proportions in provisions for choir, clergy and diocesan gatherings: the choir and sanctuary now stretch over 65 feet from the first steps to the end wall; there are eighteen fixed stalls for clergy within the sanctuary; and movable forms in the wide centre aisle allow for many more. Butterfield's meticulous interior plan and furnishings seem to have been followed with precision, and the scheme remained in place until lightning struck the spire in 1911 and occasioned substantial rebuilding, including raising the tower another 40 feet – giving it the height, if not quite the shape, that Butterfield and Medley had originally intended.

During 1851 the modest quiet space that Butterfield had designed in place of the original cloister was pulled down, and a bold high-peaked transept with an emphatically tall and narrow window appeared, repeated on the north side, surely to Butterfield's design. In the following year the tower was slightly shortened, and the spire set back behind the parapet, with lucarnes added to its surface and finials framing it. These were changes made perhaps to limit snow-shedding, punctuate the winter skyline and lighten the severity of Butterfield's sloping planes. The late adjustments seem to have come with Butterfield's advice and consent, since Medley acknowledged at the consecration in August 1853 his friend's continual guidance through all the stages of the cathedral's final evolution. Anna Maria Head, the skilled artist who was the Lieutenant Governor's wife, depicts Christ Church nearing completion (fig.13) from the south-west, the persistent viewpoint from which it would become the city's landmark. In that view it is, from porch to east window, almost entirely Butterfield's church, measured, restrained and casting its gaze back towards the best in the moral and aesthetic history of a homeland from which it has drawn its principles.

introduced at the south-west corner of the nave; a transept and cloister running south from the aisle as it met the tower took the place of the chapter house and library; and the stone-walled collegiate precinct to the south was apparently abandoned. The total height of the tower was stretched to 160 feet and stripped of turrets and lucarnes, the stair turret compressed, and the finials given more weight and less delicacy. The library of 1700 books that Medley had assembled for the instruction of clergy would now be housed in the sacristy. This was a notably plainer and more powerful church, and it diverged completely from the notion of replicating an English original, finding a language entirely of its own to complete the scheme.

Indeed, though Wills can be largely credited with the west end, nave and aisle, it is Butterfield's sturdier vision of a great south porch, broached spire, boldly gabled transept and high chancel that governs the site, attaining on a footprint not much larger than a decent parish church the impression of cathedral scale by letting volume and structure carry the profile and poetry of the building. The decoration is limited to bold, functional elements,

18 (above)
St Ninian's Cathedral, Perth: perspective for proposal, 1850, reproduced in A.J.B. Hope, *The English Cathedral of the Nineteenth Century*, John Murray, London, 1861

19 (below)
St Ninian's Cathedral, Perth: view of the chancel dressed for Eastertide, photograph attributed to Magnus Jackson, probably 1873

ST NINIAN'S, PERTH

The rump of the Anglican communion left in Scotland by the late eighteenth century was a beleaguered, endangered and scattered minority. Its perceived association first with a refusal of allegiance to William and Mary, and then with the rebellions of 1715 and 1745, had seen its members ferociously inhibited from access and rights to worship in their tradition. Proscriptions were slowly relaxed at the turn of the century, and for the next fifty years, though the number of adherents was small, Episcopal dioceses and parishes were re-established. Their historic structures had largely passed to the Church of Scotland, so the principle that where there is a bishop there must be a cathedral could only be followed if new ones were erected.

The idea of establishing the first of these was the brainchild of two young Oxford undergraduates, sons of peers of great wealth, George Frederick Boyle and Horace Courtney Gammell Forbes, who saw in the tiny Scottish church and its distinctive liturgy a promising field in which to develop a model of the rites and social commitment of the Tractarian movement. They proposed Perth in the diocese of St Andrews as a site for a collegiate church to advance this, and – with Forbes's father, the premier baron of Scotland, in the lead – the ageing Bishop Torry of the diocese was approached in the summer of 1847 with the idea of establishing what Lord Forbes called a 'missionary episcopate'.[3] Torry at once indicated a preference for a full cathedral, and formed a committee to advance it, with the initial idea, which proved impossible, of rebuilding the ancient seat at Dunkeld. There were at that time two small congregations of Episcopalians in Perth. They and their different interpretations of Anglican orthodoxy would be at loggerheads for the next fifty years. One, at an 'English Chapel', followed the current usage of the established Church, refusing to acknowledge the authority of the bishop; the other, in a hall on Athole Street, followed the Scottish rite – and it was with the latter in mind and close to their hall that the new cathedral was planned.

The site was that of a lost priory running not much more than 200 feet east to west on the north-

eastern perimeter of a mercantile and garrison town of about 15,000. Trade had declined when the river was allowed to silt up, and Perth now survived on small industries and piecework that left most of its people poor, in overcrowded conditions and subject to dread disease. Among the middle class there was a dearth of schools. Once the decision to build in Perth was made, servicing these two local needs – assisting the poorest and educating the comfortable towards duty – became the principal objectives of the cathedral, along with the regular performance of choral services in the Scottish rite.

With a mere £3000 initially available, discussion turned to which part of the cathedral to build first, with the bishop declaring in January 1848 in favour of starting with a choir and chancel. Butterfield drew the scheme of the entire cathedral, with twin towers at its western end, completing drawings in December 1848. He would have preferred to start with the nave and leave a permanent chancel for later, but, overruled, proposed that the first bay of the nave and aisles be constructed for use and the wall of the entire south aisle built to form a yard, as a reminder of the promise to complete and of the design it was to follow. Butterfield's plan took the rough measures of Scottish cathedrals like Dunkeld – 200 feet long, 60 feet wide and 70 feet high – adjusting the proportions slightly to fit the size of the site. Construction was in local sandstone and tile. The foundation stone was laid in September 1849 and Butterfield's design for the completed work, published in perspective (fig.18) and plan, circulated widely.

The consecration took place on a day of bitter frost in December 1850. For many, like John Mason Neale, it was an event more than comparable to that when the Canterbury college opened. He arrived the evening before, walking over every two hours to find workmen still installing details and completing its fittings, none of his party able to sleep for excitement as it dawned on them that they were seeing the first new cathedral to be erected in Britain since the fifteenth century.[4] It was a startling achievement that within a year had also established a model for the movement to extend churches into the burgeoning and troubled provincial towns of mid-century Britain, with missions to the poor on one hand and a pioneering experiment on the other of a 'middle class school' in which students could pursue either classical studies for university preparation or modern studies for commercial and professional life, according to the wishes of their families. Almost at once, a new bishop, Charles Wordsworth, who was determined to align the Scottish Church with the English in matters of tenor, rite and authority, began challenging St Ninian's status and threatening its very survival. To which the *Morning Chronicle* could point out that Scotland and its tiny Episcopal Church had realised what the established Church in England could scarcely imagine: 'In no large English country town could a few Churchmen band together, and in a short time rear a cathedral church, people it with a zealous and working chapter – connect it with educational establishments – and send it forth . . . to preach the faith among the squalid alleys of thick civic population.'[5] But the bishop's distaste for his cathedral persisted; its fortunes declined, along with those of Forbes and Boyle; and the prospect of completion lay far distant.[6]

It was built with the sparest of means, with the east wall almost bare, a simply carved oak pulpit and only four very simple elbowed stalls for the clergy in the chancel, the other seating being on even simpler benches and forms. Plain wrought-iron coronas provided the lighting. All the splendour in this soaring, subtle and beautifully windowed empty cavern sprang from the chancel screen, where polished marble columns made three pointed arches for the trinity, with oculi at their spandrels of deeply carved foils, all set above the plainest but still gleaming rails and gates (fig.19). The first writers for the *Ecclesiologist* saw the 'austerity' of St Ninian's clear planes and unadorned closings as eccentric and 'Mannerist', while another, returning four years later, found it 'neither so clever, nor so stately, nor yet so *abnormal*' as Butterfield's better work. Given the tiny ground plan, minimal budget and the austerity of its character, its fitness as a cathedral was also questioned. Others saw it very differently, finding in it that 'chaste magnificence' that Butterfield sought; and he himself loved what he had achieved, telling a friend at the end of his life that it was the work of which he was most proud, its circumstances having compelled him – by asking for a work of magnificence to appear from the slenderest means – to invent a design in which grandeur came entirely from adherence to essentials, expressing nothing but an '*absolute honesty of purpose*'.

NOTES

1. John Medley, *Elementary Remarks on Church Architecture*, P.A. Hannaford, Exeter, 1841, pp 7–8.
2. The Fredericton project was of extraordinary interest to the high-church party in England, with Medley reporting progress regularly to the *Ecclesiologist* from 1847 to 1852, and to public meetings on his annual fundraising visits to England, where his addresses, on which I have drawn, are widely reported in the local press. See also Phoebe B. Stanton, *The Gothic Revival and American Church Architecture: An Episode in Taste, 1840-1856*, Johns Hopkins University Press, Baltimore, 1968, and Paul Thompson, *William Butterfield*, Routledge & Kegan Paul, London, 1971, p.441.
3. The fullest account of the project is 'A Detailed History of St Ninian's Cathedral, 1847–1914', undated, available on the cathedral website, on which I have drawn, along with A.J.B. Beresford Hope, *The English Cathedral of the Nineteenth Century*, John Murray, London, 1861, pp 78–9; *Church Bells*, 1872, pp 229–30; and *The Ecclesiologist*, December 1847, pp 137 and 140, and February 1851, pp 24–9, and December 1859, pp 376–8.
4. Eleanor A. Towle (ed.), *John Mason Neale, D.D.: A Memoir and Letters*, 2 vols, Longmans, Green & Co., London, 1906 and 1907, vol.1, pp 186–7.
5. *Morning Chronicle*, 22 October 1851.
6. *The Guardian*, 13 April 1853.

CHAPTER 3

'CHA TILL MI TUILLEADH', 1848–78

COLLEGE OF THE HOLY SPIRIT, GREAT CUMBRAE

THE COLLEGE OF the Holy Spirit grew from the efforts of the young George F. Boyle to provide Episcopal schooling and services for the family summer estate on the isle of Great Cumbrae at the mouth of the Firth of Clyde.[1] Boyle has left us a full account of the progress of his scheme, which began with the engagement of a chaplain and making of a schoolroom to teach local children along with some gentlemen's sons from the mainland; continued with Butterfield's chapel of St Andrew, built for the townspeople on the family estate and opened in August 1848; and culminated with the acquisition of a large swathe of hillside for Butterfield to develop a modern version of the medieval clerical college and collegiate church, with a choir school, Latin grammar school and probationary fellowship of those aspiring to

ordination.[2] A quarry was opened on the site; the task of restructuring an entire hillside was begun; a cemetery was built for the local community; and the foundation stone of the church laid at Whitsuntide in 1849. It was conceived as a place with a persistent recollection of the times and temper of St Columba's isle of Iona, and the words of Iona's saint as he first set forth on his mission – 'Cha till mi tuilleadh' (I shall never return) – were carried as its motto.

In 1872 the college prepared a very fine edition of Bishop Alexander Ewing's 1866 study of *The Cathedral or Abbey Church of Iona* with heliotype illustrations. In addition to showing the ruins of Iona, three heliotypes were also made to represent the architecture of the college (figs 21 and 23), in an epilogue by the provost that accounted for its history. Ewing, a highlander, saw Cumbrae as the prospective cathedral of his vast diocese

College of the Holy
Spirit, Great Cumbrae:
view from the west,
heliotype, from J.G.
Cazenove's essay 'The
Collegiate Church and
College, in the Island
of Cumbrae', within
Alexander Ewing's *The
Cathedral or Abbey
Church of Iona*, Grant
& Son, Edinburgh, 1872

of highlands and islands and its college as a new
Iona, returning to the missionary work among the
isles that Columba had embarked upon 1300 years
before. The soft contrast and grey tones inherent
in the heliotype technique lend a suggestion of
antiquity to Butterfield's work, heightening the
resonance intended between the architecture of
the new college and that of Columba's Iona.

THE CHURCH

A preliminary sheet of measured studies (fig.22)
shows the plan of the church; full south and west
elevations; an east elevation; a partial north
elevation; and a section looking east to show the
vestry with its oratory window and the lean-to
passage leading to the canons' house to the south.
The basic ideas all carry forward to the built work,

with only three significant adjustments – raising
the height of the tower and spire; eschewing the
north windows shown on the plan in anticipation of
an eventual north aisle; and slightly modifying the
eastern aspect, vestry and connections as the client's
ideas of usage changed. The eastern light is a wheel
or rose window, with a drip moulding to protect it
in the form of the sheltering wings of the dove. This
would be replaced by a window of three lancets with
quatrefoil heads and a bolder Pentecostal bas-relief,
based on models in medieval manuscripts, of the
dove descending to breathe the fire of faith into the
land. Straddling the edge of a shelf 200 feet above the
sea, the most striking characteristic is the scale and
proportion. The entire church is only 70 feet long,
its nave as narrow as 20 feet and its chancel only 15.
Yet the roof ridge is nearly 40 feet above the floor of
the nave, and the top of the spire, some 80 feet in the
drawings, would when built, carrying a windowed

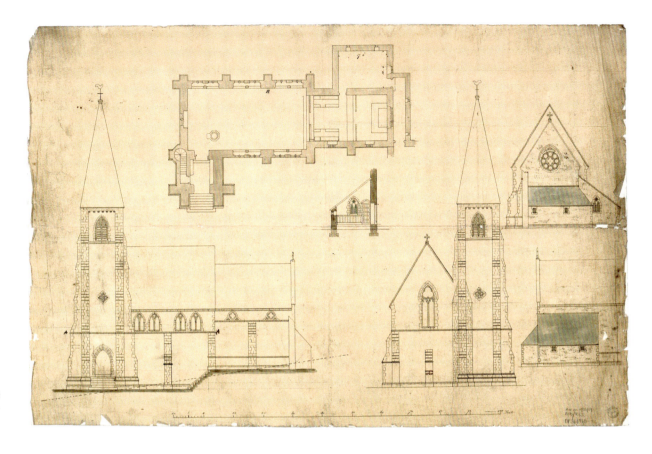

College of the Holy
Spirit, Great Cumbrae:
preliminary design for
the church, 1848

College of the Holy
Spirit, Great Cumbrae:
view to the chancel,
heliotype, from J.G.
Cazenove's essay 'The
Collegiate Church and
College, in the Island
of Cumbrae', within
Alexander Ewing's *The
Cathedral or Abbey
Church of Iona*, Grant &
Son, Edinburgh, 1872

arcade in its final stage and lucarnes around its
steeply tapered spire, rise to 120 feet – three times the
length of the nave and six times its width.

Entering the church, the chancel arch is the
dominant and unifying element (fig.23). It is a
work of complete originality, in which an arched
and traceried open screen of stone above polished
Aberdeen grey granite columns fills the entire
upper portion of the dividing arch between nave
and chancel, with a huge Celtic flowered cross
carved of Caen stone at its centre. Except for bands
of different-coloured stone in the window arches
and the myriad flaming points of gas light around
the walls, the nave was plain, and the decoration
of the chancel, which to modern eyes might seem
surprisingly vivid, was then considered chaste and
simple, since it lacked sculpted stonework, its stalls
were plainly carved, and flat tile patterns along its
surfaces of wall and floor sufficed for ornament,

College of the Holy Spirit, Great Cumbrae:
design for altar frontal, *c*.1851

along with open scrollwork and simple flame-shaped finials at the gates. Figures of the ferns and dog roses that abound on the island fill the roof and come together in one of the altar cloths (fig.24), where a rosehip is shown as it splits to seed in a symbol both of regeneration and the dispersal of faith. The border above is scattered with seeds, and the draped front with stars, showing that the earthly and heavenly are shaped to the same design.

THE COLLEGE

It took two years to build the church, which opened at Whitsuntide in 1851. Meanwhile work proceeded on the two residential buildings flanking it. The canons' house to the south, connected to the vestry on the ground floor and abutting the chancel, was ready for occupancy in November 1850. It is marked in the landscape by an elaborate stair tower which anchors the composition, offsetting the falling

25
College of the Holy Spirit, Great Cumbrae: view from the south-east, heliotype, from J.G. Cazenove's essay 'The Collegiate Church and College, in the Island of Cumbrae', within Alexander Ewing's *The Cathedral or Abbey Church of Iona*, Grant & Son, Edinburgh, 1872

away to the south and resulting irregularity, while extruded chimneys and unusually large dormers are carried up to a quite unfamiliar scale. The slightly monastic ground-floor windows facing west are actually enormous, of modern plate glass, and flood the two libraries they front with reading light. The house was originally designed to house the provost, chaplain, two or three canons and a group of senior foundation students, who would be young men assisting in mission work and tutored in preparation for the universities or ordination.

As completed, the built work largely followed the west and south elevations as they were presented in Butterfield's preliminary designs (fig.26), except at the rear and north. Here a 'common hall' was added, running west to east with a single large tripartite east window, carrying distinctive stone tracery under its arch and an open roof of the simplest ridge, collar and rafters. Then a cloister was ranged against the east side of the canons' house and the south of the hall, 'forming two sides of a small quadrangle, intended to be completed hereafter', but which never was. Added to the changing approach to oratory and vestry, these substantial and semi-discrete extensions seem to have appeared quite rapidly, resulting in a general scheme that one writer complained of as 'disjunctive' – an accumulation of parts in different dimensions and orientations, with independent roofs rising to different heights, hipped, open-gabled or gambrelled. In fact, there is something satisfying about the irregularity: a cascade of roofs, arcades and chimneys that we see so pronouncedly from the south, like a village, a farmyard or an ancient abbey with a long history of accretions and happily ready to acquire more.

The choristers' house was completed in October 1851. It was originally designed for sixteen choristers and scholars, a matron, a servant and a resident organist and chanter. It stood free, set back from the furthest terrace, and was shaped like a large Hebridean farm building, with a gambrel roof, without ornament and unselfconsciously simple.

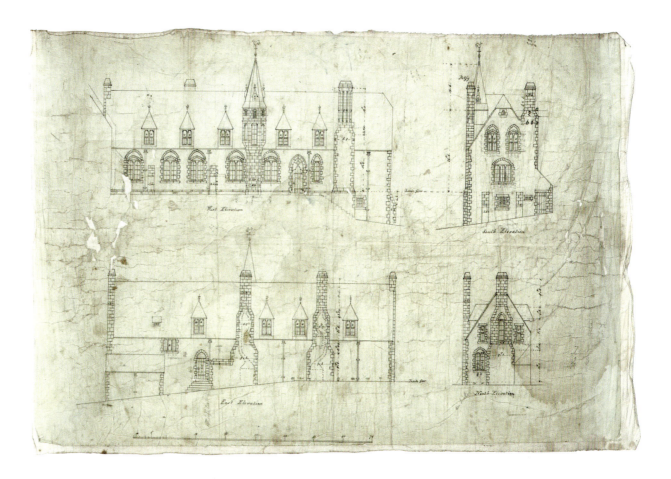

26
College of the
Holy Spirit, Great
Cumbrae: canons'
house elevations,
*c.*1848

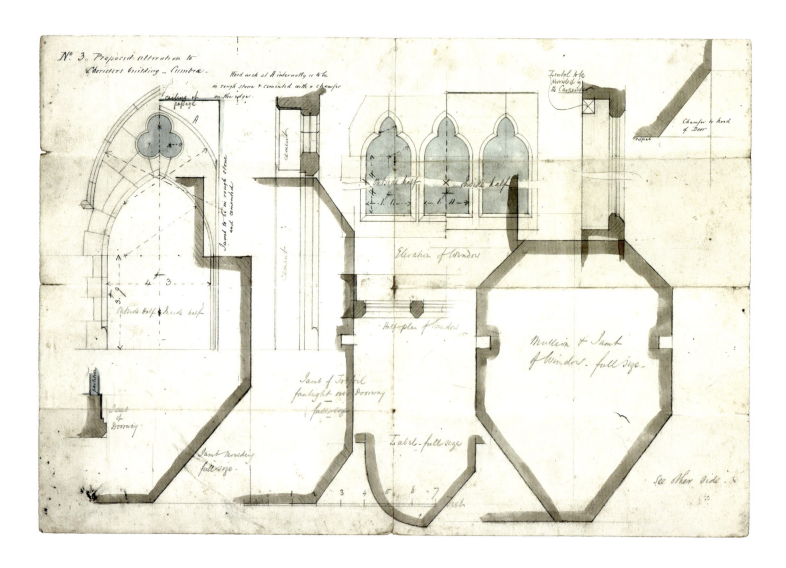

27
College of the
Holy Spirit, Great
Cumbrae: alterations
to choristers' building
– details of door
and library window,
c.1853–4

Changes were made by Butterfield throughout the first years, as the purpose shifted to housing candidates for university and undergraduate reading parties, but, with some very restrained refinement of the main entry and the windows of common rooms, the additions continued in a markedly rustic vein. A sheet of detail drawings (fig.27) shows the windows and door shaped to gain more presence through trefoil heads and a transom light, the stone not traceried but simply cambered.

THE VISTA

A photograph by James Valentine taken from the top of the Presbyterian church (fig.28) shows the ensemble completed, Butterfield finding a structural logic in the moorside, forming terraced earthen planes and cascades of stone steps, paths and platforms, with a walled burial ground opening to the town below and anchored by a great stone cross, which Butterfield had mounted on an ancient plinth, as sentinel.

While the canons' house continued to take a small number of graduate theological students, there was resistance from the new national college at Glenalmond, and another of its original missions – which was to furnish retreat, repose or refreshment to working clergy – became more important. Advertisements stressed the 'seclusion from the Dangers of great cities', and we know from men like the great poet and priest John Keble and Gladstone's vicar son, Stephen Gladstone, who came back many times, that it provided an atmosphere of

28
College of the Holy Spirit, Great Cumbrae: view from the north-west photographed by James Valentine as *Cathedral of the Isles, Isle of Cumbrae*, 1878

respite, prayer, thought and quiet debate stimulated by buildings that stood so aloof from the world. Meanwhile the college provided a second small parish church and primary school for the poor of Millport, a town of 1200 in the winter and 4000 in the summer season; cottage and barn missions, for which a canon rowed 5 miles across the water; and lectures for the townspeople. The greater missionary aspirations among the isles remained unfulfilled, as the Boyles' fortunes were ravaged by bank failure and the college was placed under the trusteeship of the diocese. But a new bishop in 1874, George Mackarness, sought to reawaken the task that he called its 'first love', carrying a renewed 'old catholic' faith, in Gaelic and English, to the far-flung people of the diocese upon which it gazed; and two years later he consecrated it 'Cathedral of the Isles', reminding us that 'Every wave that beats upon the rocky shore reminds us of St Columba and his missionary labours . . . Cha till mi tuilleadh'.[3]

In January 1888, exactly forty years since its inception, with the college now facing closure, a newspaper writer could walk through, regretting its uncertain future but astonished by the degree of attention Butterfield had brought to its making, both in detail and in the whole, 'as if the salvation of the artist depended upon the perfection of his work'.[4] And so – then and ever, in all his projects – did Butterfield feel it did.

NOTES

1. The information on the college's origins is drawn largely from two collections in Archive Services, University of Dundee: College and Collegiate Church of the Holy Spirit: Papers; and Diocese of Brechin: Correspondence of Alexander Penrose Forbes and George Frederick Boyle.

2. The account of the project at Great Cumbrae is drawn principally from George Frederick Boyle, 'Short Account of the History, Constitution, & Objects of the Church and College at Cumbrae', manuscript dated Isle of Cumbrae Lent 1852, Archives and Special Collections, University of Dundee; J.G. Cazenove, 'The Collegiate Church and College in the Island of Cumbrae', appendix to a new edition of Alexander Ewing, *The Cathedral or Abbey Church of Iona*, Grant & Son, Edinburgh, 1872; letters of J.G. Cazenove in the collection of the author; *The Guardian*, 17 July 1850; the very thorough description in *The Ecclesiologist*, December 1859, pp 379–83; *Morning Chronicle*, 15 June 1851, 17 May 1854, and especially the long description of 6 July 1854; *Scottish Magazine and Churchman's Review*, vol.1, 1852, pp 315–17; *Churchman's Companion*, vol.19, 1856, pp 443–50; *The Cumbrae College Calendar*, James Parker & Co., Oxford, 1872, including founding documents; and *Irvine Herald and Kilwinning Chronicle*, 20 August 1881. See also William Perry, *The Oxford Movement in Scotland*, Cambridge University Press, Cambridge, 1933, pp 52–63; Gavin Stamp, 'Cathedral of the Isles', in Peter Howell and Andrew Saint (eds), *Butterfield Revisited*, vol.6 of *Studies in Victorian Architecture and Design*, Victorian Society, London, 2017.

3. Mackarness, quoted in numerous press accounts of the college's consecration as a cathedral, for example *The Buteman*, 6 May 1876.

4. *Ayr Advertiser*, 20 January 1888.

II 'PAROCHIALIA'

CHAPTER 4

THE NEW PARISH SOCIAL SYSTEM, 1845–51

THE CUSTOM OF THE COUNTRY

A S BUTTERFIELD CAME of age in 1835, the state of working people in the towns of England was famously distressed, but the countryside where his work as an independent architect first took flight was often even poorer. There were long-neglected older parishes with churches in ruin, vicars in absentia and education left to a dame school. There were outlying districts devoid of all services except the victuallers', to which villagers had moved to work. Squatter hamlets of subsistence farming had arisen where labouring families had been driven out by the widening of landed estates and the mechanisation of farming. Uncertainty and distress had brought the countryside into fiery, destructive and deadly rebellions throughout the 1830s, first with the Swing Riots of 1830 and then as Chartist risings spread to the countryside in 1839–40, Welsh farm people revolted against tolls and taxes,

and discontent over low wages and high food costs brought bread riots to market towns, burning hay ricks to farmland, and sabotage to bridges and carriages on country roads.

Out of these circumstances, and the threat posed by leaving them to fester, grew the idea of reviving the Church as an agent of social amelioration and control through moral and educational progress. Much of the movement on the ground grew out of humanitarian efforts among young country gentlewomen to nurse the sick poor, tutor neglected children and rescue youth from the influence of godless homes and riotous taverns. But it was also seen as an essential defence against rebellion, an argument that soon won the day against the claim that bringing education among the poor was in fact the *cause* of their disaffection. In reality, the uneasy peace of the twenty years that were to come derived more from a long wave of rural prosperity after 1850, as foodstuffs and mineral resources met the demand of a rapidly growing urban population, and from the widening reach of the regular army, volunteer militias and the courts in the policing of property and public order.

The four principal agencies of the growing movement for 'parish extension and revival' were all fundamentally architectural: a well-ordered, warm and dry church, fit for a reverent service, its pews free and open for the poor; a conspicuous and comfortable parsonage in which a clergyman might be ready to live within his parish; a walled, well-tended graveyard to respect the dead and in which to assemble for muster and mourning rather than riot and sport; and hygienic and accessible schoolrooms for young children, to draw them away from the loose conditions of their homes, and to learn essential habits of social decorum, skills in domestic craft among the girls, and a modicum of arithmetical and language literacy for the boys. Since it quickly became apparent that schools would only become effective when a modern cottage could be offered to attract a competent teacher's family, the 'schoolhouse' began to appear alongside them.

Much of this architectural programme was untested, so that, summoned to the aid of reforming country vicars in the high-church circle, Butterfield was peculiarly well-placed to produce prototypes of the modern vicarage, rural church, mission chapel, churchyard and village school. Some were invented *de novo*, and others – like the lychgate, the litany stool, the lectern and the churchyard cross – revived the forgotten furnishings of an everyday religious life. Then, as the movement grew through the 1850s, he refined – with scrupulous regard for variety, with system but without formula, with respect for local building tradition but without rustic sentimentalism – these new building types as they began to spread nationwide to improve and quiet the 'custom of the country'.

'AN EDUCATION OF HEART AND WILL': MONRO AT HARROW WEALD

In its Christmas issue for 1866, the popular weekly *John Bull*, looking back twenty years, reminded its readers of those 'dark ages in the state of parish work' when established institutions had failed and 'fresh lines of thought and action' had been needed to meet the needs of the countryside.[1] Among the boldest were those of a young vicar at Harrow Weald, a large agricultural village that had begun, once the railway opened nearby in 1845, slowly to edge closer to the life of the metropolis. Edward Monro came to the parish in 1842 at the age of twenty-seven. He had been at Oriel College, Oxford, in the first heady days of the Tractarian movement. Born to the Scottish family of physicians who had served for many years as wardens of Bethlem Royal Hospital (popularly known as 'Bedlam'), and the brother of two pioneers in the new field of psychology, Monro and his wife Emma would never have children, but he was fascinated by youth, and moralising tales for boys appeared almost annually among his flood of publications.

By 1846 Monro had established a parsonage and new parish schools and begun to replace an inadequate and unseemly modern chapel with the first stages of a modest ecclesiological church, working with James Park Harrison, antiquarian, architect and colleague of Butterfield in the Oxford Architectural Society. Having got to know the boys of his parish, Monro developed a radical new plan for their improvement. In March 1846, with the hesitant acquiescence of his bishop and the enthusiastic support of Earl Nelson, Gladstone, the Earl of Selborne, John Keble and other high-church luminaries, he issued an appeal to support a free residential college where 'the sons of poorer classes might be trained for service in the Church as deacons or schoolmasters and be taught early to practise self-denial and self-discipline'. By July Monro had 'taken 16 boys from their homes' to launch 'St Andrew's College' on a site three-quarters of a mile from the parish church where Butterfield began a series of buildings for the college, all in economical red stock brick. At its first anniversary in July 1847, a dining hall was in place, doubling as a temporary chapel, with a schoolroom and bedroom space for twenty-five boys. By its second, Butterfield and Monro could welcome visitors to a fully fledged college, 'wonderfully improved', with a library and a small chapel, making an architectural ensemble which the *Guardian* hailed as 'the most perfect union we ever remember . . . of simplicity and economy with good and right taste'. The assembled grandees were astonished by the demeanour of these raw country boys: 'merry, but without coarseness; full of life and fun, but interfering with no one, – and yet with not a person near them to exercise any control . . . the best proofs of the success and efficiency of their training' – a training that Monro described as 'an education of heart and will' in which freedom of thought and nascent individualism were respected, but models of restraint and self-discipline that allowed that liberty were set by four head boys as 'patterns and examples . . . in word in conversation in charity in spirit in faith in purity'.

Some saw this as a foolhardy exercise in the 'transmutation of raw ploughboys into sweet choristers'. But what emerged was something truly useful and democratic, with a cricket club, prizes in modern history, classical poetry and oration, a debating society, collections of natural science, a quarterly student magazine, a printing press, a chemical laboratory, a glass-painting shop and choral lessons directed by the great liturgical music pioneer Thomas Helmore: at once an industrial college, a choir school, a teacher training college, a miniature public school on a liberal model, and a form of apprenticeship, with students 'placed out' in the summer. By 1851, London's high-church weekly, *The Guardian*, could proclaim it a triumph, 'not a plan or a scheme, but an actual education, which has been tried and has borne fruits'. Butterfield remained involved in the life of the college, introducing a drafting class and a prize competition for architecture. By its fifth year, he had further extended the college for a complement of thirty pupils, including an ambulatory cloister, all still in plain red brick, 'in the simplest and cheapest way, but with a very religious effect'. At that time, Butterfield also took Harrison's simple little parish church in hand, converting it into a chancel and adding a nave with a shallow roof and a porch. It was built with expansion in mind, with foundations and structure ready to support a tower and a roof of higher pitch once the wealth of the parish could sustain it.

Monro conducted another experiment which he christened the 'Nursery', a self-governed parish lodging house for fifteen young farm labourers. 'Collegiate life is good for other ranks at this stage when young men enter into adult life, then,' Monro asked, 'why not for the poor?' The Nursery offered its tenants, who paid five shillings and sixpence a week out of their labourers' wages, civil and hygienic living conditions, a light cycle of daily prayer, the guidance of a vicar, instruction in modern husbandry and farming, training in woodwork, a library, and a mild but strictly enforced code of conduct. From two to four acres of market gardening land was obtained to support the little fellowship; and the product of this common nursery helped feed the community and bring in some shared income. The Nursery began in hastily converted dwellings, but by 1851 it had moved into a new building by Butterfield, designed 'in cottage style', with a separate bedroom for each tenant, a common dining room, a 'room for household prayers', a kitchen, kitchen gardens and ambulatory. The Nursery was a genuine and much-copied success. 'Nursery-Men' found work more readily, were found by medical examiners to be strikingly more healthy, and – introduced to reading, productive gardening, cooperation and civil discourse – were made more ready 'to enter adult life with gladness'.

At the height of Monro's success, in 1853, letters reporting 'grave errors of judgment and practice' came to Butterfield from Monro's wife, Emma, and he passed them to the college trustees, whose confidence in the vicar was now lost. Monro sustained the college for a time with fee-paying students, but by 1860, when he took a parish in the centre of Leeds, its short life ended. During three or four years of good health remaining he conducted parish schoolrooms and evening classes for child labourers with such love and commitment that when he died in 1866, at the age of fifty-one, more than two hundred children left their schoolrooms to walk behind his coffin as it was drawn to the Leeds station. At his burial in the churchyard at

Harrow Weald countless 'Old Andreans' contributed eulogies; and the entire labouring class of the village gave up their wages to honour him with a day of mourning. Butterfield's brick college was first let out for housing, and then partly demolished in 1879 to make way for the suburban encroachment of London. Old collegians rescued the stained-glass windows they had themselves produced, and – while much building material was dismantled and reused – fragments of both college and nursery seem to have been worked into housing that still stands.

MORAL AND SPIRITUAL SUPERINTENDENCE: HOLTHOUSE AT HELLIDON

There is a central tableland in England, where springs and ponds feed streams that flow east to the Wash, west to the Severn and south to the tributaries of the Thames. Part of it rises on the eastern edge of Northamptonshire, where, just below Arbury Hill, sit the ironstone villages of Hellidon and Catesby, to which the 30-year-old Charles Scrafton Holthouse, whose family had inherited the rights to their rectory, came in February 1845. He was the third son, delicate in health and of no great intellectual

29
Church of St John the Baptist, Hellidon: view from the south, mounted albumen silver presentation print, after 1881

pretension, who had gone to Oxford with the path of a clergyman always in mind. He determined to remain unmarried, because of the uncertainty of his health, but was deeply attached to the emerging idea of the family and 'hearth' as the vital incubators of a moral and dutiful life. The 600 people in Hellidon and Catesby – a large rural village for its day – were almost entirely supported by arable farming and grazing. Younger children worked in the fields as seasons demanded, and most left home to be sent out to service between the ages of ten and twelve. There was the site of a vicarage, but the structure itself had gone, so he took lodging at a farmhouse. On his first examination of the church, he fell into one of the pits that had appeared in its sinking floor; was told there had been no resident vicar within the memory of man; and found a churchyard overgrown with nettles and used as a playground.

Holthouse at once applied himself to the recovery of the Hellidon church, turning to Butterfield for a survey and plan, which he had ready to report to the *Ecclesiologist* by the end of April – one of the first published accounts of a proposal for restoration.[2] Butterfield's survey showed a roof that had been progressively lowered and was now unsafe, and the walls of the nave, rebuilt in mock-Gothic in the early eighteenth century, 'so decayed as to render their safety very doubtful'. Rebuilding the nave, repairing the arch of the porch and the buttresses on the outer wall, and raising the roof to its medieval ridge line was costed at £600. Work began early in 1846, and the church reopened, after £800 was spent, in February of 1847. It was the first of Butterfield's many reclamations of degraded village churches and established a procedure he would follow for forty years: searching the archaeology for essential remains, motifs, rhythms and proportions and then using them to inform a rebuilt structure true in its outlines to the probable original at its principal time of construction, incorporating and restoring stable elements and rebuilding those that were lost or irreparably degraded. The results were crisp and clean, without any nostalgic regard for 'patina', but with an overriding concern for durability, producing compositions of ravishing simplicity.

30
Hellidon Grange
Parsonage and
School: view from the
north, photographed
c.1870

Holthouse then turned to the matter of a vicarage. Raising funds through the sale of land attached to the living, he acquired an 'unsightly' farmhouse with stone outbuildings on a hill south-east of the church. Butterfield surveyed the house, finding it 'so dilapidated and decayed as to render it expedient that the same shall be in part taken down and a new house built'. Holthouse then asked for a plan to develop it as both a home for the vicar and a boarding school for boys between nine and fourteen. This was to be an establishment with modest fees for 'sons of farmers and tradesmen', whose primary object was 'the formation of character, . . . to mould them by the teaching of the church of England, and to form within them that manly Christian character by combining the regularity and discipline of school with the confidence and affection of home life'. Bodily health would be promoted by fresh air, open country, swimming ponds and woodland, and moral hygiene by the village's inconvenient distance from the vicious temptations of a town. Boys would attend daily service in the church. The school would begin with four to six boys and a resident matron, with a curate assisting the teaching. Plans for the alterations were first filed in January 1850, and construction of the vicarage, with a schoolroom in the barns, was completed in 1851. Butterfield essentially built a new shell around the core of the existing farmhouse and a link to the range of

granary and barns, where a loft was converted into the schoolroom. There is a rough eloquence to Butterfield's work, dominated by the texture of the soft brown ironstone of these hills, dressed only lightly with plainly cut York stone, and furnished with rustic fireplaces, window seating, a gabled bay and panelling in oak and deal. Concrete is exposed, no constructive element is concealed and, where they serve a purpose, the old window openings of the farmhouse are left in place. Yet there is an absolute precision and refinement of proportion and detail behind the simplicity. It is without a hint of sentimentality – a celebration of the powers and pleasures of the common country home and hearth.

By 1860, when demand had risen, Butterfield had returned for the first of a series of expansions. Over the next seven years new residential and dormitory wings were added behind the vicarage to the east, with the striking additions of a double-height rear bay for the 'best bedroom and study' and a new entrance hall facing the street. The south front was revised; and the land in front of the main service buildings was cleared and lowered, so that a ground floor and courtyard were created for the school, which now stretched the length of the old granary range, a great window replacing the little dormer in the original schoolroom, a dining hall formed beneath it, an outdoor staircase, a timbered gable and a bellcote. By 1870 there were twenty-six pupils with assistant teachers in the new field of 'modern studies': history, geography, languages and natural science. The additions show growing refinement, in the cuts and joints of the undecorated stonework and the lines of the timber-framing and gables, but retain a beautiful severity in eschewing ornament to let the flat planes of wood and masonry sing.

With the Grange in hand, Butterfield and Holthouse turned to the improvement of the village school. This had been conducted from time to time in a thatched schoolroom, but more recently in the premises of a tavern, whose innkeeper was the salaried schoolmaster. By 1861 the thatched school had been replaced by two adjoining schoolrooms with tiled roofs, the attached cottage converted into a teacher's residence, and the school brought into the Church's National system with a trained master

Hellidon: view towards
the church and village
school from the
upper terrace of the
Grange, showing the
extension of the east
wing into a double bay,
photograph by Alfred
Newton, *c.*1890

and mistress. A third classroom for infants, with a
higher roof for the steeply tiered benches that had
become the standard seating to aid the instruction
of the very young, was added at the rear in 1881.

The experiment at the Grange in educating
boys entering puberty on the kindly model of the
family hearth was a notable success, pupils looking
back on their time at Hellidon – from careers in
trade, skilled artisanry and military or civil service
– as a sort of childhood paradise. But Holthouse's
attempts to bring 'pastoral superintendence' to
the everyday life of his disorderly parish had him
working 'constantly uphill', and his health weakened
with the strain. In a Sunday confirmation class
in 1881, the vicar's head fell to the table, and he
died among the children he so loved. By then such
remote stretches of rural England were well into
a long cycle of impoverishment and decline, and
Hellidon's population, which had peaked at close to
650, was now rapidly falling into the 400s. In such

straitened times, Butterfield and Holthouse's plan to
add a cottage hospital to the parish ensemble failed;
and, within three years of Holthouse passing, a new
vicar issued a prospectus for 'Hellidon Grange', now
a preparatory school 'for the sons of noblemen and
gentry', ending the life of the model economical
school in which young boys from the middling classes
of countryside and country town were prepared to
enter working life.

PARISH INSTRUMENTS: PROTOTYPES FOR SCHOOL, CHAPEL AND VICARAGE

East Farleigh was a Kent village of 1500 inhabitants
serving a new railway, a flourishing canal trade and
the now vast market for the hops to season the ale
and porter that, until cleaner water came to the
nation's towns, were among the only cold drinks that
could quench the thirst without endangering health.

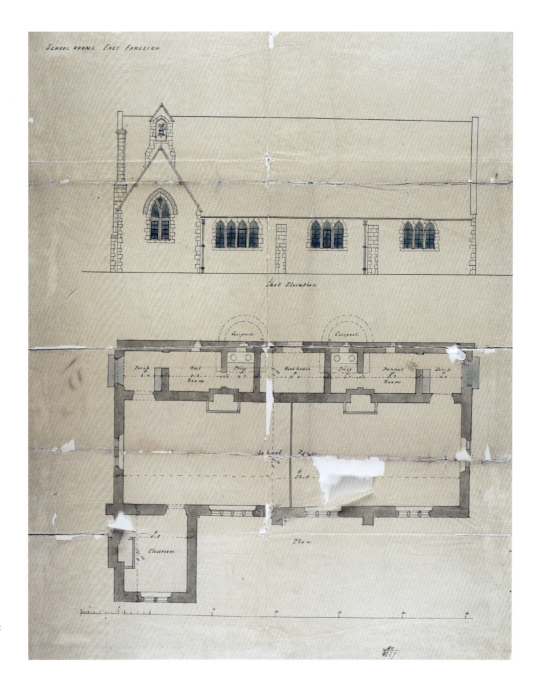

Butterfield's school establishes the system of a single
well-ventilated, high-roofed hall for the schoolroom,
divided if needed by a curtain; tall windows set
above a child's head height, rising over a high
washable dado on which charts and images could be
posted; a secondary, raked-seat classroom, largely
for infants; porch, boot and bonnet rooms in which
boys could be segregated from girls and young
infants in their charge; and separate doorways
opening to boys' and girls' yards and washing and
latrines. East Farleigh was walled in the humble

medium of 'Kentish rag' – large field stones laid at
random right to the supporting corners, with blocks
of cut stone trim around the doors and windows.
It was the first among many of Butterfield's essays
in using local building traditions to realise designs
of more dignity and ambition than was usual.
'The whole', said the *Ecclesiologist*, 'is treated in
a bold and masterly way, with a happy avoidance
of any mere chapel effect. We fully expect to see a
characteristic style arise for our church schools.
The demand is very great and must be supplied.'[3]

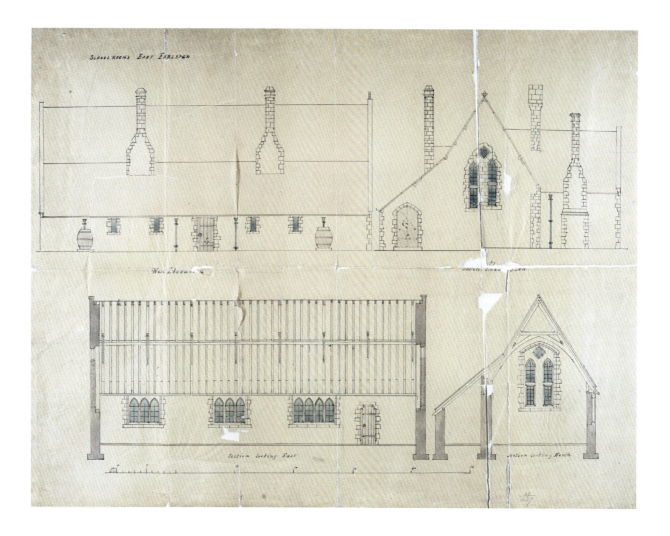

33
East Farleigh School: elevations and sections, 1845

Visiting a year later, the school inspector found East Farleigh closed due to the difficulty of attracting and maintaining instructors, but Butterfield added a teacher's house late in 1847, and the school then flourished.

Butterfield's theory of the national Church derived from working in disparate and often isolated sectors of the country, neglected by the Church, with no sense of a common or national life. Hamlets and households within a single parish might speak a different dialect to their neighbours, and so great was the localisation of culture that learning the common language, comportment and conversation of a town – or of a country house for those entering service – was a painful and dangerous process. Butterfield's Church would therefore be the instrument for advancing a common ethical culture, building for the entire nation 'a memory of its national history and . . . reviving a particularly

English moral character'. In this the primary school would be the fundamental agent. East Farleigh, with its visible echoes of an old abbey school and the sense of external dignity and internal decorum that it offers children, is a vivid architectural expression of that intent. An even more persuasive instance is the utterly beautiful schoolroom and schoolmaster's house that appeared in 1848–9 at Aston Cantlow. Shaped in a great L of stonework, it sheds the slight solemnity of East Farleigh to fit itself with a sort of comfortable, rambling, lyric grandeur into the lush water pastures of Arden, echoing without imitating the stone barns and farms of the region where Butterfield's career had begun. From thence forward, historical echoes grow progressively fainter, as Butterfield develops a specific aesthetic grammar for the country school, inscribing into the rural landscape little poems to civility and aspiration, each deriving its exact character from its

St Edmund in
Dunchurch,
Thurlaston: school,
schoolhouse and
chapel, later the parish
church of Thurlaston,
photographed *c*.1890

own locale, but clearly signalling its adherence to a national life and purpose.

Butterfield told a friend that William Butler of Wantage 'dropped upon him one day with this order: – "Build me chapel for a hundred pounds." "What do you mean? It's impossible." "No, I mean it; I can only afford 100 pounds. A Dissenting preacher has set up his pulpit in one of our hamlets; I know I can preach him out in a month". The chapel was built, and the work done'.[4] The chapel, at Charlton, served as a day school on weekdays and a church and Sunday school on Sundays. In stock brick covered in roughcast plaster, with elm benches and kneelers covered in leather, crowned with a little wooden bellcote, and widely noticed, it served to pilot a new concept of the 'chapel-school'. In 1848–9 in John Sandford's model Warwickshire parish of Dunchurch near Rugby, a more adventurous version was attempted. Sandford's *Parochialia* of 1845, detailing his experiments at Dunchurch as a pilot for the socially responsive country parish, had been widely noticed and followed by country clergy.[5] At Thurlaston, a hamlet growing large on the outskirts of Rugby, Sandford took his experiments a step further with an unprecedented typological combination, following a suggestion made by his friend Thomas Arnold of Rugby, of installing in a single structure all the elements

of what he called 'an incipient church'.[6] Here Butterfield works in exposed brick, attaching a tower for the schoolteacher house to a high-roofed schoolroom with a raised dais at the east end to turn into the chancel of a church on Sundays. The model was of immediate interest to colonial bishops, some of whom adopted it, and Thurlaston itself was a marked success, the school (as intended) finding new quarters as the village grew, and the chapel then becoming the church of a new parish of St Edmund, with the schoolhouse adapted, as Butterfield's design anticipated, into the bell tower at its western end.

Butterfield undertook another experiment in consolidation and economy at the same time for Sir John Taylor Coleridge in the little village of Alfington near Ottery St Mary, where he was restoring the church. Coleridge was the proprietor of this village, where he determined to build on his own modest resources a church, school, teacher's house and parsonage that would demonstrate the simplicity and efficiency with which a complete parochial ensemble could be installed. The church was a simple chapel covered in roughcast concrete, pierced with a sparing set of narrow deep-set lancets, the three at the east end with windows by Pugin, finished without tracery, and the roof was a delicate web of open timbers, the last of its bowed arches carrying a simply carved rood. The domestic buildings were all woven together into a single interlocking structure, resulting in a great economy of construction, materials and maintenance. The complex was completed in 1852 with the addition of a simple buttressed bellcote to the church.

In 1847 the high churchman James Bliss was appointed to the parish of Ogbourne St Andrew in Wiltshire. The parish was a large one, incorporating three villages, some outlying settlements and a population of nearly 700. There was high grazing land for sheep; arable land and cattle pasture below; racehorse breeding and coursing; and a gravel pit to supply the road and rail laying for the new town and train yards of Swindon, 9 miles to the north. The area had been one of the centres of the rural revolt of 1830–31, when a number of farms had been burned and crops destroyed;

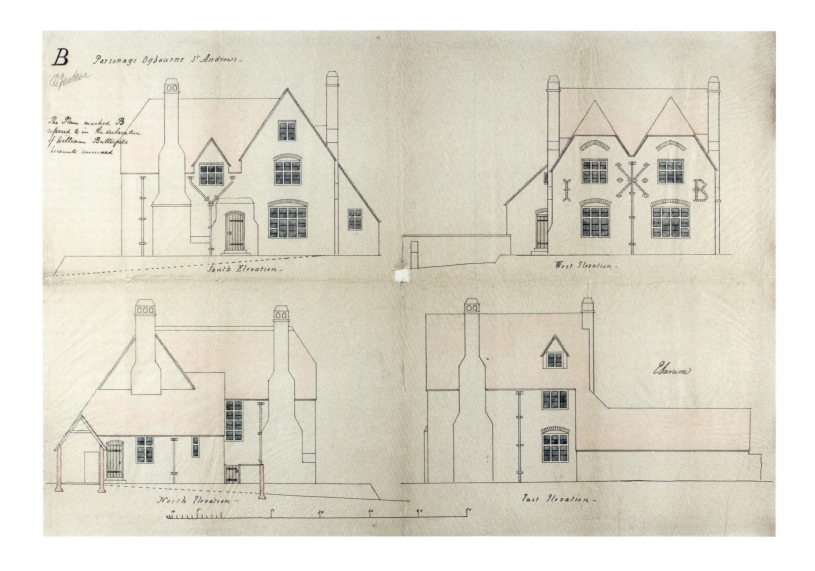

The Plan marked B referred to in the declaration of William Butterfield hereunto annexed

B Parsonage Ogbourne S.t Andrews

South Elevation

West Elevation

North Elevation

East Elevation

35

Ogbourne St Andrew Parsonage: elevations, c.1847

and its parish life had since been much neglected. The old vicarage stood apart from the village, a little to the south, above the east bank of the river, on the north-east corner of a substantial plot of glebe land. Bliss found the church, with its gallery, high pews and vacant chancel, inadequate for the size of the parish; unsuited to a decent form of service; and discriminatory towards the poor. As for the vicarage, due to the 'extreme poverty of the previous incumbent', it had fallen into ruin and could no longer be inhabited. He turned at once to Butterfield for solutions to both projects.[7] Designs and specifications for an entirely new vicarage at the considerable sum of £1200 were filed in March 1848; groundwork began in May; and it was ready by the autumn of 1849, when the church reopened on Butterfield's new plan, with gallery removed,

expanded seating on low open pews, many of them left free for the poor, and a chancel tiled, stalled and equipped for communion.

Elements of Ogbourne rectory – the combination of a hipped roof end with steep pointed gables and dormers; the orientation of principal rooms to a vista rather than a ceremonial entry; and an absolute delight in brick and the means of laying it – reappear in nearly all Butterfield's subsequent domestic works. Adopting local building features in local materials, often with village builders whose craft in employing them was long tested, he avoids the picturesque by stripping down details and emphasising structure, lending a vicarage gravity to the comfortable and familiar. There are four striking features – the great fall of roof at the roadside; the symbolic hearth-shape of the south porch; the three enormous extruded chimney towers that anchor the composition; and the subtly asymmetrical west front, which carries in the brickwork, at a startling scale visible to shepherds on the high downs across the valley, the unusual sacred monogram 'IXB', for 'Jesus Christ, helpmate'. The whole west front of the parsonage, with the eyebrows of its upper windows raised to an exceptional height, with a welcoming door and gate into the yard and pantry for the poor to claim their bread and coal, epitomises the idea of a display of dignity and service that Keble called the necessary 'remonstrance' of a parsonage. There is still a shock upon seeing this house, with its readiness to follow the functional logic of the plan, even to extremes, so that planes are all unembellished in a uniform monochromatic palette; gables, folded and plain, are strikingly acute; and the kitchen roof falls near to the ground against the cold and windy north on a sheer incline of 28 feet at 60 degrees. Specifications fill a dense twelve-sheet manuscript, with extraordinary attention to weatherproofing, waste and drainage, and to a dry and stable substructure, for which Butterfield mixed the stones of the derelict old parsonage, ancient sarsens as post and anchor, and modern concrete to seal and secure the fill. Above, he called – the first clue we find of his intensive curation of brickwork – for 'good hard rock burnt red stock bricks, the most even coloured selected for the facing of walls . . . to be laid with a neat close joint struck in fine mortar'. Elaborate specifications for mortars change the width and colour of the bonding at certain levels to bring horizontal lines into the composition and strengthen the bearings without the expense of stone courses.

He may not have been entirely happy with the result since, for his next brick parsonage, at Woolston in Buckinghamshire, Butterfield bought the brick himself and shipped it to the site, along with exacting specifications on how to cover the waiting pile against weather, and with precise recipes for the mix of mortars, stating how much, at what times of day and in which weathers to prepare them. Expanding on such building manuals as John Reid's *Young Surveyor's Preceptor* (1845) and Alfred Bartholomew's *Specifications for*

Practical Architecture (1840), Butterfield's lengthy specifications, filed in the County Records Office, moved a step forward from Ogbourne towards the most advanced hygienic and sanitary systems, accounting for every detail of plumbing, whether in toilet (where a newly patented cistern and privy apparatus is called for), well or scullery, particularly to protect against waste deposits, spillage, grease accumulation and poor drainage of effluents. Walls and floors of service areas were to be finished in specific washable surfaces, window mullions and closing latches are meticulously described to overcome drafts, and the placement of ventilating bricks is precisely identified.

NOTES

1. The account of the Monro collegiate projects is drawn principally from Edward A. Monro, *Parochial Work*, second edition, J.H. Parker, London, 1851, pp 189–98; *Buckinghamshire Herald*, 17 July 1847; *Churchman's Companion*, 7 August 1847; *The Guardian*, 1 October 1851; and 'Common Lodgings for the Poor', *The Guardian*, 14 May 1851.

2. The account of Hellidon Grange is drawn from written documents in the Holthouse Papers at the Northamptonshire Record Office, including builder's accounts, Holthouse's short memoir and manuscript chronology of parish improvements, obituary notices, his open letter to parishioners, and a draft prospectus and final perspective sketch by Holthouse of the school; as well as from Butterfield's 1851 drawings for the parsonage filed in the records of the Church Commissioners there; and *The Ecclesiologist*, May 1845.

3. *The Ecclesiologist*, April 1846.

4. Arthur John Butler, *Life and Letters of William John Butler*, Macmillan, London, 1897, pp 57–8.

5. John Sandford, *Parochialia; or, Church, School, and Parish: The Church System, and Services, Practically Considered*, Longman, Brown, London, 1845.

6. *The Guardian*, 24 January 1864.

7. The account is drawn from the extensive specifications, proposal, contractual documents and building accounts for the Ogbourne parsonage, which are filed with the drawings in the records of the parish at Wiltshire and Swindon Archives.

CHAPTER 5

CHURCH EXTENSION, 1845–57

NEW MODELS OF A COUNTRY CHURCH:
COALPIT HEATH AND WEST LAVINGTON

T IS 1846, AND 'JOHN BUNYAN' is by now well known to the literate classes of Bristol. He is the notoriously lazy mount of Joseph Leech, a young Irishman who arrived from County Clare in 1839, and, at the age of twenty-four, became proprietor and principal writer of the high-church, high-Tory *Bristol Times and Mirror*. Every Sunday, John Bunyan, with assiduously recorded reluctance, carries Leech on a pilgrim's progress round the city and its outskirts to report on the condition of local churches. Leech is relentless in his assault on absenteeism, laziness and cant among the clergy, and no less sparing in listing the crimes of architectural convenience perpetrated by churchwardens and diocesan architects. This Sunday, however, he walks over to Butterfield's new stone church in Coalpit Heath, now one year old, and declares: 'We do not think we have seen for years a sacred building, so beautiful in itself, harmonizing so sweetly with the rural character of the surrounding scene. There is in it and the adjoining parsonage, even to the eye of the indifferent traveller, something eminently simple, solemn, and pastoral, which shows that more than mere architectural skill – namely, feeling, and sentiment – must have been employed in preparing and effecting the work'.[1]

The commission for a church and parsonage, some 7 miles north-east of Bristol, apparently came by competition, but Butterfield was well-connected in the city. His mother's sister had married into the Wills family of tobacco magnates, with whom he stayed often as a youth. As a student in London he had submitted drawings for the famous Clifton

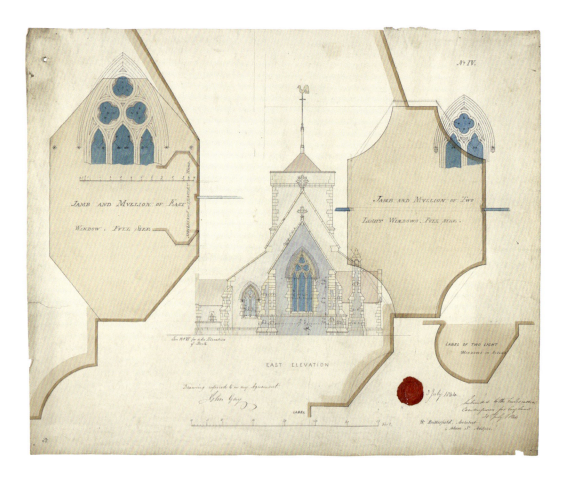

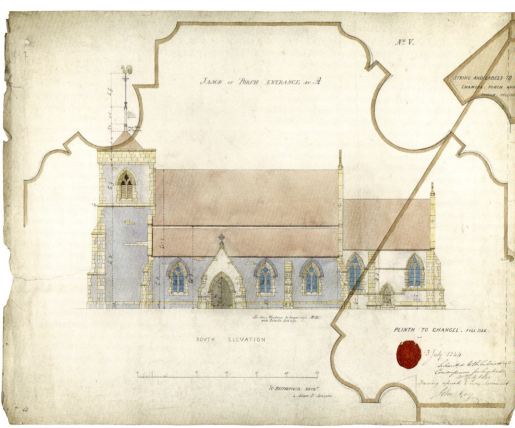

36

St Saviour's Church, Coalpit
Heath: east elevation and
window details, 1844

37

St Saviour's Church, Coalpit
Heath: south elevation, 1844

Bridge competition, and just a year before Coalpit opened, completed his first church – a punctiliously ecclesiological Congregational chapel in the Bristol suburb of Highbury. His drawings for the church at Coalpit Heath were presented to the Ecclesiological Society in May 1844 and greeted with acclaim; the agreements with a local builder, John Gay of Downend, were completed by the end of July; and the church and its walled yard were ready for dedication in October 1845. The cost of the church, dedicated to St Saviour, was £2700, raised largely by small subscriptions, and £900 for the parsonage, completed by Butterfield on land adjacent in 1846. It has a lovely complexity of form but is rather cold, celibate and austere – unlike Butterfield's vicarage at Wilmcote, built for a large family at the same time, which, facing carefree on its gardens, carries many more hints of tracery and the ecclesiastic but reconciles them with a world of children and country pleasures.

It is an unusually large village church, seating over 500, with a 60-foot-long nave, 20 feet wide and serving 'a very poor population . . . quite 2000 in number' who had left the fields behind to work the shallow coalfields – 'proverbial for vice and irreligion' – that served the growing city nearby. It was built in bricks of mixed grey stone from the local quarries, with cut stone blocks and moulding for the quoins and trim. A number of then unfamiliar features startled the conservative press: the high open roof with its timber structure unpainted and fully exposed; the fretwork wooden screen beneath the chancel arch; the gable crosses; a font with an elaborate wooden cover; the use of encaustic tiles with symbolic devices; and bold iron strapwork. All would have been common to a church of the sixteenth century but had since been destroyed or stored unused. The drawings do not show the low buttressed wall that surrounded the church and its then small yard; but it too was an innovation, and one particularly dear to Butterfield, in whose work the making of distinct perimeters, enclaves and divisions would remain a persistent concern. This was not just to conform to the rubrics of the Prayer Book but to implement that emerging Victorian concern for the categorisation of space into

hierarchies of function, an idea of the visible order of things that was becoming essential to the psychic comfort and social order of a volatile mass society. The reputation for vice and irreligion was rapidly dispelled: by the time of Leech's second visit, he found its people, leading the perilous and unhealthy lives of miners, 'interesting themselves with almost alacrity' in their church, raising a subscription for an organ and clock, and asking for an evening service to be added to the morning daily prayer to meet the colliers' twenty-four hours of shifts.

Coalpit is a young architect's work. Rhythm and proportion that would later come by instinct here arrive by measure: each step in the elaborate sequences of interval and level and every turn of moulding is mathematically derived; and the plan adheres strictly to ecclesiological rubrics on such matters as the placement and scale of the porch. This was, as a result, the first and last of Butterfield's churches to reap unqualified plaudits from the ecclesiologists, but it lacks the intense characterful presence on the ground, and the liberating spatial freedom within, that would soon after – as at West Lavington – become the signatures of Butterfield's work.

In 1849 Butterfield completed a small village church, school and parsonage in Henry Manning's Sussex parish of Lavington for a new living. Manning's curate and confessor, Charles Laprimaudaye, had taken on the care of the district and bore the entire cost of the church. His wife was sister to the London merchant John Gellibrand Hubbard, an associate of Butterfield in the Margaret Chapel Engagement who had helped to establish the St Saviour community in Osnaburgh Street, whose family would go on to initiate Butterfield's church at Newbury in Berkshire, and who undertook himself the creation of his London masterpiece of St Alban in Holborn. The site was a sloping rabbit warren, which Butterfield terraced into long shelves of earth, riding the church, in local Wealden sandstone, on the top of them and crowning it with a shingled bell tower and short spire, typical to the Sussex Downs. He laid it out on an unusual plan, reportedly drawn from that of a local thirteenth-century church, the porch at the far west end, and all his fixed low seats

THE FUNERAL OF MR. COBDEN: THE INTERMENT IN WEST LAVINGTON CHURCHYARD.—SEE PAGE 356.

38

Funeral of Richard
Cobden – interment
in West Lavington
churchyard, detail
from *Illustrated
London News*,
15 April 1865

aisle and defiance of the 'traditionary' practice
of placing the entry in the second bay. Was 'our
eminent architect' now 'registering the first traces
of an excessive reaction' from 'architectural rules'?
Indeed he was, and to modern eyes the adaptation
on a smaller, more informal footprint of the plan
of Coalpit Heath, loosening it from the fanatically
regulated progressions and solemnly measured
proportions that make Coalpit a little tight and
discomfiting, has produced a form in which the
play of light upon its internal structure induces
calm and serenity through its freedom and vitality
– a paradox that will spell 'Butterfield' for fifty
years to come.

West Lavington became the local church, on his
retirement, of Richard Cobden, who had remained
a Sussex countryman and conservative member of
the Church of England throughout a career as the
radical advocate of the interests of new classes in
the nation's towns. Delegations from workingmen's
associations all over the industrial towns of the
north marched from the station to join the Liberal
and Radical political establishment at his funeral
in 1865 (fig.38), and, as a pilgrimage site for the
working-class movement, the little church for years
thereafter became one of the best-known country
churches in the land.

set into a block 12 foot wide, leaving two wide-
open aisles, like cloisters, each with a window at
either end, and fitting the chancel into a long and
narrow eastern extension. It is a tiny church whose
open rafters rise to a dramatic height but avoid the
shadowy effect of a great roof over a small space
through the light-filled aisles. These, along with a
radically pointed west window, illuminate capitals
of carved leaves, adapted from his survey notes at
Teversham, and a chancel arch whose heads are
thickly moulded into stone ferns like those he had
studied at Southwell Minster in Nottinghamshire.
The interior is mostly of local chalk, increasing
the effect of lightness. The porch, shockingly
un-ecclesiological in being almost flush to the
south-west corner of the nave, 10 feet square and
reaching to the drip lines of the roof, is of English
oak timber framing on a substructure of masonry. It
is in wonderfully disproportionate scale, to shelter
mourners and encourage rich and poor to linger
together, and is in sympathy with the belfry and
spire of the same material and structure.

The *Ecclesiologist* was troubled: 'an interesting
and excellent design very sympathetic to Sussex,
but deprived of much of its beauty by . . . the
"crotchets" of its author', who is charged with a
number of errors, including hints of inadmissible
later Gothic in the windows, the lack of a centre

THE YORKSHIRE PARISHES OF VISCOUNT DOWNE: SESSAY, COWICK AND WYKEHAM

In April, 1848, in the last days of a great famine,
with the memory of rural agitation still fresh, and
at the height of anxiety over the threatened Chartist
revolution, Butterfield quietly completed at Sessay,
near Thirsk, a new ensemble of church, school and
schoolhouse.[2] It was the first in a remarkable series
of works through which William Henry Dawnay,
7th Viscount Downe, endeavoured to transform
the moral, educational and domestic well-being of
those living in and near his rapidly accumulating
portfolio of vast estates – in Surrey, Rutland, the
Humberhead Levels, the Vale of Pickering, the
North York Moors and the riverine lands between

Ripon and Thirsk. He was, as his wise chaplain, the great Yorkshire memoirist John Atkinson, noted, 'A good, right-thinking earnest-minded man . . . largely interested in the well-doing and well-being of the many tenants who held under him as well as more generally of the parishioners at large'.[3] Born two years before Butterfield in 1812, Dawnay had made his country home with his uncle at the rectory of Ashwell in Rutland, where he had been its reform-minded Tory MP. Though he had sworn to his rural constituents to uphold the Corn Laws, he was sufficiently affected by the hunger and famines of the early 1840s to reverse his view, joined the prime minister Sir Robert Peel in effecting their repeal, and consequently pledged not to seek re-election – a matter that became moot on inheriting his father's Irish peerage in 1846, along with the rectory-manor of Sessay, one among five such parishes over which his father and grandfather had held rather careless title as rector, developing the Sessay rectory into a comfortable country home and either neglecting parish work or leaving it in the charge of curates.

Sessay, a scattered parish of just over 400 residents, lay not far from the line of the coming Great Northern Railway. It was a mixed arable, orchard and grazing community of slightly undulating flats, still discernibly carved into the ridge-and-furrow pattern of medieval farmland. The ancient parish church had been moved from a distant site in the seventeenth century to be closer to the rectory-manor for the convenience of a growing lordly estate, and entirely reconfigured into a 'miserable Italianised structure' in which only occasional 'points of interest' from the medieval fabric could be discerned. Viscount Downe turned to Butterfield at once to bring it into order, and their solution was one that Butterfield would adopt in many subsequent instances, effectively building an entirely new church on and around the existing footprint and foundation, and redeploying the finer masonry saved from the older church into a new design of his own.

The new school was built first, to house services during construction, with materials and features matching those of the church, but shaped in a cottage manner that begins to shed the monastic character of East Farleigh. Building works on the church itself, St Cuthbert's, commenced by the summer of 1847. The cut stone was magnesian from a quarry 15 miles to the south-west, grey slate covered the graded slopes of the roof, and weathered local oak shingles clad a spire in the simplest geometry of a 'Rhenish helm', its weathercock rising 72 feet from the ground. A stone and oak-covered lychgate with a sexton shed and boiler house guarded the entry; the burial ground was levelled and its ancient ruined cross rebuilt; clear paths and buttressed stone perimeter walls appeared, along with geometric swathes of common and a well-tended roadway crossing the brook to the south over a new stone bridge by Butterfield that bore the Dawnay arms. All these wove school, schoolhouse and church into an ordered open landscape. Local writers saw at once that the use of simple forms and surfaces in a consistent palette of local materials had introduced a new type of country church, calling it a 'veritable rural temple' based on 'the best and purest models of early English' – a landmark of the 'pastoral ideal' that could be seen for miles from the passing train.

That pastoral ideal was then extended to a set of model cottages in which Butterfield and Viscount Downe demonstrate hygienic, durable and comfortable brick dwellings for the working people of the village. The work began in 1851, and by the time of an 1858 survey, following the Viscount's death the previous year, three groups of new cottages in three different typologies had been completed along Church Lane, which carried this linear village north-east on a semicircular boundary deriving from monastic gardens, mounds and fisheries. There are a line of three double houses within their own fruit and vegetable gardens, with entry porches to the side, each facing in a different direction; a pair of street-side semi-detacheds for agents or managers; and an intriguing short terrace facing the street but opening behind to a large common orchard for tenants. All are marked by high well-ventilated roofs, dormers and gambrels, and a complete disregard for the formal and ornamental conventions of the Gothick estate cottage. They are simply and very beautifully realistic and laid the

39

Model cottages,
Sessay: one of the
double cottage units,
photograph from
stereoscopic view,
taken by H.S.
Goodhard-Rendel,
*c.*1920

groundwork for Butterfield's model rural housing
that followed soon after – at Ashwell, Baldersby,
Ruston in Yorkshire and Great Bookham in Surrey
for the Downe estates, and outside Leicester for
James Beaumont Winstanley – with which they
constitute a portfolio, blooming in less than a
decade, of almost lyrical realism, variety, common
sense and ingenuity.

In 1843, Dawnay had married Mary Isabel
Bagot, daughter of a reforming bishop who is said
to have given his blessing on condition that Dawnay
would build four new churches in the course of
his marriage. On becoming Viscount Downe, he
inherited the family seat at Cowick Manor in the
sprawling parish of Snaith, a great hall that had lain
empty for some years. The manor lands were not
extensive, but the surrounding area was scattered
with remote hamlets on terrain often hard to travel
where Viscount Downe exchanged portions of his
own land to obtain sites for three full parish groups

– two in areas out of reach and a third, in which the
mother house of the new district would sit, in fields
to the north of the hall. This was watery country,
much of it land reclaimed in the eighteenth century
and barely rising above sea level amid a web of
rivers and drainage channels feeding the Humber.
New railways and the massive Aire and Don canal
moved chemicals and coal through to the new port
of Goole, and onwards to the Baltic, bringing back
Riga timber, cut in the yards down river, to build the
cities of Yorkshire. There were peat moors and water
meadows; and a microclimate suited to cash crops,
including hemp for the ropes of shipping. The signs
of a long-built human history were few; there was a
scent of the Low Countries to the brick vernacular;
but the land looked as it looks still – like absolutely
nowhere else in its emptiness within the British Isles.

The selection of sites was difficult, not only
because of scarce buildable land, but due to the very
straggling character of the place. The strategy seems

to have been to find a location on roadways between small population centres, in order to make them convenient for as many as possible: the Hensall group was south of the village on the road to the locks of the Aire canal and the hamlet of Heck; Pollington's between Pollington and Balne; and the mother church of the new parish at East Cowick, closer to a village and to the manor but looking north across a vast estuarine expanse. In each place, working in concrete for infrastructure, cement for interior walls, and a lovely Lincoln brick, to a repeatable system of extreme economy, Butterfield built a unique towering church and graveyard, with parsonage, school and schoolhouse beside them, of startling modernity at startling speed.[4]

Foundations were laid on a single day in July 1853, and they were consecrated over a single week in November of the following year. Schools and parsonages were built like the churches all in brick, with steeply pitched roofs and large hipped dormers, with coverings of Welsh slate at schools and red tile at parsonages, Hensall's quickly becoming known as 'The Red House'. Windows were uniformly modern wood-frame sashes, with some casements for ventilation in the schools. The parsonages have a vertical presence and the schools a horizontal. The different character given to each of the three churches is remarkable. Pollington, lying along a slight treeless rise or dyke, houses nave and chancel under a continuous high ridge, and is dominated inside and out by its skyline of spine, the sheer drop of the roofs and the uninterrupted vertical thrust of an extruded belfry and flanking buttresses. Hensall, settling into the slightest dip, with a bell tower at the porch overlapping the narthex, speaks more to a sense of clustering and ensemble. The Cowick church, Holy Trinity, rose from a completely level plain of open meadowland, seating close to 400 with stalls for the patron and a choir of eighteen; it is scaled slightly larger, taking its measure from a 75-foot tower (St Paul's, Hensall, is 65 feet and St John the Baptist's, Pollington, 60), and has a more complex rhythm of roof timbers, more moulded shafts and a western face of three fierce deep-set buttressed lancets that commands the landscape along the road and dominates interior vistas.

Close by, the effect at the churches is one of high sacred drama inside and out, achieved through the decisive independence of their stance on the land, the intensely steep pitch of roofs, uninterrupted monochromatic planes of earth-red brick and tile, and bold structure clearly revealed. The Cowick ensembles – church, school, schoolhouse and parsonage – all develop a vocabulary of form first essayed in full at West Pinchbeck in 1849 (where the church is in stone) in the equally forbidding flatlands of Lincolnshire's South Holland district.

The human success of the experiment was modest. Ten years later vicars reported difficulties in bringing in congregations, the 'scattered' pattern of dwelling still being an obstacle, especially in bad weather. Farmers in the parish demanded labour on Sunday. Night schools were unrealistic where schoolrooms were difficult enough to reach by day. By then, however, both day and Sunday schools had begun to flourish. Pollington, out of a total population of 863, had 90 children on the register for day school, and Hensall could support both a master and mistress. But children had all gone away into labour or service by the age of twelve. As these nine austerely beautiful and efficient buildings rose, Butterfield's great friend John Duke Coleridge, then an art critic, antiquarian and struggling lawyer, would present a paper in Exeter, reporting his discussions with Butterfield on 'the necessity of modernism' in sacred architecture, begging for an exploration of new forms of splendour built from modern materials, produced to a system and deployed with simplicity.[5] No works could have illustrated that argument with more force.

In 1851, Dawnay's uncle Marmaduke Langley died without issue, and bequeathed him the vast properties of Wykeham Abbey and the adjacent manor of Hutton Buscel, set in rich champaign at the west end of the Vale of Pickering and encompassing a great swathe of the moors behind it. The house stood by the ruins of an abbey church in the valley, within which lay a small medieval parish church, reworked in Italianate fashion a generation before for the convenience of the abbey and to house its family monuments. It was both unwelcoming and increasingly inconvenient for villagers, who were

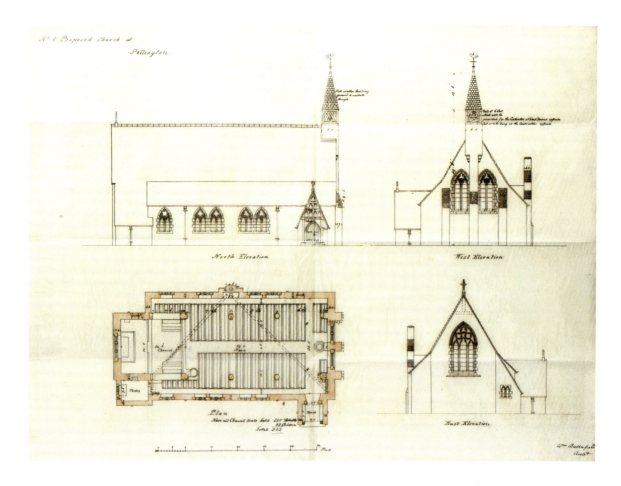

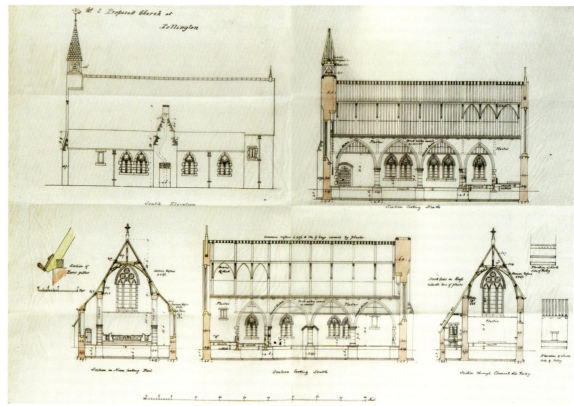

40
Pollington Church:
trace copy of elevations
and plan, 1852

41
Pollington Church:
trace copy of elevation
and sections, 1852

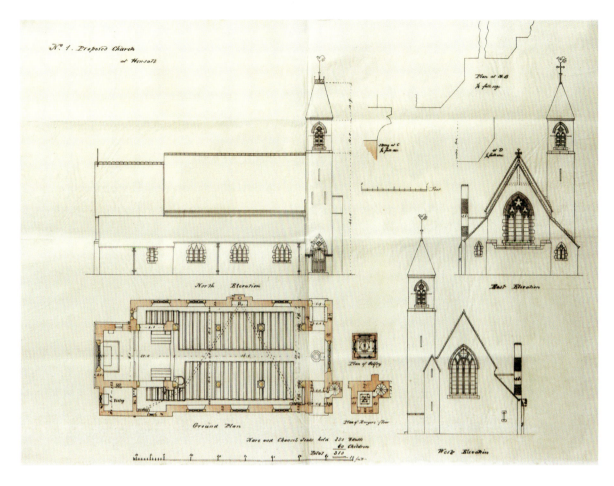

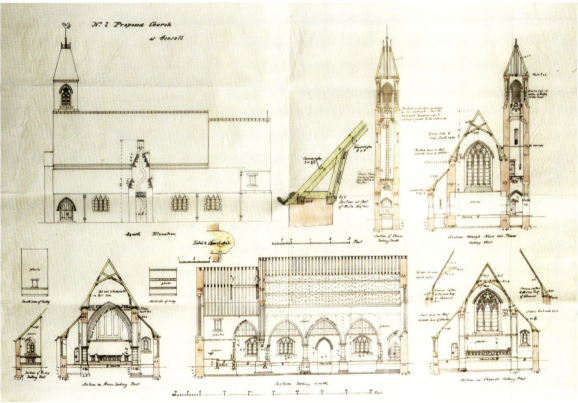

42
Hensall Church: trace copy of elevations and plan, 1852

43
Hensall Church: trace copy of elevations and sections, 1852

44
St Helen's Tower and
All Saints' Church,
Wykeham: view
from the south-west,
photographed *c*.1900

determined were the original, pre-Italianate lines of the old one. In a daring move, Butterfield then rebuilt the ruined St Helen's Tower on its site to serve as a lychgate and added an entirely new belfry and spire. Everything is in a single tone of yellow sandstone, with varying degrees of cut and finish. The whole ensemble was in place by November 1854, and the church – looking compact but actually seating 340 – fits so comfortably into its difficult position that it could easily be passed by, looking as if it had always been there – as, in a way, it had.

THE COMPACT CHURCH: WARESLEY, LANDFORD, MILTON

Waresley Park in Cambridgeshire was among the estates of the Lords Feversham, the Duncombe family, whose properties on the North York Moors made them neighbours of Viscount Downe at their summer seat in Danby. In 1841 it had passed mostly into the care of Octavius Duncombe, who took a very similar interest in his tenantry and manor, building a new village centre with model housing close to the crossroads, and there, in about 1853 just as Wykeham was nearing completion, he and his family engaged Butterfield to build a new parish church. It was a wheat and barley district with a population of less than 300. The existing church dated from 1728, when, the old parish church having been destroyed by a windstorm, it was built as a replacement in a very rough imitation of Christopher Wren's chapel at Pembroke College, Cambridge, which had the advowson of the parish. It lay inconveniently in its ancient graveyard in an isolated position, had not been well maintained, and 'was totally devoid of all ecclesiastical character'.[7] Butterfield demolished it, placing a stone memorial cross on the site of its altar and a grove of lime trees to show the footprint of the medieval nave, and extending the burial ground so that it could now serve as the parish cemetery. The new church, in stone with a north aisle, its broached spire rising 100 feet above the plains, a semi-transept for the organ on the north, and the whole seating at least 120, was consecrated in the summer of 1857.

settled further north near the road to Scarborough. There stood the remains of an earlier village, known as Marton, with a church of St Helen's, which had burned down long before and lay in utter ruin, except for the remnant of a medieval tower. The Viscount asked Butterfield for a new parish church, a school and teacher's house and a parsonage, all to be close to the site of the ancient ruined church.[6]

Butterfield built up the land above and a little east of the ruin, supporting it with a massive buttressed retaining wall against the road, and then terraced the crest of the berm to provide a site for the new All Saints' Church. The vicarage, just east of the church site, using its sloping site to play a symphony of staggered levels, was constructed first, with a hall between vicarage and church site to serve as a temporary chapel during construction and a parish hall thereafter; the school and schoolhouse were constructed in stone soon after, just below the high road. The old church at the abbey was pulled down in 1853 (the site of its altar marked with a cross), its sandstone blocks harvested to build the new church, which closely followed what Butterfield

45
Church of St James
the Great, Waresley:
ink study sketches
for south and east
elevations, 1853

Study sketches in the estate archives seem to date from the spring of 1853, when design was in development. A rough plan and elevations with the chancel somewhat undetermined (fig.45) examines the spire starting at the line of the roof ridge, while a more finished perspective (fig.46) shows the bell tower raised above a parapet that lies higher than the ridge tiles of the nave. It is the second option that was built, though the position of the tower was reversed, so that it attaches to the entrance bay of the north aisle and faces its great splayed buttressed porch to the road. Loving attention is paid to the geometry of the shingled helm, which is shaped in cambered planes similar to the spires at Wykeham and Sessay. A consecration report in the Cambridge press found it 'one of the neatest and most appropriate village churches we ever saw'.[8]

The parish church for Landford lay on the north-east corner of the New Forest, adjacent to a manor long held by the Eyre family, to whose vast north Wiltshire estates Butterfield's friend Earl Nelson and his mother were both attached. It was a difficult and isolated parish, eking out a living from gravel pits, lacemaking and the gathering of forest products and provender. Lady Nelson had begun a National school with a resident teacher at the crossroad centre of the village as early as 1842, which she soon after extended to Butterfield's design, and through its influence there was by 1856 some hope for the Church's ability to reach the people.[9] His survey of the existing church, a tiny chapel which bore some elements of great antiquity, made it impossible to see how – much repaired and sunk deep into the ground – it could be safely

north West View

Church of St James
the Great, Waresley:
ink study sketch
perspective from the
north-west, 1853

restored and extended from its existing ninety-three
seats to serve a parish population that had grown to
over 400.

Butterfield was ready to retain some elements
of the older structure, but the vestry voted to build
an entire new church on the existing 'ancient site',
relying on brick from the long-standing works of the
Crook family in Whiteparish nearby, and on William
Crook as builder. At Butterfield's urging, the Norman
door, the altar, the font and the bells were restored
and repositioned within the new church – the great
door being carefully protected by a double porch –
and monuments of the Eyre family were removed
and rehung in a south aisle. He raised the new
church nearly 3 feet above the old foundations and
followed a new footprint, but – 'chaste and restrained'
– it conveyed a subtle sense of its precursor in the
proportions of the west front and the general sense

of containment. Completed in 1858, it is the first
brick country church after the group at Cowick, with
an evident debt to Pollington and Hensall, and an
enormously important first essay in weaving courses
and trim of pale stone into the pattern of brick.
Butterfield would return to add a memorial reredos
to Lady Nelson, who largely funded the endeavour,
and – as the parish and its people prospered – to add
a vestry and transept in 1882.

The village of Milton was an outpost of
the parish of Adderbury, south of Banbury in
Oxfordshire, in a district of great poverty whose
population peaked in the 1850s at about 175 people,
many on poor relief, with a famous public house
for travellers that kept it alive. Butterfield was
engaged to design a minimal church for a site on
a glebe meadow next to the tavern. A foundation
stone was laid in the summer of 1856, with the

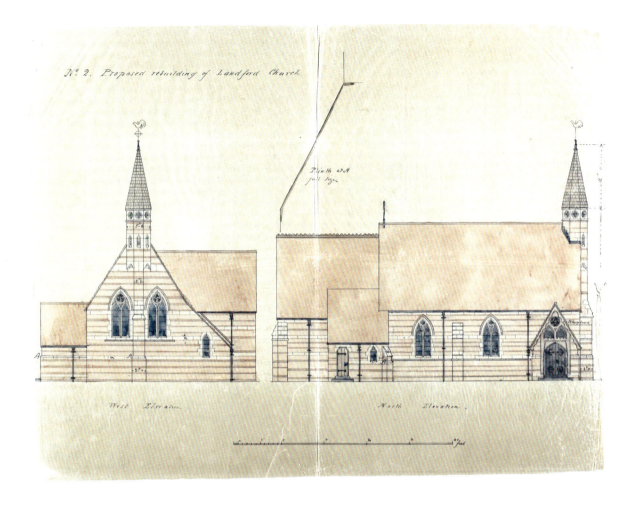

No. 2. Proposed rebuilding of Landford Church

West Elevation.

North Elevation.

47

Landford Church: elevations for rebuilding, 1857

48

Church at Milton, near Adderbury: view from the crossroads at the south-west, postcard, *c.*1890

architect present for a solemn service followed by 'a merry dance on the village green'; Butterfield shared his plans with the writer in *Jackson's Oxford Journal,* and the wonderfully logical oddity of the scheme delighted him.[10] It is a tiny church for a hundred congregants, eight singing men, no organ but space for a village band, and, with no resident incumbent, room for a sexton as custodian of graves and fabric. The nave is 38 by 20 feet, but a full 30 feet is allowed for a choir under the bell tower and a tiny chancel with a raised floor and drastically lowered roof. It is in the beautiful amber ironstone of the district, laid in small rubble blocks and trimmed with limestone under roofs of red tile. Deep placement in the yard, a bold wooden porch, a simple stone lychgate with a roof that echoes the tower: all create the dignity of decisive separation from the ragged hamlet and famously crowded tavern grounds about it. It was the most unusual and compact of a body of experimental minimum churches for outlying country districts that had begun at Cautley near Skipton ten years before and would now come in a short inventive burst of economical examples at Belmont near Durham and Etal in Northumberland in stone; and in brick at Gaer Hill in east Somerset and Braishfield in the New Forest, all dating from 1855–7.

A TEMPLATE FOR THE TOWN: ASHFORD

Ashford was a Surrey village that had suddenly been brought into the western-facing metropolitan orbit of London, first by the arrival of the railway and then with the appearance of the Welsh School, which was leaving Grays Inn Road for an expansive new campus in park and farmland, bringing more than 200 children and staff to a village already expanding to accommodate a newly arrived dormitory population. 'Cottage homes' and other new institutions for the refuge, welfare and education of young people soon followed the Welsh School's path to the borders of Ashford, the most extensive being the West London District School, housing more than 800 needy children, which arrived in 1872. There were fewer than 500

residents in 1861, shortly after Butterfield's church was built, and nearly 1000 ten years later.

The ancient parish church, neglected and largely in ruins, had been pulled down in 1796 and replaced by a 'mean brick chapel' to serve a few pew-holding farmers and gentry, with a mere thirty-two free seats for the poor.[11] On a budget supplemented by the Welsh Schools, Butterfield tore the little 'preaching box' down and built entirely anew on the south-west corner of the churchyard. The result is the model of a suburban church for the great town, its south face and entrance porch facing the highway, so that it would become a landmark integral to the built fabric of a growing community, rather than set aside in a country glade. The foundation stone was laid in July 1857 and the church opened in 1858. It is a 90-foot-long double-aisled church, the nave and aisles roughly 60 feet long, with the roof rising to 48. The body of the church is unusually broad at 64 feet, in which 520 members of the congregation could be seated for regular services, of whom 300 were children from the Welsh and parish schools. It is in hammered ragstone, with structural Bath stone quoins and courses constituting the extent of external decoration. The roofs are of red tile. Inside, short piers, low aisles and arcades lead to an intensely pointed chancel arch and support a clerestory whose large windows bring light and ventilation from above the surrounding landscape. Surfaces are flat and monochrome, allowing pitch and height to turn an almost rectangular nave into a soaring vertical space. The powerful effect was immediately grasped by those who saw it at the opening, 'its noble and lofty proportions . . . impressing the beholders . . . that there has entered into the conception of the designer . . . something of the dignity and majesty due to him whose presence chamber it is to become'. The restrained detail is akin to the three Cowick churches, with simplified capitals, columns and arches, and a porch and west front showing a precise plainness in stone that is comparable to the meticulous simplicity of the Yorkshire work in brick. Joseph Norris of nearby Sunningdale was Butterfield's builder, beginning forty years of an extraordinary architectural partnership.

49
St Matthew's Church, Ashford:
interior view looking east,
photograph by Francis Frith, 1895

50
St Matthew's Church, Ashford:
view from the south-west,
photograph by Francis Frith, 1895

NOTES

1. The account of the Coalpit Heath project is taken from 'The Church-Goer' [Joseph Leech], *Rural Rides; or, Calls at Country Churches*, second series, John Ridler, Bristol, 1850, pp 96–107; *St James Chronicle*, 21 May 1844; *Bristol Mercury*, 15 June 1844; *Bristol Times*, 11 October 1845; and *The Ecclesiologist*, May 1844. For further references, see Paul Thompson, *William Butterfield*, Routledge & Kegan Paul, London, 1971, p.428.

2. The account of the Sessay project is primarily drawn from the *Yorkshire Gazette*, 24 July 1847 and 2 June 1848; *Durham Chronicle*, 14 September 1849; Edward Royle and Ruth M. Larsen, *Archbishop Thomson's Visitation Returns for the Diocese of York, 1865*, Borthwick Institute, University of York, 2006; and *Sessay Village Conservation Report*, North Yorkshire Council, October 2017.

3. J.C. Atkinson, *Forty Years in a Moorland Parish*, Macmillan, London, 1891, p.48.

4. The account of the three Downe churches at Cowick relies principally upon a compilation made by Kenneth Sayner of Snaith of copies of records from the county archives, especially within the papers of Clark & Sons Solicitors of Snaith, which he generously shared with me. See also *Morning Post*, 11 July 1853, *Morning Chronicle*, 28 October 1854, and Royle and Larsen, *Archbishop Thomson's Visitation Returns*, op.cit.

5. John Duke Coleridge, 'The Necessity of Modernism in the Arts, Especially When Devoted to the Service of Religion', *Transactions of the Exeter Diocesan Architectural and Archaeological Society*, vol.4, 1854, pp 335–60.

6. The account of the buildings at Wykeham draws primarily on a report in the *Morning Post*, 9 November 1854. See also Royle and Larsen, *Archbishop Thomson's Visitation Returns*, op.cit. Numerous traveller's and topographic guides and histories recite the history of the Wykeham abbey, its church, All Saints' and St Helen's Tower; the simplest and most reliable (as for Baldersby and Sessay) is *A History of the County of York, North Riding*, vol.2, Victoria County History, London, 1923.

7. *Cambridge Independent Press*, 1 August 1857.

8. ibid.

9. The account of the church at Landford draws from the faculty of October 1857 with Butterfield's detailed proposal, held in the parish records at Wiltshire and Swindon History Centre, together with a copy of notes prepared by the rector on the history in 1872; and from a report in the *Wiltshire Independent*, 14 October 1858.

10. *Jackson's Oxford Journal*, 16 August 1856.

11. The account of Ashford parish church draws from reports in the *Windsor, Eton and Slough Express*, 14 July 1857, and *Ashford, Windsor and Eton Express*, 3 July 1858.

SIMPLIFICATION: FIVE COUNTRY PARISHES

St Cuthbert's Church, Sessay

St Cuthbert's Church and School, Sessay

All Saints' Church, Parsonage,
and School, Wykeham

Holy Trinity Church, East Cowick

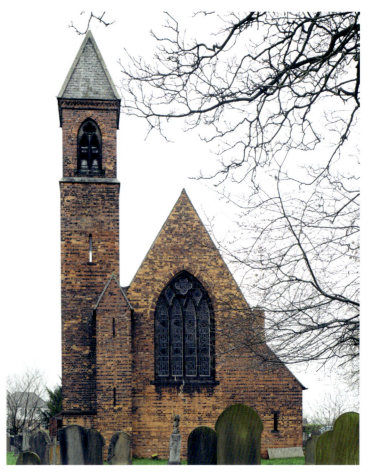

The three churches at Cowick:
Pollington, Hensall, East Cowick

The three churches at Cowick:
East Cowick, Pollington, Hensall

CHAPTER 6

THE FLOWERING OF THE COUNTRY SCHOOL, 1857–73

THE PROMISE OF UNIVERSAL EDUCATION

N 1844, WROTE a Church monthly, 'The country is now engaged in the holiest war it has ever waged, – a war against ignorance, vice, and infidelity . . . Education should be universal; since it is only while knowledge remains a distinction that it can engender discontent, or tempt men to desert their sphere'.[1] It may be chilling to read that the rapid movement for early-childhood education was first commenced as a means of encouraging people to accept their rank and condition. But by 1856, the accelerating impetus towards social hygiene no longer had need to plead its cause on the grounds of suppressing discontent, and the *Ecclesiologist* could observe 'schools of every description, schoolhouses, parsonages . . . rising in abundance; and an excellent unpretending type of appropriate architecture for these classes of buildings seems to be developing'.[2] Butterfield's first country schools had pioneered that exploration

of an appropriate architecture for the educational mission of the Church. And he continued to develop the approach, with increasing simplicity, in such examples as West Pinchbeck, Hellidon, Wykeham, Baldersby, West Lavington and Cowick. But a later long burst of new village schools and schoolhouses, starting at Baldersby, was completed in 1857 and, continuing for fifteen years of astonishing invention, carried those developments into adventurous new territory, first on paper through a wealth of lovingly made contract drawings, and then scattered on the land as one of the great imaginative masterworks of Victorian architecture. For Butterfield to have lavished such care on constructing such a particular grace upon each community shows the enormous mnemonic and moral value he saw in these 'unpretending' sites for the construction of a more civil life, both in their uses and in their presence on the rural landscape.

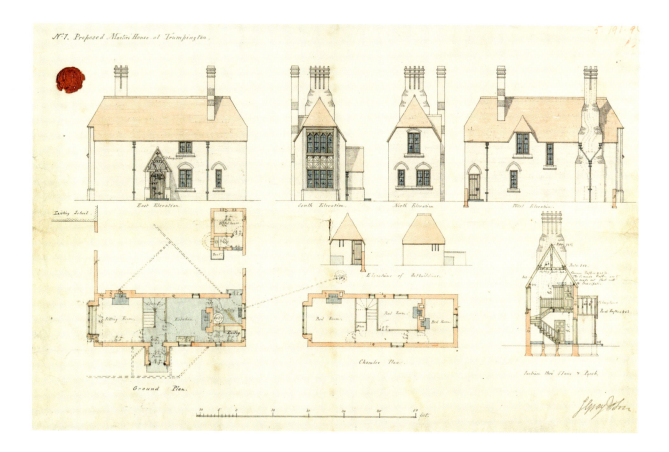

51
Master's House
at Trumpington:
elevations, plans
and section, 1857

By 1862, the pace at which new parish schools were being supplied had reached more than 100 a year, bringing 28,000 new children into the Church's National system each year. These were four times the new schoolhouses and new pupils being annually provided by all other denominations combined, and the figures are out of all proportion to the low relative figures for Church membership or attendance. Though the primary school system had been initiated by the Nonconformists, the Church had effectively taken over the first level of education for the nation at large, and the parish school, secular and standardised in the bulk of its curriculum and led by lay teachers increasingly trained together and to a common end, was slowly asserting itself as the anchor point of civil life. Here children learned to function in a common culture, speak a common language, sing common songs, learn common fundaments of knowledge (including a national history) and adhere to common notions of ethics, morality and deportment, cast in the common phrases of the English Prayer Book and King James Bible.

SCHOOL AND SCHOOLHOUSE

Good teachers required good lodgings, and the new master's house at Trumpington near Cambridge was built to replace a dwelling that had decayed. It was one of Butterfield's few freestanding teacher's houses, and with its great gabled bay, porch, hall and fine staircase, perhaps a little more generous than the attached teacher's dwelling that he most often was called on to provide. The narrow plan was governed in part by the desire to offer a large enough garden to feed a family. There are characteristics that Butterfield would use in all of his schoolhouses: a kitchen large enough to dine in and opening from the common entry and stair so that it could serve as a common room for pupil teachers or assistants; a back bedroom to accommodate an assistant; washable floors throughout the ground floor, sitting room excepted; and an orientation for door and private quarters that turned them away from the schoolyards and school privies – in this case adjacent to the dwelling.

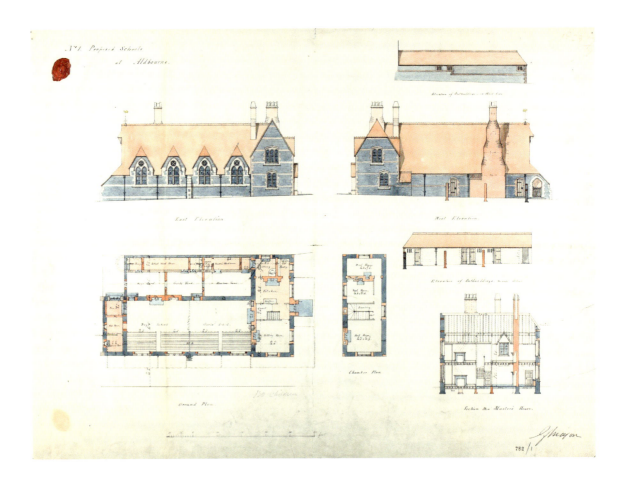

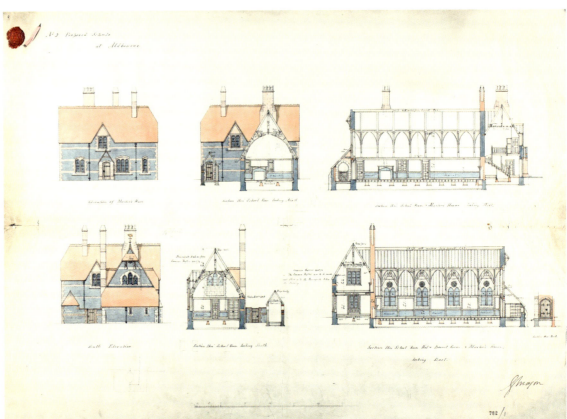

52
Schools at Aldbourne:
east and west elevations,
section and plan, 1858

53
Schools at Aldbourne:
elevations of master's
house (north), school and
service entrance (south)
and sections, 1858

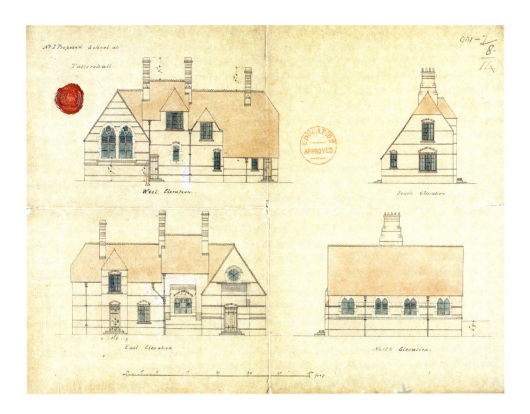

School at Tattershall:
elevations, *c*.1860

Storerooms and water closets were in outhouses. Trumpington was one of those early exercises in gables, asymmetry, wooden window frames and great extruded chimneys that caught the eye of the Arts and Crafts movement.

Aldbourne was a large parish in north Wiltshire, and the new school was designed for 130 pupils, a master, a mistress and a pupil assistant. The schoolroom was 51 by 20 feet with a dividing curtain, and the linear schoolhouse organised on the same lines as Trumpington. But this was a tight plot adjacent to the church in a village centre, and a lot depended upon its walling and the management of a narrow yard. It was in flint, the most economical material in the region, with stone trim, red brick and tile, and it followed exactly the rubrics for a large classroom: a high ceiling with large venting windows on at least one side; a high washable dado on which imagery could be attached; and enough distance between teacher and pupils to limit exposure to disease, provide space for children to present their work and permit good visual supervision. Boots and bonnets – and perhaps lice and dirt – were isolated in the porch; and an

elaborate system of doors and divisions kept boys apart from girls and infants when using the porch, yard or latrines. The entry faced the village square, and the great windowed school itself faced the churchyard, where its four windows carried tracery heads of noughts and crosses. A separate infant school was added to the front porch in 1873; and the school, unusually, was demolished in the late 1950s.

The great landholding Fortescues of Castle Hill in north Devon had taken an unusual interest in schools, lecturing and writing on the new topic of 'middle-class education' and driving the formation of a county boarding school for farmers' sons, which was meant to address one of the central problems of rural education – the reluctance of farming smallholders to support their boys' education beyond the elementary level. There are two Butterfield National schools for which the Fortescues of Castle Hill were responsible. At Tattershall in the Lincolnshire fens, where their landed interests extended, they erected perhaps the most exciting of Butterfield's school-and-schoolhouse combinations, in which dwelling, schoolroom, classroom and entrances – each with different characteristics and

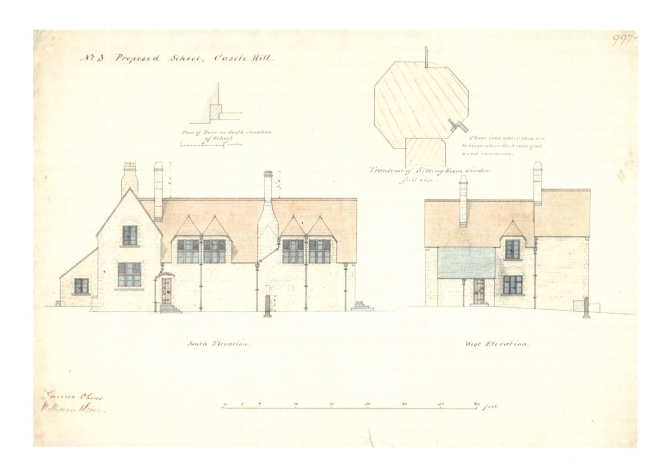

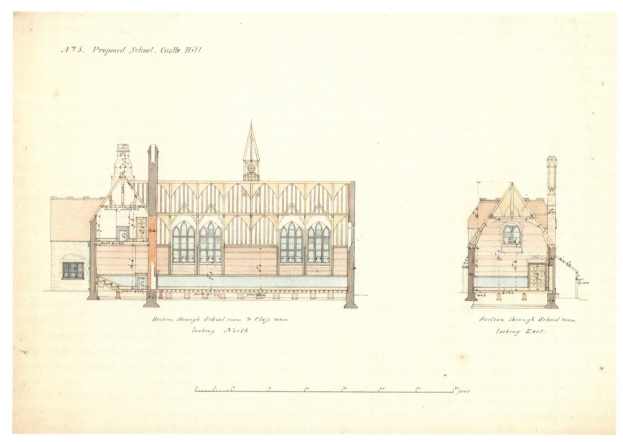

55

School at Castle
Hill: south and west
elevations, *c.*1860

56

School at Castle Hill:
sections looking north
and east, *c.*1860

at different scales – are brought together in an overlapping collision that, while entirely functional, looks on paper to be an almost random landscape of volumes, windows and roofs. The patterns of brick and stone are informed by those of the famous brickwork of the castle keep, lying a short distance away but well in view. The school at Castle Hill was in fact a new National school for the parish of Filleigh in the valley below the Fortescues' estate, which rises into Exmoor. It resulted from a bequest by a son, dying young, to provide for the children of the community and has room for ninety-nine pupils, assuming a number from the working families of the estate as well as the local tenantry. It is an impressive structure of Codden Hill limestone, offering four bedrooms rather than the usual three; and we find a cycle of pupil teachers, starting at the age of twelve and staying for up to five years, with a married couple of master and mistress providing extra tuition in the teacher's house for them. Plans here, as in other Butterfield teachers' houses, provide the kitchen as a warm social space for pupil teachers, with ready access to the secondary bedroom in which they are housed, and the master's study and living room carefully separated. The system at Filleigh worked very successfully, with pupil assistants gaining entrance to the national teacher training college at Battersea.

AN ALTRUIST'S MODEL SCHOOL

'A child left to himself bringeth his mother to shame' was the text of the sermon preached by the village curate at the opening of Kirby Muxloe school in June 1858. Kirby Muxloe was a small village on the far outskirts of Leicester.[3] Its economic life, like Leicester's itself, centred as much on the framework knitting of its women as on the labour of its menfolk on its agricultural lands. Most of those lands, along with its ruined castle and manorial rights, had been acquired by the Winstanleys of nearby Braunstone Hall, a parliamentarian family from Lancashire who had purchased the manor from ruined Royalists in 1650 and since amassed vast estates in the area. In 1855, through a rather odd

sequence of early deaths, the entire estate fell into the hands of an unlikely heir, James Beaumont Winstanley, a quiet young scholar, a friend and follower of Auguste Comte (who first articulated the philosophy of positivism), and who was committed to an altruist's creed of benevolent capital, demonstrating models for a more equal society. A young curate, John Haigh Scott, had taken the joint incumbency of Braunstone and Kirby Muxloe two years before. Scott quickly and controversially introduced liturgical reforms to his two churches, including choral services and an organ; undertook some building improvements; and then began a campaign to raise funds to erect modest daily and Sunday schools at Kirby (the larger of the two little villages in his curacy). This was launched in September 1855, and a design from Butterfield was contracted. By the end of 1856, with the majority of funds still lacking, Scott appealed to his new patron, and Winstanley stepped in to provide the entire projected cost not only to build and equip a complex of schoolroom and infant school, with an attached teacher's house, but to adapt it to an unusually dignified and generous model. In May of 1858, the 'very handsome commodious school-room, with accommodation for 70, the average number attending – with a house for the master and mistress' were opened.

The model of the long monastic or manorial hall in stone with its row of Gothic windows, applauded by the *Ecclesiologist* as a model country schoolroom when Butterfield introduced it at East Farleigh, has here been left entirely behind in favour of the comfortable, familiar and domestic. Like the school at Tattershall, which takes its constructional and aesthetic cues from the great brick castle-keep beside it, the lower level takes its proportions of brick to stone and the shapes of its principal openings from the moated ruins nearby of the fortified brick manor of Kirby, while the upper sections follow local patterns of domestic architecture from the fifteenth century in the open pattern of the half-timbering and the extraordinarily shallow gables. These historical and regional echoes are sounded in strikingly plain and modern tones. A similar character drawn from the local cottage

Kirby Muxloe School
and schoolhouse: view
from the south-west,
photographed *c*.1860

and farmyard vernacular was given to Butterfield's village school and schoolhouse at Great Bookham, begun with Viscount Downe near his Surrey home and completed by his family in his memory at the same time as Kirby Muxloe. There, too, all sense of the monumental and monastic was abandoned, and school and teacher's house are wonderfully jumbled together, facing in all directions on an irregularly assembled plan that looks forward to the wandering collage of the Arts and Crafts villa. Bookham indeed was promptly sketched and much admired by Philip Webb just as he began work on the first such villa – the Red House for William Morris.

THE SIMPLE VILLAGE SCHOOLROOM

The hamlet of Horton-cum-Studley lay on flat lands north-east of Oxford, just below the rise on which stood the Elizabethan manor house of Studley Priory, within the rectory of Beckley, whose landed incumbent was George Theophilus Cooke,

a fellow of Magdalen College, Oxford, and rural dean. Until 1867, the priory chapel served as the village church, and two small mixed schools in rudimentary buildings taught some forty pupils. In 1866, just before Butterfield began designs for Keble College, Cooke appointed a curate for the hamlet, and they began a building programme to furnish a new church, graveyard, school, schoolhouse and parsonage, and to repair and refurbish an almshouse of Jacobean date whose inmates were obliged to attend services.[4] For the church, Butterfield deployed a bright palette of yellow, scarlet and blue bricks that stands out like a haystack strewn with poppies and cornflowers in the meadows of Otmoor. The same light tones are used in the school that lay just to the east of it, while for the teacher's house and vicarage, the cruder red stock brick of Keble was used. The simple teacher's house can be seen facing the boys' playground, with a common shed for fuel and storage. The 30-foot mixed schoolroom is in the standard configuration of two sections with a variable aisle between, the girls' end having its

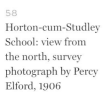

58
Horton-cum-Studley
School: view from
the north, survey
photograph by Percy
Elford, 1906

59
Horton-cum-Studley
School: the schoolroom,
photographed before
1906

own rear door to the east, leading out to the girls'
and infants' playground, which was walled off from
the boys'. The steep pitch of the infant classroom
allowed for stacked seating and curtailed the
spread of infant infections. A photographic survey,
anticipating rebuilding, was taken in 1906 (fig.58),
looking at the school and its yards in a neglected
condition, but interior photographs filed with it
date from a considerable time before (fig.59) and
show the same activities as would have been typical
fifty years earlier: the boys are writing an exercise,
and the girls, with pupil monitors supervising, are
at needlework. The door to the entry porch is open,
though the two side casements of the high windows
above it, louvred to allow for ventilation, are closed.

Two of Butterfield's later Wiltshire schools, each
with a divided main room and a small classroom,
show increasing economies of construction, space
and aesthetics, and produce works of almost

exaggerated plainness, modernity and functional
beauty. Dinton, in brick on a roadside and turning
its narrow end to the highway for an entry, dresses
its street front with banded porch columns, a little
diapering and a cross, but leaves every other surface
unadorned, and its six windows are based on a single
rectangular module and are hung on a single lower
line. As in all Butterfield's rural schools, readily
movable classroom furniture allowed temporary
conversion to other uses, from coroner's inquests to
public lectures and from seasonal feasts to Sunday
services when churches were in repair or restoration.

Dinton's National school appeared in a community,
 west of Salisbury, where private initiatives had
supported some schooling for a generation.
Poulton's arrived in a community of great poverty
in which nothing had been done for the young, and
teachers through its early years reported enormous
difficulties: distances to walk to school were long
and, for the many without boots or shoes, impassable
at many times of the year; smaller children were
called away for tasks in the fields; desks for eighty
were often filled with no more than a quarter of
that number; and the 'pennies' paid for tuition were
often simply too hard to find. It was almost a decade
before improved attendance was noted, after the
gravelling of the main path, the formation of a parish
boot and shoe club and the removal of fees.

St Michael's Church at Poulton, one of the finest
in Butterfield's rural corpus, replaced a decayed
and inconvenient predecessor on another site on
this nearly flat shelf of arable farm, quarries and
meadowland at the southern end of the Cotswolds.
It is a work of almost surprising simplicity that
was immediately celebrated as recapturing a
particular regional character and investing it
with extraordinary dignity and calm. Poulton's
school, completed just to the south while the
church was in progress, is part of the same almost
rhapsodic refinement of Cotswold simplification.[5]
Its front faces west over meadows to a brook and
was approached, as would be the porch of the
new church and the vicarage, from a network of
footpaths rather than the busy road running to
the east, whose borders were taken by cottages.
A single centre window 8 feet high and 4 feet off

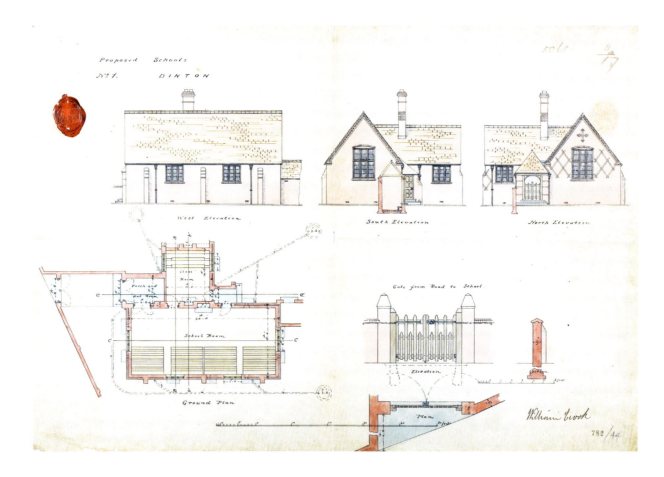

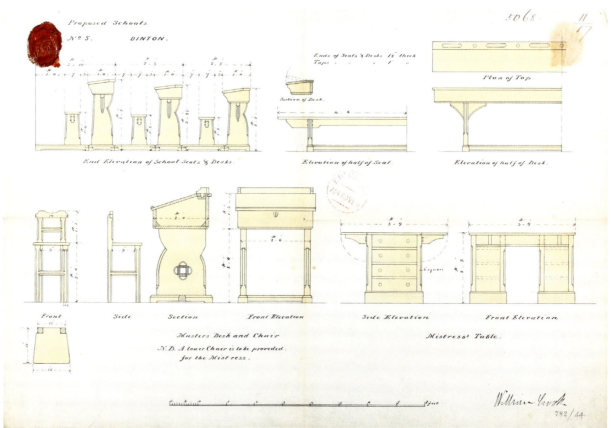

60

Schools at Dinton:
plan and elevations,
1873

61

Schools at Dinton:
desks and seating,
1873

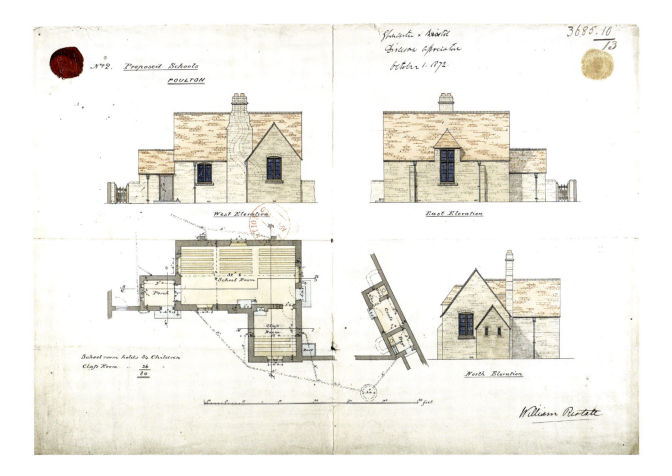

62
Schools at Poulton:
elevations and plan,
1872

the ground breaks the slope of the roof under a
hipped gable to bring in morning light – the only
case where a single window was used for the long
wall behind the divided desks in the schoolroom.
It is one of the key elements in the composition
that take the traditional stone architecture of farm
buildings and carding sheds in this district and
adapt it to the scale, height, finish and hygiene
of the school. The builder was William Restall of
Bisley, who constructed the new church alongside
it and would bring the same impeccable skills in
masonry to Butterfield's great church and parsonage
at St John Clevedon in Somerset. There are no
careless drawings in Butterfield's corpus, but there
is exceptional refinement to this one, in which
tones are made paler to indicate the exact degree
of recession, details are rendered with fanatical
precision and the tiled roofs are animated with
shafts of sunlight.

NOTES

1. *Ecclesiastical Gazette*, July 1844.
2. *The Ecclesiologist*, June 1856. The Minutes of the
   Committee of Council on Education, from 1841 onwards,
   are especially informative for this study in the years
   from 1844 up to the introduction of the transformative
   Education Act of 1870. This is the era when systems,
   qualifications and structures were codified; these include
   the rich reports of the government inspectors and model
   plans for schools and schoolhouses.
3. The account of the Kirby Muxloe school project draws from
   reports in the *Leicester Journal*, 6 September 1857, and
   Leicester Guardian, 29 May 1858.
4. The account of the project at Horton-cum-Studley is drawn
   principally from obituary notices of George Theophilus
   Cooke, county histories, gazetteers and guides.
5. The account of Poulton school is based on an article in the
   Gloucester Journal, 5 June 1909.

III 'THE HEARTH, THE ALTAR, and THE GRAVE'

CHAPTER 7

'SETTING APART', 1854–71

THE IDEAL VILLAGE

N 1853, THE BUSINESS of the railway entrepreneur George Hudson collapsed, and William Henry Dawnay, Viscount Downe, acquired his house and estate of Newby Park at Topcliffe on the Swale, renaming it after the nearby village of Baldersby. Completed to Colen Campbell's designs in 1721, it is regarded as the first Palladian villa in England and a landmark in the architectural history of the country house. It was set in a wide plain of open agrarian land. Estate farm workers, agents and tenantry were widely dispersed and, along with the villagers of Baldersby, poorly housed and served, with neither an established church nor a National school. Among a population of over 700, more than three quarters of those who declared a Church were Nonconformists. Viscount Downe at once determined to provide more services and better housing. By 1860 he and Butterfield had

built in the village of Baldersby a large model house for the land agent, a smaller single dwelling with a shopfront and a terrace group for three tenant households.[1] Predominantly in red brick with black diapers under fine tiled roofs, they feature occasional half-hipped or half-timbered gables, trimmed in wide blocks of local stone and rising to a dignified height, and carry large windows, substantial chimneys and compact gardens. They read not so much as model rural cottages but rather as prototypes for modern dwellings in the country town and suburb.

Meanwhile, Viscount Downe and Butterfield had begun an entirely new settlement between Baldersby village and the Park, for the centre of a new district with school, parsonage and church, to be called St James. By May 1856, foundation stones could be laid for all three buildings, and they rose with great rapidity, to be completed in September of the following year. The great church, seating up to 600, with eight bells and a spire rising 160 feet above the plain, has long been celebrated as Butterfield's rural masterpiece. It was dedicated to St James the Great, built of rough-cut stone under fired red tile, with ashlar trim and banding and a brick-lined interior. Outside, the spire commands the entire landscape of its people with a nearly reflective surface of finished grey stone, broken by twelve shallow scalloped bands, establishing a pattern that is repeated in the roof beams and reredos inside the church. Patterned brick walls line the nave within, lightly coursed with Huddleston stone and set under a high open roof in which the collar and cross beams are cut like cloud forms. The interior gains in density and decoration as the chancel is reached, past a low carved stone screen and a scrolled ironwork rail, up to a floor tiled in a blaze of colour beneath a sanctuary that dissolves into a cloudy marble haze of whites, pinks and greys.

The principal windows establish a narrative sequence culminating at the east end with a *Transfiguration* from the prominent studio of Michael O'Connor & Son, in which intense light shines through the mandorla and white raiment of the central figure, commanding the axis and internal vista of the church. Beneath it is a pale alabaster reredos in high relief in which a white cross emerges within a clouded nimbus. That evocation of the heavens echoes in the dance of curves carved into the stone screen, in the scalloped timbers above the nave, in the streaked white marble dado round the chancel walls, and in the lustrous night sky of starry silvers, blacks and blues that Butterfield came back to paint on the chancel ceiling. Inscribed on the walls and tiles, like a runic script, are tiny geometric figures. These are motive fragments of the underlying melody upon which the grander elements of a transcendent *melos* are grounded, laid down as if clues towards comprehension of the inexpressible. It is a lovely demonstration of what John Duke Coleridge, crediting Butterfield for the ideas, had called for in his 1853 manifesto *The Necessity of Modernism*, when he asked for

a religious architecture that would 'invest the shapes which are embodied with an awful and angelic beauty, which may lift the mind above all associations merely human, and make it touch the heavens'.[2] From now on, we will see Butterfield inscribing his major works again and again with these tiny suggestive devices from a symbolic geometry, like the key signature on a sheet of music.

Facing the church are the school and teacher's house, wedded together in an L shape and cast mostly in the same snecked stone with ashlar trim, but sporting a wonderfully overscaled half-timbered gable above the main entry porch that faces the church. The same material and details are used in radically different proportions and scales, to establish the difference between the domestic and the educational, and the plan turns in different directions to keep them engaged but separate. It provides an extreme instance of those discordant collisions of shape and scale that Butterfield's schools so delight in. Behind the church, and reached from a track bounding the east side of the churchyard, is a capacious parsonage, in a similar mix of stone and exposed, steep pitched roof and folding gables. Both school and vicarage were in place by the time the church opened in the autumn of 1857. But the leafy close of new brick dwellings west of the church and the row of almshouses across from it were still in contemplation, probably built in 1860 at the same time as the last of Butterfield's brick dwellings for old Baldersby village.

There are four brick-based dwelling structures. On the south side of the road, set back behind a garden, are a pair of attached one-storey alms cottages, largely in timber-frame, with extraordinarily large gabled windows facing the road, so that the passing world and the great spire reaching to another were both evident to a seated pensioner, who could be observed in turn. Across from them, and reached from a gate leading to the graveyard, are three lodges in a single turned terrace, banded and windowed in stone, probably intended for parish officers – sexton, clerk, assistant curate, choirmaster, assistant teacher. They are designed with internal water closets, and each lodge faces a different prospect with an entry from a different point, presenting themselves to the world as an almost urban group. Laid out informally to the west of them are two double cottages with gardens attached for the workmen on the estate, built entirely in plain brick. Developing the Sessay model, they carry their finely tiled and sealed roofs to hygienic heights previously unknown to the country cottage and provide windows – the upper ones under deep half-hipped gables – of unusual generosity. Each is oriented differently, with individual walled vegetable and fruit gardens, separate entries and private outdoor privies, but with shared chimneys, coal and woodsheds. The village is a varied and scattered group of buildings, deploying a consistent palette of materials, with window shapes following the same pattern in school, church, terrace and parsonage, in different proportions to reflect the social and functional hierarchy, but conspicuously working together as a built representation of a collaborative community with different ranks and duties. The landscape is united by long lines of boundary wall at a single height and in a single pattern of brick and stone. The same collage of stone and brick is used for the walls of the Dalton churchyard ten years later, and Butterfield carries them inside the church itself to form the base of the chancel screen (fig.75), laying the familiar and the ordinary as groundwork for splendour.

The first of the tombs in the new graveyard was that of Viscount Downe himself, who died after a long, weakening illness in January 1857, his body laying at Topcliffe for some months until Baldersby church and churchyard were consecrated, so that he could be buried close to the chancel walls of the last and finest of his works with Butterfield. In a single decade of work together they had built close to a hundred efficient and beautiful architectural demonstrations of the educational, ecclesiastical and domestic instruments that could generate a better rural life, none entirely alike. They are a memorial to one great landlord's exhausting dedication to the welfare of his tenantry, and they constitute together, perhaps, his architect's most affecting, flawless and unpretentious work.

'THE GRAVE'

A human soul is fed
On food which kindred natures crave;
On him their threefold influence shed
The HEARTH, the ALTAR, and the GRAVE.
– John Moultrie, 'Alice Gay's Bridal', 1854[3]

John Moultrie was one of a host of early Victorian writers and poets whose work was made for the fireside, to be read aloud and quickly grasped – either telling cautionary and improving tales, like the incomparable fabulist John Mason Neale; awakening simple spiritual sentiments like Keble's *Lyra Apostolica;* or, as in Moultrie's encapsulating 'home truths', in simple easily learned and repeated instructive rhymes. One who knew Moultrie's conversation well described his thought as invariably and unwittingly looking at the quotidian and the ordinary and finding them 'suggesting the ideal', evoking 'the sensation that the outward practical working life had beneath it something which transcended and ennobled it'.[4] In his collection *Altars, Hearths and Graves* of 1854, he dwells on three familiar sites – the altar, or common sanctuary; the hearth, or private household; and the grave, as a marker of remembrance and mortality. In this construction, the altar or sanctuary should be both distanced and accessible, a visible tabernacle bringing us into acquaintanceship with (in Matthew Arnold's words) 'something not ourselves'.[5] In the same way, the grave and graveyard should be seen and tended as the site through which the rhythm of life and death and the history of a people is learned: Moultrie was censured as a boy at Eton for running off one day to ruminate in the graveyard at Stoke Poges in which Thomas Gray's well-known elegy was composed. Above all, perhaps, Moultrie – like Holthouse of Hellidon – argues that the hearth and home are as integral to the development of a religious life, a civil comportment and a private conscience as the school or church, and believed (as Butterfield constantly asserted) that the material character of a household should reflect its moral role, and serve to awaken a spiritual sensibility.

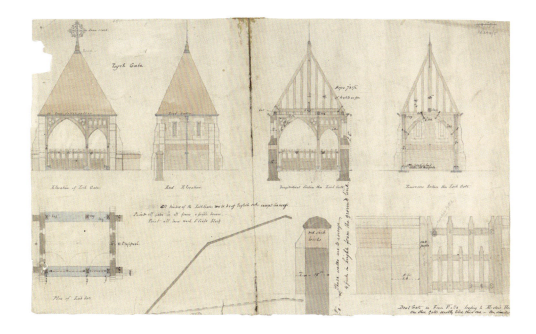

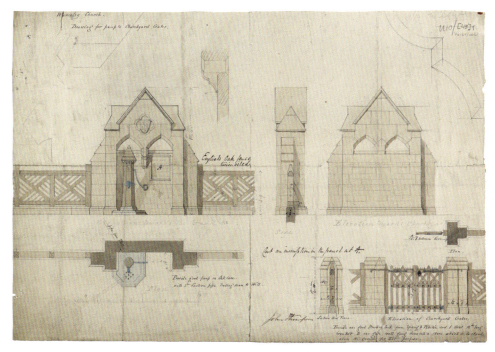

63
St James's Church,
Baldersby: lych gate,
gate and fence walls,
*c.*1857

64
Church of
St James the Great,
Waresley: pump and
churchyard gates,
*c.*1855

In many country villages the churchyard had long been the only open land across which to move without trespass. Butterfield studded the first series of *Instrumenta Ecclesiastica* with designs for simple tombstones, lychgates, churchyard crosses and other markers of memory for the burial ground, and as the first of these *Instrumenta* were being published, the *Ecclesiologist* – in August 1844 – addressed 'Church-yards' in a lead article probably written with Butterfield: 'No renovation of a church will be complete until the consecrated precinct about it have also resumed the decent order that becomes the resting-place of Christian bodies.' It remains 'the one dormitory of the whole parish' and can no longer be left disfigured by uneven ground, cluttered by headstones with rhymes of extravagant eulogy, or made hierarchical through tombs separated by railings. The addition of a boundary wall is recommended, along with a churchyard cross – once ubiquitous but universally destroyed during the Commonwealth – 'to excite the devotion of the living, and to secure the repose of the departed'.

By 1840 there were only a handful of surviving fragments of the ancient covered lychgates, many of them carved in twining wood, under which a bier could be laid and its bearers and mourners rest at vigil – sometimes for days – before a priest attended to escort them to the burial. They almost certainly derived from funerary practices established before the coming of Christianity to England. Butterfield's pioneering revivals of the form began in 1844 with a heavy masonry double portal at Coalpit Heath, like the gates of a fortified manor, and a set of simpler open sheds with light tile or shingle canopies and arched wooden braces first introduced in Jedburgh in the same year, and then in many varied instances – perhaps at its plainest for Milton (fig.48). They were initially greeted as eccentricities but soon widely adopted, not only for funerary purposes but as a liminal space in which sound and light changed on entering the sacred enclosure, and the memory of the dead could be evoked. Baldersby's double gate shows a third, quietly monumental approach, for which there may be Nordic precedents, with a towering, sharply peaked pyramid roof of tile, ruggedly thick and slot-windowed side walls, and an enormous flowered and ringed metal gable cross, which would be simplified and carved in stone at the same scale above the porch. The arches of boldly patterned tracery woodwork anticipate the vaulting and screens of the nave in the church to follow.

In legend often a haunted as much as a sacred space, the churchyard was still in part the province of traditions associated with burial sites from long before the introduction of a vicar and church into rural England, with its mystic ash-grove, sacred yew, healing thorn bush and ghosts of All Hallows' Eve, its lychgate still serving funeral rites unknown to the prayer book, and the adjacent village green holding pagan festivals of the May, wrestlings, Pace Eggs, mummeries and the pretended apparitions of the Green Man. Here the Church comfortably converged with folk tradition and superstition, reinforcing the many reasons why country people who might disdain the doors of the squire's church could be persuaded to respect the sacred enclosure that had been there long before him. Country vicars, like Viscount Downe's chaplain, J.C. Atkinson, and the incumbent of his widow's church at Dalton, Sabine Baring-Gould, were among the most enthusiastic and assiduous recorders and publishers of rural legend and folkways, and themselves instigated within the church itself such Victorian revivals of ancient custom as decorating the nave as a forest chamber for Christian festivals (see fig.19) and replacing the noisy and unruly harvest home of long tradition with its mid-century reinvention as a Church feast and religious 'harvest festival'.[6]

At Waresley, where an entirely new church was situated on a lightly bounded version of the village green at the crossroads, a wonderful scheme for fences and gates was designed, with a village pump taking the landmark position to the east and sporting a shield bearing the arms of the patrons. With the pump Butterfield evokes the association of churchyard and the Christian rebirth by water with pagan spring spirits and healing wells; at Ashwell he built an entire wayside temple form around a venerated spring, topping it with a cross and Christian inscription; and added a similar community pump for fresh water outside the gates of his great slum church in Holborn. Baldersby and Waresley both established a model for the lightly walled and fenced enclosures Butterfield would build around new town and suburban sites, especially where – as the cemetery movement proceeded – no burial ground would be provided, but a sense of separation is essential to his plan and siting, to ensure that the church sits, visible but apart, in dedicated solemn ground.

'THE HEARTH'

John Sandford, then Archdeacon of Coventry, came to the rectory of the country town of Alvechurch, a Worcestershire parish of some 1700 inhabitants with a mix of light industry and agricultural services, in 1854. There was an inadequate rectory house, distant from the church, that Sandford decided to replace; and his curate had already

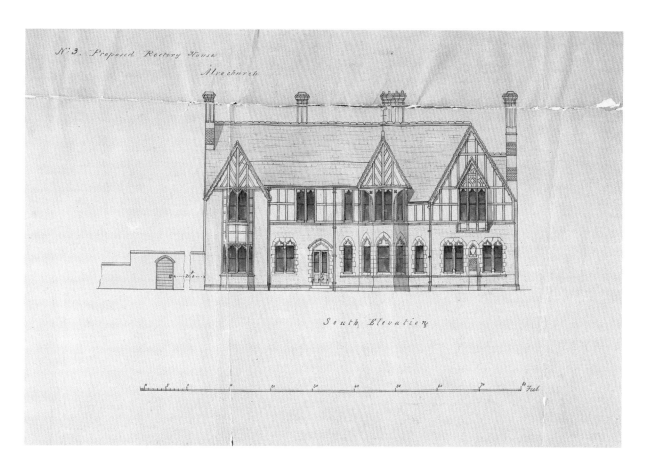

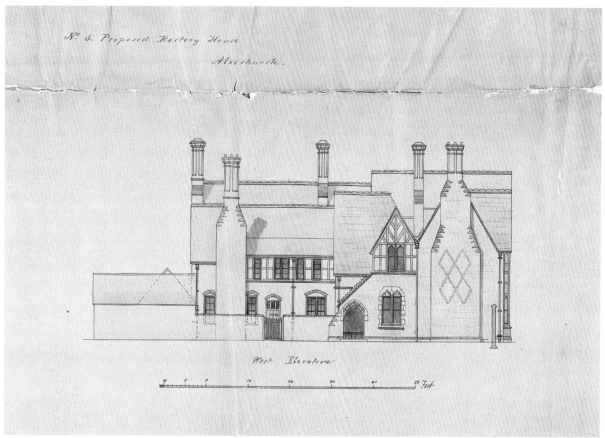

65
Alvechurch Rectory:
south elevation, 1854

66
Alvechurch Rectory:
west elevation, 1854

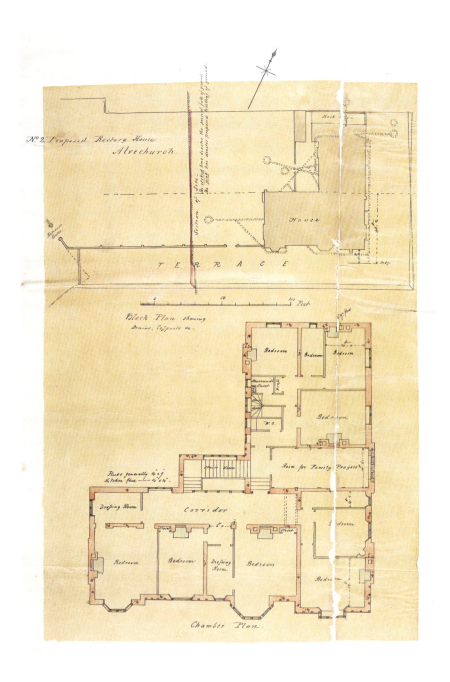

Alvechurch Rectory:
block plan and plan of
chamber floor, 1854

The site was a triangular swathe of glebe land sloping southwards down the hillside on which the church sat, a little way to its east. There were 350 feet along its northern boundary and 105 feet bordering the west, where the ground then fell more steeply into meadowland. Butterfield levelled the entire plot into a single earthen platform and extended it another 15 feet out to the south to form a terrace. He set the house into an L-shaped plan towards the north-eastern edge of the levelled site, building in the diapered brick and half-timbering that had marked the domestic architecture of the locality since the sixteenth century. The study, library, living and dining rooms are placed in a line, with sliding dividing walls opening space for receptions inside and doors leading out to the paved terrace and sloping lawn to the south. The entrance court faces west into walled gardens, with a carriage drive to the north. A diapered brick pattern marks the rector's study, and the entry sequence includes a long hall. Nearly half of the building's footprint is for the service wing and staff accommodation, encompassing the north portion of the L, fronting a walled service court to the west, a terrace to the east, to ensure morning light and a ventilating perimeter, with a hedge dividing it from the family terrace. The most remarkable feature is the south terrace, 25 feet wide, set behind a wall and running the entire 240-foot length of the levelled site, to serve as an ambulatory and – with a gate leading off the driveway – as a site for summer assembly and entertainment. All sense of ceremony and noble prospect is ended, with the principal façade facing into the garden, and the public approach made towards an unpretentious porch with a door of a gently ecclesiastical character.

A prayer room, with a fine ecclesiastical window, facing east and framed in stone tracery, sits above the corner between the two halves of the household, uniting them for prayers; but, for the rest, this is a comfortable small country house governed by its relationship to the out-of-doors and divided very simply into two blocks – for the server and the served – with generous passages and stairs for circulation. To the architectural community it was a revelation. A whole new vision of the English

engaged in a long campaign to fund a new National school. His wife, a writer of improving manuals on domestic life, had died shortly before the move; most of the male children were gone; and Sandford rather suddenly married again, to the twice-widowed and hence twice-wealthy Lady Erskine. Between her means and the support of Lady Harriet Windsor-Clive, soon to become Baroness Windsor, who had family attachments to the parish, a new rectory on a scale fitting a prelate of the Church became possible.[7]

house was embodied in the pragmatic collision of forms and rooflines, the rejection of a traditional avenued approach and symmetrical entry front, the incorporation of garden and terrace into the plan, the deployment of great windows where they served the most purpose, and the suggestions of vernacular informality in the use of local brick and building techniques. Butterfield knew its significance, providing the most elaborate specifications, drawing the plot plans of the whole garden scheme with as much precision as the interior detail, and establishing a succession of workshops on site to fabricate the components to the highest standards.

The cornerstone of the new National school by Butterfield was laid in August 1856, opening in May 1857, close to the church and to the just-completed rectory. By 1859 there were over 200 pupils, where the old school of the 1830s, one of the first in the National system, had taught no more than 110 in notoriously unhealthy quarters. By then, Butterfield's restoration of the 'mutilated sanctuary of St Laurence' parish church was also afoot, conceived with Sandford as a demonstration of how to produce a dignified and noble effect with a moderate outlay, by the use of simple materials. The brick-clad interior, vibrant and majestic through the great effect Butterfield achieved by restoring the roofs to their original height, was at once held up by the national press as the model of an economical modern church, and Butterfield followed its interior character of brick patterned with white stone at Hitchin in Hertfordshire and – for Baroness Windsor again – at Penarth in southern Wales. The stone tower, which had long been drastically cut down, could not be rebuilt to its true height at this stage, leaving the old and new in a temporarily odd disparity which still persists. Upon its reopening in October 1861 the Worcester Architectural Society – which Sandford himself had initiated – noted in amazement that this great advocate of bringing moral and spiritual reform into country life through architectural means had achieved in one town, in a mere six years, 'exactly what the society he was most active in founding set out as its principles'.

Bamford in the parish of Hathersage lay on the River Derwent along the busy toll road from Manchester to Sheffield. It was a typical instance of the growth of a mill village in an era when cotton accounted for 50 per cent of the country's industrial production and nearly 40 per cent of its exports. Like many villages in the industrial and mining country of the north, it was a community almost entirely populated by millworkers, where children worked a half day in the mill, meaning that – whatever the cost to health – school attendance and discipline at a young age were much superior to those where pupils were tied to irregular farm work; most stayed at school after the age of ten and few were sent away to service. The family of Samuel Moore arrived in the 1830s to take over a corn mill and convert it to spinning thread for lace. When they came to the village it was a small hamlet of thirty houses, but they remodelled the whole place, building cottages for their workpeople and a school for their half-timers and all the children in the village. In 1840, it was still a half-agricultural mill village of just over forty households, but not long after, Samuel's son, William Cameron Moore, opened a second mill to spin cotton yarn, and by the end of the decade, the Moores had become proprietors of virtually all the land in the district, and their company was employing 170 people.

Working closely with Butterfield and the vicar of Hathersage (whose ancient and splendid church Butterfield had just restored), William Cameron Moore had the schoolroom licensed for services, rented a house as a temporary vicarage up the valley, and set about building a church and churchyard.[8] In 1859 the foundation stone of the church was laid, and a year later it was completed. It was a very substantial and finely made structure for a relatively small congregation, seating 150 adults and fifty children, almost entirely funded by the Moores at a cost just over £3500. The site runs along a steep slope rising to the north, so Butterfield laid the building on a narrow footprint 90 feet long, with the body of the church only 30 feet wide. It is built for shelter in a moorland climate. A great tower, on four deep, thick supports, holds the north-west corner, covering the entry, which leads into a low passage that runs across the west front and ends by jutting out into a room for the sexton. The wonderfully

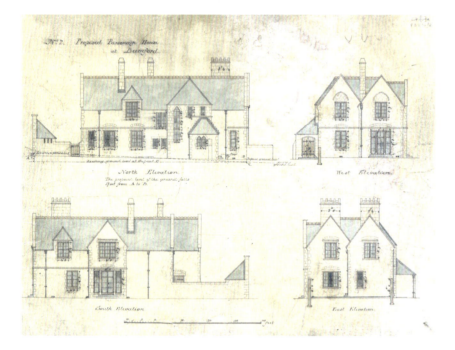

south to the river, the parsonage house was a readily visible part of a self-contained village life.

The rectory at Landford was built to replace a garden parsonage near the gates of the manor park, where Butterfield's brick church now stood. Butterfield 'examined it thoroughly' in 1869, hoping to retain a portion of the old house; but he found that the foundation posts had disintegrated entirely, and 'reluctantly' concluded that he would have to build from scratch.[9] It follows a very similar plan to that at Bamford, though at slightly smaller scale, and, at a cost of £1400, much more economically built. Both are distributed on a rectangular plan of two floors with no inhabited attic, under a single principal roofline, with simple two-storey gabled extensions. Family and reception rooms are oriented to a slope of gardens, with a great central bay and much of the rest of this garden front left windowless. In both, the approach is towards the narrow west front, with an unostentatious entry, at Bamford through a facing porch, with the vicar's study to its right, and at Landford just around the corner to the north, with the study marked from the road by a diapered cross. The hierarchies of space are clearly and simply defined, with none of that carefully crafted disjunction – great extruded chimneys, collisions of line, half-timbered gables, shifts in height or scale – that is typical of Butterfield's earlier parsonages and schoolhouses.

'THE ALTAR'

The decade of early essays in the compact church – starting at Cautley in 1847 and ending with Milton, Gaer Hill, Landford, Braishfield and Belmont – had tested Butterfield's ability to produce a persuasively devotional space with the simplest of means and smallest of footprints. When a further spate of commissions for small village churches appeared ten years later, he was ready to produce a profusion of different compact ecclesiastical spaces, in the varied landscapes and conditions to which each was adapted. They appear at Emery Down, deep in the New Forest; Ravenswood, on intractable heathland near Wokingham in Berkshire; Bursea,

68
Bamford Rectory and Church: view from the south-east, postcard, before 1905

69
Bamford Rectory: elevations, 1855

tapered stone tower and spire – based on a glimpse recollected from a train journey through the Swiss Alps – rises 108 feet and carries a peal of six steel bells. The rectory was completed shortly afterwards, just as cotton fortunes and millworkers began reeling from the Civil War blockade in America, so that the carriage yard, with rooms for servants and stables, was delayed for some years. It is in local stone on a relatively large plan, with six bedrooms, a service stair and a full hall for entertaining. Adjoining the churchyard, close to the centre of the village, facing a great swathe of open land falling

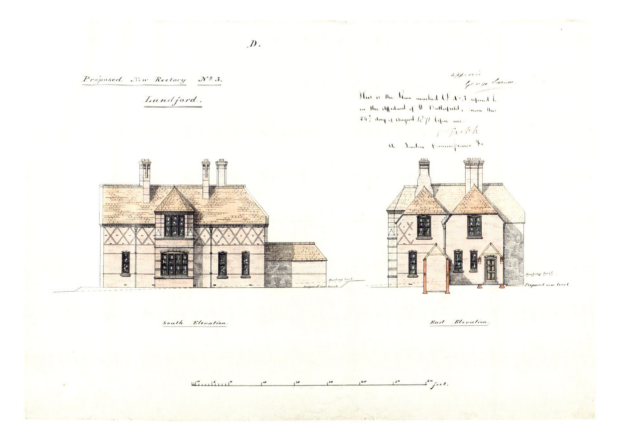

70

Landford Rectory:
north and west
elevations, 1871

71

Landford Rectory:
south and east
elevations, 1871

72
St Anne's Parsonage,
Dropmore: view
from the south-
west, photographed
c.1867–9

73
St Anne's Church,
Dropmore: view from
the south-west upon
completion, 1866

a distinct persona that derives from the landscape of the *locus* and its building culture. A sampler of examples from 1866–8 shows him finding decisive means to realise conspicuous boundaries; a clear and ordered approach including shelter at the point of entry; and marked separation within the church itself, ensuring that, however compact the volume, a boundary between the common ground of the nave and the transcendence of the sanctuary would remind churchgoers of the division between the bonds and bounds of the world and the infinite and dissolving sacred realm beyond it.

In 1864 the Fortescues of Bocconoc in Cornwall inherited the Dropmore estate on Littleworth Common in Buckinghamshire and promptly – at the young Harriet Fortescue Phillimore's urging – set about establishing a new district with a cottage-built school, and a church and parsonage by Butterfield, all rising within four years.[10] The church came first, in chequered flint under a continuous roof, with plain brick supports and an emphatic horizontal stringcourse of cut stone, rising as it reached the east to denote the raised floor of the chancel. The materials of the boundary walls show the same mix of materials and textures as those in the building; and wooden porch, outer gate and bell tower are all assertively shaped and dressed, in consonance and alignment, to mark the point of entry from a distance. The bellcote can be seen from the gardens of the parsonage house, completed a little later. There, the diapered brick, wood-framed windows and simple half-timbered trim are interrupted by bands of flint which stretch out into boundary walls like those of the church, in similar alternating rows of flint and brick, so that the dwelling stays both properly apart and distinct from its church yet in demonstrative material relationship to it.

The new parish of Elerch or Bont Goch was the inspired idea of its first vicar, Lewis Gilbertson of Jesus College Oxford. Here he established a church, school and parsonage, all by Butterfield, endowed by his family as an experiment in bringing the catholic practice of Anglican worship in the Welsh language to a people attached to their chapels. Services had been conducted in Butterfield's schoolhouse since 1862, erected in the same randomly coursed stone

on the watery levels of Yorkshire's Spalding Moor north of the Humber; Bont Goch, at the head of a mountainous valley of sheep, quarries and mines in mid-Wales; Horton-cum-Studley, in Flora Thompson country on the Oxfordshire pastureland of Otmoor; Beech Hill, amid lower Thames Valley watermills, woodland and grazing; Dropmore, in what was rapidly becoming parkland on the western perimeter of London; and back in the levels of Swaledale, at the Downe memorial church in Dalton. They are an extraordinary celebration of the difference and variety that could be achieved working within a similar footprint and envelope, and of the ability to invest into a well-contained shape

as he would use for the church. Built by their own
and for their own, the people of the valley took to
the church with enthusiasm, sitting with women
on one side and men on the other, and singing with
'vigour and heartiness' from the start, with Thomas
Helmore adapting his chants to the Welsh texts for
their use.[11] Dedicated to St Peter and completed in
1868, its plan is close to that of Milton ten years
before, bespeaking containment and economy at
every step. As the *Guardian* reported,

> the new church stands in the midst of the
> Plinlimmon range of hills, and on a spot . . .
> chosen for its commodious access to shepherds
> and miners, but by no means attractive for
> its natural beauty. Yet here . . . we find this
> unassuming structure . . . according thoroughly
> with the character of the neighbouring hills, and
> harmonizing with the finest of the old churches
> around . . . So entirely plain were the plans and
> drawings of the church, that it was built (with the
> exception of a mason employed for the freestone
> in the windows and door-frames) by the native
> masons and joiners on the spot.

Butterfield knew his old Welsh churches, and this
church, with its shallow chancel and powerful cap,
seems in shape, texture and spirit to be kin to them.

Ten years after William Henry Dawnay died,
Lady Downe and Butterfield began a model
small village church in his memory in a low-lying
settlement in the parish of Topcliffe known to locals

as 'Dalton-i'-t'-muck', on land recently surveyed and
found to be in the Dawnay possessions.[12] Distant
from the parish church, it had become the spiritual
province of Primitive Methodist and Wesleyan
chapels. A church, a parsonage, and a burial ground
for all would perhaps redress the balance. It is a
narrow little church, merely 18 feet wide with a
continuous roof ridge only 28 feet from the ground.
Built and furnished for £2500, Dalton – with its
four simply buttressed narrow window bays and
undecorated porch – seems at first too severe, just
a narrowly pierced wall in grey stone blocks under
a continuous roof of steel-grey slate with a slender
red-tile ridge. But the masonry is cut and placed
with extraordinary finesse. The small bricks of
rough snecked stone are thickly mortared to make a
rippled surface, rest on smooth bands of amber local
sandstone that diminish as they rise and are broken
by the white Huddleston limestone that frames and
moulds the openings. It is a pattern that paints in
shifts of tone and texture the weights and lines of
its structure. The tower manages to frame a great
west window without supporting buttresses, rising
from a square base on an enormous anchor, then
passing through a tapered ringers' chamber to a
delicate octagonal belfry, and ending in a pyramidal
cap covered with thirteen bands of thin stone slabs,
seven carrying the same scalloped texturing that
is used at Baldersby, so that the little spire, like its
modest bells, would echo the great steeple with its
eight great bells that lies across the fields in St James.

Inside, the brick-clad walls, like those at
Baldersby, are forged from a vivid mosaic of colour
and detail in inexpensive manufactured materials,
though a modest array of polished marble finds a
place in the reredos. They manage to be animated
with pattern, motive and line without ever losing
unity or calmness, working with the busy rhythm
of the wagon-beam roof to engage the eye so
completely that the boundaries of the tiny space
dissolve. The fabric and its furnishing are entirely
the work of local master masons and carpenters. But
the lightly coloured windows that complete the effect
are among the earliest works of the William Morris
studio. For the single wide lancet at the west, placed
within the broach of the tower, Edward Burne-Jones

Proposed New Church No. 9.

Dalton.

Details of Chancel Screen.

Cope
full size.

line of
cope.

½ Plan at CD.
full size

the dotted lines show the
tracery and casping

centre line

centre line

½ Plan at AB
full size

Base
full size.

A   B

Section.

Signed by me in so far as
anything in this drawing is
connected with my Specification
and Tender   Francis ...

Signed by me in so far as
anything in this drawing is
connected with my Specification
and Tender.

Richard Raworth ...

A   B   Plan.

Half Elevation.

75

Church of St John
the Evangelist,
Dalton: details of
chancel screen, 1867

provided the figure of St John the Evangelist, after whom the church was named, and Philip Webb the symbolic decoration above. The six-foiled window above the altar carries a Christ in Glory, again by Burne-Jones, with William Morris's heavenly choir singing praises on either side. The David and Moses in the north windows of the nave are by Burne-Jones, but it was Morris himself who furnished the extraordinary Annunciation that fills the wonderful double window in the north, archangel and virgin separated by one of the delicate dove-grey shafts that Butterfield would thereafter introduce to so many of his ecclesiastical works.

Butterfield's own symbolic polychrome is anchored in the blood-red, five-petalled flower on either side of the reredos and in geometric tendrils,

blossoms, seeds and seedpods that form lines around the chancel walls.

In 1866, when work commenced at Beech Hill in Berkshire, some asked why another new church on the outer perimeters of Reading was needed, in a district only lightly populated.[13] Land and endowment had come from the Hunters, a local family who found the 3-mile journey to the parish church inconvenient, and who wanted a suitable resting place close to their seat at Beech Hill House for their departed, while local newspapers pointed out that the scattered rural district was marked by great poverty, isolation and need. Its first incumbent, Edward Hobhouse, made an even more compelling case, for the proprietorship of the poor. He argued that in a new church with free seating

76

St Mary's Church,
Beech Hill: interior
view looking east,
half-plate glass
negative by Philip
Osborne Collier,
*c.*1905

for all, workers and tenantry could feel, however mean and unsettled their lives, that this would be a sole fixed place of their own and one so firm and lasting that it could harbour generations of family memory. The church sits on a site where two roads join on a hilly corner of the Hunters' home farm, and was constructed by Wheeler Brothers of Reading for £2500 in a riot of brick pattern-making inside and out, with a shingle bell turret, a north aisle, a short chancel and a vestry and organ chamber on the north side. As at Dalton, the challenge of suggesting the divisions between nave, choir and sanctuary in a minimal space is met with a wooden screen, the slightest recession for the altar and three dispersed east windows, to suggest the infinite but avoid too clear and forceful a flood of light.

NOTES

1. Principal sources for the Baldersby projects include *The Builder*, 10 and 24 October 1857; *Yorkshire Herald*, 24 May 1856; and *The Times*, 11 August 1856.
2. John Duke Coleridge, 'The Necessity of Modernism in the Arts, Especially When Devoted to the Service of Religion', *Transactions of the Exeter Diocesan Architectural and Archaeological Society*, vol.4, 1854, p.15.
3. John Moultrie, in his collection *Altars, Hearths and Graves*, Hamilton, Adams & Co., London, 1854, p.8.
4. Bonamy Price, letter to Derwent Coleridge in the form of a memoir, April 1875, in *Poems of John Moultrie*, vol.2, Macmillan & Co., London, 1876, pp xxxii–xxxviii. For a typical, immensely popular and wonderful example of the fireside tale, see John Mason Neale, *Evenings at Sackville College: Legends for Children*, Joseph Masters, London, 1852, reprinted throughout the English-speaking world well into the twentieth century.
5. See Matthew Arnold, *Literature and Dogma: An Essay Towards a Better Appreciation of the Bible*, Smith, Elder & Co., London, 1873.
6. See for example S. Baring-Gould, *Yorkshire Oddities, Incidents and Strange Events*, John Hodges, London, 1874, and his *Further Reminiscences*, John Lane / Bodley Head, London, 1925, which includes a vivacious account of his experience as Lady Downe's parson at 'Dalton-i'-t'-muck' in 1867–71 (pp 18–27). See also J.C. Atkinson, *Forty Years in a Moorland Parish*, Macmillan, London, 1891.
7. The account of the Alvechurch project is drawn largely from reports in the *Coventry Standard*, 29 May 1857; *Worcester Herald*, 30 May 1857; *Worcester Chronicle*, 22 May 1861; and *Bromsgrove Messenger*, 12 October 1861.
8. The account of the Bamford project draws from the *Derbyshire Advertiser and Journal*, 2 November 1860, and from a full history given in the *Derbyshire Daily Telegraph*, 26 October 1911. The plan is filed with the Incorporated Church Building Society, Church of England Record Centre, hereafter ICBS Archives.
9. The account of the Landford project is drawn primarily from the report, papers and specifications accompanying the drawings in the parish files at the Wiltshire and Swindon Archives.
10. A report on the Dropmore project appeared in the *Building News*, 25 May 1866.
11. The account of the Bont Goch project draws from a report in *The Guardian*, 22 July 1868.
12. The account of the Dalton church draws from Baring-Gould, *Further Reminiscences*, op.cit. In a letter, William Morris references the Dalton windows, which were still in his studio in March 1869 and shown to clients as models of the new work the firm was undertaking: see William Kelvin (ed.), *The Collected Letters of William Morris, Volume 1: 1848-1880*, Princeton University Press, Princeton, 2014, p.75. Butterfield includes the little Dalton church in his very short list of works for biographical directories at this time, clearly regarding it as one of major importance.
13. The account of the Beech Hill project draws from reports in *The Builder*, 6 October 1866, p.749, and *Berkshire Chronicle*, 19 October 1867.

IDEAL VILLAGE AND MINIMAL CHURCH

Village of St James, Baldersby

Village and Church of St James,
Baldersby
also overleaf

Church of St John Evangelist, Dalton
also overleaf

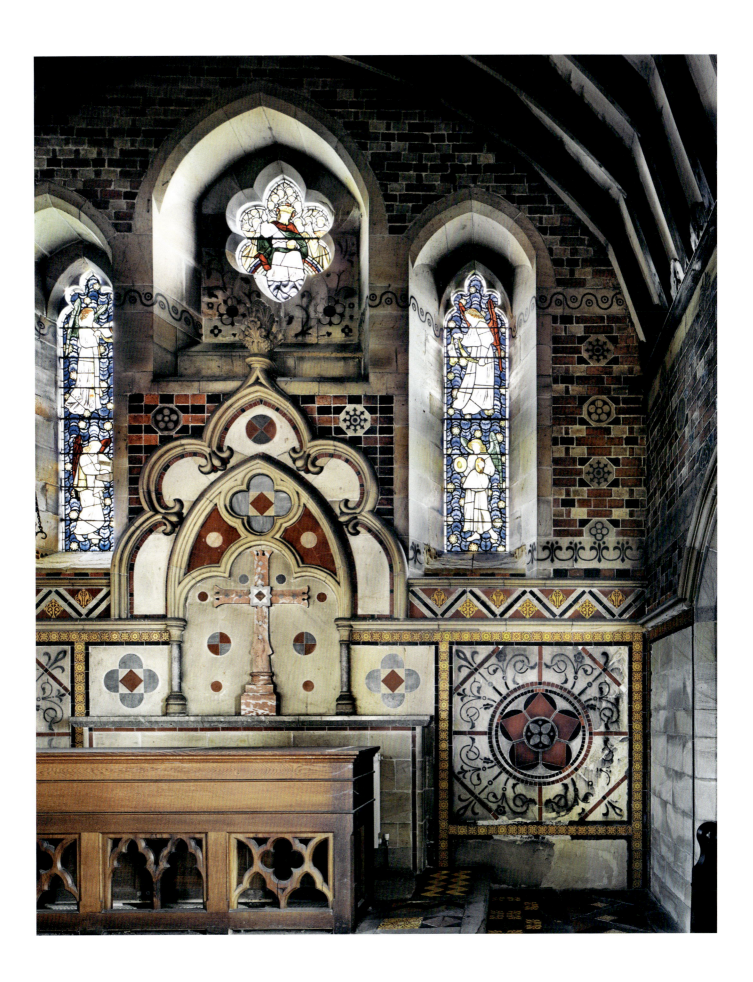

Church of St John Evangelist, Dalton

CHAPTER 8

RECUPERATION *of the* PARISH CHURCH, 1847–73

AMESBURY AND GREAT MONGEHAM

N 1878 THE *Saturday Review* marked the death of the remarkable antiquary Sir Stephen Glynne by looking back to the casual disregard in which country churches were held fifty years before, when Glynne first began a lifelong quest to inspect and record these neglected centre-points of the national landscape. 'Grand ecclesiastical architecture had always its votaries and its more or less erudite exponents,' said the *Review*, 'but any definite idea of science or art attaching to village churches would have been absolutely unintelligible. They were simply the playgrounds of the churchwarden and the victims of the pewed and cushioned squire.'[1] The movement to recuperate such parish churches began to spread rapidly in the second half of the 1840s. In this Butterfield played a signal part: a single monthly issue of the *Ecclesiologist* in January 1847 could list five

new Butterfield restorations under way. The most conspicuous was at Wavendon, a Buckinghamshire parish church where funding from the Hoare family allowed him to produce a revolutionary template for external restoration, in which the 'skeleton of the church is built up again precisely on the former plan, and with the use of the old materials',[2] while, inside, everything that obscured the basic structure – from galleries and box pews to organ loft, stoves, a dropped ceiling and a high pulpit – was cleared, leaving a fully exposed nave dominated by its ancient arcade and vaulted high above with timbers, something not seen in a village church for 300 years.

In many country towns and villages, the larger and once more distinguished parish churches had suffered the most depredation, like the great collegiate church from which a society of priests had once served the surrounding country but whose parish population had dispersed to the overgrowing towns, or the abbey and priory church whose stones were reclaimed for housebuilding after the Dissolution. Yet they served as evocations of the half-forgotten rural world that so many had left behind, lovingly recommended by traveller's guides and gazetteers, their fragments of sculpture and tracery printed in antiquarian studies, and views of their charming ivy-clad dilapidations amid overgrown churchyards printed to hang on parlour walls and lie in library cabinets. Encouraged first by Sir Walter Scott and then by writers such as William Harrison Ainsworth, by John Keats's Romantic poesy conjuring up St Agnes's Eve, by the historical scene paintings of artists like Paul Delaroche, and by the sudden fashion for pageants and tournaments, the culture was now deeply infected with medieval fancies. This encouraged the earliest initiatives in recuperation, but as they progressed, any perceived changes to these survivors of the chivalric age would be contested; and as we reach the later period of Butterfield's work – with its regard for the durable, the crisp and a lively palette – many protested against his readiness to discard incidental accretions and scrape away the corrosive patina of time. In fact, though he had no fondness for the dust of memory, he often pleaded with his patron to retain elements of no particular distinction – such as a rough western tower or an add-on Perpendicular porch – to keep alive the outline and memory of the long familiar.

Amesbury was a small market town at a crossroads on the Wiltshire Avon which, until the railways took travellers away, had a lively business in innkeeping and the coaching trade. It had originally grown up around a medieval priory, whose once splendid church had served the parish prior to the Dissolution and was thus spared destruction. By 1851, when Butterfield was invited to survey the church, it lay in the patronage of the Coutts banker Sir Edmund Antrobus of Amesbury House, or 'Abbey', which lay adjacent to it. Antrobus found the abbey itself in a very poor state, pulled most of it down and embarked upon a rebuilding programme, which he suspended until retirement from city life approached, when he began to establish his place

in Amesbury not by resuming that work at once, but by turning first to the needs of the parish. Butterfield found a very damp, cold and disorderly church.[3] It was built on a cross plan with a grand south transept and chancel, a narrow low nave with south aisle, a rough-and-ready east window and a small private chapel, outbuildings and service sheds lying north of the chancel. This already awkward arrangement had been meanly modified by churchwardens of the preceding century who had lowered the entire chancel roof; extruded a plain porch at the southwest corner of the aisle; rendered the windows, gable, door and facing of the south transept into classical Georgian; and encumbered the interior with box pews, a high pulpit, huge wall monuments and a gallery across the west window, to all of which a seventeenth-century staircase to the tower added even more unnecessary incident. Faced with the haphazard accretion of seven centuries, Butterfield's proposal let much of the church's history lie and focused on what was essential to restore its internal vistas, bring the best of its early fabric back to life, increase its seating capacity and make the church dry, comfortable and fit for a dignified form of worship.

Written exchanges on the 'proposed new works' start in 1849. Butterfield summarised the project in simple detail:

> The present fittings including the gallery are to be removed; the whole Church to be refitted and reseated with oak furniture, the Church to be drained, the floor raised to ensure dryness, and repaved with tiles and stone in the passages, and with wood beneath the seats, the walls to be scraped, cleansed and coloured . . . the belfry to be repaired and made weathertight . . . The chapel in North Transept is to be fitted up as a vestry, with a screen. A room for a furnace is to be built, and hot water pipes in drains laid round the Church . . . and a new oak roof covered with stone slate, at a higher pitch than the present one, is to be put upon the Chancel.

The outbuildings to the north were to be swept away and a low wall built 'to enclose a yard, and protect

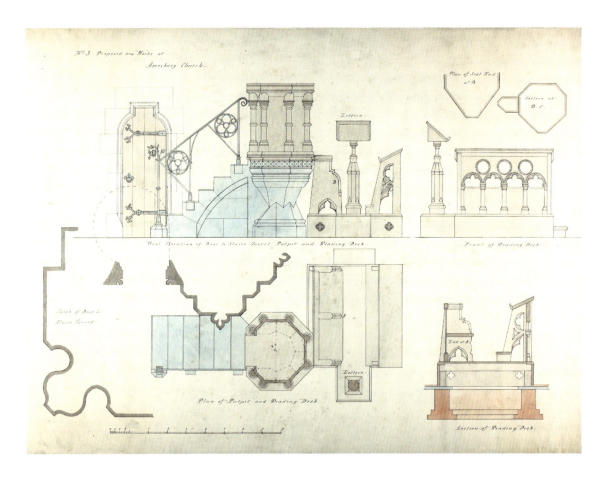

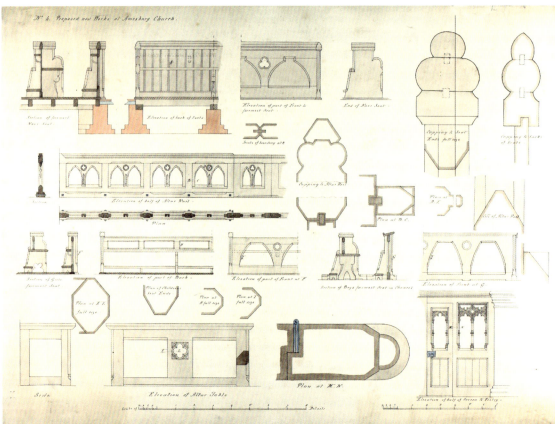

77

Amesbury Parish Church:
pulpit and reading desk,
c.1850–52

78

Amesbury Parish Church:
furnishings, *c*.1850–52

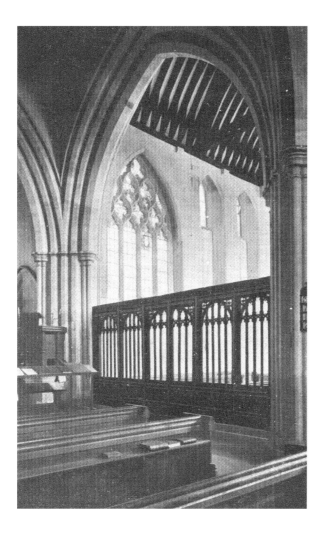

Amesbury Parish
Church: interior
view looking north-
east from south
transept to chancel,
photographed *c*.1907

the Church'. Seating, with children accommodated in the north transept, and a boys' choir derived from the local grammar school in the chancel, would now increase by fifty-four to a total of 655.

To these fundamental changes – whose costs of £4000 were borne largely by Antrobus – Butterfield obtained gifts from clergy and lay patrons for further improvements: a new east window in character and scale with the body of the church; a new west window; the rebuilding of earlier sections of the nave; and a new gable, lancet windows and doorway for the south transept, which would be brought into harmony with the thirteenth- and early fourteenth-century portions of the fabric that Butterfield was most concerned to recover. While each of these steps would go a long way towards recapturing the sense of an early English church, with its dignity and spaciousness, everything

depended upon the grace and synchronicity of the new fittings that would unite the whole. To these – all following a consistent repertory of detail and scale, from the iron straps on doors to the fretwork of the vestry screen – Butterfield paid the most minute and beautiful attention. As the London *Morning Post* remarked soon after its completion, in December 1853, nothing quite like this had been done before, recapturing the lost splendour of an obscure but once 'glorious building' in a remote country town, and it was hailed as a landmark of the Church revival.

Great Mongeham was a large Kent parish church of very early origin that served what had once been a market town but had now dwindled to a small village of granaries, maltings and breweries supplying the infamous merchants, seamen and boatmen of Deal, off which shipping from the continent would ride in the shallows at anchor (or be wrecked on the shoals). Lying among cornfields and visible from the water, the picturesque rustic church stood in wonderfully nostalgic contrast to the raucous urban disorder at the coast, and artists of the early nineteenth century delighted in the overgrown romance of its ruins. When Edward Penny arrived to take up the vicarage in May of 1849, he made its revival the first goal of his ministry, and, given the degree of its dereliction, it would remain so for the rest of his life. The little porch was almost falling to pieces, the mullions of most of the windows were crumbling, the west door was in ruins and the roof of the chancel was so bad that rain poured through it and birds made their nests inside. The church was an assembly of disparate parts: a very short nave, 45 feet by 30, leading to an unusually high chancel, over 40 feet long with a very narrow girth of about 15 feet, which was the oldest part of the church, probably built soon after the Norman Conquest. There were two chantry chapels. That on the north side, with a side door, was now dedicated to the storage of farm equipment for the family on whose land the church stood and whose fortunes had failed. The southern chantry had long gone to ruin, and a south aisle had begun to collapse in the sixteenth century, when the town was already in decline, and been

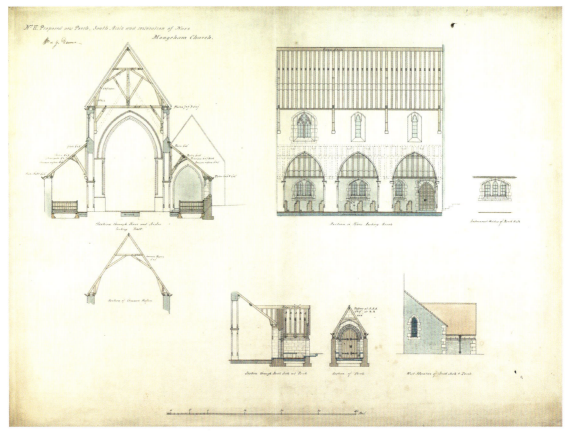

80

Great Mongeham Church:
east window and details of
chancel, *c.*1849–51

81

Great Mongeham Church:
new porch, south aisle and
restoration of nave, *c.*1884

the fourteenth century of any distinction, opening the opportunity to restore it to a consistent Early English condition enlivened by some fragments of Norman and twelfth-century work. Some complained of the lack of decoration in the many plain lancet windows employed in the oldest of the walls, with Butterfield in response saying that the essence of the earliest English architecture lay in simply piercing walls. Others were bitterly opposed to his removal of later accretions, believing that a part of the history of the church was destroyed by erasing the memory of more recent eras to re-create the sense of a cohesive church of the twelfth to fourteenth century.

ST BEES PRIORY

In about 1842, students at the Theological College at St Bees in Cumbria issued two engraved views by one of their number showing the priory church in which it had been founded and housed for more than twenty years.[5] The college had been organised to provide a path to ordination for those unable to find or pay for a place at one of the universities and to increase the numbers of priests available to fill the particular needs of the burgeoning population of the north. Its regime and two-year curriculum were stringent, with students boarded simply, at their own cost, in approved lodgings. Its success was remarkable, St Bees often ranking close to the great universities in the annual list of new ordinands. Students were drawn almost entirely from the professional and trading classes where many – coming well into their twenties – had been working. This was a revolutionary change for a Church that had for so long equated her clergy with the privileged third sons of the landed gentry. The college hall was built in late Georgian Gothick style within the ruined choir and chancel of a great Benedictine abbey church associated with St Bega, a seventh-century Irishwoman whose ship had foundered on these shores.

The nave was used as the church of a parish of 20,000 people, embracing the new port of Whitehaven, the grammar school which had grown

82
St Bees Priory Church and College: view from the north-east, engraving by F.B.A. [Francis Busteed Ashley] produced for sale to raise funds for the student missionary society, *c*.1842–4

83
St Bees Priory Church: view from the north-east, Valentine & Sons postcard, *c*.1895

demolished, with its wall roughly propped up some sixty years before. There had been enlargements and improvements from the twelfth to the fifteenth centuries, including the very impressive tower, a clerestory and the arcades of the nave.

Butterfield's work began in 1850 with the restoration of the ancient chancel; a new porch and south aisle were built in 1853, when the nave was re-roofed; the north chantry was tackled in 1860, and the south chantry, west window in the tower and western door in 1861, with stained glass added to the east window at that time.[4] In some ways, this extreme case of neglect worked to the advantage of the restorers, since there was little work since

84

St Bees Priory
Church:
design for chancel
screen, 1886

85

St Bees Priory
Church: interior
view looking east,
photographed 1886

up beside it and the new seminary, all of which
made its condition even more shocking to the
Ecclesiologist, which, in September 1842, lamented
'the miserable condition of the conventual church
of St Bees'. So much of the priory ruins had been
mined for building materials that some aspects were
unrecoverable, but, starting in 1847–52 when he
began to restore and rationalise the west bays of the
college hall, and then in 1855–6 when he first opened
the transepts and space under the tower, Butterfield
worked for forty years to slowly reconstitute a
coherent church; to reorder its college buildings,
grounds and walks; and finally to embellish its
interior with a flourish of extravagant beauty.

In 1865, his free-standing New College Hall
appeared, with lecture room, library and a gravelled
and railed 'dandy walk' for ambulation along the
river. The college retained most of its Regency
pavilion on the eastern foundations of the priory
church; but the new hall facilities released all of the

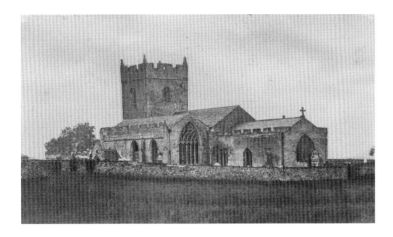

the old priory church remained a landmark for the traveller; and postcards, souvenirs and magazine engravings continued to write its image into the common culture. Photographer James Valentine captured the priory church in the 1890s (fig.83) from the same viewpoint as college student Francis Busteed Ashley's sketch fifty years before (fig.82). It now lay in one of those ordered Butterfield enclosures which restored a site from a picturesque ruin to a working precinct of the parish. The emphatic approach to rebuilding the tower and belfry lends authority to the church's place in the distant view.

IN THE WESTERN DISTRICT: BRIGHAM AND LAMPLUGH

The western district of Cumberland was a volatile country of fast-growing and fast-declining coal ports shipping fuel from the vast Cumbrian seam to the burgeoning industries of Ulster; clothiers, hatmakers and weavers; rolling plants for steel; and quarries, lime kilns and copper and iron mines, whose useful lives were shorter than those of the men who worked them. 'Precocious towns' like Maryport grew at furious speed, peopled with migrants from throughout the country who crowded into lodgings rife with disease. Parish boundaries were vast, so that a vicar like the poet's son John Wordsworth in the village of Brigham – where most of the 800 local people were spinning flax or working in quarries and lime kilns – might find his charge stretching to the manufacturing town of Cockermouth 2 miles distant and as far as Workington on the coast. Gradually, as rail travel allowed, Brigham also began to house some of their middle classes and shipping and mining magnates; and it was at their instigation that a movement to restore the ancient parish church began. There was very little sectarian jealousy in this. The parish in these circumstances was a civil institution; its subscription lists for restoration were filled with members of Dissenting chapels; it married and buried families of all sects; and the leading figure in reconstructing its history and advancing Butterfield's work was the Quaker member of parliament Isaac Fletcher.

86

Brigham Church: view from the south-east before restoration, photographed 1863

87

Brigham Church: view from the south-east after the second phase of restoration, photograph by Dr Thornburn of Tadcastle, 1876

rest of the church for worship, so that Butterfield could rebuild the south transept in a manner that brought the old and new buildings into harmony. In a final phase completed in 1887 he raised the roof over what had been the first bay of the original choir to create a shallow chancel, with a high lunette and interior walls in a relief of pink and white circular geometries; restored the tower and capped it with a commandingly severe pyramid; raised the nave roof to its original ridge line, on a wonderful span of open timber beams; and finally, in a stunningly bold move, filled the entire chancel arch with an enormous metal screen, the lower part showing the façade of a battlemented temple rising on iron shafts, and the upper section a filigree Eden of vine and blossom fretwork through which, haloed with a mandorla, an open cross rises from the parapet (fig.84).

The college began to lose students late in the 1880s and closed before the turn of the century. But St Bees developed as a bathing and walking resort;

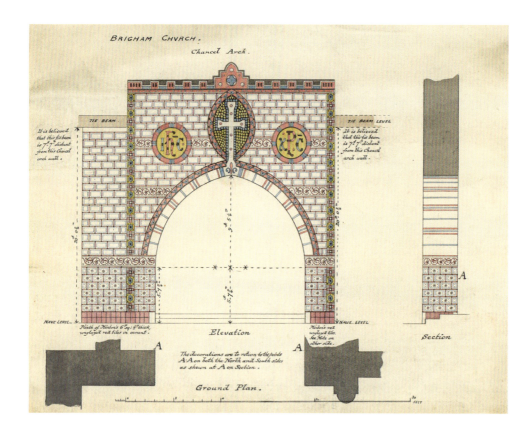

BRIGHAM CHVRCH.

Chancel Arch.

Elevation

Ground Plan.

Section

It is believed that this tie beam is 7ft 9in distant from this Chancel arch wall.

The decorations are to return to the points A:A on both the North and South sides as shown at A on Section.

88 (left)
Brigham Church: elevation, section and ground plan of chancel arch, 1876

89 (right, top)
St Michael's Church, Lamplugh: view from the south-east after rebuilding, photographed *c*.1875

90 (right, below)
St Michael's Church, Lamplugh: interior view looking east, photographed *c*.1880

St Bega's was a semi-fortified church of local red sandstone with a nave and tower of the twelfth century and a Decorated south aisle, from the time of Edward III, of real beauty and sophistication. The tower was said to carry the only ring of bells in the western district, though only three of the six were in place when Butterfield was called in. His plan for restoration was approved in 1864. Much objection had been raised to the demolition of galleries and box pews by those who held them, but objections were overcome when it was found that a large bequest to fund the work stipulated their removal. Nave and aisle were completed in 1865, with Butterfield bringing back to life an extraordinary corpus of Norman carving.[6] Work on the chancel and in extending the graveyard were to be completed by a gift from Lord Lonsdale, but were delayed, first by an exorbitant rise in building labour costs, then by the effects of the crash of 1873, and finally by a miners' strike that drastically depressed the income of landowners. Work on the exterior was nevertheless completed by 1876, soon followed by Butterfield's remarkable scheme of painted decoration for the

chancel. A surviving drawing for the east side of the chancel arch (fig.88) shows the same rose pattern in the dado as that which covered the ceiling. Fletcher looked back at those prosperous, uncontentious and flourishing years in the western district before the long depression that followed 1873 'almost as a dream of a golden age'. Crushed by adversity, he killed himself in 1879, and Butterfield's Cumberland builder, ruined by failed speculations, hanged himself in a barn three years later.

Lamplugh was a scattered sheep-rearing, mining and wool-making parish in the western fells south-east of Cockermouth. Its church had been rebuilt more than once, so that by the time Butterfield was called to address it, the nave consisted of no more than a plain whitewashed box of the 1770s with square sash windows. There were some elements of a chancel, a family mortuary chapel, and loose fragments of medieval work remained – all probably moved from another site when the centre of the parish shifted. Butterfield's restoration was occasioned by the boom in iron ore of the 1860s, when the parish population rose to nearly 1200

and landowners with mineral rights had funds at hand. He built an entirely new nave, mostly in red sandstone, and a wonderful double bellcote carrying a single plain west window, as at Lindisfarne. He rebuilt a chancel on the traces of its predecessor and restored the chapel as a south vestry. The surviving archaeological fragments were incorporated as gargoyles on the outside and above the crossing arch inside, where the entire restored head of what must be the old east window is placed. Two luminous photographs of a date astonishingly close to its completion in 1870 (figs 89 and 90) show the church as Butterfield completed it, with, as the local paper reported, two of the windows and the gargoyles of the old church 'cleansed and reintroduced into the spic and span of its replacement'.[7] There is indeed a crispness and clarity – a realistic, unsentimental and unapologetically durable freshness – that brings to mind Halsey Ricardo's reflection that throughout Butterfield's work 'everything is trim and yare – a strong contrast to the shallow sentimentality which calls for effects which are endeared to it by associations that cannot again be repeated'.[8]

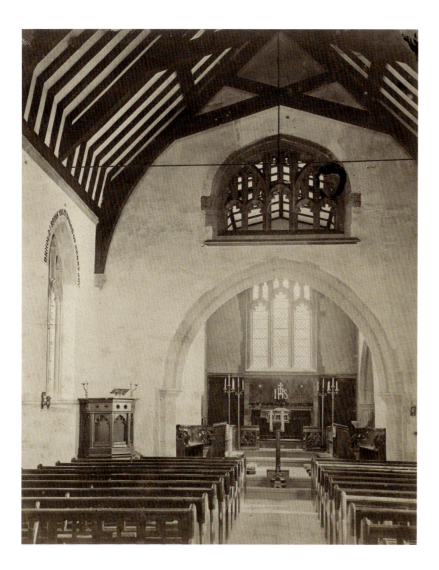

NOTES

1. *Saturday Review*, 9 February 1878.
2. The account of the Wavendon project is taken principally from the *Buckinghamshire Herald*, 15 September 1849, and *The Ecclesiologist*, June 1848.
3. The account of the work at Amesbury parish church is taken primarily from correspondence and accounts in the parish records, Wiltshire and Swindon Archives, and from the long reports in the *Salisbury and Winchester Journal*, 10 December 1853, and *Morning Post*, 12 December 1853.
4. The account of the work at Great Mongeham church draws from *The Ecclesiologist*, December 1854 and January 1855, and a summary history in the *Dover Express*, 23 May 1902.
5. *The Ecclesiologist*, September 1842. The St Bees project history relies extensively on the work of Ian McAndrew and Doug Sim on 'The Priory Church', on the remarkable village website: https://stbees.org.uk.
6. The account of this project is taken from Isaac Fletcher, 'Brigham Church', in *Cumberland and Westmorland Antiquarian and Archeological Society Transactions*, vol.4, 1878–9, pp 173–7, and *Carlisle Journal*, 22 January 1864, 15 April 1864 and 13 October 1865.
7. The account of the Lamplugh project draws from reports in the *Penrith Observer*, 29 June 1869, and *Cumberland Pacquet*, 30 August 1870.
8. Halsey Ricardo, 'William Butterfield', *Architectural Review*, August 1900, p.21.

CHAPTER 9

'ARREARS of NEGLECT', 1865–84

REBUILDING: WHITEPARISH

We could tell of churches, and that perhaps
within sight of noble residences, of which the
dirt and desecration would hardly be credited in
another age; of chapels used as lumber rooms, of
chancel arches blocked up with huge and hideous
galleries, of family pews with fire-places and glass
shutters; in short of pens and snuggeries, and
a wretched system of exclusiveness in the place
where rich and poor meet together.[1]

SO WROTE JOHN SANDFORD, remembering
the state of the Church when his clerical
career began late in the 1820s. By 1867,
the movement to restore such churches
in country parishes had so gained ground
that the poor people of Whiteparish, a dispersed
agricultural and stone-cutting parish on the edge
of the New Forest, themselves appealed to their
clergy to redress the shame they felt at the neglected
condition of their church compared to neighbouring
parishes around them.

Butterfield himself obtained photographs to
record the contrast between what was and what
became.[2] Though prints and paintings of the early
century show the body of All Saints' Church as a
sturdy, heavily buttressed, wide-girthed edifice in
flint, virtually nothing of that historical texture
remained, and the interior was dominated by high
boxed pews and a gallery. The task was effectively
as Butterfield labelled it on the photographs when
completed: 'rebuilt by me for Lord Nelson'. The shell
of the chancel was mean and unimpressive, but it
had been sympathetically paved, roofed and refitted
in 1853, to accommodate a memorial window, and
was left alone. The banded chancel arch was very
old and left in place, and some early remains were

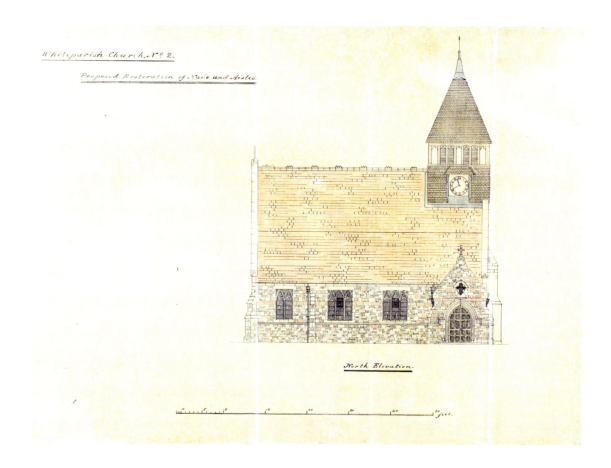

Whiteparish Church. Nº 2.

Proposed Restoration of Nave and Aisles.

North Elevation.

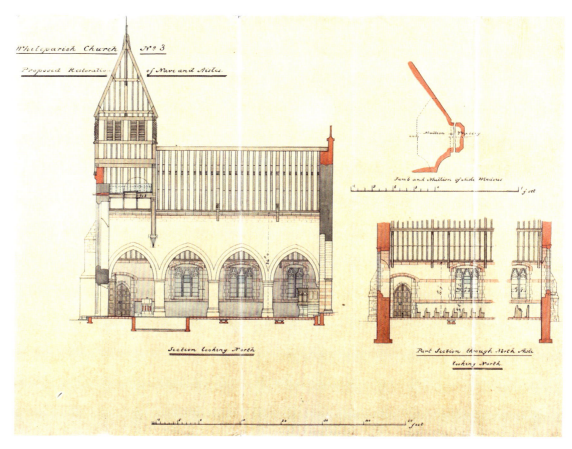

Whiteparish Church. Nº 3

Proposed Restoration of Nave and Aisles.

Jamb and Mullion of Aisle Windows

Section looking North

Part Section through North Aisle looking North

91

All Saints' Church, Whiteparish: restoration of nave and aisles – north elevation, *c.*1867–8

92

All Saints' Church, Whiteparish: restoration – sections looking north, *c.*1867–8

93
All Saints' Church,
Whiteparish: view
from the north-west,
photographed *c*.1870

found and reinstalled, notably a Norman priest's doorway, which was fitted into the south portal. As rebuilt, the church had open free seats for 300, in place of 230 sittings which had been allocated by the churchwardens on a yearly basis. The cost was £2000, and the builder was the local firm of William Crook with whom Butterfield worked throughout Wiltshire. Flint, the cheapest building material in the district, was mixed with a vivid red ferruginous local sandstone; a new font was provided of multicoloured marbles within a white stone top and base. All that was said at the start was that 'another blot on their part of the diocese' might be removed. But much more was achieved, as a church of the stunning scale and solidity their grandparents knew was returned to its people, reflecting the colours of the stone and ground around it and seeming to sit astride the land like a saddle.

RECONSTRUCTION: HEYTESBURY

Heytesbury in the Wylye Valley of west Wiltshire was another scattered parish of some 1300 people, living in the remains of what had once been a

town of 5000, with a large almshouse, a lockup and market square. The parish church, largely of the thirteenth century, had been established for a collegiate body of clergy, serving a wide area, so that the plan was closer to a small cathedral than a village church, with a lengthy chancel flanked by cloistered side aisles, north and south transepts and a vast and lofty crossing. In 1846, its condition came to the attention of the *Ecclesiologist*:

> However incredible it may seem . . . The spacious chancel and transepts . . . are disused, being blocked off from the nave by a wooden partition, in which is a small door, generally locked. Over the west arch of the tower is Lord Heytesbury's flying pen. There are other galleries in the nave, and the pulpit &c. stand at the west end . . . The altar is of course quite out of sight, and the chancel, with its fourteen stalls, made useless. The chancel aisles have been destroyed.[3]

Plans for improvement had been made in 1840 by Wyatt & Brandon and another scheme proposed by Owen Browne Carter in 1848, but in 1865, when Lord Heytesbury approached Butterfield for a

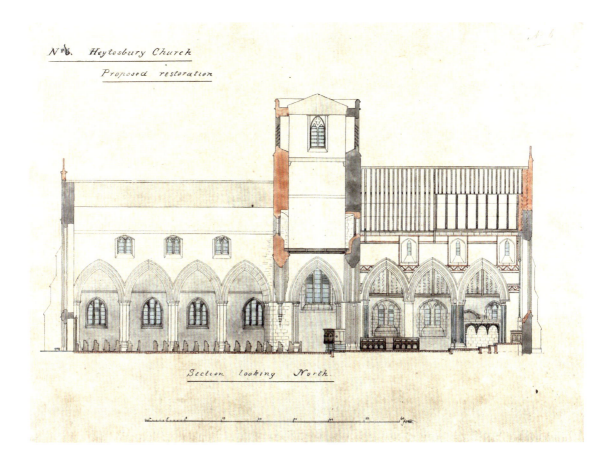

survey and recommendations, the general condition remained.

The church was closed for two years and reopened in September 1867 after costs of £6000 for building and major donations for windows. Butterfield reported on his work, a combination of extensive restoration and reconstruction:

In the interior of the Church the galleries were taken down, all the fittings were removed, and the Chancel and tower, which for many years had been entirely shut off from the Nave by one of the galleries, were made once more available for Divine service. The two transepts were also thrown open to the Church, the one on the South had been closed in and used as a Vestry Room, and that on the North, originally a Chapel . . . much beautified by the Hungerford family, had been built up and appropriated as a burial place for the à Court family . . . The Hungerford screen was restored, the old windows were reopened, and the space filled with seats . . . It was found necessary to rebuild from the foundations the piers of the Nave, and also the South and West sides of the Tower, which were in a very dilapidated and crushed state; this enabled the Architect to widen the western Arch of the Tower . . . The arches of the Chancel aisles, which had been filled up, were reopened, and the aisles, which had been taken down, were rebuilt. The East Window was restored to its original length, and the flat roof of the Chancel raised to its former high pitch. The old heavy stone tile of the Church [roof] was removed, and replaced with slate.[4]

Sections (figs 94 and 95) show Butterfield's reconstruction of the internal arcades of the chancel, using what he could of the remaining shafts, leaving one on each side in a rough cylindrical state like a Roman column, but developing the others into banded and polychrome clusters of stone and marble, like the medieval arch mouldings above. Thin columns of deepest blue marble are repeated on either side of the blind arcades at the east window, carried up in two stages and rendered pencil thin to frame the window with an effect at once subtle and startling. He stripped and reseated the nave and restored or rebuilt where necessary its sturdy octagonal shafts. The rare treatment of the east window as a single lancet within a blind arcade is one of those 'oddities' of medieval architecture in which Butterfield took such delight. Without decoration it made little sense, so he reconstructed a highly unusual painted geometry following the faint residue of pigmented lines on the walls. The whole effect of the interior is both serene and thrilling, with Butterfield and Alexander Gibbs introducing in the windows a monumental drama of light and colour complementary to that in the stones.

A CASE HISTORY: ARDLEIGH

In 1872, Thomas Walter Perry took up the incumbency of St Mary the Virgin, the parish church of Ardleigh, halfway between Colchester and Dedham in the estuary lands of Essex. The village stretched over 5000 acres, housing 1600 people, 1400 of them living and working in the parish, of whom 1200 were 'of the poorer class'.[5] The parish church, in the centre of the 'township', had first been built in the twelfth century as an outgrowth of St John's monastery in Colchester, but survived as a largely fourteenth- and fifteenth-century town church of moderate proportions, graced by a porch of great vigour and a tower of impressive proportion, both in a late Gothic style typical of this region, the tower capped with a parapet in the sixteenth century. The body of the church had been largely rebuilt in 1760, when much of its medieval character was first lost. Then, between 1835 and 1840, its churchwardens, perhaps fearful of collapse, had seen fit to replace the remaining fourteenth-century stone shafts along both sides of the nave with iron columns, and to tear down most of the north and south walls in order to build unsightly aisles. The entire roof had been progressively lowered and was now completely re-covered, with a pair of rudely gabled clerestory windows above the south aisle. A random accumulation of galleries, belfry stairs and 'ugly pews, high and low' furnished

the nave and aisles, and the chancel – in the rector's personal care – was now little more than a brick shed tacked on to the east end. Seating 275, and uncomfortably laid out, it had become inadequate for the parish's population, especially for children and the poor, badly lit, cold and unsuited to any but the most rudimentary liturgical practices. Its roof was bowing; its thin, poorly sealed new aisle windows let in air and water; the tower was blocked off; and the clerestory windows were mostly boarded up. As the *Church Builder* noted, describing its 'shocking' condition in April 1880, Ardleigh was typical of pockets of Essex and East Anglia that the 'Great Restoration' movement had passed by, leaving 'arrears of neglect . . . and errors in alterations or repairs – well meant at the time – which require to be rectified'.

Confronted with the degraded and now dangerous state of his church, Perry began to survey its condition himself before undertaking repairs. He established that the tower and porch were built in 1460, but found no provable trace of the original twelfth-century church 'owing to the havoc to which it has been subjected'. He took a number of his own photographs to record the 'lamentable appearance' and, in 1875, finally located the foundations of the original chancel, discovering that its dimensions were fully 17 feet longer. Further research produced no description or drawing of what the chancel might have looked like: it had been entirely torn down and rebuilt some years before, in brick, to a length of 'one pace'. He reported that the lower portion of a Perpendicular stone chancel screen remained in place, though repaired with rough plaster casts of broken tracery. Over the next four years, Perry attempted to 'patch up' the church, but had to report that it was 'in worse condition year by year', and that the annual costs of urgent piecemeal repairs were likely to exceed those of a full-throated attempt at correction and conservation. By 1879, he was ready to start a movement for complete restoration. An intimate friend of Butterfield's Canterbury client Alexander Hope – who by then was known as Beresford Hope, having inherited the Beresford Hall estate in Staffordshire – Perry turned to Butterfield for a survey and plans. The surviving records, drawings and photographs concurrent with the work are so thorough, and were made and retained with such rare care, that Ardleigh not only provides a prime example of how Butterfield's late restorations were conducted, but is quite possibly the one he wanted us most to recount and remember.

Butterfield surveyed the church early in the summer of 1879, and on 1 August sent his report to the vestry:

> The parish church of Ardleigh is in a state to speak for itself to almost any eye. An architect's report is almost superfluous. It has a fine tower and south porch in generally substantial condition. Both, however, need restoration and renewal of their best ornamental features very largely. The rest of the church may be described as a ruin. It has been gutted internally by the removal of the piers and arches which once separated the nave and aisles, the north walls have been badly rebuilt, and the chancel has not only been meanly rebuilt but reduced to half its original length. The case is one for almost re-building, with the exception of the tower and south porch.

But, he stressed, 'The new work, which I have proposed in the plans . . . is guided largely by the small indications of the old lines and treatment which still remain.' The proposal was therefore to re-create what may perhaps have never been – a consistently worked small fourteenth-century parish church of nave, aisles and chancel, in a considered amalgam of flint and rubble, leaving intact the later medieval accretions on the perimeter – porch, tower and west window – to stand as a record of a parish church as it had adapted to the changing circumstance of earlier times.

Butterfield's specifications were terse. Seating was raised from 275 to 333, with an allocation for children and the elimination of rented pews. 'The existing Tower, the western portion of the nave, the west wall of the north aisle, the porch and the chancel arch and respond of south aisle are to be carefully kept standing.' All else was to be removed, including the entire chancel, which would be replaced on a longer and wider footprint,

with a vestry to the north. A mix of tile, stone or Portland cement was to be used for interior facing, and the windows were to be 'glazed with cathedral rolled glass in diamond lead lights, tied with copper ties to wrought iron bars, and . . . provided with gunmetal casements in certain lights for ventilation'. Some small restorable portions of the nave walls were to be retained, where possible, and all new walls to be of stock brick faced on the outside with rubble and flint 'to agree with the best parts of the existing walling', with Bath stone dressings. The nave arcade and all internal responds, arches and doorways were to be in Bath stone. The reredos too was to be of Bath stone, with arcading on each side inlaid with Minton's tiles, the heads of the Evangelists in gilt mosaic medallions to either side, with the existing engraved alabaster cross becoming its centrepiece, and a marble shelf above the table.

Butterfield draws attention to the progression of stone steps rising in the sanctuary and specifies Minton tile floors wherever wood was not specified (in a pattern whose drawings he would supply) and simple red Minton tiles for the lower parts of nave and chancel aisles and vestry, too. The relatively simple new roofs, raised to the weather-lines that indicated the original height and pitch, were to be of Memel fir, plastered over to leave only the principal rafters and leading timbers exposed. Wherever possible, existing aisle roof timbers were to be repaired and re-used. The main roofs were to be tiled and the aisle roofs clad in lead with lead gutters. Dryness, comfort, equality and hygiene were critical. He calls for two stoves for heating, with a flue for one rising up the tower and a chimney on the north for the other. Pipes and lead gutters were to carry water from roof to cesspools; air bricks were to be used in external walls to ventilate below the wooden floors; low open bench pews and kneeling benches (rather than hassocks) were designed, both in the interests of hygiene and to ensure a closeness and absence of distinction between rich and poor. The existing chancel screen was to be repaired and refixed, but all other fittings, including stalls, pews, sedilia, doors and pulpit, were to be newly made of walnut and Riga oak, except the altar rail, in wrought iron and brass, with a thin walnut rim.

98

Church of St Mary
the Virgin, Ardleigh:
enlargement,
restoration and
refitting – south
elevation, 1879

99

Church of St Mary
the Virgin, Ardleigh:
enlargement,
restoration and
refitting – east
elevation, 1879

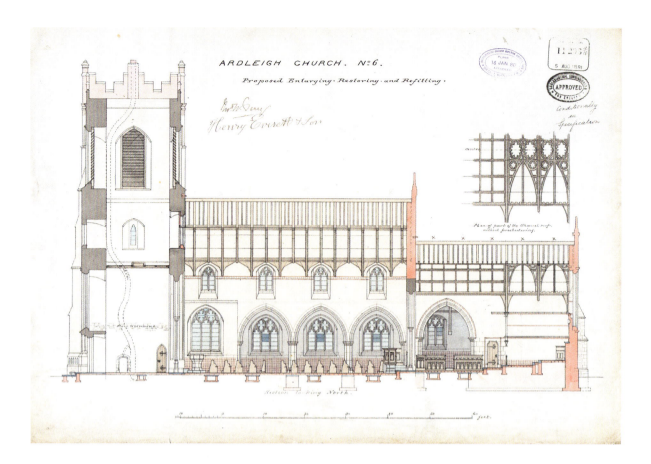

Church of St Mary
the Virgin, Ardleigh:
enlargement,
restoration and
refitting – section
looking north, 1879

The vestry approved, based on an estimate of
£4000. Applications for aid were prepared, a grant
of £500 was promised in January 1881, based on
a full set of Butterfield's drawings, and in August
1881, the Church Commissioners gave approval to
proceed. In late January 1882, the diocese issued a
faculty, approving Butterfield's specifications, and
by March sufficient funds had been subscribed to
start construction. The builders who won the tender
– Henry Everett & Son of Colchester – were initially
asked to begin with the new chancel, in order to
allow continued use of the church for as long as
possible, and to ensure that full funding was on
hand before proceeding to completion. As it turned
out, full funding appeared to allow for the entire
work to be accomplished in a single campaign.
Accordingly, the last service in the old church was
held on 18 June 1882, and 'the following day the
work of pulling down the whole of the old Church,
except the Tower and the Porch, was commenced'.

Butterfield and his builders found much to
surprise them in the course of work: portions

of an ancient east window appeared within the
walls of the little rebuilt chancel of 1760; much
of the original north arcade was found as rubble
composing the 1840 buttresses of the north
aisle; a Gothic saint's niche – probably for a lost
representation of St Margaret – appeared beneath
layers of plaster; and a piscina was found, turned
over to do service as a stone within a wall of the
1835 south aisle. With these features in mind,
Butterfield modified the details of his designs
for the reredos and for the altar rail – providing
drawings to his craft metalworkers, Hart, Son &
Peard, for a simpler and more striking pattern
that better catches light and the eye. Late in the
project, Butterfield realised that the upper portion
of the tower with its battlements was too insecure
to restore, and he rebuilt it. On the ground he had
discovered before the start of construction that
soil had been allowed to accumulate around the
footprint of the entire church for some centuries,
making a wide mound of damp earth that rose
16 inches above the base of existing walls. This

was removed and spread across portions of the churchyard to render the burial ground more level, and paving was laid against the new walls to prevent further encroachment. The whole church was ready for service just over a year after the first demolitions, and re-consecrated in August 1883. Furnishing continued into the new year, and in August 1884 Butterfield's final bill was presented, five years to the day since his proposal to rebuild this modest country church.

In 1885 Perry issued a pamphlet of lithographs prepared from photographs showing the church before and after rebuilding, to provide the older parishioners with a 'memorial of their former Church and its many Sacred Associations with their past lives'. It seems unnecessary, for surely the most striking effect of what was to all intents a new Butterfield church was how comfortingly its external aspect echoed its antecedent, and how comfortably parishioners returned to its reordered graveyard to honour the memories of their dead. Ardleigh is conspicuously, as are all Butterfield's restorations, a monument to the continuity of the parish church, a demonstration – from its elaborate heating system to its durable manufactured surfaces – of how it could be made fit for the conditions of his time while investing new life into the memory of place that these 'centre points' of the nation's life embodied.

NOTES

1. John Sandford, address to the joint meeting of the Oxford and Worcester Architectural Societies, 1854, reported in *The Ecclesiologist*, October 1854.
2. The account of the Whiteparish project is based on reports in the *Salisbury and Winchester Journal*, 2 February 1867 and 30 April 1870.
3. *The Ecclesiologist*, April 1846.
4. These extracts and the account of the Heytesbury project are taken from Butterfield's reports and correspondence in the parish files at the Wiltshire and Swindon Archives.
5. The account of the Ardleigh church project is taken primarily from minutes and other records of the vestry and parish of Ardleigh in the Essex County Archives and from the plan and pamphlets filed in the ICBS Archives.

101 (above)
Church of St Mary the Virgin, Ardleigh: view of the chancel after restoration, photograph by S.B. Angle & Co., 1884

102 (below)
Church of St Mary the Virgin, Ardleigh: view from the north-east after restoration, photograph by S.B. Angle & Co., 1884

IV OVERGROWN TOWNS

CHAPTER 10

'THE CLASSES *and* THE MASSES': LONDON, 1850–70

'HERE AT LAST IS A LONDON CHURCH'

WRITING FOR the popular *Daily News* in April 1854, a knowledgeable critic from Oxford reported that:

> In an obscure street in the metropolis there is now rapidly advancing toward completion a church perhaps the most costly and brilliant of its size ever attempted to be built in England in modern times or old. Most of our readers . . . in their wanderings among the streets to the north of Oxford-street, must have caught a glimpse of a queer-looking spire, rising between two and three hundred feet from the ground and built of slate and tiles instead of stone.

Beneath the spire, the critic continued, lay something

> though odd and original in the extreme, by no means deficient in eye satisfaction. After a while the sense of oddity wears off, while that of pleasantness and appropriateness increases; and the first distinct criticism, after the exclamatory mood has subsided, will, probably, be 'Well, here at last is a London church, built with London bricks, with a regular London street front,' and without any sacrifice of the orthodox 'ecclesiastical' forms.[1]

PREVIOUS PAGE:
All Saints'
National School,
Margaret Street

THE EVOLUTION OF ALL SAINTS' MARGARET STREET

In 1845, the notion of building a model high church for a crowded city arose at the Margaret Street Chapel, a drab meeting house buried on a nondescript street in Fitzrovia where, under the eventual ministry of William Upton Richards, some of those affected by the first stirrings of the Church revival gathered for services. Pusey and Keble were

NEW CHURCH OF ALL SAINTS, MARGARET-STREET, CAVENDISH-SQUARE.

THE CHURCH OF ALL SAINTS, MARGARET-STREET, REGENT-STREET.——Mr. Butterfield, Architect.

103 (left)

All Saints' Margaret Street: perspective published in *Illustrated London News*, 24 March 1855

104 (right)

All Saints' Margaret Street: interior perspective published in *The Builder*, June 1859

its guides, and Butterfield, one of its number, was house architect, progressively ameliorating the interior of the chapel and – once the decision was made to rebuild – selected to accomplish this model of an ecclesiological church in the national capital. Neighbouring land was obtained and sufficient funds put in place by 1849 for Butterfield's drawings and plans to be developed, and by Easter 1850 the last service at the old chapel was held, the old building was readied for demolition, a temporary hall was constructed for the interim, and Pusey,

quietly on a cold winter morning, had laid the foundation stone of the great new church.

Beresford Hope – as one of its principal patrons – was, as he had been at Canterbury, Butterfield's client and associate. Much of Butterfield's work on the built envelope of the precinct and church was complete by 1852, but it would take another seven years and a major gift from the banker Henry Tritton for the internal decorative work to be completed. The painstaking and quickly degraded fresco work in the east end was especially problematic, proving Butterfield's point that traditional decorative techniques and materials were neither appropriate nor economical in modern British conditions and justifying his own commitment to modern manufactured tile and glass mosaic, especially for narrative and figurative elements in murals. The essential design drawings, taken to Paris for the world's fair of 1855 and then displayed for thirty years behind Butterfield's desk at Adam Street, have now disappeared; but contemporary print and photographic representations are extraordinarily rich, allowing us to see the interior of the church as it first emerged and was then embellished and perfected by Butterfield over the forty years he contributed to its refinement.

The excitement generated by the church as it rose from the ground between 1850 and 1852 was extraordinary; by 1853 renderers for the illustrated architectural monthlies and the weekly popular press had begun publishing engravings of the completed shell of the church, and visitors were being welcomed to it. John Sandford, visiting the church with Butterfield in its raw 'architectural' state about this time, could already read in it a profound symbolic programme that came not from painterly portrayals or decorative details but from the very sense of the space and its fabrication: 'The forms, the proportions, the materials, the colours, – each brick and stone seem to have been arranged . . . [to] foster veneration in the human soul. Some will call this a rhapsody; but I can tell you . . . that it is possible for an architect, as it is for a painter and a poet, to be a great religious teacher'.[2]

Since the site did not allow an east window, a frescoed wall above the altar, reaching up to the vaulting, had been commissioned from the painter William Dyce, who was then at work on the Arthurian frescoes in the Palace of Westminster. Dyce framed the work within gilded tracery on the model of High Gothic screens, and they darkened rapidly, leaving an east wall that Butterfield struggled to reconcile with his general scheme. It would also take six years before the wall was far enough advanced to bring the interior into condition for consecration. At that time a number of elaborate engravings of the interior appeared, some seeming to portray further murals in some form on the north and south walls, which did not appear in the final form of tile mosaics for another twenty years. But Butterfield's lower portion of the east wall (perhaps the decoration was still undetermined) was always shown raw.

The earliest among the flood of reports and critiques in the popular daily and weekly press dwell on the subtly faceted and tapered tower, then 220 feet high. One writer compared its compelling effect on the low-lying metropolitan landscape of his day to that of Giotto's campanile at Florence upon which Dante could not stop gazing. Initial reactions to the aspect from the street involved a fascination with the severely patterned red and infused-black brick façades expressing nothing – bar capping gable crosses of stone – but the logic of their own purpose in a pattern of windows, walls and roofs without balcony, cornice or bay to relieve. As appreciation grew of the ingenuity with which the whole disparate precinct was woven into the constricted site, the purpose of the reductive approach became clear, containing but not crowding a tight space within a volatile and disordered streetscape, and leaving all ornament to the laying of the bricks themselves, where they curve to mould the window openings and follow courses to mark the line of the floors. The sternly beautiful character of Butterfield's ideal street front and city court remained a sadly solitary example of ingenious planning among the plethora of routine new buildings that soon overtook the streetscapes of an expanding London.

It was the extraordinary and unexpected effect of the great height of the nave and groin-vaulted chancel that first caught critics' attention; then the open rhythm of the great nave arcades, with their clustered shafts of polished marble, dense leafy corbels and capitals, and spandrels covered in geometric polychrome stone mosaics, like the apses and pavements of churches in Venice; and finally the wide stone arches flanking the choir to screen the chambers in which the two halves of the great organ sat, where the elegance of the columns, and the high stone tracery and filigree metal screens that filled them, were all without precedent. Discussion of decoration at first centred on Dyce's work, on which opinion was divided, and on the principal windows by Alfred Gérente, in which all were disappointed. It took time for the surprise wrought by the overall design and high colour of Butterfield's polychrome decoration to settle in the mind, and its unity was not fully apparent until the climactic lower wall of the chancel was first draped and then inlaid in pattern geometry that gathered the ornamental

scheme together, Butterfield finding thereby an extraordinarily simple means of reconciling the jagged High Gothic of Dyce's tracery with the much smoother and more original aesthetic he had deployed throughout the body of the church. More gradually observers came to recognise the fundamental restraint of Butterfield's handling of such a wealth of gorgeous materials, in which the luxury came from revealing the character and hue of the stones themselves, and in which common and precious materials were united with such democratic ingenuity. Carving was minimal; paint and gilt were eschewed; the constructional brick was at times left raw; there was no woodwork at all in the nave, and it was kept discreet in the stalls of the choir. By the 1870s, the reception had evolved to the point where writers talk of the conversation between the patterns of surface colour and the patterns of built form that shaped the space and came to recognise a 'savage beauty' in the simplicity that underlay the gorgeous effect.

By 1864, the initial decoration of the east end was largely complete, and a series of half-plate souvenir photographs were published by the studio of William Henry Davis (figs 105 and 106). They show Butterfield's marble decoration of the super-altar, dating from a gift of 1864, when the temporary curtained wings, patterned in chevrons with frames of cross and quatrefoil, were probably also added. The baptistery beneath the tower catches shafts of light from above and a flood of light from the entry as the visitor turns. Red, grey, blue, sienna and green marble columns rise from a hexagonal base of Mansfield red to support the basin, with busts of Church fathers in the architraves and in roundels, foils and triangles in the spandrels. No further carved figures of the human form appear in the church – and the pulpit follows a very different, almost Islamic system of abstract surface pattern – but virtually the entire palette of colours and symbolic geometries that decorate the walls is established at the font in capsule form. The ubiquitous reappearance of these simple figures, applied in flat plane or low relief, brings a subtle unity to an interior in danger of becoming too elaborate as it worked to meet the expectation that

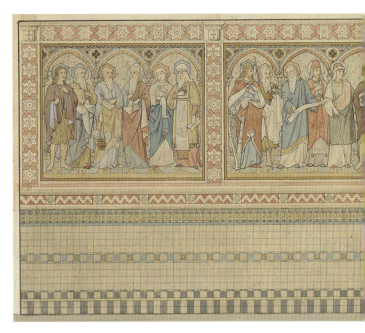

it would display a repertoire of modern ecclesiastical decoration, almost as a gallery of motifs, materials and techniques. Butterfield's ingrained structuralism works to contain this potential for excess by confining the most exuberant ornament to points at which it can be seen to grow out of the constructive form – the capitals, the tracery that braces the delicate wide arches and narrow columns that flank the choir, the flowering corbels that carry the weight of the great chancel arch, and what Butterfield's most astute admirer, the poet Gerard Manley Hopkins, called, when visiting in 1874, 'the touching and passionate curves' of the metalwork in screens and lectern.[3]

Butterfield's ornamental scheme called for murals on the entire length of the north and west walls. When Richards died in 1873 the church proceeded with the north wall mural as his memorial, in tile mosaic designed by Butterfield, painted by Alexander Gibbs and installed by Poole & Sons in 1876. It is introduced by two panels of prophets and kings, centred on the nativity, and completed by early apostles, saints and martyrs. The studio drawing shows the 'classical' and 'architectural' approach, especially in the constructive geometry of the draperies. Their pictorial character and relation of picture to surrounding decoration suggests a debt to Giotto's frescoes in the upper church at Assisi and the Arena Chapel at Padua, which Ruskin had published not long before; and the stillness and avoidance of expression in the physiognomy are close to the mysteriously compelling stasis of Piero della Francesca, whose *Baptism of Christ* had hung in London's National Gallery since 1861 and whose great *Nativity* had just been acquired.

A year later, Gibbs and Butterfield replaced Gérente's original west window, based on the Tree of Jesse at Wells. The colours did not accord with Butterfield's master palette for the church, failed to introduce the light he wanted and carried an

107 (above)
All Saints' Margaret Street: design for brass lectern, *c.*1855–9

108 (above, right)
All Saints' Margaret Street: design for north wall mural, 1874

exaggerated archaism. Given the height at which the window lies, Butterfield and Gibbs again portray the human features neutrally, restrain the dynamics to movement of the vines, and render fully half of the surface area of the higher panels in light tones to catch the western skies. When the second vicar, Berdmore Compton, left in 1886, the west wall fresco was replaced with another mural in tile mosaic, as a testimonial, of the Old Testament 'types' of Christ, centred on Moses's rod of the fiery serpent, here depicted in the shape of a cross which lies directly beneath the Crucifixion in the apex of the great window. In 1891, a final Butterfield tile mural of the Ascension was laid high into the blind arch at the south-west corner of the nave (see page 6), completing the narrative circle with an open composition under a light-blue sky to trap the western light as it crossed from the city skies to those of ancient Palestine. The drama of the scenes is eschewed in favour of a certain monumental stasis so that the events are read not as the telling of a tale but as summaries of the sequence through which the mysteries of the faith are revealed.

Two works by Butterfield open the great survey of new church-building in England by Hermann Muthesius: Rugby Chapel and All Saints' Margaret Street.[4] These Muthesius regards as the clearest

examples of the original and 'non-archaeological' basis of design that set Butterfield apart from the Gothic revival, in which buildings expressed a new modernity by allowing each to determine a governing idea of its own to follow, so that it exhibits a distinct and unrepeatable character. Muthesius's photograph of All Saints' (fig.110) was taken between 1889, when the altar cloth we see was made, and 1895, when changes began at the time the spire was shortened and rebuilt. It is perhaps the last and best record of the chancel as it reached its finished state under Butterfield's supervision. Much of the stationary improvements are evident in Muthesius's plate, notably the super-altar and inlaid decoration of the lower portion of the east end and the green altar cloth of the Agnus Dei, embroidered in silk after medieval samples Butterfield had studied, its panels divided and bordered to echo the north wall mural (fig.109).

We can now see the cohesion of the symbolic and decorative programme as all of the elements come together, integral to the structure and in a unified palette of colour and matter where incident dissolves into an overall pattern. The real power of All Saints' now comes alive, which is the shaping of its voids: the opening to a soaring height to find light from a near-continuous row of tall windows

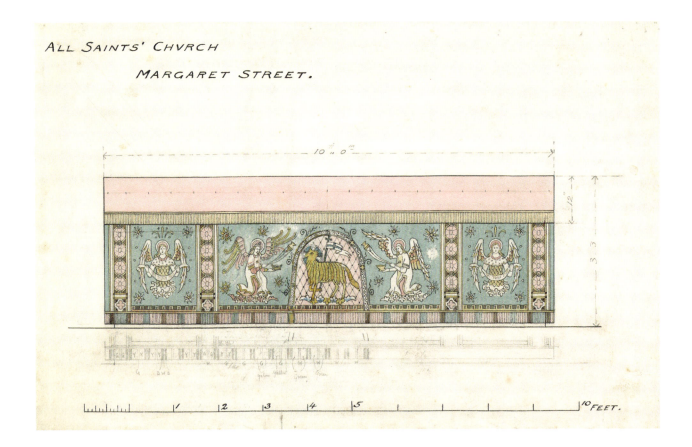

ALL SAINTS' CHVRCH
MARGARET STREET.

in the clerestory; the cloistered shelter of the high-roofed aisles; the division of the nave into just three wide bays of a sprung arcade; the dark-chambered spaces flanking the choir seen through screens in constructive geometry of almost ethereal delicacy. Essential to these effects is the experience of reaching them, which some condemned for its severity: the passage between the high-peaked walls of clergy house and choir school, which rose like a curtain against the city, through a gate whose arch of dark brick and stone anticipates the geometries that will appear inside, into a quiet dense-walled courtyard, changing mood from the clamorous city and shifting a sense of scale, so that, when the turn into the church arrives, it seems to open into an impossibly lofty space, transcending its own meagre footprint in a climactic experience of suffused light, shape and colour.

As Muthesius recognised, All Saints' was built with a licence to invent, effectively proposing a renewal of the building art for modern times. In this Ruskin felt it had triumphantly succeeded:

It is the first piece of architecture I have seen, built in modern days, which is free from all signs of timidity or incapacity. In general proportion of parts, in refinement and piquancy of mouldings, above all, in force, vitality, and grace of floral ornament, worked in a broad and masculine manner, it challenges fearless comparison with the noblest work of any time. Having done this, we may do anything; there need be no limits to our hope or our confidence.[5]

THE MARGARET STREET CITY SCHOOL

The Margaret Street schools were a pioneering if complicated attempt to weave together a set of high-roofed, hygienic open schoolrooms for children, segregated by age and gender, with a four-storey town dwelling for two separate teachers' households (one for male and one for female teachers), all confined in an impossibly tight and irregular urban site. Segregation extended in the

All Saints' Margaret Street: interior view looking east – plate II, 'Allerheiligenkirche in Margaret Street, London', from Hermann Muthesius, *Die neuere kirchliche Baukunst in England*, Ernst & Sohn, Berlin, 1901

teachers' quarters to separate coal sheds, stairways and kitchens for as many as six unmarried masters and mistresses, and served to manage and separate the movements of some hundreds of boys, girls and infants, and to accommodate evening classes for young working males and sewing and clothing circles for confraternities of girls in the parish. The site, just across the road and to the east of the church, prompted the use of complementary materials, a more economical red Fareham brick than the extravagant and beautifully finished rose-coloured masonry of the church, but much more busily trimmed in extruded Bath stone, perhaps suggesting a character for city institutional building that might be more readily emulated than the bare monochrome planes of the clergy houses and choir school across the street.

Opened in 1870, it was adopted as one of the first new 'board schools' of London; but as commercial enterprises poured into the district,

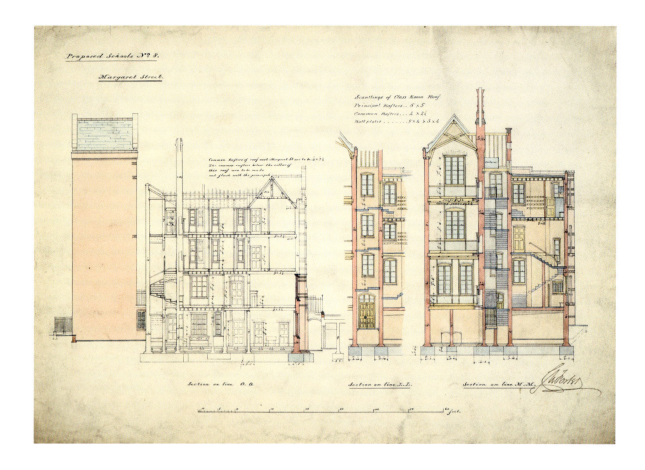

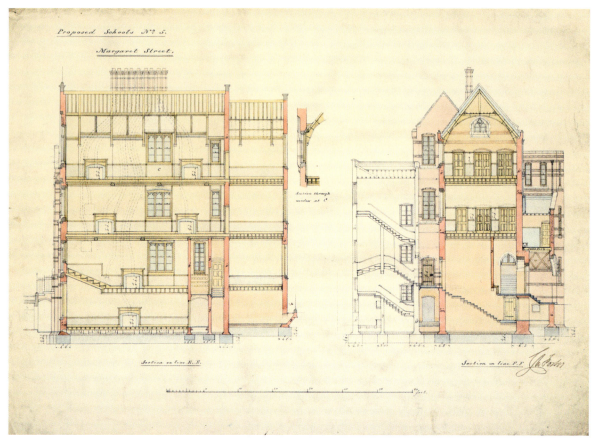

111

All Saints' National
School, Margaret Street:
sections looking west
and north, *c.*1869

112

All Saints' National
School, Margaret Street:
sections looking east
and south, *c.*1869

much of the working population was forced out, and the small, poverty-stricken residential area covered by the Margaret Street parish dwindled. Lacking a settled population of day pupils, the parish used it increasingly as part of the mission of All Saints Sisters of the Poor, who – as Edward Walford describes them in the fourth volume of his *Old and New London* (1878) – went out to 'teach in the night-school of the district, and visit and nurse the poor and sick at their own houses; and . . . take charge of orphan girls, and receive aged and infirm women, incurable sick women, and young serving girls into . . . an industrial school, in which all kinds of plain needlework are done'.[6]

ST ALBAN'S, HOLBORN

In 1858, as he was returning home with a friend along Gray's Inn Road from a Sunday service at his new church at Stoke Newington, Butterfield led his astonished companion into the squalid little alley of Baldwin Gardens to show him a particularly mean spot, in the midst of the infamous den known as 'Thieves' Kitchen', where he was about to build a great new church.[7] The land was a gift of Lord Leigh, and the patron of the church and incumbency was a merchant prince whose family business had grown with the Russia trade, John Gellibrand Hubbard. A mission in advance of the new church was established in 1858 under a curate of St Andrew's Holborn, Alexander Mackonochie, who had worked with Butterfield at Wantage. Work commenced in April 1859 on a church dedicated to the poor with 800 seats, none encumbered. Completion was delayed for many reasons, including the death of the artist, Henry Styleman Le Strange, while his decoration of the blind east wall was in progress. With Frederick Preedy taking over the east mural, the church was consecrated by Bishop Tait in February 1863.

Butterfield set the church back from Baldwin's Gardens to the north, making space for a walled and gated court to give relief and a patch of light where the narrow alleys opened into a wider thoroughfare, designing at the gate a pump and water fountain providing fresh water to those in the alley, and raising the floor of the church well above the level of the street, so that a grand flight of steps rises up to the great north portal to welcome, in a rich profusion of coloured brick, the poor to whose service it was dedicated. Butterfield's solution to the confined site was to raise both the nave and the slightly lower chancel to a great height, find a pattern of open beams that softened the shadows of the roof, and flood the nave with light from large clerestory windows. Only small windows at either end broke the high wall of the north aisle to shield it from the clatter of the street. To the south, where the aisle was well windowed, the church was reached by passing from Brooke's Market through a gate lodge within the clergy house, and then turning west along a long passage to a porch projecting from the church and facing east. The two entries then met in a towering narthex 50 feet by 14, with a central font – a space of assembly, greeting, respiration and quiet – lit with shafts of light from the west.

Its architectural character departed so conspicuously from accepted conventions of form and plan that it left some even of Butterfield's admirers most uncomfortable. As late as 1872, when growing familiarity had largely turned opinion in its favour, Charles Eastlake – though spellbound by the extraordinary grace of the arcades (derived from Butterfield's drawings of Tintern Abbey) – could 'scarcely avoid the conclusion that the guiding principle . . . is rooted in a determination to be singular . . . at any sacrifice, whether of tradition, convenience, or grace. Architectural features which it is the fashion to elaborate he reduces to the severest and most archaic form.' But the great purpose he acknowledged: Butterfield, in 'marked contrast to Pugin', aims not at the picturesque but 'at grandeur and effect'.[8] It was the occasion for the designer and antiquary Edward William Godwin to launch one of the first salvoes of the Aesthetic Movement, as – with a cruel reference to the disfigured face of Victor Hugo's Joker – he placed Butterfield at the head of

the odd clique . . . whose love of originality or rather singularity is so great that rather than have faces like the rest of the world they would cut off

their noses and make Gwynplaines of themselves.
That this latter phase of the Gothic school may
have had its origins in a wholesome horror of
the hard and artless formulae which [. . .] found
in every old dimension some new rule [. . .] is
so far commendable. But because one longs for
freedom – because one desires to escape from
deadly restraints – it is surely no reason why
we should strive to be ugly. We may regret the
expressionless character of everything around us,
but this is hardly a justification for performing
the operation of *Bucca fissa*.[9]

This picture of an architect glorying in excessive
originality and 'ugliness' – first conspicuously
attached to the architect of St Alban's by Godwin,

Eastlake and others of the progressive generation
who came of age in the 1850s – would establish
the familiar portrait of Butterfield well into our
own times.

   The Church would build close by a set of
hygienic lodgings for the working poor, infant and
primary schools and – adapting the mission room
that Mackonochie had established in 1858 – a parish
hall for lectures, night classes, entertainments and
meetings of labour unions, guilds and working-class
friendly societies. The front court and narthex were
now on the processional routes of workingmen's
organisations, some of them initiated by the Church
itself, and this alliance with Radical and socialist
causes probably accounts for the ferocity of the
assault upon it for the ritual practices for which,

St Alban's church, Baldwin's Gardens, Holborn; as seen from staircase window in South Square, Grays Inn; – the intervening houses in Grays ✠ Inn Lane being pulled down at the time of my making this sketch, viz: Aug 13. 1883.
J. Drayton Wyatt.

Grays Inn Lane

115
Church of St Alban
the Martyr, Holborn:
view from the west,
watercolour sketch
by J. Drayton Wyatt,
13 August 1883

following Disraeli's punitive 1870 law on conformity, Mackonochie was twice condemned. Lavish performances of liturgy – Arthur Stanton, the great curate of St Alban's, argued – brought comfort and understanding into the often desperate and colourless lives of an illiterate metropolitan poor, preaching through spiritual splendour rather than moralistic sermons. The unusual narrative scheme of the east wall was conceived by Butterfield to the same purpose, as a visual summary of the faith for the unlettered. It showed each of the redemptive mysteries recited every Sunday in the Litany in short phrases familiar to all. Butterfield, with his severe views on piety, was, along with Hubbard, soon ill at ease with the ritualistic approach to worship and with the clergy's readiness to adorn

the church with a picture-book presentation of the Christian story, which kept him sadly from the doors of his most original and powerful city church. The carriage trade was, however, extraordinary. Though much mocked for sporting 'sables in the slums', the great ladies who came so attired on Sundays and saints' days were commonly back the next morning in street clothes as lay visitors to the abandoned young, sick, old and distressed of the parish. On an average autumn Sunday in 1886 it was much the best attended of Butterfield's new London churches, reporting 767 people at the morning services and 533 in the evening – men to the right, women to the left, and rich and poor together.

The choice of site, a stone's throw from the prosperous mansion terraces just to the north,

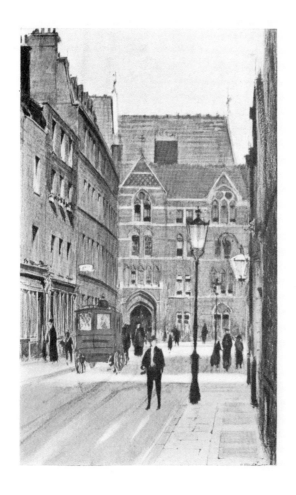

116

St Alban's Clergy House, Brooke Street: view from the south, plate by William Walcot, *c.*1909, from George W.E. Russell's *St Alban the Martyr, Holborn: A History of Fifty Years*, George Allen & Co., London, 1913

hunger, child mortality and infectious disease. They were slowly being regulated and policed, and by the 1880s would start to be torn down as the march of commerce reached their quarters. By now, a building that had been a puzzle or an outrage when it was first constructed had become the most admired of Butterfield's works, and many views appeared when the startling west front was briefly but fully exposed during clearances of the common lodgings in 1883 and 1884.

A subtle and scrupulously urban ecclesiastical character marks out St Alban's clergy house from its neighbours fronting Brooke's Market, on land acquired off the south-east corner of the church, highly visible at the end of a short street from High Holborn which, at the time of building, was about to become a wide boulevard leading from the west end to the City. Housing chorister school, service confraternities and sisterhoods, meeting halls and a household of resident clergy, it was at once a clerical college and a mission hall, a sentinel of the Church for the poor and a secluded retreat for those serving them. Butterfield – by inviting a rigorously functional block of metropolitan chambers to adopt signal moments of ecclesiastical expression at its crest and base, with a full if tempered Gothic arcade above the entry – displays at once its religious character, but weaves that into something that clearly belongs to the fabric and life of a city street. The open-gated entrance arch, with a porter's lodge to the left, turns west into a walled walk that runs along the flank of the church to its south porch, a quiet cloistered moment of decompression.

Butterfield had made an equally urbane intervention at very nearly the same time for the vicarage of St Michael's Burleigh Street, built just below Covent Garden as its marketplace was extended and its approaches regularised in the late 1850s. Here he managed to fit a large household and parish office five storeys deep into a narrow triangular plot like that at Osnaburgh Street, sinking services into a lower floor, rising the entry level above the street, and handling the angle of the site with three short street fronts, with an impressively articulated and demonstrative public floor. Its arched door to the world faced

followed an argument set out in the year of its consecration by John Sandford, proposing that, since opulence and misery live side by side, new churches be sited at the junction of those worlds to make a place in which both come together and 'the one may forget his grandeur and the other his destitution'. Nor, he continued, should they be built and furnished with the economy and plainness that a site among the tenements of the poor might suggest, but furnished in decisive contrast to the mean surroundings, recognising that this may be the only thing in a poor man's life to convey 'the idea of the beautiful' on which spiritual awareness is founded.[10] The best-known view of the church (fig.115) shows its belfry rising above the 'common lodgings' along three squalid undrained alleys that ran to Gray's Inn Road. These overcrowded and unsanitary rooming houses had grown up throughout east London to house newcomers, day labourers and street workers of all varieties, and were notorious sites of crime,

straight down towards the Strand and the *mêlée* of theatres, chophouses, hotels and indoor circus that was beginning to turn this quarter into a city of the night. Making a precinct out of a semi-corner, it presented a new model of the city townhouse. Viollet-le-Duc took another of Butterfield's rare red-brick interruptions into the rhythm of London's streets – the 'church house' of 1870 built for the missionary societies on one of the few streets of dwelling and chambers left amid the Westminster of the Foreign, Colonial and India Offices – adapting it, fully acknowledged, as a 'prototypical city house for London', which he published not long after.[11]

NOTES

1. Anon., 'A Remarkable New Church in London', syndicated from the *Daily News* in *Northampton Mercury*, 29 April 1854, and elsewhere. My account of the Margaret Street church draws upon many sources, but the history in the *Survey of London, Volume 51: South-East Marylebone, Part 1* is an exhaustive point of reference, as is Paul Thompson, 'All Saints' Church, Margaret Street, Reconsidered', *Architectural History*, vol.8, 1965, pp 73–94. The *Survey* has been relied upon for all surviving works in London that it covers. See also William Allen Whitworth, *Quam Dilecta: A Description of All Saints' Church, Margaret Street*, W. Gardner, London, 1891, by its vicar, including a detailed record of the church's architectural origins and progress and a fine schematic plan.

2. John Sandford, address to the joint meeting of the Oxford and Worcester Architectural Societies, 1854, reported in *The Ecclesiologist*, October 1854.

3. *The Journals and Papers of Gerard Manley Hopkins*, Oxford University Press, Oxford, 1986, p.248.

4. Hermann Muthesius, *Die neuere kirchliche Baukunst in England*, Ernst & Sohn, Berlin, 1901.

5. John Ruskin, *The Stones of Venice, Book 2*, in E.T. Cook and Alexander Wedderburn (eds), *The Works of John Ruskin (Library Edition)*, George Allen, London, 1903, vol.11, p.229.

6. Edward Walford, *Old and New London: Volume 4*, Cassell, Petter & Galpin, London, 1878, pp 441–67, transcribed in British History Online: www.british-history.ac.uk/old-new-london/vol4.

7. The account relies in part on George W.E. Russell's remarkable, partisan and witty *Saint Alban the Martyr, Holborn: A History of Fifty Years*, George Allen & Co., London, 1913.

8. Charles Locke Eastlake, *A History of the Gothic Revival*, Longmans, Green & Co., London, 1872, p.257.

9. E.W. Godwin in *The Architect*, 2 December 1871.

10. John Sandford, *The Mission and Extension of the Church at Home* (Bampton Lectures for the year 1861), Longman, Green, Longman & Roberts, London, 1862, pp 183–6.

11. *Building News*, 30 March 1877. For this and other London metropolitan works, see also Nicholas Olsberg, 'Common Place', 12 November 2018, on drawingmatter.org.

PRECINCTS OF LONDON

All Saints' Church, Margaret Street

All Saints' Margaret Street:
entry court, clergy house and choir school

All Saints' Margaret Street:
choir school and clergy house

St Michael's Clergy House, Burleigh Street;
All Saints' National School, Margaret Street

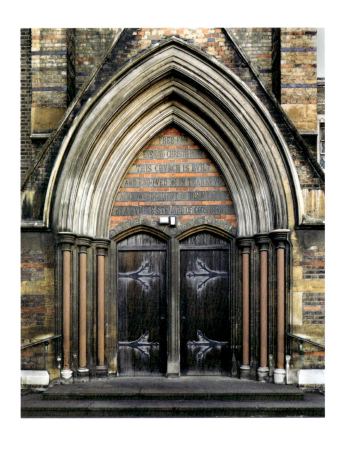

Church of St Alban the Martyr,
Holborn: north porch, south
gateway; clergy house

Church of St Alban
the Martyr, Holborn

CHAPTER 11

'NORTH AND SOUTH', 1848–65

THE INDUSTRIAL OUTLOOK: HUDDERSFIELD

NDUSTRIAL HUDDERSFIELD has an unusual history, having grown up almost entirely on the lands, rivers and canals of a single family, the Ramsdens. In September 1846, Butterfield received an invitation to propose a new church to cater to a growing and underserved district in the north-east of a parish now accommodating some 30,000. The Ramsden estate was in trusteeship at the time, with Sir John William Ramsden, the heir, still underage. His mother Isabella Ramsden (née Dundas) and his uncle, Earl Fitzwilliam, were trustees, with George Loch, the accomplished estate manager, guiding them. The request for a church and school had come from local people in Birkby, Bay Hall and Hillhouse, and it was taken up by Mrs Ramsden as a memorial to her husband, who had died in 1836. There was no high-church feeling in the family, so it might be assumed that Butterfield's

name came to them from Viscount Downe, no high churchman either, who had just begun to work with him at Sessay. In his efforts to advance (and exploit) Huddersfield, the absentee young Ramsden proved just as ready to fund a Nonconformist chapel, and pledged to withdraw support for any church with tendencies to ritual. Indeed, the impetus to build the church to improve the moral condition of millworkers newly arrived in the towns and to tie it to property development, from which its patrons could benefit, was a reflection of the improving, business-minded, confident and pragmatic spirit of capital in the industrial north, as Elizabeth Gaskell characterised it in her 1854 novel *North and South*.

The choice of site remained uncertain for a long time, with Isabella wishing to acquire a large plot of new land where she might profit from the presence of the church by developing it for middle-

class housing. The land finally settled on was on the common adjoining Bay Hall, in the southern section of Birkby, most of it on the northern side of the beck that bordered the common.[1] A set of approved plans and estimates were in place by July 1850, apparently adapted from Butterfield's first proposals of 1846. It seems that the site designated for the church was then reconsidered, as being too low; and it was not until July 1851 that final specifications were produced, the contract with the builder, Joseph Kaye, agreed, and a new quarry opened near Marsh Wood to begin the structure. The amount of earth-moving to build a level site and the challenge of supporting so tall a tower were both very impressive, as can be seen in the plan (fig.119). Consequently, the estimate now ran to £7000, twice the original budget, though still reflecting extensive cutting back at the trustees' request.

The drawings retained by Butterfield all show the site and church in a shape close to what was built. The great north porch, its steps, and the terracing of the approach, all wonderfully original, anticipate the coming of a road along the beck below. The continuation of the north aisle to a subsidiary east window lights the interior for morning services very effectively. The nave windows lie under a pronounced horizontal line of drip mould; this forms a frame with the buttresses, which drop deeper and intensify as the gradient drops. The windows, their varied tracery bearing the only ornament inside or out, share some of their shape and sequence with those at Merton College

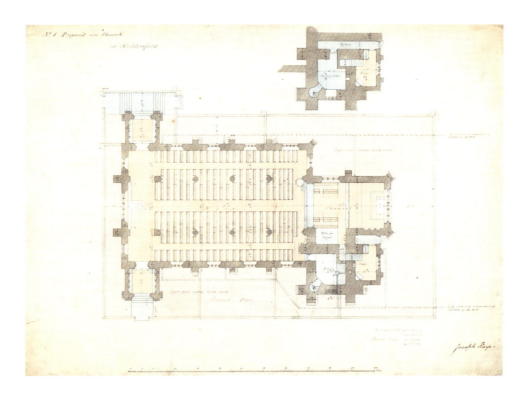

St John's Church,
Birkby, Huddersfield:
plan, *c.*1850

chapel, Oxford, which Butterfield was restoring at
the time. By 1900, when the local photographer
Smith Carter recorded an image of the interior,
there seemed to have been little stained glass, and
this church on its hill above the worst of the smoke
and steam needed no clerestory to be bathed with
light. Between the drawing and the completion of
the 220-foot tower in 1852–3, the two louvres of the
belfry were reduced to one, drawing the eye to it as a
fulcrum around which the church revolves.

For the laying of the foundation stone in October
1851, the young baronet, now twenty years old,
made his first visit to Huddersfield. Butterfield and
Kaye led a masonic procession in full regalia from
the parish church to the site, where crowds gathered
to catch a glimpse of the man who would become
their landlord a year later. The church, dedicated
to St John the Baptist, was largely completed
and in use by 1853 and consecrated in 1855, after
adjustments to heating and repairs to the tower. In
1858 the visitation records show all seats either free
or at very low pew rents. There were 250 on Sunday
mornings and 300 in the evening service (higher
evening attendance was a clear sign that working
people were a major part of the congregation), 300

at Sunday School, two mixed day schools run by the
church, and 4000 now living within the new parish.
Many were from remote country settings, and so
few had been exposed to religion that baptisms for
entire families were a weekly occurrence.

Seating 530 in a nave over 80 feet long and 48
feet wide, with a broad western passage and two
generous porches and paved approaches, the church
at Birkby established the soaring spacious template
for Butterfield's town churches, contrasting
markedly with Coalpit Heath five years before,
where 550 were accommodated in a space well
under two thirds of the volume. Smith Carter took
a series of photographs of the church about 1890,
after the landscape had matured around it and the
rims of stone had darkened (fig.120). He shows the
church still standing solitary on its common, facing
north to the mills and back-to-backs of its growing
parish of Birkby across the beck to the north. To
the left are the first of the 'St John's Villas' in the
belated middle-class suburb that the Ramsdens
had hoped the church would stimulate, and for
which Butterfield's vicarage (behind the church) was
designed as a model. Carter's camera stands halfway
to the centre of Huddersfield, right on the edge of

St John's Church,
Birkby, Huddersfield:
view from the east,
photograph by Smith
Carter, *c*.1890

arcade window, there is an underlying sense of
tension, discordance and the incomplete, like many
great medieval works that point towards an ultimate
perfection of design that human genius can seek,
approach, but not attain. 'Gothic architecture',
proposed the *Ecclesiologist* at this time, in a piece
that seems to speak for Butterfield, 'to be perfect
must be imperfect . . . The eye must be carried
from the visible to the ideal; it must go beyond
what is expressed, and deduce from it something
which, though unexpressed, . . . is of more primary
importance to the spirit of the design, than that
which is presented at once to the outward view.'[2]
In this most 'Gothic' of all his parish churches, that
sense of quivering uncertainty is supremely present.

THE LOST CHURCH OF THE LEYLANDS, LEEDS

St Thomas's, Leylands, was built to serve one of
the most destitute, disease-ridden, under-serviced
and overcrowded working-class slums of Leeds.
It rose out of a mission that held services in an
improvised schoolroom nearby, and by the time of
its consecration in February 1852 the clergy were
running a lending library; a Sunday school of 300;
evening lectures for young working people on
Wednesdays and cottage meetings for the older;
and a team of home visitors to identify cases of
need.[3] Built in stock red brick to a programme
that required both scale and economy, the building
of the church was planned in phases, with nave,
aisles and schools to appear first, and chancel and
tower to follow. Its sponsor was Matthew Rhodes,
a member of the Margaret Street Engagement
whose grandfather, starting as an operative in the
dyeworks, had risen to wealth in the district. Rhodes
reverted to Rome soon after the work began, and
support for more building was not forthcoming,
so that only the first phase was completed. A few
damaged contract drawings are among the scant
records that remain for this, Butterfield's great slum
church and his first work in polychrome brick. Light
was brought in through high east gables suggesting
transepts; there was a vast west window; the roofs

its now vast agglomeration of mills, chimney stacks,
streets, canals, terraced housing and tram lines, all
crowded along the river, railway lines and canal at
the base of the valley. The solitary church was a vital
landmark, seen from this aspect by nearly the entire
town of now 95,000, its stony masses stepping
up from the porch to a crest of the steepest pitch,
exaggerated by that shockingly large east window.
The shifts in scale, which look so eccentric rendered
on one plane on the elevation sheet, become
supremely satisfying.

Yet in those shifts of scale and in that single
emphatic horizontal stone course above the nave

121
St Thomas's Church,
Leylands, Leeds:
west and south
elevations of nave
and aisles, 1849

cascaded; and the outer red-brick walls were
animated, to carry the eye upwards, with diapers
and a chequerboard of bricks infused with black
earth pigment. The great entry porch at the south-
west corner would serve as the first stage of a 'lofty
shingled tower' to come. The foundations of a crypt
and chancel were also laid down for the future.

Leeds was the site of the great high-church
experiment in the overgrown town, where a whole
programme of church building for new districts
centred around Walter Hook's new parish church
of St Saviour, built with a gift from Pusey. But it
was at heart a Methodist and increasingly a Roman
Catholic town, where any high Anglican church
would rest on stony ground. This was not aided
by the almost invisible situation of St Thomas's,
backed by the vast Brunswick brewery and fronted
by squalid dwelling courts. Visiting in 1855 Hook
already called it 'a dirty district',[4] and regretted
the low-lying site, which discouraged attendance.
Marriage notices in the early years suggest a
relatively settled congregation of skilled artisans;
but the dwelling courts rapidly deteriorated and
became overcrowded with an immigrant population.
By 1870, 'Our Rambler in Leeds', writing in *The
Architect* of 3 December, came across it by chance

in a 'dingy side street'; though mightily impressed,
he found it closed and was unaware of the name of
its architect, a fact which was kindly supplied by a
local correspondent in the next issue (10 December),
who agreed that it deserved every encomium, but
was sadly unappreciated by the people of Leeds.
Fortunes revived in the 1880s when the church
purchased a good organ, its first full choir was
formed and its abandoned school was brought back
to life. Butterfield was now called in to complete his
chancel, assigning supervision to a local firm, and
in April 1893, forty-one years since the church had
opened, the chancel was consecrated. Butterfield
was continuing to work on the stalls, fittings and a
great tile reredos in January 1897, the last recorded
designs in his oeuvre. But by then the Leylands
had been inhabited by entire colonies of refugees
from the pogroms of Eastern Europe, and Jews now
represented 75 per cent of the parish population.
The church ran special services in Hebrew and
welcomed missionaries for the conversion of the
Jews, but with little effect. By 1910 the housing
had been razed for slum clearance and its people
resettled. The result was a magnificent church
seating 800 but lying abandoned in a wasteland,
and in summer 1938 it was demolished.

THE MARCH OF BRICKS AND MORTAR: STOKE NEWINGTON

When Edgar Allan Poe went as a schoolboy to live in Stoke Newington, he found 'A misty-looking village, where there were a vast number of gigantic and gnarled trees, and where all the houses were excessively ancient. It was a dream-like and spirit-soothing place'.[5] By 1840 it had grown into one of the most extensive of the decorous 'sober suburbs', short on taverns and long on improving institutions, to which the professional and managerial class of London had moved to lead quieter lives than the metropolitan streets afforded. As the suburban railways began to reach the area and rows of cheaper houses approached the open fields to the south-west, where the parish bordered Hoxton and Dalton, it was determined to carve out a new parish, where, with support from Butterfield's great friend Robert Brett, a mission had been developing to serve the fast-growing poorer population. Once the bounds of the new parish were set, land was offered as a site for the parish church in a large triangle of market gardens, hayfields, horse barns and grazing meadow.[6]

Butterfield and his party settled on a wild site in its south-west corner, looking west to the empty Foy estate, south to a road with a small row of garden villas, and north and east to open fields. In 1848, on the south boundary of the building plot, Butterfield erected National schools, which would also serve as a temporary church while the process of funding, designing and building the new one was under way. Services were choral, under Thomas Helmore, whose hymns and 'noted chants' laid the lasting basis for sung worship in the Anglican Church, and the liturgy was advanced, so that the 'church-school' quickly became a famous landmark, both for the high-church community, living in modest sections just to the west and south, and for the opposing forces from fiercely evangelical Islington, to whom it raised a red flag that would draw mobs and disrupters with increasing intensity and violence to the doors of St Matthias's and its wardens for the next twenty years.

Butterfield's design for the church itself was unprecedented. It carried a broached saddleback tower that was virtually unknown in England, though there were many and lovely examples in parish churches of northern France. Both aisles were carried east to form quasi-transepts flanking it. The shallowest of chancels carried the largest of east windows. The tower in an uncomfortable early perspective was dressed with four tall finials and its cap carried over it above a heavy cornice. Porches rose above the roof of the aisles, and the two west lancets seemed to stand independently. This rendering was published by the *Ecclesiologist* in August 1850, without Butterfield's consent and to his distress: it made the originality of the scheme

122 (below, left)
St Matthias's District Schools, Stoke Newington: view from the south-east, lithograph by Standidge & Co., *c.*1849

123 (below, right)
St Matthias's Church, Stoke Newington: perspective from the north-east of final scheme, *c.*1851, reproduced from church archives by T. Francis Bumpus in *An Historical London Church*, T.B. Bumpus, London, 1913

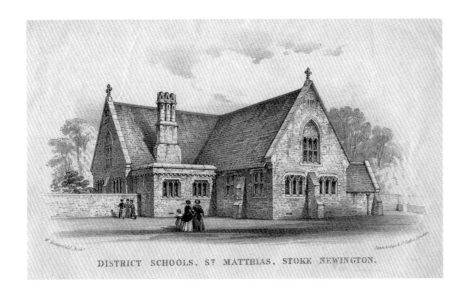

DISTRICT SCHOOLS, ST MATTHIAS, STOKE NEWINGTON.

S. MATTHIAS CHURCH, FROM A DRAWING BY MR. BUTTERFIELD,

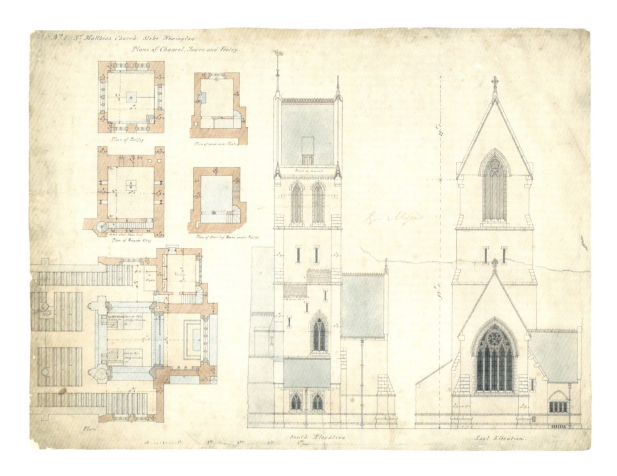

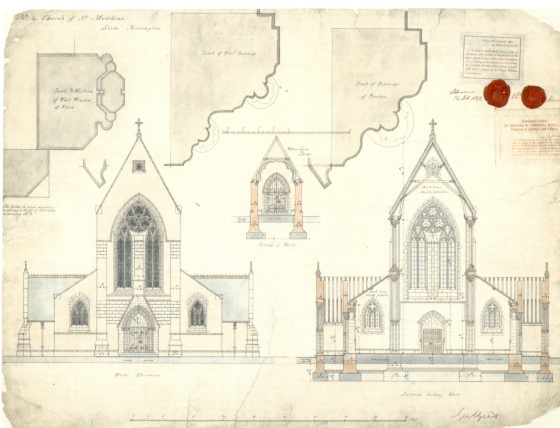

124

St Matthias's Church, Stoke Newington: plans of chancel, tower and vestry, south and east elevations, *c.*1851

125

St Matthias's Church, Stoke Newington: west elevation, section looking west, details of porch mouldings, February 1852

both harder to comprehend and very difficult to like; Butterfield's lifelong opponent, the historian E.A. Freeman, promptly took to the pages of the magazine to ridicule and condemn the design, with the editors springing to Butterfield's defence in a subsequent issue. By that year a much more consistent design was in place, the tower greatly simplified, the composition balanced by placing its principal buttresses at the west end of the tower, and the whole body of the church carried higher, to ride above a large new development of 'Poets' Roads' dwellings just beginning to appear across the western boundary of the church. At this point the west end was modified so that the window was divided by a central buttress flanking the doors at its base, shaped like a two-pronged fork entering the ground, and cradling a wheel of tracery in the head.

Upon completion there was a parish population of 3000, seating for 750 and a choir of eighteen men and eighteen boys, with a boys' choir and schoolroom above the vestry. Visitors came from far and wide, said Thomas Francis Bumpus, a writer on the churches of London who belonged to the church, to see this great novelty in the London landscape: 'The quaint treatment of the west front puzzled them. The clerestory was unusually high; the window tracery was wholly unlike any other.' But the 120-foot tower was the main attraction: 'an enigma; nothing of the kind had ever been seen in London or out of it'. The use of common stock brick shocked some, and the disproportionate height of the relatively narrow nave disturbed Eastlake, since it seemed to override every other impression; but he added that – as he acknowledged at St Alban's, where the same overriding logic of proportion seems to exaggerate the width of the nave – such carrying out of a principle to its extreme was part of 'the secret . . . which distinguishes Mr Butterfield's work from others which arc less daring in conception, and therefore less liable to mistakes. Mr Butterfield has been the leader of a school and it is necessary for a leader to be bold.'[7]

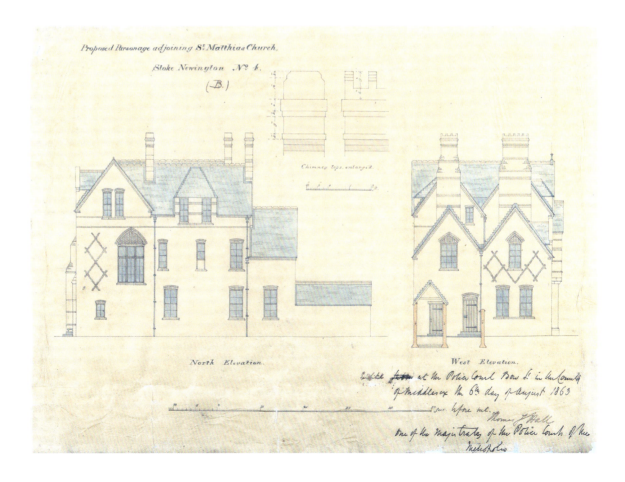

126
St Matthias's Parsonage, Stoke Newington: north and west elevations (Scheme B), 1863

127

St Matthias's Parsonage, Stoke Newington: view from the south-west shortly before completion, photographed 1865

The school complex was further developed with a Butterfield infant school just to the south of the church; funds were eventually found to fence and pave the walkways around the church; and in 1863 Butterfield was asked for designs for a parsonage. This was sited within a garden plot just across from the north-west porch of the church. It is a good early model of Butterfield's 'English house' which, like his country rectories, turns away from the road to face its gardens. The path running to the east was slowly turning into a road, and the vista there of field and trees was likely to fill with terraced houses. The plan takes account of this and is highly unusual. The entrance was on a narrow front facing east – the porch is visible on the drawing of the north elevation – where diapers of darker brick mark the point of entry. Stairs from the hall lead up to the first-floor drawing room and principal bedrooms, while a door to the left enters an anteroom and then a book-lined vicar's study, with a large window

facing south beneath the wide dormer of the drawing room. It seems to propose a plan suitable for a professional family in the relatively crowded landscape of an inner suburb, in which the study could serve as a doctor's surgery or a reception room for a solicitor's clients.

The parish grew fast. Until the 1890s there were still some households capable of supporting the church; but, as the last of the land filled in with meaner terraces and lodgings, the parish described itself in 1913 as that of a uniformly poor population of people, most of whom had resettled from the capital's East End. The area was almost entirely destroyed in the Blitz, but the walls of St Matthias's stood, and it was rebuilt in the 1950s. The wonderful parsonage was lost altogether.

NOTES

1. The account of the church at Birkby is developed from reports in the *Huddersfield Chronicle* and from summaries in a descriptive calendar of the Ramsden correspondence, presented online by the Kirklees Archive, which was closed for consultation during the period of my research.
2. *The Ecclesiologist*, March 1845.
3. The narrative account of St Thomas's Church is primarily developed from reports in the *Leeds Intelligencer* from 1850 to 1900. Brief notices appear in *The Builder*, 14 February 1852, and *The Ecclesiologist*, February 1854.
4. *Yorkshire General Advertiser*, 6 January 1855.
5. Quoted in T. Francis Bumpus, *An Historical London Church: A Record of Sixty-Five Years of Life and Work in the Church and Parish of St Matthias, Stoke Newington*, T.B. Bumpus, London, 1913.
6. The account of St Matthias's, Stoke Newington, is developed primarily from the extensive newspaper and journal reports, especially the *Morning Chronicle*, 15 June 1853; from Thomas Waugh Belcher, *Robert Brett of Stoke Newington: His Life and Work*, Dutton, London, 1889; from T. Francis Bumpus, *London Churches, Ancient and Modern*, first self-published in London in 1881 but with additions in 1885; and from Bumpus, *An Historical London Church*, op.cit., from which the quoted texts derive. The disputed drawing and subsequent debate in the *Ecclesiologist* can be found in successive issues of the journal from August to December 1850.
7. Charles Locke Eastlake, *A History of the Gothic Revival*, Longmans, Green & Co., London, 1872, p.257.

CHAPTER 12

FRESH AIR: RESORT *and* COUNTRY SUBURB, 1845–91

'SEA-AIR AND PROSPECTS': NEW HUNSTANTON

HENRY STYLEMAN LE STRANGE was an antiquary, artist and proprietor of a number of properties on the western shore of north Norfolk. He came into possession in 1839 of Hunstanton Hall on the northern corner of the west coast, including the small village of Hunstanton, which faced towards the open sea and had begun to attract visitors for sea-bathing. In April 1841, he began to develop a plan to convert the cliffs and seafront to the south as a health resort. Le Strange began working with Butterfield early in 1845 on plans for an 'entire town *de novo* all in the Old English Style', built around a green to which the remnant of the thirteenth-century village cross would be moved.[1] An announcement was published on 1 May 1845, with a first prospectus for shareholders, proposing 60 to 80 residences on the 'celebrated Cliff of Hunstanton, and the fields adjoining, to afford Families in Norfolk and the neighbouring Counties, an opportunity of enjoying the advantage of Sea-air and prospects, which this part of the Coast so abundantly furnishes.' There would be a 'commodious Inn and other ornamental and useful Buildings', including a bathhouse, library and shops. Butterfield offered three different house plans at an average cost of £700–800, with full specifications in prescribed materials, rough-cut randomly laid local brown carrstone predominant. The room layout and articulation of each scheme, especially at the rear, could be taken as a 'suggested plan' to be varied according to individual need. By the end of August, a printed prospectus for potential leaseholders was issued, with a plot plan (fig.128) and an invitation to consult Butterfield's model house plans either at Le Strange's agents in Lynn and Hunstanton or at Butterfield's office in London.

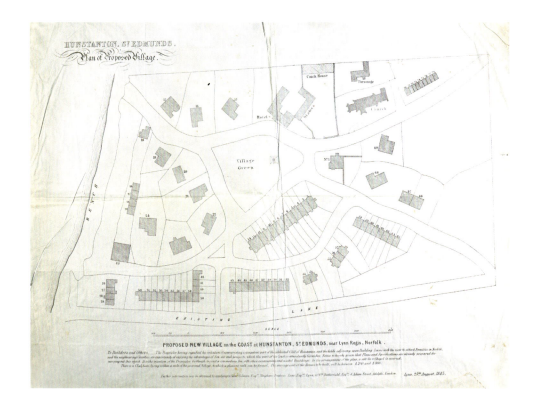

128
'Hunstanton
St Edmunds: Plan
of Proposed Village',
prospectus published
in Lynn, 25 August
1845

Butterfield's family hotel, a 'New Inn' soon to be known as 'The Golden Lion', was built at once, to help market the plots for dwellings, and appeared in 1847 in a form, a reporter later noted, 'every line of which shows the master's hand'. It must have struggled, since it was listed for lease more than once within the first ten years of operation, with the following description: 'Built in the year 1847, by an eminent London architect, in the most substantial manner, at a great outlay, . . . replete with every convenience, including salt and fresh water baths (hot and cold), . . . a coffee-room, a drawing-room, seven private sitting rooms (commanding full and uninterrupted sea views).'[2] There were twenty-two bedrooms, a bar, a kitchen garden, a carriage house and stalls for eleven horses. Cottages for builders and the town agent were built just to the east. It followed very closely the block plan at the top centre of Butterfield's plan (fig.128), and a remarkable early photograph (fig.129) shows it standing alone, a severely dignified entrance façade facing the remains of the ancient village cross, now installed on an octagonal pyramid of steps to Butterfield's design. The public rooms were in this wing, with a six-bayed garden front of private suites facing

towards what was then known as the 'German Ocean', the whole of the ground floor set behind a wall of floor-length French windows.

In 1850 the general plan was modified. The informally distributed short terraces and the park and garden land between them remained, while the plots for large seafront villas or boarding houses were removed and the Green extended to the cliff top, making a large open civic park. By September 1850, the seventy or so house plots within Butterfield's triangular swathe of carefully distributed and oriented terraces around the southern arc of the enlarged green were being staked out. Omnibus service began from Lynn in summer 1854, and steamer and coach connections to the railway at Wisbech were soon in place. Some reports suggest that the first three plots were then taken up, built and occupied, as a demonstration of each of the three basic house types.

But progress was slow. One who had been there as a child about 1853 remembered more than forty years later that 'the now flourishing little town of 1800 inhabitants then consisted of an inn (The Golden Lion), a bricklayer's cottage, a bathing machine, two donkeys, and a stone

resort proceeded apace. The first 'St Edmund's Terrace' of seven demonstration houses seems to have been ready for occupancy by 1864, along with one of the large end-of-terrace lodges close to the shore; and the entire park-planned ensemble was completed during the next five years, conforming in many details and all principles to the 1845 plan of short terraces with differing grades of house, built to a common system and displaying a consistent but varied profile in the same brown stone, with white stone window casements, brick trim, hipped and half-hipped dormers. By 1879 'Hunstanton St Edmund's' formed the quiet grassy centre of a resort furnished with an iron pier, a church by Preedy (seen in the distance in a photograph taken around that time, fig.130), a large railway hotel on its southern corner, and a home for forty-six convalescents built by the Prince of Wales (whose acquisition of the nearby Sandringham estate provided an enormous boost to the popularity of the resort). Le Strange had drawn an ambitious 'country suburb' plan of northward expansion based on single picturesque villas, but we can see the residential resort now expanding to the north behind the Golden Lion in more conventional terraces and lighter stone by architects from Lynn. Butterfield's loose assembly of lodges, boarding houses and private dwellings, to the south, all laid down to catch the breezes and vistas, remained untouched, much admired and much visited, as excursionists followed the wandering paths of his village green. Writers continued to be fascinated by the 'genteel, clerical air' and casual coherence of this little garden city, noting its 'picturesque houses with mullioned windows, built of the local carr-stone, after Butterfield's design, which fringe the green in irregular groups, instead of being left to the red brick and stucco of the speculative builder'.

THE ART OF ANALOGY: BABBACOMBE

The Devon resort of Torquay, on the slopes beside a little south-facing bay at the north end of Torbay, first emerged as a residential adjunct to the vast westward anchorage for warships and troop

129

New Inn, Hunstanton: view from the south-west, reproduced *c.*1900 from a photograph by Samuel Smith dated 1853

130

The Green, Hunstanton, photographed *c.*1880

cross'.[3] The project depended for success on the arrival of a much-contested and long-delayed new branch railway, and then on the building of accommodations, demanded by railway investors, that would sustain another level of tourism from the 'quietly clerical atmosphere' of Butterfield's 'St Edmund's Village'. But after Le Strange died in 1862, his son and trustees were able to complete the railway project, and the development of the

carriers headed west to the Americas to fight the French. The shore's health-giving properties were quickly noted; a small harbour was built; and within a few years of peace there was a settlement accommodating more than 2000 people, two hotels and a little trading fleet devoted largely to contraband brandy. By 1848, with a railway branch line in place, there were nearly 12,000 inhabitants and over 2000 guest rooms for visitors. Pleasure sailing and carriage drives to local beauty spots had become an essential part of resort life, bringing visitors and summer residents to the cliffs and coves just to the north in what was then called Babbicombe, while the picturesque outcrops and natural amphitheatre of coloured carboniferous limestone that lay about it provided settings for excursions and *fêtes champêtres*. Since the mid-eighteenth century, that compressed limestone, polished to resemble marble, had fed a trade in decorative stonework and mosaic that grew in importance in the 1850s and 1860s, during the eager quest for native building matter.

Life in Babbacombe – its name would be prettified as its prestige rose – still bore little resemblance to the prospering bayside resort to the south. It was an outlying settlement of the parish of St Marychurch, whose church and commerce lay about a mile away. Villagers maintained a small fishing (and smuggling) fleet from boats drawn up on the steep pebbled shores of its coves, and a few villas and retreats for summer visitors with a taste for wilderness had begun to appear on 'the downs' immediately above the cliffs. But the principal employment was in the marble quarries, in home crafts gathering stones to work into spouts and paperweights, and in making simple vessels from the simply worked deep-red local clay, a home craft which was just becoming organised into full-scale industrial potteries. There was a long association between St Marychurch and the family of Judge Sir John Patteson, who funded the restoration of its church and whose children (one of whom became the martyred Bishop of Melanesia, John Coleridge Patteson) summered at the rectory in the 1830s and 1840s, remembering it as a sort of dream

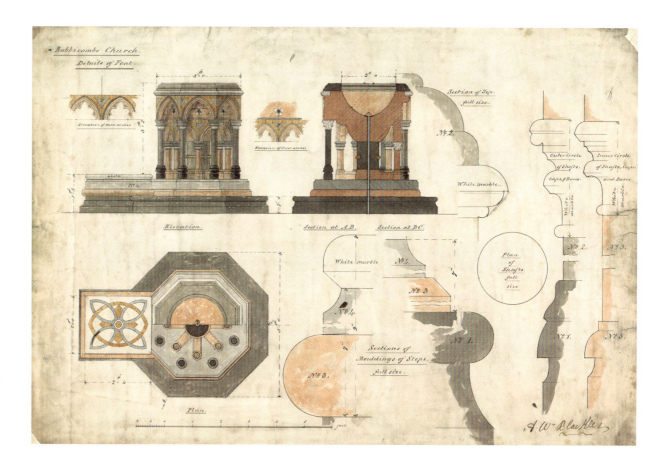

132
All Saints' Church,
Babbacombe: details
of font, *c.*1865–7 –
design signed off by
A.W. Blackler for the
Royal Marble Works

world of free roaming in a dramatic landscape of
cliffs and rocky outcrops.

The parish church was too distant to reach
the working population of Babbacombe, where
a young high-church curate, John Hewitt, set
up a missionary service to the sick and poor and
held services and catechism classes in a small,
uncomfortable schoolroom. When Patteson's
daughters, Joan and Frances, moved to Babbacombe
after their father's death in 1861 to run a guesthouse
on the cliffs, they took up the cause of Hewitt's
mission and, with him, set about making a separate
parish, raising interest and funds among the
Coleridge and Yonge families with whom Butterfield
was so closely associated. Hewitt obtained land in
open fields south-west of the village centre, secured
backing from Bishop Phillpotts at his palace of
Bishopstowe nearby, and asked Butterfield for a
'town church' spacious enough for an urban centre
that did not yet exist.[4] Butterfield's response was
the design of a great church of mixed red and grey
Petitor sandstone, in blocks of varied size, randomly

coursed like the natural conglomerate in the cliffs at
nearby Watcombe and exposed in the same fashion
on the interior. Within, a spatial and decorative
narrative would preach by analogy to those whose
working lives were so closely bound to quarry, cliff,
rock, fossil and pebble through the spiritual truths
that could be discerned in the structure, pattern,
progressions, tones, moulding and incision of stone.

A phased project leading to a church with
eventual capacity of 800 was agreed, a new
ecclesiastical district formed, and funds found
sufficient to build and equip the nave. Aisles, tower,
porch, vestries and chancel would be deferred. The
foundation stone was laid in 1865 and, once the
nave had risen, a loan was obtained to add the aisles
and porch, allowing the body of the new All Saints'
Church to open in November 1867 with nave, aisles
and great south-west entry porch all in place. It was
long, wide and low, with light almost entirely drawn
from the rows of aisle windows, which, 10 feet high,
drew light from the high coastal downs on to eight
enormous shafts of highly polished local marble,

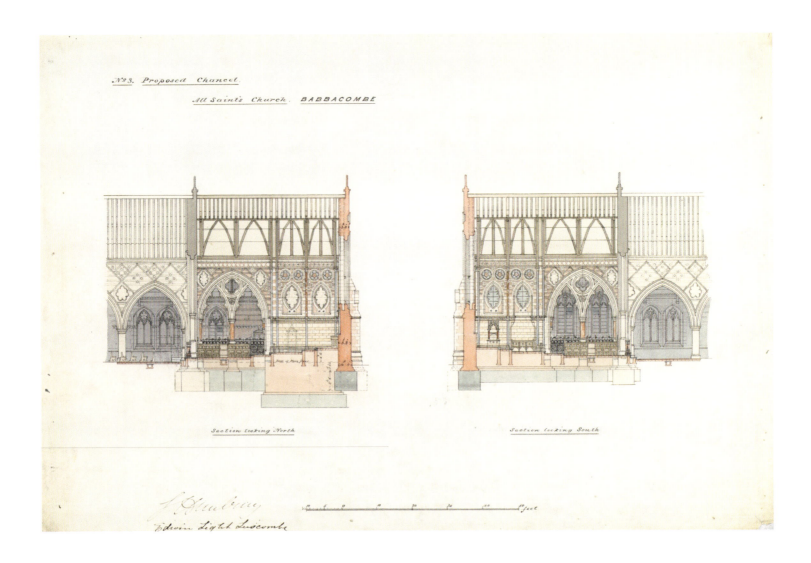

Section looking North

Section looking South

Edwin Light Luscombe

133

All Saints' Church, Babbacombe: sections of chancel looking north and south, *c.*1870

each constructed of five drums of different hue and grain, rising from light to dark. Gas brackets, each carrying eighteen jets of white flame, were placed in the spandrel above each column. A high cornice of white freestone captured a band of light below the roof, whose open beams formed a shallow bow, grazing the point above the cross on the chancel arch and creating a striking tension between mass and line. A cleverly columned, pierced and inlaid font of Devon marbles – sourced, cut and assembled by the Royal Marble Works – anchored the west end. An adventurous marble pulpit, installed a year or two later, was a fanciful miniature of a multi-arcaded classical temple, such as that of Solomon in illuminated manuscripts, playing with intersections of planes, voids, layers and illusory perspectives.

Sooner than anticipated, Babbacombe and its environs began to turn into a retirement suburb;

the church drew resident families of great wealth into its circle; and a drive to build the chancel began. On Bishop Phillpott's death his palace was acquired by Sampson Hanbury of Truman's Brewery, who became churchwarden and provided funds to commence, encouraging Butterfield to develop a more richly ornamented design. Ground was broken in spring 1872, the foundation stone was laid in September that year, and the new chancel was consecrated in November 1873. The shaping, construction materials and methods for the chancel are the same as those deployed for the first phase, but extending to the same width and height as the nave and a full 45 feet eastward. The scale and rhapsodic treatment of the choir and sanctuary have a richness that no one in 1865 could have anticipated. Although the roof is virtually continuous, Butterfield makes a decisive division between the two halves of the church, so

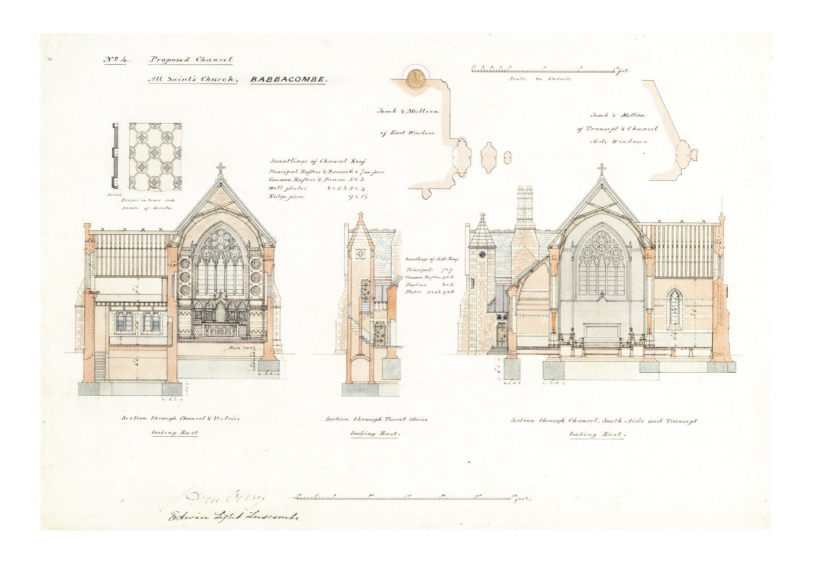

Nº 4. Proposed Chancel

All Saint's Church, BABBACOMBE.

Jamb & Mullion
of East Window

Scale en Details

Jamb & Mullion
of Transept & Chancel
Aisle Windows

Section
Diaper in lower side
panels of Reredos

Scantlings of Chancel Roof
Principal Rafters & Braces 6 × 7 on face
Common Rafters & Braces 5 × 5
Wall plates   8 × 5 & 5 × 4
Ridge piece   9 × 1½

Scantlings of Aisle Roof
Principals   7 × 7
Common Rafters 4 × 5
Purlins   5 × 5
Plates 5 × 4 & 4 × 3

Section through Chancel & Vestries
looking East

Section through Turret Stairs
looking East.

Section through Chancel, South Aisle and Transept
looking East.

Edwin Light Luscombe

134

All Saints' Church,
Babbacombe:
sections of chancel
looking east, c.1870

that choir and sanctuary read, with their high, light-coloured ceilings, like a glowing grotto which the plainer nave and aisles embrace by flowing around it into the transepts. Wide openings to the transepts from the choir are framed in cusped and moulded double arches; and the sanctuary is walled in a film of marbles, with pairs of high moulded windows above, glazed on the south and filled with Salviati glass mosaics on the north. Motifs from the nave are reiterated throughout – in the marble and metal chancel screen and gate, in the carving of the choir stalls, in the sculpted walls, and within the brass lectern and altar candlesticks, so that the extraordinary variety of events is unified at every scale.

A rare early photograph (fig.136) shows the matching shafts of the nave arcade, built in 1866 out of five stacked drums of local marble, each of

different hue and grain, and polished to a reflective sheen. Above, the camera catches the blocks of pale freestone in which fossil forms have been inlaid through the silversmith's 'niello' technique of filling incisions with molten metal. Six years later, Butterfield picked up and enlarged these figures from geology as devices in the chancel pavement and adapted one of them for the catherine-wheels carved beside the east window. This machine-age translation of a familiar medieval sacred motif into the cogs, bearings, spokes and teeth of the flywheels and circular saws used for stonecutting would have been noticed at once by the working people in the congregation. We can see the continuous light-catching lattice of diamond and pentagram in the walls, which Butterfield repeats at small scale in trellis stonework on the outside of the church, condenses and flattens in a diapered frieze above

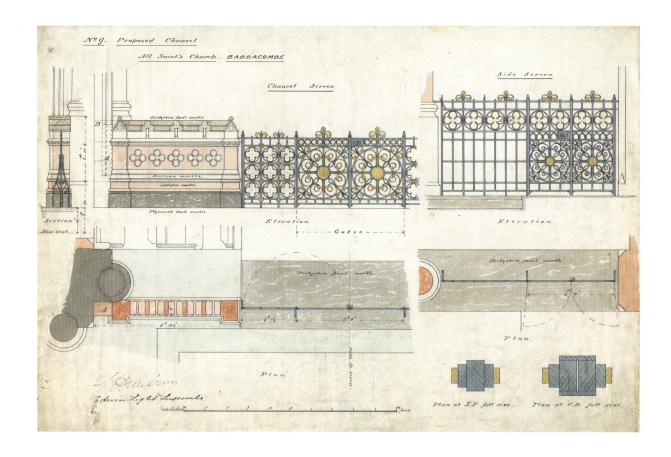

135
All Saints' Church,
Babbacombe:
elevations, plans and
sections of chancel
and side screens,
*c.*1870

136
All Saints' Church,
Babbacombe: view of
the nave looking east,
photographed *c.*1880

ALL SAINTS' CHVRCH. BABBACOMBE
Nº 1. Proposed Tower & Spire.

Plan of Belfry

Plan of Intermediate floor

Plan of Bellringers' floor

West Elevation.

Section looking West.

Edwin Lightfoot Luscombe

137
All Saints' Church,
Babbacombe: tower
and spire, c.1873

the east window, and then deploys as the underlying structural geometry in the pattern of the chancel pavement. The same webs or tartans were used in scientific works at the time to display the geometry of compression in crystal and calcite, and they are close to the representational analysis, just then emerging, of molecular structures in minerals. As the marbles and tile move towards the sanctuary and its altar, they grow tighter and richer on the ground, and vaguer and more unearthly on the

walls, where a high dado is laid of cloudy polished pink Petitor in bands of contrasting depth and lightness, like a dawn and a twilight. All are part of the same sermon in stone, in which the structures, modes of material transformation, and path to endurance of minerals stand as metaphors for the metamorphosis that takes in the lives of the faithful. Gerard Manley Hopkins spent most of a day in August 1874 struggling with its peculiarity and with its unaccustomed sense of closeness to the quarry before slowly recognising, by sketching its motifs, 'an interior line of unity', which he came to recognise as an exercise in suggestion and analogy, in which the tangible and finite are woven into a pattern that leads to the infinite and absolute. He referred back to this matter of 'erring on the side of oddness' – a tendency which he felt he shared – in a letter to Robert Bridges in 1879 developing the idea of 'inscape', as he discerned it at Babbacombe, deriving from parallel contrapuntal forms that realise its central purpose, which is the evocation of 'fancy': the imagining of otherworldliness.[5]

Flanking the chancel to the north were a three-storey transept of sacristies for clergy and choir, a tiny oratory with a fine north window and a vestry. Open semi-cloister passages on either side of the crossing left voids of repose and provided for movement and procession to and from the chancel. A high-gabled, firmly buttressed porch had been built at the west end of the church in 1867 to establish the foundations and footprint of a tower to come and to furnish its lowest level. With the chancel complete, a gift was received from Sampson Hanbury and his wife to complete this final phase, with a peal of bells added in her memory when she died in Cannes not long after. Tower and spire proceeded rapidly, to a more ambitious design (fig.137) that had to bear the weight of a massive peal, which Butterfield managed to support on its original narrow foundations by carrying the buttresses to a great height and providing the thickest concrete walls. One of a number of towers reflecting Butterfield's long study of Saint-Pierre de Caen, it was to anchor the east end of a wide avenue within a ribbon of parkland stretching for a quarter of a mile towards it as the central parade of a great residential resort, with the All Saints' tower as its climax.

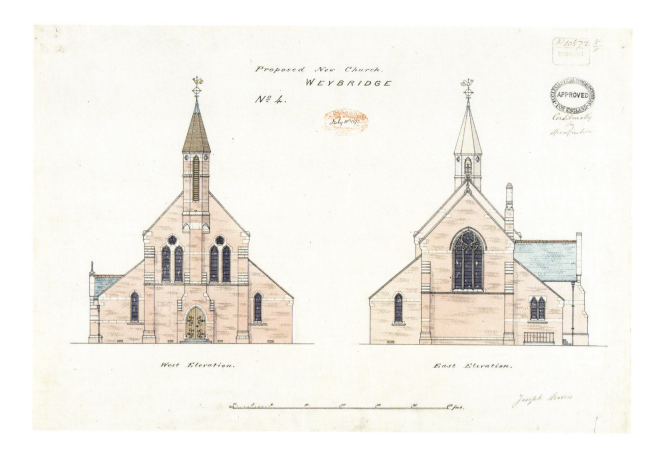

St Michael's Church, Weybridge: east and west elevations, approved May–July 1873

The development of the resort stalled in the long dull wake of the 1873 financial crisis, so that when Francis Frith recorded it in 1889 (fig.131), the church still stood in open fields beyond the fringe of the village. But a slowly reviving economy had just produced a set of villas in the near northerly distance, and by the turn of the century – when the church was sadly distorted by the introduction of window gables above the aisles – 'Cary Park', once to have been that open boulevard to the great west tower, was simply a road going nowhere between two casual lines of suburban villas.

RIVERSIDE AND PARKLAND: WEYBRIDGE

The small Surrey town of Weybridge, 19 miles from London, had fallen into the trading and transport orbit of the metropolis when the first canals were developed, but with the arrival of the first stage of a railway to Southampton in 1838 its economy shifted to one of the earliest dormitory suburbs and

leisure resorts on the new railways. A new parish church had been built in 1848, with 278 seats to serve this growing population, soon expanded to house 600. In 1861 the census counted a population of 2600 with close to 400 children enrolled in the parish schools; a new town of villas and terraced houses was developing to the north of the parish church; boathouses and rentable punts welcomed picnic parties to the rivers; the Duke of York's Oatlands estate to the east had been turned into a grand hotel, advertising healthy gravel subsoil and fresh air as inducements to the invalid, a mere 45 minutes from Waterloo; and portions of the great park had been divided into parcels for large villa retreats. A mixed settlement of detached middle-class villas and terraced housing began to appear a mile to the south, around the crossing of the highway to Kingston and the main-line railway. Butterfield's St Michael's was to serve that rapidly expanding district and absorb the overflow from the parish church.[6] When completed in 1874, this new district church was described by the local press

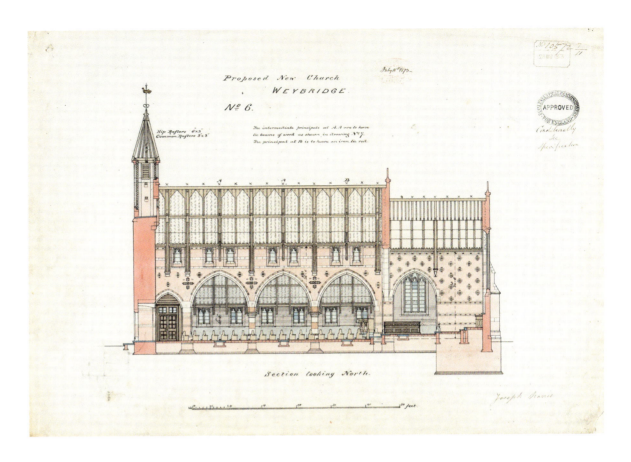

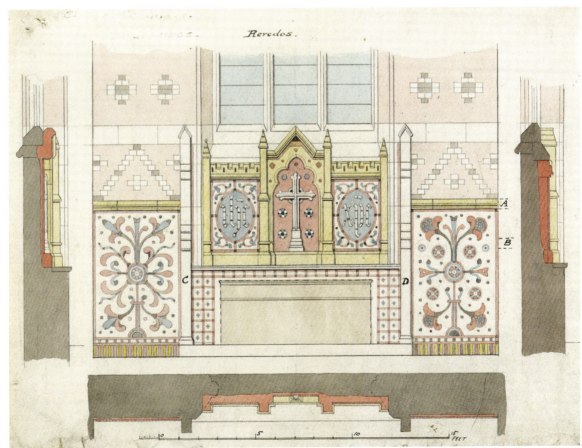

139
St Michael's Church,
Weybridge: section
looking north, approved
May–July 1873

140
St Michael's Church,
Weybridge: reredos,
*c.*1873

as 'of red brick, stern and deterrent outside, but pleasanter within'. It lies within the confines of a single rectangular house plot, one among a row laid out between a busy road and the main-line railway for middle-class garden villas. In the confines of that suburban setting and with a modest budget, Butterfield had to fit a footprint large enough to seat 550, with a full chancel, choir, organ room and vestry, and a bell tower.

He set a lofty nave between wide aisles with gently beamed roofs and very simple double windows; placed small ventilating windows in a clerestory high above the arcades, away from the dust of the road and smoke of the trains, and catching light from over the shadows of the leafy suburb; kept to studiedly plain exterior surfaces, relieved by the mere whisper of a plaque and diaper above the entry porch; and shaped the vestry and organ chamber into a garden setting at the north-east, in a domestic scale and manner. These steps, along with the scrupulously scaled and patterned churchyard wall, reconcile what would otherwise be a towering and intrusive object to the temper of its suburban setting, while on the powerful west front, facing trains leaving the station for Waterloo, evident structure – the blocks and courses that bear its height and weight – carries all the burden of ornament.

Within, a more urbane drama was wrought by the breadth, poise and balance of pattern and proportion. The east wall, of tile mosaics in a restrained palette of pink, dove grey, graphite and dun, is one of the first expressions of the vines and fruits that would become the symbolic language for the tiled sanctuaries of Butterfield's country and suburban churches. Here we see two types of the lily – first in bud on the prophetic panel to the north and then bearing the harvest of redemption to the south. Within a decade, the compact, quiet and serene analogy of nature as a portrait of the divine was too sober for the taste of the times, and the chancel was reworked with gilding, holy pictures and filigree in the 'richer' idea of sanctity then (and since) sadly prevailing. The church was demolished to build flats, without protest, exactly 100 years after it began.

SERENITY AND SATISFACTION: CLEVEDON

Clevedon first grew up on the cliffs above the mouths of the River Yeo, which drove the fulling mills on which it prospered, and it is there that the ancient church of St Andrew's lay, to be made famous by Alfred Tennyson as the resting place, in 1833, of his close friend and fellow poet Arthur Hallam. Well before the health benefits of saltwater bathing began to take hold, its interesting seascape, blessed by famously salubrious breezes, had been a romantic subject and a summer retreat, where Coleridge celebrated life in a simple cottage among 'its wooded hills and green lanes and rich meadow'. By 1838, when Lady Elton of Clevedon Court drew the scene for a famous lithograph from a viewpoint not far from the site on which Butterfield's church of St John the Evangelist would rise, summer villas were already abundant, and her husband, Sir Arthur Elton, had begun a lifetime of devotion to developing the land as a sea-bathing resort with an air of propriety and a sense of 'serenity and satisfaction'.[7]

A branch railway line, hotels, a pier and the day-tripper arrived, and with that came new pockets of deprivation typical of resort towns into which the rural poor had flowed to serve visitors, with mean housing, on short contracts and for low wages. Their neighbourhood had grown up around the station, just below a portion of the eastern hill that was ripe for villa development. A mission school and a temporary church were established there in the late 1860s, and, on his wife's death, Elton decided to raise it into a full-fledged church for a new ecclesiastical district that would straddle the slope between the working poor below and the middle class settling above.[8] It was fiercely opposed by the closest of the three existing Anglican churches, with an expression of contempt for the lowly to whom its doors were closed, but was vehemently supported by a bishop who found his churches filled with the middle classes and scandalously neglectful of the lower. Butterfield and Elton worked together in great harmony and friendship to build a church in pink Mendip stone with roofs of graphite slate,

required, so that the grounds could become a garden, where severe terracing with only evergreen plantings could all be designed by Butterfield himself as part of an architectural scheme in which stone is softened by greenery, and straight lines by rounded. Butterfield returned to complete the interior in 1884 in a symphony of delicate wall decoration, polished Babbacombe marbles, a chancel arch with an enormous white marble cross, and a high reredos in the form of a portal and canopy like the Porta della Carta of Venice. The majestic effect of unfolding from entry to east wall through a bath of light at the crossing did not survive additions and changes wrought not long after. The church's high-church practices remained in contention for many years, but the new parish was unusually successful in improving the lives and prospects of poorer young people in the lower town. As intended, it also encouraged terrace and villa building on the eastern hill, which now followed a manner and mode of construction that were remarkably in keeping with it, Butterfield's parsonage setting a residential tone in sympathy with the church.

The flourishing charitable society of St John's was very much in keeping with Clevedon's growing reputation as the resort of young unmarried women purportedly in search of husbands, 'with no men in sight and scarcely a curate either!'[9] but with an endless round of charity teas and Sunday-school duties, cruelly satirised by the humourist John Latimer of the *Bristol Mercury* in the 1880s, but portrayed with just sympathy by George Gissing in his lament for brilliant 'left-overs' condemned to idleness and quiet good works in *The Odd Women* (1893).

AN EVENING HYMN: BOURNEMOUTH

The town of Bournemouth had grown up to house returning India hands, retired military and those with hearts and lungs weakened by London fog, who came to breathe a little more easily and, perhaps, like the Kebles in 1866, to die a little more comfortably. About 1888, Henry Twells turned to his friend of forty years to build a church on its

141
Church of St John the Evangelist, Clevedon: postcard view from the south-east with the vicarage seen behind, Valentine & Sons postcard, *c.*1900

142
Church of St John the Evangelist, Clevedon: interior view looking east, photographed 1884

laid across the incline of the hill, and a barely ornamented saddleback tower at its south-west corner of extraordinary rigour and force. It was an irregular configuration lent symmetry by great east and west windows at the same scale and with the same tracery, eschewing exterior ornament to take a near-Romanesque delight in sturdiness, stone and structure.

The foundation stone was laid in October 1876, and the church consecrated, with a school and parsonage, in April 1878. No churchyard was

143
St Augustin's Church,
Bournemouth: view
from the north-
east, photograph by
Debenham & Gould,
plate from W.C.
Ingram, *A Memoir of
the Rev. Henry Twells*,
Wells Gardner & Co.,
London, 1901

Debenham and Gould,   Bournemouth.

ST. AUGUSTIN'S CHURCH, BOURNEMOUTH.

eastern hills to attend in his retirement and comfort his widow when he was gone. By then, much of Bournemouth had become, like 'Seabourne-on-Sea', Radclyffe Hall's portrayal of it in her 1924 novel *The Unlit Lamp*, a town of estranged wives and widows of the dissolute, unfaithful or invalid, who sustained a host of new churches appearing in its fast-growing suburbs of pine and sandhill.

Like the Weybridge church, St Augustin's was sited on a house plot in a similar though somewhat more spacious villa development, most yet unbuilt. It recast the Weybridge design in a beautiful rough stone, scarcely trimmed, adopting exactly the same framework – 100 feet long by 50 wide and 50 high, with the same point of division between nave and chancel, a nearly identical western profile and a similarly impressive approach to the northern porches and vestry.[10] Here, the site allowed a second porch to the south, giving Butterfield a final rare chance to render the narthex as the 'western passage' that so delighted him; and on a brightly lit site there was, like Babbacombe, no need for a clerestory. The aisles are therefore lined with three bays of wide, high windows, and in a sign of shelter the nave roof is allowed to drop down to nearly kiss that

above the aisle, exactly as Butterfield had done at Hensall. Wall decoration seems to have been discreet throughout, so that the interior must have felt like a nearly amorphous glow of light within a cloister. But a wonderful open cascade of spiralling vines and blossoms at the east end described another world, to which Twells addressed his sermon in the octave of consecration, taking from the Song of Solomon the lines: 'Let my beloved come into his garden, and eat his pleasant fruits'. This was Butterfield's last new church, and, in its reduction to what can be expressed most simply through wall, roof, gable and opening – a poem written out of the mere assembly of the planes and shapes of a building in themselves, by one for whom the greatest poetry lay in the most useful and unpretending – perhaps his most elegiac. Twells was known everywhere for his 'evening hymn' on the trials of age and the joys of a final departure.[11] He and Butterfield died a month apart in the fatally cold winter of 1900, and one can feel, both in the sturdy enfolding stone, standing in recollection of the nation's earliest Christian tombs and temples, and in its exuberantly delicate evocation of the gardens of paradise, that this was Butterfield's 'evening church'.

NOTES

1. The account of the work at Hunstanton is drawn principally from letters from H.L. Styleman Le Strange to William Earle Lytton Bulwer, 1845, in Bulwer of Heydon family papers, Norfolk Record Office, including announcements, prospectuses and plan; a report in the *Norfolk Chronicle*, 3 May 1845; 'Hunstanton Heritage Gardens Conservation Plan', Kings Lynn and West Norfolk Borough Council, February 2016; and Kath Fryer, *A Fine Strong Boy: The Life and Times of Henry L'Estrange Styleman Le Strange*, Hollinfare Publications, Hunstanton, 2000.

2. *Norfolk News*, 27 February 1847; *Cambridge Chronicle*, 3 March 1855.

3. The commentary on Hunstanton in this paragraph derives from the *Saturday Review*, 4 August 1883; *Ipswich Journal*, 24 August 1888; and *Blackwood's Magazine*, September 1897.

4. The account of the Babbacombe project is drawn largely from many newspaper and journal reports, but especially: *Illustrated London News*, 16 November 1867; *Western Morning News*, 4 November 1867; *Western Morning News*, 5 November 1873; *Plymouth and Exeter Gazette*, 8 November 1873; *Building News*, 14 November 1873; and *Torquay Times*, 18 July 1874. There is an extensive project history by 'Criticus' in *Torquay Times*, 20 April 1906.

5. Hopkins records two visits to All Saints', Babbacombe, once soon after the first phase opened in 1867 and again in August 1874 with the chancel complete: *The Journals and Papers of Gerard Manley Hopkins*, Oxford University Press, Oxford, 1986, pp 254–5. Among the many discussions of Butterfield as seen by Hopkins, see Norman White, 'Hopkins and All Saints' Babbacombe', *The Hopkins Quarterly*, vol.20, no.1/2, 1993, pp 40–43; Martin Dubois, '"Pure Beauty of Line": Gerard Hopkins and William Butterfield', *Postgraduate English*, no.16, September 2007, University of Durham; and Kumiko Tanabe, *Gerard Manley Hopkins and His Poetics of Fancy*, Cambridge Scholars Publishing, Cambridge, 2015, chapter 3.

6. The project history of St Michael's, Weybridge, is documented in manuscripts, clippings and transcripts in the parish files of the Surrey County Records Office. Butterfield's plan is filed in the ICBS Archives.

7. See, for example, *Handbook for Travellers in Wiltshire, Dorsetshire, and Somersetshire*, John Murray, London, 1882 edition, pp 370–71.

8. The account of the church at Clevedon is taken from reports in the *Weston Mercury*, 7 October 1876; *Weston-super-Mare Gazette*, 21 October 1876; *Western Daily Press* and *Bristol Mercury*, 1 May 1878; and from Margaret Ann Elton's centenary history of the church, published as a pamphlet by Clevedon Printing Company in 1978, which is an extraordinarily informative and accomplished essay in local building history, with an appendix containing Butterfield's own 1878 guide to the church.

9. [John Latimer], 'Aunt Dorothy's Advice to the Young Ladies of Clevedon', *Bristol Mercury*, 1, 8 and 15 February 1886.

10. A full account of St Augustin's, Bournemouth, is given in W.C. Ingram, *A Memoir of the Rev. Henry Twells*, Wells Gardner & Co., London, 1901. The original plan, plot plan, section and elevation are in the Bournemouth planning office, with detail drawings in the collection of the Getty Research Institute.

11. Henry Twells, 'At Even, Ere the Sun was Set', 1868.

V 'THE WAY WE LIVE NOW'

SOCIAL HYGIENE *and* CIVIC ORDER, 1857–76

CHAPTER 13

'SAVE THE STATE'[1]

N 1851, THE CENSUS reported just under 18 million people in England and Wales, of whom slightly over half – or 9 million – were housed in towns of 10,000 or more. Forty years later, with a population now approaching 30 million, 70 per cent were living in towns of at least 10,000, while the number in the countryside stayed stable. There was nothing remotely comparable to urbanisation at this pace in the rest of Europe, where even the Low Countries, by far the continent's most urbanised lands, counted no more than a third of their population in the towns. So recent was this shift that a memory of country life was still ingrained among urban people. In a charge to his clergy of 1862, the Bishop of London, Archibald Campbell Tait, made a desperate plea for new churches to be set up in a metropolis of now near 3 million, arguing that only an engaged Church

working in districts of manageable size could realistically provide a 'system of relief, even of the poor's temporal wants', and making a special case for the parish church as the primary agent of this welfare, because:

> our poor in London come from country towns, where they have been accustomed to their parish church, and all the kindly influences which gather round it . . . and shall their advent to our neighbourhood deprive them of religious and social blessings which they might have enjoyed at home? If we neglect them, it will be at the peril of the nation.[2]

The Church's effort to extend into outlying areas of the overgrown towns was not only a social cause, but also – perhaps above all – an architectural and

PREVIOUS PAGE: St Cross Church, Clayton

representational mission, in which the presence of the churches themselves served as what Keble called 'remonstrances' – sentinels of order, probity and continuity in a volatile landscape, and demonstrations of that 'respectful bearing' that marked a settled civil life. This was a rhetorical purpose that Butterfield most strikingly achieved. His contribution to the number of new town churches was a tiny one, and others in his time built many more – there are at least 150 by John Loughborough Pearson, and those of Ewan Christian are nearly uncountable. But the sixteen new town churches Butterfield built between the Crimean peace of 1856 and the Golden Jubilee of 1887, starting at Newbury in Berkshire and Hammersmith in Middlesex, mark an entirely original and assertive contribution to the cultural landscape, tuned to an imaginative reading of each site's history, circumstance and probable prospects, adapting to constraints of site and budget, and – with one notable exception in Kensington – bringing a model of sturdy, quiet and sometimes stern restraint into the townscapes of an era clamorous with the display of prosperity, civic pride and the entertainments of the middle class. They were transformative in themselves, as cautionary, even reproachful, monuments of grave dignity among the increasingly mannered, immoral and lavish expressions of the moneyed life characterised by Anthony Trollope in 1874 as 'The Way We Live Now'.[3]

'GRAVE SEVERITY': NEW URBAN DISTRICTS IN NEWBURY, HAMMERSMITH, HITCHIN AND MANCHESTER

The church of St John the Evangelist, for a new district on the southern perimeter of Newbury, was built with funds from John Gellibrand Hubbard, patron of St Alban's, Holborn, and his sister at the behest of their brother, who became its vicar.[4] It was erected in anticipation of new housing and commercial development growing up around a revived market in grain, and placed in a semi-rural sector south of the canal port, just below the station. Butterfield's drawings first propose a turreted bell

tower set forward from the west wall, with a great window inset between its supporting buttresses (fig.144). He then altered this profile into a much more assertive built silhouette with an open double belfry (fig.145). Both schemes are marked by the great height of the nave and chancel and by the virtually continuous band of high, bright windows along the aisleless south wall. In the first scheme the roofs are of slate, and in the second red tile is used to cover, making a monochrome fall of planes like the churches of Cowick. The whole church is raised on a platform to float above land that falls away to the west slope. The lines of stone diapers and stringcourses in the brick are an unerring reflection of the church's structural logic, marking where vertical and horizontal stresses fall and are carried and repeated in the high course of brick pattern-work within.

In one of his earliest field photos (fig.146), the Oxford photographer Henry W. Taunt captures the unity of a church in which the columns and arches of the font and above the crossing of the timbers in the roof are as central to the cohesive effect as the great north arcade and chancel arch, and shows the almost illusory distance to which the nave rises among the gracefully pointed web of collars and rafters of the roof. Butterfield's technical drawing shows how ingeniously a system that looks as light as a lattice was made to bear the weight of a roof pitched to this extreme. The Valentine studio's tinted photograph from around 1900 (fig.147) is printed in imitation of an oil painting on a raised and varnished surface in which the figures, ingeniously left in black and white, provide a striking indication of the great shift in scale through which Butterfield has transformed the simple profile of a country chapel into a town church, now entirely dominating the crossroads and revealing how firmly it rides above the drop to the north. The lowest band of stone that marks the floor of the church hovers well above the heads of those walking the pavement. A Sunday school was built in 1864–6, to Butterfield's design, south of the crossroads, soon expanding for day pupils from the overflowing parish school. But the anticipated southward expansion of the town was slow in

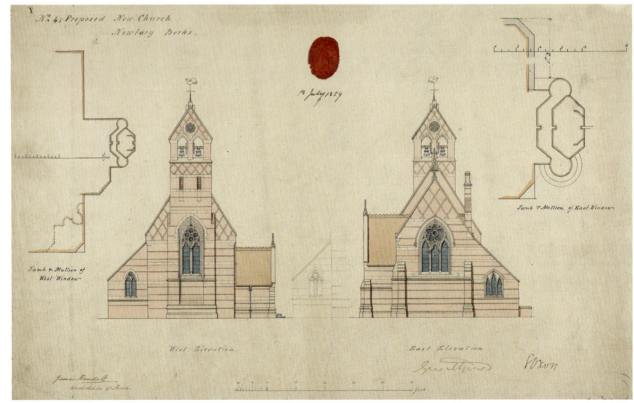

144
Church of St John
the Evangelist,
Newbury: study
for south and west
elevations, *c*.1859

145
Church of St John
the Evangelist,
Newbury:
east and west
elevations, 1859

was in a field of rough land adjacent to a scattered settlement of shacks and sheds housing labourers drawn to the nearby brickfields, commercial nurseries and new freight yards. This was one of a number of shed cities in the western perimeter of London into which Tait himself famously went to preach and lead evening prayers. The church – dedicated to St John the Evangelist – grew out of a mission to the district run by laymen of St Matthias's, Stoke Newington, and had a firm high-church bias. Means were small and the need urgent, so the great brick church was built without a tower for the time being, and with much of its interior fittings left for a future date.

By 1864 it was well established, the district was more settled and Butterfield's parsonage and schools could be built at the rear of the site. It was a lofty, spacious, conspicuous and beautifully gas-lit church in a tight but discrete enclosure, structural brick and timber work carrying all its ornament, inside and out. James Thorne's *Handbook to the Environs of London* of 1876 celebrates 'its altitude, breadth and boldness of character', but notes especially in the parsonage and schools a tendency to realism that reaches a 'grave severity'. And Thorne could now observe a Hammersmith in which 'the builder has very nearly supplanted the gardener and farmer . . . The mansions of the fashionable torn down and given place to schools, factories, or subdivisions, while the wealthy seek more distant and romantic regions for their summer and autumn retreats'.[5] Ten years later, the tower had been erected; a street of hygienic modest terraces laid out on Church land just to the east, with a mission chapel for overflow from the church; tramlines ran along Glenthorne Road; and the vicar's annual report recorded 225 pupils in the infant day school, 1500 per week at the various Sunday schools and a team of laypeople working among the poor of this now very mixed and populous district that was held up as the model of the mission of a London parish. It was very effective among those nearest to where it lay, but there were vast new districts in Fulham and Hammersmith where the growth and drift of population had been so rapid that parish community services had been left far behind and the social fabric of society broken down.

146
Church of St John the Evangelist, Newbury: interior view looking east, photograph by Henry W. Taunt, *c.*1870

147
Church of St John the Evangelist, Newbury: view from the west, [J. Valentine] tinted art postcard, *c.*1900

coming and had barely matured by the time the church was laid waste in a bombing raid in 1943.

In July 1857, when the drawings were completed for a new church in Hammersmith, the site lay to the west and north of what was then a small rural river town. A long row of modest detached villas was being built on a road to the east, running north from the terminus of the new Junction Railway, and two terraces of poor housing were about to be developed along the east side of Cambridge Grove below the church. When the foundation stone was laid, it

148 (left)
Church of St John
the Evangelist,
Hammersmith: view of
church and parsonage
from the south-east,
postcard, c.1910

149 (right)
Holy Saviour's Church,
Hitchin: view from
the south-west after
the additions of full
aisles and south
porch, photograph by
Thomas B. Latchmore,
c.1884–1900

Holy Saviour's, Hitchin, appeared on the outskirts of a market town of basket-weavers and hatters, in what began as a haphazard residential community of working people moving in from meagre farmland towards the freight yards of a railway junction and that would gradually evolve into a neatly terraced workingmen's suburb. The district church at its opening was a variation on the Newbury model, shorter and squatter, graced with two aisles, gentler on the outside and much busier within.[6] It was 110 feet long and 44 feet wide, seating 400, with narrow, shed-roofed aisles designed for further expansion. Like the churches at Cowick, Hitchin relies on concrete for its shafts and framework, but here, rather than the monochrome of that beautifully finished deep-pink Lincoln brick and tile, Butterfield took a mix of red and black from the rougher stock of a local yard, whose proprietors were the builders, to set up a rhythm, with scattered pale stone trim, in which surface pattern rather than surface itself would dominate. As Hitchin moved eastwards, streets of more genteel terraces appeared, and Butterfield widened the aisles of his church, built substantial covered entries, and walled and railed the street frontage to lend it more presence and decorum. By the time these extensions were complete in 1884, Holy Saviour's offered reading and garden clubs, temperance societies, Bible classes, football and cricket clubs, girls' sewing circles and weekly choral and bell-ringing practice – all a bulwark, said its bishop, against the new

threat from artisans' societies 'diligently spreading rationalism and socialism' among young working people.[7] There were four overflowing services on Easter Day 1883, each moving 600 people into and out of the church.

Another severely grave, and gravely beautiful, brick town church appeared at the same time as Hitchin to centre an amorphous district not far from Manchester. It follows the pattern at Hammersmith, with a galilee west porch and a free-standing south-west tower. It lay amid arable fields now increasingly dotted and channelled with steel mills, canals, railway lines and chemical and locomotive works, and first emerged to serve the scattered clusters of 'operatives' cottages' growing up around them. The settlement lay in the western edges of the parish of Droylsden, a substantial township of 8000 close to Ashton-under-Lyne, then one of the largest towns in England, with a population of 35,000. St Cross grew out of a school and mission established by a young Droylsden curate in the late 1850s, with the church completed in a single campaign and opened under licence for its first evening service in April 1866.[8] Set off in a large walled churchyard, with a thin high tower and a line of large, repeated windows in the clerestory, it echoed the volumes of brick and glass, narrow chimney stacks, windowed workshop walls and plain surfaces of the mills in its surrounding landscape.

The church and school were built with funds from the banker Peter Hoare, on the western

and by the great emphasis Butterfield placed on the lighting essential for a town church with so much activity in hours of darkness. Large gas lanterns lit the approaches, while within the church myriad points of white flame shone from the wall brackets, standards and coronas of nave, choir and chancel. In a photograph taken just as the school was extended in 1895 (fig.150), terraces of substantial housing for working people on North Road have begun to appear, and a small municipal park to the west of the schools is in construction, fronting a dense development of more rudimentary terraced houses on what is now the eastern fringe of Manchester.

portion of his largely abandoned manor, Clayton Hall, the habitable portion of which was converted into a vicarage. St Cross seated 650, had a large organ transept and stalls for a substantial choir, was lit from a great clerestory set high above steam and smoke, and carried within an unusual air of austere grandeur, with bands and frames of brown and amber stone crossing rising patterns of black-diapered red brick in a play of horizontals against the intensely vertical thrust of arches and timbers. The cost of £14,000 was twice that spent to furnish churches of similar capacity but less commanding scale nearby, and the evangelical Bishop of Manchester questioned, at its belated consecration in 1874, whether the sight of such splendour was not a deterrent to the humble and penitential devotion he sought to inculcate among the poor.

Lee noted then that among the 800,000 people of his diocese of Salford and Manchester, less than one third had ever seen the inside of a house of worship of any denomination. St Cross was in fact a triumph of intervention. Sitting just to the north of Butterfield's busy National school on the main Manchester-to-Ashton road, it rapidly became both the visual and social landmark of a new community, burying its dead, running a cricket club on its own ground beside the church, maintaining a travelling choral society, and providing 6.30 a.m. weekday services to fit the timetable of working people. Attendance was greatly encouraged by the appearance of gas lamps on the 'lonely and dark' Ashton Road in 1870,

'PREACHING CONTINUITY': THE 'TOP CHURCH' AT PENARTH

Penarth in 1851 was a fishing village of twenty-four dwellings below the cliffs that commanded the entrance to the bay and port of Cardiff, which were growing rapidly around new coal docks built by the Marquess of Bute. In 1855, Baroness Windsor, proprietor of coal-rich estates almost as extensive as Bute's, saw greatly improved efficiency and profits by building rival docks of her own at the mouth of the bay. Opened in 1865, this involved a massive work of civil and marine engineering. Within fifteen years Penarth itself was a considerable town with a population over 5000 and nearly 800 dwellings, its enormous coal harbour on one side of the cliffs, a residential town on the slopes and valley below the head to the west, and public promenades, villas, pier and hotels of a pleasure resort on its south-west shore, serving what was now a Cardiff of 165,000 people.

As work began on the docks in 1859, Baroness Windsor decided to anticipate growth by replacing the tiny hilltop village church, associated with the ancient abbey of St Augustine's, and extending its burial ground, bringing in Butterfield – with whom she had worked at Alvechurch – as architect.[9] The site was on the very crest of the headland with pleasant downs riding to the clifftop at its east. The short saddleback tower of the old church and the three-light east window had been in clear

There are two extraordinary archaisms in the church: very thick low shafts with wide unornamented capitals form the nave arcades, like those of a Norman abbey, alternating between cylinder and octagon in an irregular sequence; and aisle and clerestory windows, like the plain openings of the bell tower, are simply narrow, barely pointed lancets pierced virtually without framing into the fabric of the walls – so that every sense the church arouses is of stone upon stone, assembled like a prehistoric outgrowth of rock thrust into the light of a clifftop and lined with the warmth of brick within. The severity of enclosure is well suited to a windy rainswept headland, and, in its stony avoidance of ornament, recollects the plain Welsh chapels and churches of antiquity, like that its villagers knew there before. It bears what a poet of our time, Gillian Clarke, who lived as a child in the shadow of the 'Top Church', calls 'a stony profile preaching continuity'.[10]

'A MODEL HOSPITAL': THE COUNTY INFIRMARY AT WINCHESTER

Winchester had established a county infirmary – the first in the country – in 1736, which had moved in 1759 into a building in the large, badly drained and disease-prone historic quarter. When this reached a state of dilapidation that needed urgently addressing, it was rather quickly determined that a new and more hygienic site should be found. The final choice was a south-facing slope high on the Romsey Road, on dry ground with good breezes in 'a new and untainted area'.[11] Since designs for a modern infirmary were almost entirely untested, Butterfield and his friend Sir William Heathcote, chair of the building committee, undertook an intensive investigation of ideas, practicalities and principles, travelling over the course of two years to new military hospitals and other medical facilities to study alternatives, and consulting at length with Florence Nightingale. Funds were highly constrained from the start, and economy became of overriding concern as building costs in southern England rose at alarming speed.

The final scheme was shown to the press in November 1863, and then vetted by the military

sight of the busiest shipping lanes in the kingdom, and played a critical role in a pilots' navigation. Butterfield therefore situated his new church around the established site, with a south-west tower close to the position of the old one, carrying a saddleback top reminiscent of its predecessor, and an east window again of three lights with a head of three foils. The interior is clad in diapered brick, with slate-blue marble columns enlivening the clerestory, and foils of the same material in the spandrels, where Butterfield follows the Welsh tradition of decorating with words by engraving the Beatitudes into the stone.

engineer Douglas Strutt Galton in 1864 for economy and efficiency before bids were finalised and construction commenced. The fundamental decision not to build according to the emerging convention of the pavilion hospital, which was Nightingale's preference, came not only through the constraints of a relatively small sloping site but from Butterfield's analysis of the relative costs of construction, maintenance and the burdens of movement. Other conventions were dispensed with at Nightingale's own suggestion, including the elimination of two medical orthodoxies – day rooms and balconies running the length of the wards – arguing that patients who reached a condition where they could enjoy them should be discharged. The only disagreement unresolved was over the location of the chapel, which she preferred in a separate building, but Butterfield with only £700 on hand to produce it, chose to incorporate on top of the east wing as a construction economy, and then took advantage of it to strengthen the public profile of a building whose trustees had otherwise issued an absolute proscription on 'unnecessary ornament'. Nightingale ultimately 'congratulated the building committee on having received from Mr Butterfield a plan for a model hospital'.

There were beds for 110, with the five principal wards ending in short balconies between lavatory towers designed to confine plumbing and waste to perimeter drainage. A central block housed medical, laboratory and surgical staff and facilities, with a massive vertical circulation space in the gabled stair tower facing north beside the entrance. 'Conventual quarters' for nurses were in a low wing next to

153
Royal Hampshire County Hospital:
view from the north-east upon completion,
photograph by William Savage, 1868

154
Royal Hampshire County Hospital:
view from the south-east upon completion,
photograph by William Savage, 1868

155
Royal Hampshire County Hospital:
view from the south-west upon completion,
photograph by William Savage, 1868

laundry on the west side of the front quadrangle, across from the gate lodge and warden's house. A mortuary was provided in a separate brick shed on the south-east corner. The entire work is in a brick manufactured by the builders to save costs, with stone trim securing the structure and drip lines and providing Butterfield with the horizontal anchors to the comfortable perception of height and to the visual comprehension of division and structure that were so vital to his aesthetic of the vertical. The geometric design of his garden below the building and his great entry court above set up the illusion of a reflected topography of the masses that rise behind them, a Palladian effect that would be essential to the success of the Keble College quadrangle. For the first decade or more, city water and sewage services were inadequate, and the self-sufficient plumbing and waste systems Butterfield had designed for the hospital had been poorly installed and were badly maintained. He returned for adjustments and repairs many times, finally resigning in despair.

The hospital, completed in 1868, begins the astonishing ten-year sequence in which all five of Butterfield's great secular complexes appear: at Rugby School, Keble College, Exeter Grammar School and the Cheddar Hospital. They could not at first glance look less alike, but a wealth of entirely original ideas flows between them; and they are united by an embrace of what Ricardo calls 'the conviction that architecture was a thing of every-day use and for every-day wear, that its business was to clothe the needs of today and express ourselves and our ambitions', with a 'frank acceptance of the requirements of our time, out of which to evolve and distil an ideal'.[12]

CATHEDRAL OF THE ARTS: ST AUGUSTINE, SOUTH KENSINGTON

St Augustine's Church in South Kensington, appearing slowly from conversations in 1865 to final decorations in the 1890s, is the first in a series of large-scale ecclesiastical masterworks for the towns and cities of the late Victorian age that stretch from Rugby, Barnet, Belfast, and Perth out (though in

unfinished form) to the other side of the globe, at Adelaide and Melbourne.[13] They show Butterfield working at a newly metropolitan order of scale and visual refinement, each work finding its own system of colour and symbolic decoration that will suffuse the space and structure, from a pattern on the outer wall to a curve of the lily in a metal rail. Although its siting was closely related to the westward growth of London, St Augustine's had a broader purpose than that of a new district church, being conceived as a second model, after All Saints' Margaret Street, of the metropolitan church as a site for the advancement of 'Christian Art' in its fabric, fittings, decoration and services, displaying with more rigour than the lavish fresco and marbles of Margaret Street how inexpensive modern materials and techniques could forge a place of nearly Byzantine splendour, coherence, instruction and invention.

The location acquired for the project was essential to the concept of a parish church that served an aesthetic and liturgical purpose, as a cathedral of the arts as well as a social agent. Below Kensington Gardens lay an enormous parcel of lands that had been acquired by the Crown Commissioners to house the Great Exhibition of 1851 and Prince Albert's dream city of learning and culture – 'Albertopolis' – that was to follow. Great swathes lay open for the extension of well-to-do households into this prime sector of the royal borough, in which, in 1864, the first suburban 'District' railway arrived. Richard Robert Chope, a charismatic curate, established a new ecclesiastical mission around the poor village of Old Brompton, set up a vicarage and built an iron-framed chapel of ease in its garden, where he introduced to staid and largely evangelical Kensington what many considered a shockingly ornamental and formal liturgy.

Chope's project attracted a number of wealthy residents and local landowners, among them John Gellibrand Hubbard, who had built St Alban's, Holborn, with Butterfield and funded the church at Newbury, and John Archibald Shaw Stewart, treasurer of the Keble College project, silent manager of William Gladstone's charitable portfolio and a great friend of the architect. With funds for an endowment from one and the gift of land from

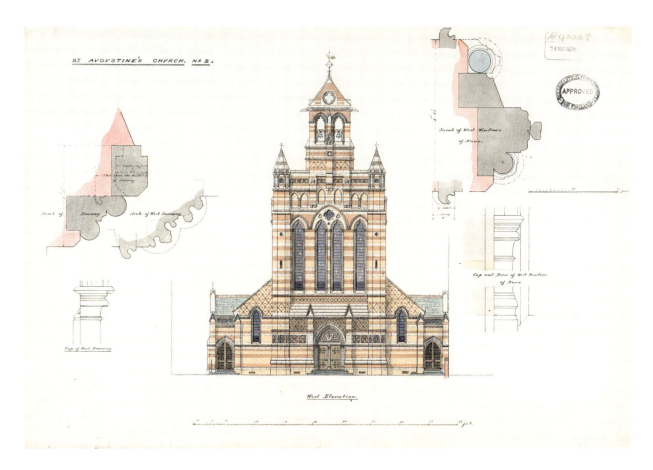

156
St Augustine's Church,
South Kensington:
west elevation, May
1876

the other, the project for a permanent church of the new district of St Augustine was announced in July 1869, with Butterfield as architect. There was a commitment to open pews with free seating for all – it would be the only Kensington church with such full access for the poor – and the announced intention of designing it to advance 'the full development of the Anglican ritual'. Bishop Tait opposed the plan, questioning the need for a new parish; and it proved legally difficult to obtain a charter with a requirement for free seating. Nevertheless, the first plans were on paper by 1868, and, with Tait's removal to Canterbury in 1869, the new district could be formed, embracing pockets of poverty in Old Brompton, and work began, with Myers as builder. Funds were raised to build the nave, west front and aisles (though designs for the full church with vestry, organ chamber and chancel had been prepared), site work commenced in summer 1870, and the core of a new church was ready for service at about the same time as the Royal Albert Hall just to its north, in 1871.

The history of the site in the years that followed gives a perfect picture of the pace and unpredictability at which the luxurious new quarters of South Kensington appeared. At the time of design there was as yet no road at all for the church to front, just a track or two and a western prospect of the new district in an undefined borderland where market gardens, stables and the remains of country estates were being slowly replaced by clusters of new 'Gardens' of town houses. A set of low-lying rural almshouses adjoined its site to the north. Everything pointed to a street pattern in which a grid would follow the south-easterly trajectory of the streets and mews to the east. But an 1880 map shows the almshouses gone, and an entire new westward thoroughfare passing along the north from the new Kensington Station. This was already lined with mansion blocks, and the streets to the south of it, including the extension of Queen's Gate itself, were starting to be laid out on the straight north–south pattern of the exhibition grounds, and beginning to acquire new living blocks, virtually colliding with the

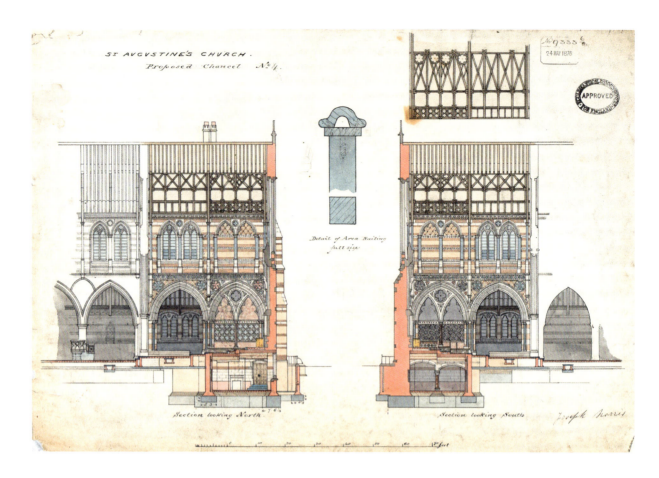

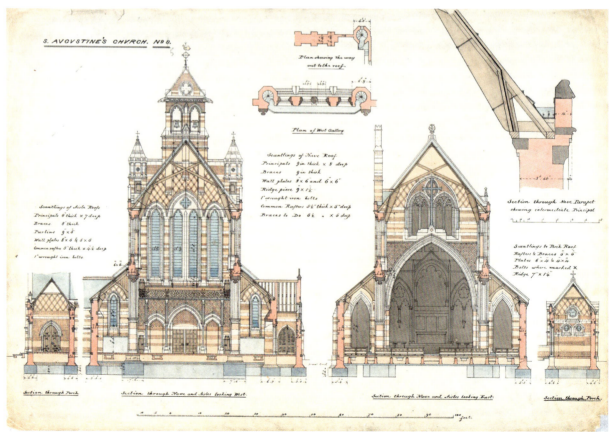

157
St Augustine's Church,
South Kensington:
chancel, May 1876

158
St Augustine's Church,
South Kensington:
sections through nave
and aisles, *c.*1876

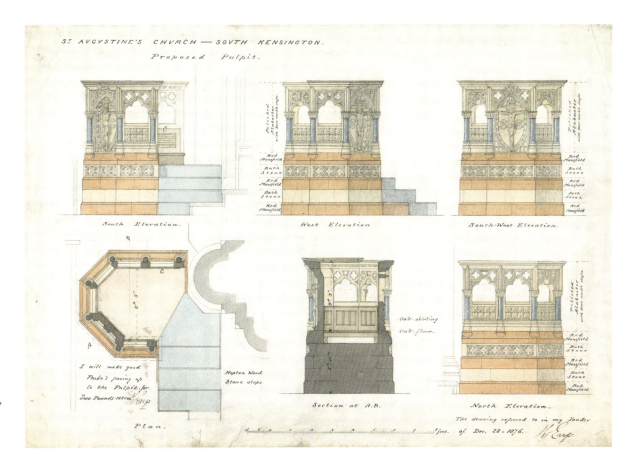

159
St. Augustine's Church,
South Kensington:
pulpit, 28 December
1876

porches of the church, denying any distant prospect of the great frontispiece and belfry and causing the front of the church to sit, not against an anticipated narrow street of low-lying terraces running south-easterly, but at an entirely anomalous angle to a great boulevard on a northward axis towards the park. An economical parsonage was added, to Butterfield's design, in the mews behind the east end in 1881, when Chope was obliged to leave the original house near the centre of the parish at Hereford Square, where development was proceeding in full force.

Like the masterpieces of Ravenna and the Venice lagoon, the power of the design came from concordance, from the field of animation and not its components. It is inside and out composed of so many incidents so scrupulously resonant of one another and so ingrained in the fabric as a whole that it was effectively without incident at all. Spatially, the greatest effect comes from the way the huge blind walls and low aisles, under a continuous 70-foot roof ridge, turn choir and nave into a shaded vault above which rise two celestial tiers of arcaded bright

clerestory and patterned roof. The two essential distinct moments are at the pulpit of layered stones, no finer than those in the columns and walls but topped with a hand-carved and pierced alabaster frieze of the Crucifixion, and in contemplation of the huge tile-painted Adoration of the Magi in the reredos, brought to life by Alexander Gibbs. Screens of wonderful wrought-iron filigree were added by Butterfield at the time of consecration in 1886; and a glass mosaic narrative of Butterfield's devising was gradually inserted into the slate tablets, foils and roundels of aisles and architraves, symbolising prophetic and foundational events in the history of Christ's Church, like those of the Margaret Street and Keble Chapel murals. Many were added posthumously in a realistic palette and manner antithetical to Butterfield's, beginning a sequence of internal 'enhancements' by which this modern masterpiece of decorative integrity and material economy descended into incoherence and vulgarity.

St Augustine's was for many years the landmark liturgical church in the westward environs of central

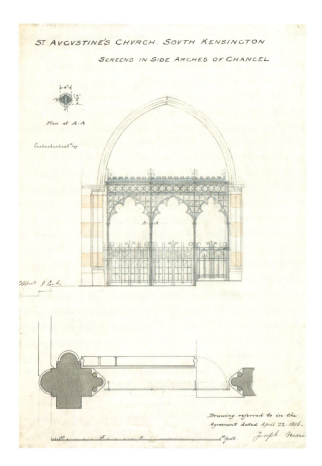

160
St Augustine's Church,
South Kensington:
screens in side arches
of chancel, 1886

collecting a photograph for the vast studio library he maintained to provide reference points for his own designs (fig.161), and finding it much more satisfying and unified than the works of William Burges which he had set out to see.[15] Echoes of Butterfield resound in his own Trinity Church in Boston, Massachusetts, designed and built through the same years as Queen's Gate; and the same delight in a clear plan carried out with savagely beautiful logic pervades Richardson's approach to the great Allegheny County Courthouse in Pennsylvania, whose designs would begin immediately upon his return.

The location of the church typified the growing segregation of London into sectors dedicated to particular levels of income and deportment. The new South Kensington bore few signs of the urban collisions described by W.J.E. Bennett when, arriving not far away as vicar of Pimlico in 1843, he had been shocked to find the different quarters of his parish mingling 'all that was sumptuous and beautiful with all that was low, wretched, and foul'.[16] It also exemplified the open condition of suburban expansion both in London and other large British towns: a lower overall density and a wider pattern of distribution than in any comparable industrial nation, with a far greater proportion of new structures designed for one or two discrete households. It made ease of movement on a neighbourhood level essential, so that whole sections appeared with a streetscape along which the privileged could pass safely and without shock to their sensitivities: the walling off of property for one purpose from that of another, the widening, structuring and cleansing of carriageway and pavement, the management of dust, clamour, dung and detritus, and the confinement of street sellers' stalls and carts to designated zones.

London. Chope's innovative enthusiasm for choral services and congregational singing won it, for a time, its intended place in London's cultural life: it became a choice site for fashionable weddings; Christmas carols were first collected, written and published there; oratorios were performed; visits to its famous Christmas and Easter decorations were announced in the press; and the church's many seasonal performances of Dickens's *A Christmas Carol* were immensely popular. But its financial position in a tiny parish composed largely of seasonal residents and their household caretakers was precarious.

Some critics found the effects most uncomfortable. In his later editions of *London Churches,* the writer T. Francis Bumpus thought it 'painfully aggressive', but many architects of the emerging generation disagreed, seeing it pointing to paths that might lead them forward from the Gothic revival.[14] Among them was the American H.H. Richardson, who visited in the summer of 1882,

NOTES

1. 'O Lord, save the state' is among the suffrages for evening prayer in Anglican Books of Common Prayer from 1662 to our own time.
2. 'The Bishop of London on the Parochial System', *Church Builder*, January 1863, p.19.
3. Anthony Trollope, *The Way We Live Now*, Chapman & Hall, London, 1875, first appearing in monthly instalments in February 1874.

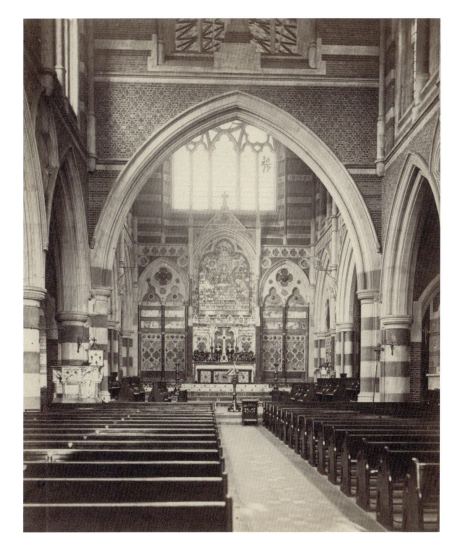

Queens Gate   South Kensington S. W.

4. The fullest account of the Newbury church project is the report from the consecration, in the *Berkshire Chronicle*, 21 July 1860.

5. James Thorne, *Handbook to the Environs of London*, John Murray, London, 1876, vol.1, pp 273 and 275.

6. The account of the Hitchin church project is based primarily on reports in the *Hertfordshire Mercury*, 21 May 1864, and *The Builder*, June 1865.

7. Report of the St Alban's diocesan education meeting at Hitchin, *Hertfordshire Mercury*, 14 and 21 June 1873.

8. Among sources used to reconstruct this history, note Roy Tricker, *St Cross Clayton: A History and Guide*, published by the parish in 1988; *Engineer and Architect's Journal*, 1 July 1865; John Higson, *Historical and Descriptive Notes of Droylsden, Past and Present*, privately printed, Manchester, 1859, pp 118–20; *Ashton Weekly Reporter*, 21 March 1857; and *Manchester Guardian*, 18 June 1874.

9. The account of the Penarth project draws on reports in the *Cardiff and Merthyr Guardian*, 9 June 1865, and *Cardiff Times*, 14 September 1866; correspondence of the Plymouth Estate in the Glamorgan County Records Office; and *Top Church*, a history and guide published in booklet form by the parish.

10. Gillian Clarke, 'Top Church', as published by permission of the author in Kevin J. Gardner (ed.), *Building Jerusalem: Elegies on Parish Churches*, Bloomsbury, London and New York, 2016, p.43.

11. *The Builder*, 21 November 1863. The history is fully recorded in minutes, correspondence, annual reports and other records of the hospital board and its building committee in Hampshire County Archives. See also Barbara Carpenter Turner, *A History of the Royal Hampshire County Hospital*, Phillimore, Winchester, 1986.

12. Halsey Ricardo, 'William Butterfield', *Architectural Review*, July 1900, p.259.

13. The design for St Augustine's, South Kensington, seems to have begun in 1865–7 for a somewhat different projected site. A drawing marked '5. West Elevation', torn from a larger sheet and gifted by the RIBA to the Metropolitan Museum in New York, shows a section through the vestibule and elevation of the west front, on a plot which slopes upwards to the south. See George L. Hersey, *High Victorian Gothic: A Study in Associationism*, Johns Hopkins University Press, Baltimore, 1972, p.124.

14. T. Francis Bumpus, *London Churches, Ancient and Modern*, T.W. Laurie, London, 1907.

15. See Mrs Schuyler van Rensselaer, *Henry Hobson Richardson and His Works*, Houghton Mifflin, Boston, 1888, p.28 et passim. Richardson's last visit to London was in 1882, when he would have collected or ordered the photograph of the church at Queen's Gate.

16. W.J.E. Bennett, 'Preface', *Sermons Preached at St Barnabas, Pimlico, in the Octave of the Consecration*, W.J. Cleaver, London, 1850, p.xiii.

161 (above)
St Augustine's Church, South Kensington: interior view looking east, *c*.1882

162 (below)
Postcard view by Charles Martin of Queen's Gate, South Kensington, *c*.1900

COAL AND COTTON, BRICK AND STONE

St Augustine's Church, Penarth

St Augustine's Church, Penarth

St Augustine's Church, Penarth;
St Cross Church, Clayton
also overleaf

St Cross Church, Clayton

St Cross Church and School, Clayton

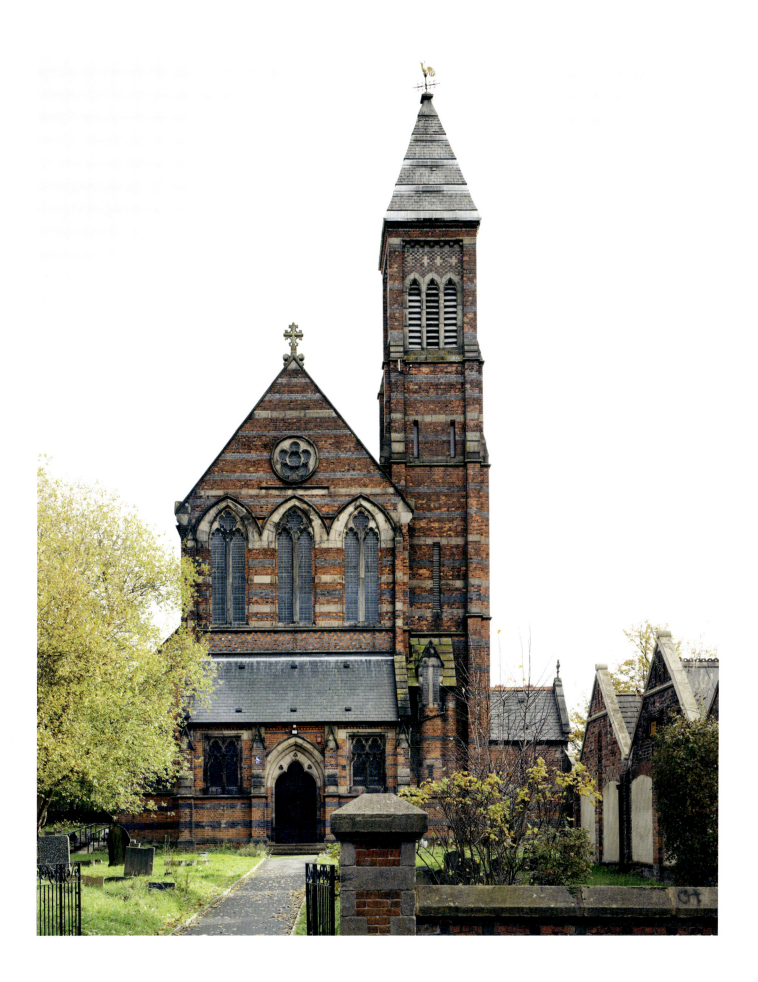

CHAPTER 14

THE CHURCH *as* CIVIC LANDMARK, 1870–96

YEARS OF JUBILEE

Look at it this way. It's to celebrate the fiftieth year of the reign of Queen Victoria, – yes: but at the same time, and far more, it's to celebrate the completion of fifty years of Progress. National Progress, without precedent in the history of mankind! . . . Compare England now, compare the world, with what it was in 1837. It takes away one's breath![1]

S O WROTE GEORGE GISSING in celebrating fifty years of perceived progress in one of the first great novels of London's suburban life, expressing a general sense that the world was getting better, and a darker sense that the way we live now had divorced people from their moral anchors. Some of the advances were real and measurable: there were 1.25 million paupers in the census of 1841; 0.75 million in a population twice as large in 1876; 28,000 committals for serious offences on average in the years from 1841 to 1851; 16,000 in 1876. And though the matchgirl strikes and police actions against socialists drew much attention in the latter decades of the century, the existence of labour agitation in itself seemed to hold out some promise of amelioration; hygiene and policing of the streets of the great towns had markedly improved; literacy had become widespread; lives were lived longer; and such improving institutions as the Young Men's Christian Association (YMCA), the Workers' Educational Association (WEA), the university extension system, libraries and workingmen's clubs were quietly appearing alongside the parade of town halls, insurance offices, banks and law courts now monumentalising the urban landscape with symbols of the hegemony of money interests and civic order.

But in many ways, the most marked change was not in the realities of life but in habits of mind. Trollope, in *The Way We Live Now*, offers perhaps the boldest satire on what he called the 'dishonesty' of an age in which social distress and moral corruption were hidden behind an accelerating belief in the triumph of progress and an unprecedented confidence that, through systematic enquiry, the problems of society could be eradicated by finding scientific means to identify and ameliorate them.[2]

A list of 'current works' the RIBA president offered in November 1870 does indeed 'take away one's breath':

> The Foreign Office, the India Office, the Home and Colonial Offices, the London University, the Royal Academy, the Learned Societies' Building at Burlington House, the South Kensington Buildings, the Albert hall, the Albert memorial, the projected . . . Natural History Museum, the Law Courts, the Thames Embankments and the new streets, the City markets, the City Library and Museum, the Holborn Viaduct, the Midland Railway Station, St Thomas's Hospital, the six Poor-law Hospitals, the colleges at Oxford and at Cambridge, the Glasgow University . . . the Liverpool Exchange and Public Offices, the Manchester Town Hall and Exchange, the Town Halls at Rochdale, Salford, Bradford, Chester, and half a dozen other large cities . . . the many Asylums and other such edifices all over the country.[3]

This is a portrait of the fabric of a new society, its urban institutions working at a new scale, and its civic culture – even in smaller towns – demanding a metropolitan gravitas for built works that represented its public life and services.

A number of signal works mark Butterfield's efforts to insert the Church into these new civic landscapes, and they balance a jubilee grandeur with a sense of weight, permanence and severe beauty that could be seen, in studied counterpoint to *The Way We Live Now*, as landmarks on the path towards a new age of integrity to which their author looked forward. They share some aspects in common. They are almost entirely in stone. They

seat some 800, extending to 1000 with open space. They are equipped with western passages and double points of entry. There are open voids or cloisters for overflow congregations, and choirs suitable for oratorio and cantata. Large vestries and sacristies look to congregational rule and a small college of clergy and choristers. Above all, they landmark their vicinities, on the street and from a distance, with a towering profile and, even in the most confined sites, a marked approach or precinct. Each is imprinted with a distinctive character quite unlike the other; but the threads and echoes passing between their details and disposition constitute a common monumental language open to endless variation.

Two took the modest and disorderly parish churches of small market towns in transformation and rebuilt them at a scale, efficiency and dignity that made them the centrepieces of the life and landscape of these changing communities. One of these was at the busiest junction in the national railway system, at Rugby. Here Butterfield raised, over more than twenty years, his final and once most readily acknowledged masterwork, in the form of a new wide-girthed stone church that folded under its monumental wings the entire nave and tower of the old parish church, architecture of no significance but some antiquity that was retained at his urging to preserve, as he writes so fondly in his handwritten proposal, 'a memory of our village life'.[4] The other was at Chipping Barnet, whose economy as the first coach port out of London to the north gradually gave way to the terraced 'villas' and grammar schools of a 'country suburb', so that the memorably rowdy crossroads became the sober precinct of a majestic Butterfield symphony in flint and chequered sandstone.

A third towering stone landmark appeared in a country suburb for the villas of merchant and industrial grandees prospering as the small port of Belfast turned with astonishing rapidity into one of the largest cities of the empire, its wealth built on linen and shipbuilding. Starting soon after the Irish Church was disestablished, high on a slope above the lough, it was built in banded tiers of red and white locally cut stone, sized, laid and bonded into near-geological composite and strata.

It carved a leonine presence in a composition of utter straightforwardness on to the developing suburban landscape of east Belfast, but shaped within – in its nave arcade, huge semi-cloistered porches, bold stone banding, hyper-scaled detail and stunning western arch, which is centre-buttressed with a slender column of polished black marble – an evocation of the spatial grandeur and atmospherics of Tintern and Rievaulx, rendered with the scrupulously Protestant austerity of tone and decoration required of the new Church of Ireland.

In the same Jubilee epoch of material optimism Butterfield was called to two remote civic projects that became his best-known later works. First was the cathedral in Adelaide, abandoned when it was to be in brick on the city grid in 1847, but now transposed into stone and on to a commanding site above the city centre, where in much-adapted form it became and remains the principal landmark of the South Australian capital. Second was a new invitation from the commanding figure of Bishop Moorhouse, recently appointed to Melbourne, for the largest and most conspicuous and time-consuming work of his career, in replacing the cathedral of St Paul at the city's transport hub. As Butterfield left that project in despair after ten years of dissension and dissatisfaction came the astonishing call to complete St Ninian's Episcopal cathedral in Perth, the first and fondest of his great town churches and, for the few short years before others were invited to ravage it with improvement, surely his most powerful.

'THE TOWN CHURCH': RUGBY

Where the giant sons of labour
Gathering, swarming, work, and wive,
Neighbour pressing close on neighbour,
In their huge, still widening hive;
Where, in haste which never endeth,
Mammon on his path doth plod;
There, a cry to Heaven ascendeth –
'Build, oh build, the House of God'
     – John Moultrie, 'Song of the Rugby
     Church-Builders', 1854[5]

In 1870, during a working visit to Rugby School, Butterfield was asked by John Moultrie, poet and vicar of the parish church, to survey the site of the old church with the intent of replacing it with an entirely new one that would stand as Rugby's 'Town Church', mother church of a rapidly growing urban parish and the moral centre of a community slowly being swallowed up in the mean streets, foul air and unnameable vices of a burgeoning shipping and trading centre that Dickens described four years before, in a famous tale, as 'Mugby Junction'. Moultrie had by then built two new churches to absorb the vast expansion of the town's population; but he began in the 1830s by expanding the old parish church, adding a south aisle in iron, to escape the constraints of a nave filled with private boxed pews, and galleries for the school. He was the first to acknowledge that the result was neither solemn, nor pleasing, nor easy to maintain, and was determined to start the campaign for a new church. When Butterfield's report arrived in 1870 his proposition was entirely unexpected, putting forward a plan in which the old tower and nave would be preserved within a larger church. Construction began in 1875 and proceeded slowly, with even Butterfield's favoured builder, Joseph Parnell of Rugby (who was one of its churchwardens), complaining of the architect's exhaustively studied attention to the decorative detail.[6] It was largely finished, its interior in a mix of Bath and Staffordshire red stone, with a 'quasi-transept' standing in for the great entry tower on the north-east, by 1878. Moultrie had since died from his service in a smallpox epidemic, and the old nave, as a second north aisle, was named in his honour. The recession of aisles to the north builds a wonderful sense of being almost lost in space, while the fold of roof upon roof it produces on the street front softens the scale in the townscape.

In 1894 a gift from a local banking family of £10,000 sufficed to complete tower and vestry, and a further donation brought in bells. By now, Butterfield's health was weak, his office minimal and his powers diminishing, but with the base of the tower built, and the core of the design long established, he was able to adjust and guide the project to its conclusion. By 1896, the entire

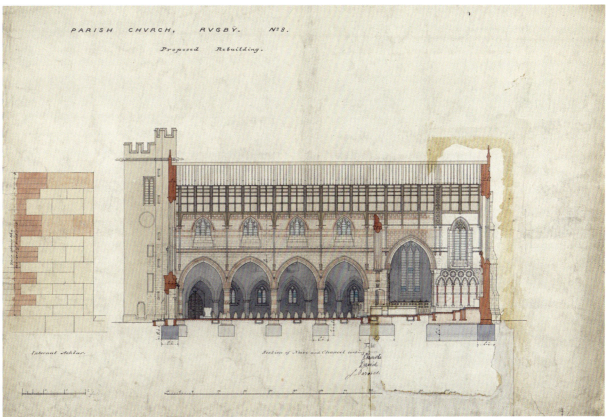

163

Rugby Parish Church: rebuilding – north elevation, *c.*1874

164

Rugby Parish Church: rebuilding – section of nave and chancel looking north, *c.*1874, additions from 1890

programme was complete, the chancel refined, the vestry added, with two answering peals of bells, a magnificent organ and an east end at once lavish and restrained, poetic and rational. It was Butterfield's last great work, and for many years it was recognised also as his finest, the drawings shown to represent him in the RIBA's 100th-anniversary exhibition, and it is the church that Ricardo seems to have in mind when, following a magnificent photograph from the north-east, he writes: 'The resolution to be true and faithful to the uttermost burns through every line . . . it charges his forms with grave steadfastness, the passion of it endues them with romance, with poetry, and the mystery that come from high aspirations . . . a character that belongs to our time and to our needs.'[7]

'THE ANCIENT AND THE MODERN': BARNET

In the words of a *Saturday Review* reporter in the late 1870s:

> The town of High or 'Chipping' Barnet, in old coaching days the first stage out of London on the great North road, has, within the last few years, been somewhat roused from the sleep which naturally fell on it after the withdrawal of the hundred and fifty coaches that drew up daily at the door of the 'Red Lion' . . . and the condition of Barnet has undergone a happy revolution. At present the town has a railway and a station of its own. The church has been reconstructed, almost rebuilt, under the care and from the designs of Mr Butterfield; and a very picturesque tower of flint and stone, worked in squares, after a fashion of which there are ancient, though rare, examples in the district, has been added on the south-west side of the nave.[8]

The small early medieval parish church at Chipping Barnet had been rebuilt in 1420 in a simplified Perpendicular manner, incorporating its tower into the body of the church, and then subject to successive improvements from the

165
Rugby Parish Church: interior view looking east, photograph by E.H. Speight, *c.*1896

166
Rugby Parish Church: view from the south-east, photograph by E.H. Speight, *c.*1896

167 (above)
Church of St John the
Baptist, Barnet: view
from the south-west,
postcard, *c.*1900

168 (below)
Postcard view of High
Barnet showing the Church
of St John the Baptist from
the east, *c.*1900

eighteenth century through to the 1830s. By 1870, when Butterfield surveyed it, the east end had fallen into dilapidation, and a general programme of reconstruction, focusing on a rebuilt choir and chancel and an extension to the south, partly to accommodate the pupils of a newly revived Tudor grammar school, was agreed. Butterfield's initial scheme took the same approach as Rugby: folding the old nave into a second north aisle and retaining the western tower by incorporating it within the enlarged structure, opening its lower stage as a baptistery within the narthex and entering it through a new and very substantial porch. The north elevation (fig.169) shows virtually all of the windows being rebuilt or replaced, but Butterfield carefully retaining the early fifteenth-century character, modelling them on those he had studied at Teversham.

In the course of preparation a windfall of £10,000 appeared from the proceeds of a land trust in the City, and a more ambitious solution was developed in which the same general scheme was applied, but with an entirely new and much larger tower added to the south, outside the footprint of nave and western passage, as a baptistry. The interior was enriched with marbles in the sanctuary and with a modern arcade of four bays in sprung rhythm along the south of the nave, capped with a high clerestory of irregular windows that bewildered the dilettanti but were in fact quite evidently drawn from a mix of forms and tracery in the older fabric. Inside, this unfamiliar rhythm, the shift in scale and style from the fifteenth-century north arcade to the distinctly modern one on the south, and the introduction of brick amid the red Mansfield and pale Bath stone – noticeable on the aisle wall in the section (fig.170) – all prompted the quip that Butterfield had mingled 'the ancient and the modern . . . in wild confusion'.

In 1878–80, Butterfield returned with ambitious steps to complete the chancel, adding stained glass to the great east window of the Ascension, with a Majesty in the wheel tracery above, and a high painted-tile reredos of the Nativity, both executed by Heaton & Butler. They both illustrate his firmly stated belief that neither perspective nor expressive

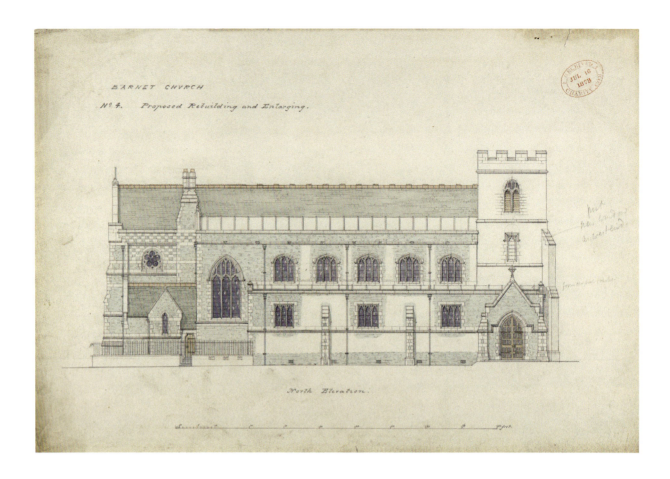

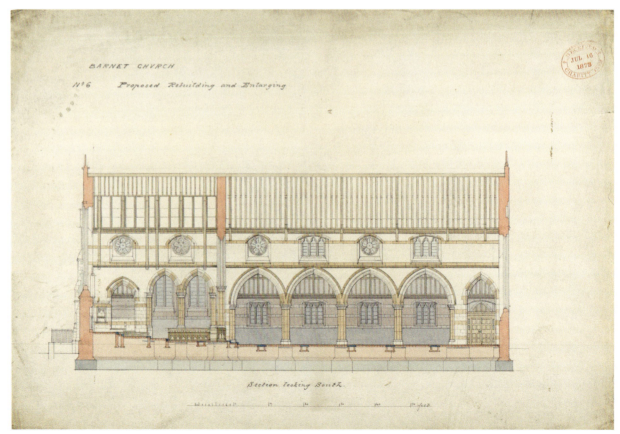

169
Church of St John
the Baptist, Barnet:
rebuilding and
enlargement – north
elevation, *c.*1872

170
Church of St John
the Baptist, Barnet:
rebuilding and
enlargement – section
looking south, *c.*1873

facial features are appropriate to glass and tile paintings, which should be regarded not as paintings on canvas but as mosaics in which 'a certain stiffness and rigidity' are desirable to lend legibility from the great distance at which they are seen: here it is over 40 feet to the east wall from the first step up from the nave, into a choir and transept of cathedral scale. The Lincolnshire architect John Charles Treylan was engaged in 1893 to redo the heating system, adding a vent in the form of a fleche, to revise the south transept for a memorial chapel, and to provide elaborately carved new fittings throughout the church that were magnificently incompatible with the aesthetic of simplification that Butterfield had established. The new tower anchored the view along the highway entering London from the north-west, while, once the middle row of shops was removed in 1891, the east end of the church took a most impressive place – filling, with a leafy churchyard behind, the entire triangular crossing on the crest of 'High Barnet' that was the centre of the town. With the flint mass of its walls showing a rainbow of colour and the wonderfully complicated recessive composition of its east end, skewed slightly to the line of the Great North Road, it closed the vista for those arriving from London as the road rose to the heights and took its turn to the north-east.

171

St Mark's Church, Dundela, Belfast: view from the south, photograph by Robert John Welch, *c.*1883

'THE LION ON THE HILL': BELFAST

The garden estate of Sydenham was developed in the 1850s as a spacious cluster of villas for the well-to-do above the railway that ran on the south-eastern shore of Belfast Lough towards Bangor. Named after a newly fashionable country suburb of London, the new suburb lay largely on the north side of the old Holywood Road in the middle of a wide area of country estates that had long been the haunt of the Anglican elite, with the manors of Stormont, Norwood and Belmont, and the bishop's palace. By 1870, at the time the Church of England was disestablished in Ireland, an Anglican congregation was meeting in a coach house and school, the city was rapidly spilling into Strandtown just to the west, with distilleries and rows of working-class housing, and a large plot of highly visible land on the upland side of the road was obtained to build a church. Constructed largely of red sandstone quarried nearby at Dundonald, its tower, nave, porches and aisles were completed by Butterfield in a first rapid campaign.[9] The church, establishing the new parish of St Mark's, Dundela, opened in 1876, with a temporary east wall set back into the future chancel arch, and the precinct left wild. The first known drawing (fig.172) has no indication of the thick banding of red and pale stone that would come to characterise the interior, but the essential features are there: a memorably delicate buttressed arch that supports the tower at the west end and screens the bright cloister behind it, and the two porches stretching out behind the tower to create long entrances that set the austere mood of the church and establish another of Butterfield's great western passages.

With the addition of a rectory in the field to the south, not to his design, Butterfield returned to the project in 1878 and 1883–4 with designs for a long perimeter wall and carriage and walkway entrances. Then in 1889 the family of the linen and shipbuilding magnate Sir William Ewart, who had steered and funded the project as churchwarden, decided to raise the east end in his memory. Butterfield expanded his initial plan to add a north transept of the same cathedral height and

172
St Mark's Church,
Dundela, Belfast:
sections through the
nave looking west and
through the chancel
looking east, 1875

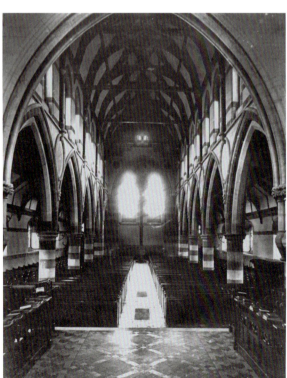

173 (left)
St Mark's Church,
Dundela: interior
photograph recording
completion, looking
west from the choir
to the divided eastern
arch of the tower, 1891

174 (right)
St Mark's Church,
Dundela: interior
photograph recording
completion, looking
east from the second
bay of the nave, 1891

PERTH CATHEDRAL.

North Elevation

West Elevation

175
St Ninian's Cathedral,
Perth: elevations for
completion phase, with
comparative elevation
of 1848 twin-tower
proposal, *c.*1888

dimensions as the organ chamber in the original
scheme, moving the organ to that side, with a vestry
and porch behind it, and adding sittings to the
south. Figurative ornament, high colour, screens
and crosses were all anathema to the new Church
of Ireland, so that Butterfield was constrained
to find a palette of tones and a vocabulary of
symbolic and aesthetic expression largely through
the striations of stonework and structure, and by
managing the fall of light and shifts in scale. The
result is extraordinarily unified and effective, with
stones cut and laid to an informal but determined
pattern inside and out, and the great tile reredos
housing the sacred monogram establishes itself as
a focal point simply through scale and geometry.
Completed in 1891, as the population of Belfast
reached a quarter of a million and was about to

double in the next ten years, this was in effect, as it
signalled so clearly in its scale and manner, a city
cathedral for the dwindling minority of adherents to
the Church of Ireland, and earned the popular name
– in homage both to the attributes of St Mark and
to the leonine power with which it raises its tawny
head to gaze from a crest across the lough below –
'the Lion on the Hill'.

CATHEDRALS NORTH AND SOUTH:
PERTH, ADELAIDE, MELBOURNE

Perth had grown quietly in the generation since
1850, when it was a town of fewer than 24,000, to
one of over 37,000, with a flourishing hinterland
in the diocese, much of the growth coming from

Butterfield proposed the boldest of all his towers, stretching the width of the nave and mounting 200 feet, to assert the presence of the Episcopal Church in the city landscape and the force of its protective grandeur, thrusting the mighty fortress of one kingdom into counterpoint with the passing parades of national arms that served another. It stalled as questions were raised about the ability of the ground to support the spire, and the tower was capped for the time being. Butterfield acknowledged that the little belfry at the crossing was now too small to complement the western spire and regretted that the engineering did not allow him to change its proportions. The reorientation of the porch to lie under a towering semi-transept at the south-west corner effectively filled a flying buttress added to strengthen the support of the tower he planned but failed to achieve. Inside it produced a cloister and narthex of extraordinary grandeur that quite offset what some had seen in the truncated church as an overemphasis on the vista towards the altar. It also presented a genuine frontispiece for the church to present to the street and allowed the west window to sink low enough to show off the blossom in its tracery head at enormous scale.

New leadership in the 1890s, determined to bring the worship and physical character of St Ninian's closer to the very orthodoxies of the English Church that its founders had fought so hard to stand apart from, engaged John Loughborough Pearson and his sons for projects of completion in which Butterfield's great church, so stringently tuned to one key, emerged entirely discordant, adorned with finials and tourelles, even the short capped tower cut down to nothing, his marvellous reredos installed to honour Bishop Torry replaced with a rococo baldacchino, and his delicately melodious chancel arch pulled down entirely.

For Adelaide, Butterfield returned in 1868 to the project of a cathedral first mooted in humble brick for the grid of an infant provincial capital twenty years before but now reconceived to lie on the prosperous mansion terraces of a hillside just to the north, looking down on a city of over 60,000. For Melbourne the first designs appeared ten years later, for a great metropolitan cathedral on the busy

176
St Ninian's Cathedral, Perth: view from the north-east, as completed, photograph by T. & M. Jackson, *c*.1890

177
St Ninian's Cathedral, Perth: view from the north-west, photographed *c*.1906

Highland migration and stimulated by dye works and distillers. In 1888, to Butterfield's delight, he was called back to complete his cathedral there, as it gained a new lease of life as a busy urban church and school. By then, the tiny triangle of its precinct was being developed into a tram-lined thoroughfare fronted with a long parade of four-storey tenements. The vision of a great west entry flanked by towers could no longer be realised, and

St. Peter's Cathedral, Adelaide.

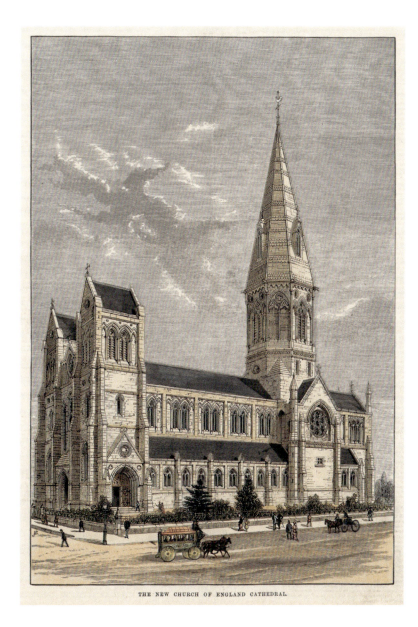

THE NEW CHURCH OF ENGLAND CATHEDRAL.

river bank at the centre of a great city on the cusp of half a million, the second largest in the empire and in its hemisphere. Melbourne's new St Paul's Cathedral, replacing a modest earlier work, would be the largest ecclesiastical work of Butterfield's career, and perhaps the most troubled. Both were regions where Anglicans, though still the largest single denomination, were less than one third of those professing a religious allegiance; but there was a sense in which, unlike Belfast or Perth, and much like Fredericton, a prominent cathedral of the Church of England was a matter of civil dignity and provincial pride, and the projects were supported by many non-Anglicans with civic interests and the enhancement of the metropolitan fabric in mind.[10]

The marvellously complex, soaring and shadowy eastern sector of Adelaide's St Peter's Cathedral, based on the church of St Lubentius on the river Lahn near the German town of Limburg, was completed by 1876: choir, chancel and transepts, with one bay of the nave as a promissory note, in much the same approach to phasing as at Perth in 1850. Although the nave and western towers were eventually completed in rough emulation of Butterfield's design, the wonderful high chamber of his chancel – a rhapsody in shadows, shafts of sunlight and plain masonry – was soon softened into an apsidal end.

Butterfield's design for Melbourne arrived in November 1878. Like Adelaide, it is geared to sharp sunlight and the shaping of cool space, and it is raised on a substantial platform above the street. The project went wrong as soon as the drawings were opened to view, with an immediate request from the committee to rotate the design on to a north–south axis, rather than following the orientation of the old St Paul's, so that the west front now faced the bridge, storehouses and service railways of the Yarra waterfront. As the project proceeded, it lost and gained bays in the nave, chapter houses and chanceries; the stonework never matched Butterfield's elaborately written requirements; the architect resigned and was re-engaged twice, and in 1888 left the project entirely. Though the western towers were missing, an oddly sited and roughly assembled but wonderfully moving and convincingly modern evocation of the great abbeys of the Scottish Borders had meanwhile been rising from the ground, and in 1891 it was consecrated. That very year the boom decades of Australia's gold rush ended with a crash and a long depression from which it would take over a generation to recover. The western completion of Adelaide and the addition of the towers to Melbourne were both long delayed, and neither cathedral emerged in quite the form Butterfield would have approved.

NOTES

1. George Gissing, *In the Year of Jubilee*, D. Appleton & Co., New York, 1895, p.51.
2. Anthony Trollope, describing the reasons for writing *The Way We Live Now* in the final pages of his autobiography, explains that it was to portray 'a certain class of dishonesty, dishonesty magnificent in its proportions . . . so rampant and so splendid that there seems to be reason for fearing that men and women will be taught to feel that dishonesty, if it can become splendid, will cease to be abominable': Trollope, *An Autobiography*, Dodd Mead & Co., New York, 1905, p.307.
3. *The Architect*, 12 November 1870.
4. Butterfield's proposal of 1870 is in the records for the project in the parish archives of the Warwickshire County Record Office, which include accounts, minutes and correspondence through to the completion in 1896, providing, with the regular reports appearing in the *Rugby Advertiser*, the principal sources from which my account of Butterfield's Rugby town church project has been drawn.
5. John Moultrie, in his collection *Altars, Hearths and Graves*, Hamilton, Adams & Co., London, 1854, p.11.
6. See note 4 of this chapter, above. See also 'Church Extension in Rugby', *Church Builder*, January 1880.
7. Halsey Ricardo, 'William Butterfield', *Architectural Review*, August 1900, p.23.
8. *Saturday Review*, 19 April 1879. The account of the church at Barnet also draws largely upon documents in the parish archive at the Hertfordshire County Records Centre; news reports in the *Herts Advertiser*; *The Architect*, 12 July 1873; *Church Portrait Journal*, May 1878; *Building News*, 19 September 1879; *Barnet Press*, 26 March 1881; and Emily S. Judge, 'A Rural Retreat', *The Sunday Review*, vol.9, 1884, pp 150–58.
9. The account is developed from plans, drawings, photographs and files that remain with the parish and the extensive working drawings and other documents in the Public Record Office of Northern Ireland. See also *Northern Whig*, 14 October 1876; *Building News*, 27 October 1876; and J.C .Beckett, *The Lion on the Hill: A History of St Mark's Church, Dundela, Belfast, 1878–1998*, Minprint, Belfast, 1998.
10. I have chosen to treat both Australian projects very lightly and to show them – as I did for another distant site at Fredericton – through the coloured perspectives by which they were viewed in context and prospect by local artists. Butterfield never saw the sites, nor steered the projects through to his satisfaction, though both had (and Melbourne retained) passages of astonishing grandeur and subtlety. I have used many original sources in newspaper, drawing and photograph collections; but both projects are very well documented in modern histories, Adelaide in the astonishingly scholarly catalogue of the South Australia State Library. It is also touched upon in G.A. Bremner's *Imperial Gothic: Religious Architecture and High Anglican Culture in the British Empire 1840–1870*, Yale University Press, New Haven, Connecticut, 2013. Paul Thompson's studies of Adelaide and St Paul's, Melbourne, are summarised in his two articles titled 'William Butterfield's Australian Cathedrals', *Country Life*, 9 September 1971, pp 622–4, and 16 September 1971, pp 686–9.

CHAPTER 15

IMPERIAL LONDON
and its ORBIT, 1872–92

THE WORKINGMAN'S TICKET: HIGHGATE, FINSBURY, TOTTENHAM, EDMONTON

FROM 1875 TO 1884 a portfolio of new Butterfield churches unfolded along the suburban rail lines as they moved north into the new dormitories of London. Most were tuned to difficult sites and great economy; but even where less constrained, at Tottenham and Enfield, the results were tempered, with inexpensive and readily worked materials deployed for ornamental purposes, and visible profiles that never marked one church out for the rich against another for the poor. They started on the boundaries of inner London on the basis of missions put in place to reach the families of carters, cabbies and other poorer families driven out to new lodgings in Dartmouth Park, where new pockets of settlement had grown up, mixing these lodgings with white-collar villas.

The new church at Dartmouth Park grew out of an effort started by the congregation of St Anne's, Brookfield, a chapel of ease in the large parish of Highgate, who had opened a mission and school in the late 1860s to reach a 'large, shifting, and rapidly increasing population, some part of it of the very poorest type' that had grown up almost overnight in open grasslands east of Hampstead Heath, known at first as 'Highgate New Town'.[1] The appeal pamphlets (fig.180) describe a whole new town of substantial houses, to all appearances 'respectable; but notwithstanding the apparent absence of the outward symptoms of poverty, several families occupy a single house; one small house . . . was found to contain 27 persons'. Nothing makes the housing shortage of a London flooded with newcomers and driving its existing inhabitants

PROPOSED : NEW : FREE : CHURCH : AT : BROOKFIELD.
DESIGNED : BY : Mr : BUTTERFIELD.
1870.

and subscriptions initiated. Work began in 1873 for the first phase of nave and aisles, seating over 600; it was roofed in the autumn of 1874 and ready for consecration in 1875. A sudden dispute over the presence of a cross in the temporary reredos led to Butterfield's resignation, but the greater dispute was over the very admittance of the poor and especially poor children for whom St Mary's had been built. Nevertheless, by 1879, services were so popular among the poor that a low, shallow chancel was added, by another, to the displeasure of some critics; but it is curiously unobtrusive, leaving Butterfield's great arch to form the climax of the church. Though the tower was never constructed, the high roof and wide-windowed clerestory served for many years as a landmark to south, west and east.

Perhaps the unstated objection was about providing something so splendid for a class considered so undeserving. As T. Francis Bumpus noted, it would, if completed to plan, have been the finest and most conspicuous of Butterfield's brick churches for London, with a tower visible for miles;[2] and what he did achieve, at a cost of more than £11,000, has a wonderful spatial grandeur. Narthex, nave and aisles lie on an internal footprint 55 feet by 90. The central arcades open a clear span 25 feet wide, with pointed and deeply grooved arches rising high above great cylindrical shafts of stone, and the crest of the chancel arch rises well into the line of the great clerestory windows. The transcendent effect comes from stripping down to an absence of interruption and delight in restraint. There are only three systems for head tracery, alternating or repeated at different scales; the palette of red and yellow brick punctuated by spots of blue and bands of white stone is maintained inside and out, with the intricate pattern of bonding after the wear of time fusing into a shifting field of pink. The sole point of decoration lies above the chancel arch, constituted by a pair of carved stone discs in low relief and a narrow cornice of figured stone. Taking advantage of an astonishing site to rise entirely into the light, it has softened the busyness and animation of Queen's Gate, Keble and Rugby into a luscious austerity of sky-wrought volume, glow and plane, through an extreme economy of surface incident.

180

'Proposed New Free Church at Brookfield': view from the north-east, detail from cover of fundraising pamphlet, 1870

out of their traditional housing quarters clearer than this picture of lower-middle-class speculator dwellings occupied as soon as they could offer shelter by displaced single labourers and migrant households crammed four or six to a room.

The prime mover was a solicitor, William Ford of Brookfield House, who was also working with Butterfield as patron of his church in Rotherhithe. Land was acquired on a hillside site expected to be scheduled for eventual housing but lying open at the time. The design was in place by 1869, with a park-like setting in mind. It was planned for free seating in a parish where pews and rents were universal, and whose low-church vicar opposed the mingling of the poor. The designs were approved in June 1870

St Clement's was on a sliver of land behind Butterfield's own simple mission hall and Sunday school in a pocket of multistorey tenement lodgings behind the city road, across from the Eagle tavern and just below the wharfside and basin of the Regent's Canal in Finsbury.[3] Completed in 1878, the church was oriented north to south, with north as the liturgical east end. A through path known as Pink Lane ran the length of the church on the 'north' or west side, hard against lodgings rising to the west, with the principal entry at a gabled porch, standing out like a comma below the nave, from which one turned left into a wide western passage, a quiet concourse, indoor and out, that suddenly opened up to a towering nave, like a clearing in a forest of traffic, roofs and walls. Butterfield somehow managed to fit 600 people in, backing the west end into the mission hall and stretching the nave and a north aisle 95 feet on a 40-foot footprint. Choir, sanctuary, vestry and organ chamber fell

into a rectangular plan at the east end, and there was a small second porch across from the entry. His response inside to the narrowness and dark is to draw the eye upwards to the light, pointing the arches sharply, raising the chancel arch into the roof, carrying the ridge line through the entire length of the church, and restricting the timberwork to rafters, so that the expanse of space is interrupted as little as possible, and the light from east, clerestory and high west windows all raised up to a line that cleared the shadows of surrounding roofs. A double bellcote rose above the east window, just high enough to make a landmark from the City Road. The little parish, still coded for poverty on Charles Booth's survey late in the century,[4] became more densely populated as railyards, viaducts and stations squeezed ever more dwellings and services out of the immediate environs of the City, and a virtual new town of Guinness Trust model lodgings for labourers appeared just below the church. The church was obliterated in the Blitz and never replaced.

The course of Butterfield's churches would then move out along the railways to Tottenham and Edmonton, where the orchards and nurseries feeding the markets of the metropolis turned overnight into terraced housing, where speculators fed off the slender incomes of skilled worker and clerical classes; then on to a 'country suburb' of privileged villas on the hill above Enfield, finally reaching open country in the horse pastures of Kingsbury, a hamlet of Brent. There in 1883–4 the last of his compact unpretentious country churches would settle in brick on to a rise in the meadows, with a western bellcote, adding to the edges of London the last of the suite of minimal rural churches in brick that had begun at Landford thirty years before.

In February 1874 a solemn party gathered at Butterfield's church of St Matthias, Stoke Newington, for the funeral of Robert Brett, the surgeon to the poor who had brought it into being and sustained it through a decade of riotous assaults by an 'anti-papist' mob.[5] The cortège then moved out in procession to walk the three cold miles north to Tottenham parish church, whose vicar Alexander Wilson was at its head, with Butterfield – Brett's most intimate friend, who had sat by his deathbed,

All Hallows' Church, Tottenham: view from the south-east, postcard by Charles Martin, *c*.1903

designed his tomb and written his obituary – immediately behind. There, in the enormous public cemetery behind the roughly built and much-degraded twelfth-century church of All Hallows, Brett was laid to rest, beside his wife and three of his children: those working among the poor of the crowded and unhealthy towns of England often died young, and their households were not spared. This was a walk Butterfield made on many Sundays. Tottenham was the home parish of his sister Anne and her husband, Benjamin Helps Starey, who would both be buried there; his nephews William and Augustin Starey would both become curates at the church, and Wilson, vicar since 1870, was the closest companion of Butterfield's later years, when All Hallows' vicarage was his second home. The cemetery behind it, the resting place of so many he loved, is where William Starey would lay first Wilson and then, beside him, on another cold February day in 1900, Butterfield himself.

Brett was laid to rest just as Butterfield's proposals for the improvement of the church reached the Church authorities. Except for a fine brick porch, added about 1500, carrying a pattern of black diapers and a nicely carved stone entry, All Hallows was unusually undistinguished and woefully inadequate for a general population that had grown from well under 10,000 to well over 20,000 in the previous two decades. A tower of uncertain origin had been truncated by a previous

generation, then battlemented and allowed to become little more than a pillar of ivy. The roof of the nave had been lowered long ago; unsightly skylights had appeared; and a gallery had been installed fifty years before when the north aisle was clumsily rebuilt in brick. Side aisles with double-pitched roofs brought in little light, and the whole place, composed mostly of rough-and-ready stonework with draughty windows, was cold, uncomfortable and ill-equipped for the conduct of the liturgy.[6]

Butterfield made a long study before proposing an eastward enlargement that doubled the footprint of the church, extending nave and aisles by a full bay, adding transepts for an organ chamber, sacristy and vestry, extending seating for the boys of the Drapers' Company school, and setting up a new choir and sanctuary behind a brick and stone chancel arch of stunning severity and force.[7] Galleries were removed, and a new superstructure in brick and stone raised the nave up to a clerestory for light and ventilation, under a central roof now steeply pitched to offer that theatre of the lofty soaring above to shelter the lowly that was so critical to Butterfield's idea of faith. The extension to the south aisle was carried out in matching rough stonework, and the large and graceful new window is patterned after tracery and mullions in the existing fabric, so that the whole south wall, though radically extended, looks as if it had always been there, and in much better proportion than it had displayed before. The new work to the east is in fine diapered red brick with wide bands of stone trim, following the palette and lines of the old porch, now gently restored and brought emphatically to light. The same pattern is carried inside, where drama and incident are drawn out of the raw dichromatic vitality of brick against stone and thick against thin, culminating in a chancel arch with a great white cross between two huge foils, and a reredos soon made famous through guidebooks as one of the richest evocations of the gates of heaven.

To the north of Tottenham, straggling along the two miles of road that connected it to Enfield, lay the 2-mile-long ribbon of the village of Edmonton. A fast, cheap rail service arrived in 1872, and the

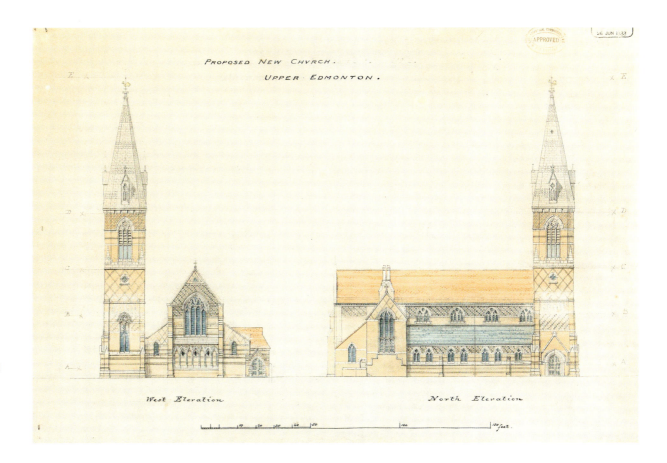

St Mary's Church,
Edmonton: west and
north elevations,
proposal as
approved by Church
Commissioners in
June 1883

population began to increase rapidly, such that,
in the words of one of its curates, 'the quiet old
suburb was suddenly drawn into the whirlpool of
London . . . Fine old houses were sold and pulled
down, while new streets of small, badly built houses
sprang up at the beck of speculating builders, with
no proper supervision from the Local Board; and
typhoid fever and other evils were the natural
consequence'.[8] There were two better-organised
'suburban villages', at either end of the parish,
with 'flagged footpaths and good roads', in which
local boosters took some pride: Upper Edmonton
on the high ground closer to London, and Lower
Edmonton to the north. Between lay a 'wilderness of
cheap housing'. For this village – neither Upper nor
Lower and designated both ways on Butterfield's
drawings – a new vicar, Henry William Burrows,
who had worked with Butterfield at Christ Church,
Albany Street, since 1850, mapped out three new
districts where, in the centre of each, a modest
church and school would be placed, to which a
neighbouring community could grow attached.

One lay along the main thoroughfare of Fore Street,
between the new town's two railway stations, just
east of the great landed estate of Pymmes Park.

Here, Burrows took a portion of land within
a commercial orchard and set up a mission room
fronting the street. He left with the new district
in its infancy in 1882, and the vicarage, in the gift
of St Paul's Cathedral, went to Robert S. Gregory,
one of the sons of the dean, who promptly set up a
permanent church at a much more substantial scale
than Burrows had in mind, giving £3000 of his own
funds to commence it. Dean Gregory had supported
Butterfield's contentious work at Tottenham, which
was also in his gift, and aided another son, Francis,
in building Butterfield's missionary college in the
highlands of Madagascar. Designs were filed in
June 1883 for a subtly patterned brick church with
a 156-foot tower at its north-west corner, set close
to the street front with paths on either side, chancel,
vestries and entry porches. To the noisy and dusty
parade of Fore Street, which was rapidly becoming
the new commercial centre of the parish, and down

deep sloped shelves inside, promised a nave bathed with light. Even in its truncated form of nave and narthex, the church, consecrated in September 1884 and dedicated to St Mary, had over 500 sittings and a choir of thirty-six. It is a capacious and impressive design, which, except for the Sienese civic flourish of the street arcade, is animated almost entirely by its assertive structure and the patterning of its surfaces.

A town hall, swimming baths, public library, Salvation Army citadel and great Independent church all appeared along Fore Street at the same time, and by 1894 the orchards behind were filled with terraced housing. The church therefore took its place among the public facilities and monuments that were everywhere coming to structure the landscape and furnish the lives of dormitory towns for the wage-earning classes. Though a south porch was later added by another hand, no tower would appear; and the church that would have culminated the remarkable quarter-century sequence of Butterfield's gravely pragmatic suburban churches for outer London was left in partial form, and demolished in 1957 for post-war development.

'SUBURBAN BABYLON': ENFIELD

Writing anonymously in the *New Monthly Review* in 1872, Harrison Ainsworth observed:

> As one glides out of any of the great London railway termini, the houses on either hand are seen to gradually diminish in size, and to increase in squalor for a considerable distance. Then, though small, they suddenly assume a cleaner and less unwholesome aspect, as one reaches terraces of more recent erection. Soon afterwards occasional spaces of waste land appear in their midst, the chosen receptacle for broken bottles and old boots. Cabbage gardens and semi-detached houses next come in view, and ere long trim nursery-grounds, succeeded by rows of detached villas, wearing an air of intense respectability about them, bear witness to the fact that one is drawing near to a modern suburb of the great Babylon.[9]

184

St Mary Magdalene's Church and Parsonage, Enfield: view from the south-west, photographed *c.*1890

which a tramway now ran, Butterfield presented two enormous buttresses, projecting 4 feet 6 inches at the base and rising 28 feet high – exactly half the measure of the ridge line. Set within them is a projecting narthex, like that of Hammersmith, here under a sloping roof of stone slabs, walled with a blind arcade of stone, set in relief against bands of brick, with three small, high floriated oculi. The nave and aisles were commenced right away, with a baffled retaining wall at the rear, a wooden vestry shed, and a short porch to the north in place of the entry through the tower. High clerestory double windows, set close to the outer shell, with

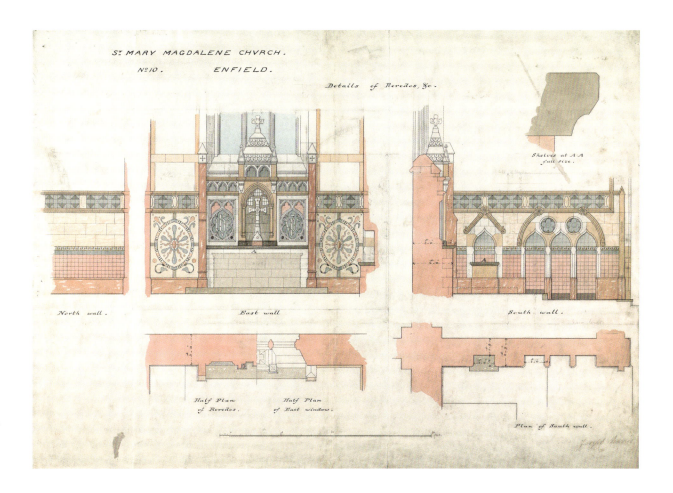

185
St Mary Magdalene's
Church, Enfield:
reredos and other
details, 1883

Enfield had been reached by rail since 1849, stimulating the growth of its Royal Small Arms Factory, which vastly expanded production after the Crimean War, employing 1000 workers by 1866 and 2400 twenty years later. The ordnance factory was at Enfield Lock, and the workers' town grew up to the east of the New River, where speculator terrace housing for London working families also began to appear after a fast new suburban railway with workmen's weekly tickets arrived. On the other side of the river was an entirely different world of bankers' and merchants' villas set among the hilly woodlands of the old royal hunting grounds at Enfield Chase, among them that of Philip Twells, brother of Butterfield's clerical friend Henry, and scion of a great City banking family. The remains of the Chase also began to expand rapidly with the arrival of a second fast rail service in the early 1870s to a terminus just south of it. It was there that Philip's widow, Georgiana, decided to place a new district church in memory of the banker, who had

died in 1880. The site was on the crest of Windmill Hill, a few minutes' walk from the new terminus, and 250 feet above the Thames – the highest point for many miles around, with a good breeze still turning the sails of a wooden mill for the last generation of the local miller's family. It lived alongside the church for a few years before falling into disuse.

Drawings for a church of Kentish rag were prepared by 1881, and St Mary Magdalene's was completed in 1883, with 500 sittings, 50 feet wide, with a 55-foot-high roof over the nave, a chancel of 20 by 16 feet, a tower of 140 feet and a precinct with stabling, coach-house and a very substantial parsonage.[10] Its exterior seems at first reticent, but on lingering the sheer strength of the tower, residing in its fortress-like bulk and visible for miles, begins to lend a forceful original character to the whole. Step inside, and the wide, high side aisles, narrow nave and unusually bowed roof give the body of the church a breadth to match, with a frieze above a high dado carrying the eye along a biblical

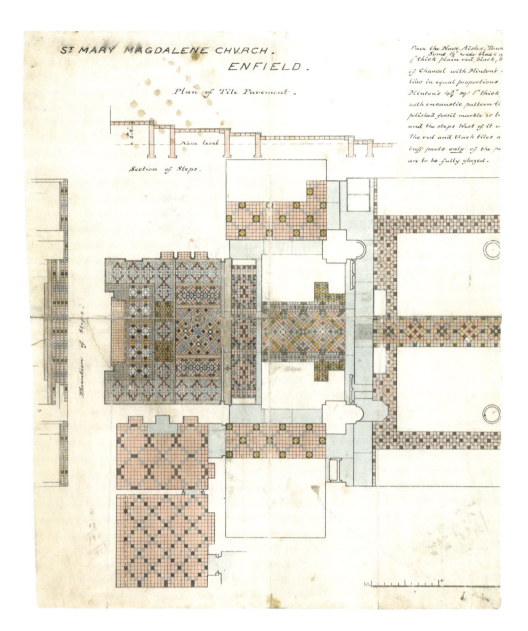

ST MARY MAGDALENE CHVRCH.
ENFIELD.

Plan of Tile Pavement.

Section of Steps.

186
St Mary Magdalene's
Church, Enfield:
plan of tile pavement
beneath the reredos
in the chancel, 1883

narrative in the side windows towards an east end
of extraordinary delicacy, using a complementary
palette of marbles and tile on a limited spectrum
of tones that together rise towards increasing
definition and progress from dark to light and an
earthen pink to the grey-blues of the sky.

The initial reception was mixed. Some were
disappointed to see yet another example of the
extreme simplicity and plainness that was said to
mark Butterfield's later churches. But others saw in
that very straightforwardness the refinement of a
rugged rural character with which 'an ideal country
church' could mark its place in the memory of a

dormitory suburb. The latter view clearly prevailed
among popular opinion, since Butterfield's stone
church – anchoring a vista with its bold tower
rising uninterrupted to the spire above a roof of
vivid red clay tiles – quickly became a much-loved
reminiscence of rural England, voluminously
recorded in painted scenes, souvenir photographs
and picture postcards.

This lofty sector of Enfield was what was known
as an 'outlet' suburb where country villas and lodges
on the model of seasonal and weekend retreats were
introduced as the full-time residence of merchant
families. Within ten years, there were more than a

ST. BARNABAS CHURCH, ROTHERHITHE.

187
Church of St Barnabas,
Rotherhithe: view to
the chancel (which
faces north), published
in *Illustrated London
News*, 6 January 1872

London's docklands in 1883 by William Adams,
the socialist poet. He continues:

By the elaborate system of sub-contracts their
wages have been driven down to 4d, 3d, and
even 2d for the few hours they are employed
. . . Hundreds and hundreds of lives are lost or
ruined by the perilous nature of the work, and
absolutely without compensation. Yet so fierce is
the competition that men are not unfrequently
maimed or even killed in the desperate struggles
at the gates for tickets of employment . . . The
streets and houses of this class are of the lowest
kind – haunts of vice, disease, and death . . . To
see these immense docks, the home of that more
immense machine, British Commerce, crowded
with huge and stately ships, steamers, and
sailors the first in the world, and to watch with
intelligent eyes by what means the colossal work
of loading and unloading them is carried out: this
is to face a sacrificial orgy of human life.[11]

hundred well-staffed 'lodges' on the leafy avenues
north and west of the church, a long row of smaller
detached villas on narrow garden plots leading
north-west, and – just east of the chancel – two
terraces of graceful three-storey shops, bay-fronted
shopkeeper's flats and professional offices on a
'Station Parade'. At the foot of the parade lay a 600-
seat Athenaeum, opened at the same time as the
church, for lectures, theatre clubs, fine art auctions,
dance and music societies. Though the station
proudly advertised workmen's weekly tickets, none
of the thirty-seven trains each day actually left
before the 8 a.m. deadline to qualify for them. This
was the merchant and brokers' suburb to perfection,
though the district stretched far enough into the
surrounding farmers' fields and adjoining railway
town that even here a Christmas fund was needed to
ensure blankets, coal and flannel through the winter
for the parish poor.

ARMS, COMMERCE, EMPIRE: DOCKLAND AND BARRACKS

'In the six great metropolitan docks over 100,000
men are employed, the great bulk of whom are
married and have families', begin observations on

Rotherhithe had until recently been a
picturesque old harbour town of merchant houses,
wharfs and pleasure grounds for the river traffic
of London. But the church of St Barnabas opened
in 1872 to serve an entirely new district in which
settlements of terraced streets had grown up to
house those who lived dangerous and unpredictable
lives as contract labourers on the new Surrey Docks,
as well as the more settled, poorer households
associated with the tar, lumber and other works
generated by proximity to those docks and the Grand
Surrey Canal. Squeezed into a small plot among one
of the better rows of new housing, with a narrow
court to one side for access, the new church was
oriented to the grid of street and alley, with its 'east'
end facing north to the sheds and floating lumber
bays of the docks, and the 'west' into a back alley
of row-house scullery gardens and domestic sheds.
For St Barnabas's, the vicar recorded, Butterfield,
'although a builder of magnificent churches and
costly colleges, was willing to design for Rotherhithe
a church dignified and beautiful but of materials so
inexpensive that it might be possible to bring the
cost within the slender means'.[12] It was in vividly

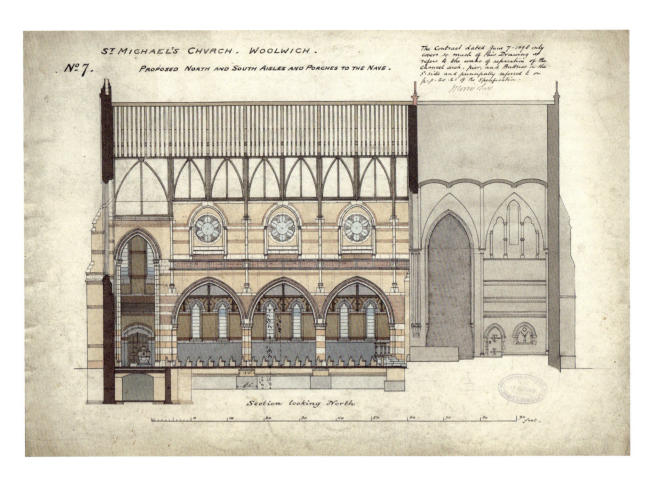

St Michael's Church. Woolwich.

No. 7.   Proposed North and South Aisles and Porches to the Nave.

The Contract dated June 7. 1890 only
covers so much of this Drawing as
refers to the works of repairing of the
chancel arch, pier, and Buttress on the
S. side and principally referred to on
p.p. 20. 21. of the Specification.

Section looking North

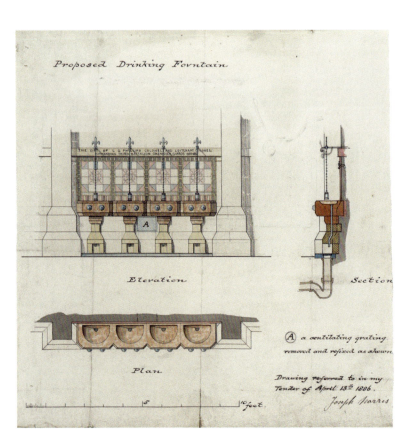

Proposed Drinking Fountain

Elevation   Section

Plan

Ⓐ a ventilating grating
removed and refixed as shewn.

Drawing referred to in my
Tender of April 13th 1886.

Joseph Harris

188
St Michael's Church,
Woolwich: section of
nave looking north
and showing proposed
aisle and porch,
approved February
1889

189
Drinking fountains
for Grenadier Guards
Barracks, Chelsea,
1886

diapered brick with a minimum of essential stone
trim for runoff.

More missionary works appeared in the port
and barracks towns growing at an enormous pace to
meet the needs of an expanding empire and its trade
routes. In Portsmouth, Butterfield's mission church
of St Michael's was built in successive stages from
1873 to 1890 in a notoriously riotous district, close
to both docks and garrison, of 'heedless, shiftless,
money-squandering . . . Jack ashore[s]',[13] studded
with lodgings and brothels for passing sailors and
soldiers and crowded with the children and women
they had left behind. It was one of the grandest of
his brick city churches, with a belfry and turrets like
those of Queen's Gate riding above the chancel arch.
Only a meagre visual record was left behind before
the church was demolished in the mid-1950s for
civic development. A similar mission in the garrison,
naval port and arsenal town of Woolwich had
brought an iron church to a desperate corner
of the town, to which a local architect, J.W. Walter,

a wide span between his lovely arcade of three bays and rose windows inset in a clerestory. A further phase, designed in 1889, would have added aisles on both sides and a tower and great porch at the north-west corner that would have been a landmark from the river and helped to anchor the church on its gradient. Though Butterfield continued to work on interior embellishments throughout his last years, this further construction was never undertaken.

The military garrisons of London and the port towns were immense generators of disease, carried to the local population by soldiers at leisure. To ameliorate this social hazard and lower the appalling natural death rate of the soldiery, the War Office from the 1860s onwards began to construct a more sanitary environment, especially for new recruits who carried illness into the barracks on their arrival. Since the connection between foul water and illness had been recognised in the 1850s, a movement for public drinking fountains in the larger towns had begun, and it was slowly extended to the parade grounds of barracks. In 1886, Butterfield was invited to design fountains for the Guards in London and Windsor, with the costs raised by testimonials and memorials. The example for Chelsea Barracks, which had been built in the 1860s and housed up to 2000 men, uses the delicate geometry of pink, white and blue tiles that we find in so many Butterfield sanctuaries, but with gunmetal and balls of small shot added, perhaps whimsically, to assert a military character. Other examples take the theme further, with portions of artillery pieces and cannonballs used to assemble the structure.

Caterham barracks appeared as part of a movement to build sanitary military facilities in fresh-air settings isolated from larger towns where order, propriety and hygiene were disturbed by soldiers in the streets and taverns. Caterham Common was a heath in the Surrey hills, above a town and valley that had become a 'parkland' outlet for country villas for London and the site of a training college for Congregational clergy. Built next to the enormous Metropolitan Imbecile Asylum, which had moved there in 1870, the Caterham Guards Depot was the largest single army base in

had added a brick chancel as part of an eventual plan for an extravagantly buttressed Gothic church, with a tower at its south-west corner. It was on a sloping and tightly constrained corner site in a 'very poor and difficult district . . . exposed to evils of a very exceptional . . . character, from its immediate proximity to . . . several large Barracks'.[14] Butterfield was brought in to develop phased designs for its completion in 1887, abandoning Walter's plan and proposing a brilliant ensemble in polychrome brick of red and yellow, inside and out. He cleared the ground and lowered the floor to give more height to the nave, making a space of real grandeur, with

192
St Mary's, Dover Castle:
view from the south-west,
photographic art postcard
by Gale & Porter, *c*.1895

the country, with six blocks of barracks for recruits by 1885, along with officer and officer family quarters, a gymnasium and large parade grounds for the drills which were the method of training.[15] Funds were then raised in the brigade for a chapel to care for the moral hygiene of the troops, to which the War Office added funds with the understanding that it would also provide for Roman Catholics, in a flanking chapel completed in 1887 with its own entrance and a partitioned sanctuary. Butterfield used stock yellow brick but mixed it generously with local flint and cut stone for chequerboard patterns in the gables, buttresses and banding.

At Caterham, Butterfield's work, usually attacked for its austerity, was at once applauded for breaking the military code to provide and embellish a church with the light, colour, wit and animation Butterfield felt due to a site of worship. The principle is taken even further at the very ancient Roman and Saxon church of St Mary's in the grounds of the garrison castle beside the Roman Pharos at Dover. A partial reconstruction as a garrison chapel by George Gilbert Scott had left it dark, damp and forbidding. Butterfield took it in hand just as Caterham was being completed, working in short phases to complete the restoration in 1892, lavishing tile covering and mosaic on the interior to near Byzantine (and marvellous) effect, and rebuilding to their early medieval state the caps of tower and pharos, the transept, the chancel,

and the lancets and portal of a nave that rose from the oldest surviving site of a church in Britain.[16] Thus, Butterfield's farewell work of reconstitution provided for those at arms in the modern empire a haptic memory of fifteen hundred years in the history of the nation and its churches, lest they forget the cause of civilisation that should govern their mission.

NOTES

1. The account of the Brookfield church project is taken primarily from plans, pamphlets and correspondence in the ICBS Archives, and from the many newspaper reports following the dispute over consecration, December 1875 to January 1876.
2. T. Francis Bumpus, *London Churches, Ancient and Modern*, T.B. Bumpus, London, 1885 edition, pp 248–9.
3. The account is taken primarily from the ICBS Archives and from Walter Harold Yeandle, *A Corner of Finsbury: An Account of the History of the Parish and Church of St Clement, City Road*, Knott, London, 1934.
4. The maps of London districts showing the economic condition of inhabitants and prepared under Charles Booth as part of his *Inquiry into Life and Labour in London* (1886–1903) can be consulted online at https://booth.lse.ac.uk.
5. For the death and burial of Brett, see *The Guardian*, 11 February 1874, which includes Butterfield's obituary, and Thomas Waugh Belcher, *Robert Brett of Stoke Newington: His Life and Work*, Dutton, London, 1889.
6. Accounts of the character of Tottenham in 1876 are taken from James Thorne, *Handbook to the Environs of London*, John Murray, London, 1876, vol.1, p.622.
7. The account of the Tottenham church project is drawn principally from faculty and other papers and plans in the parish files at London Metropolitan Archives, and from

reports and letters to the editor on the controversy which are extensive and widespread; but note especially *The Guardian*, 8 April 1874, for Wilson's defence, and the report at the time of reconsecration, *The Guardian*, 7 June 1876.

8. See Henry William Burrows, *The Half-Century of Christ Church, Albany Street*, Skeffington, London, 1887, pp 181–4, in which his curate J.R. Keble gives an extended account of the origin of the Upper Edmonton project and of the emerging dormitory town (here quoted). A letter in *The Guardian*, 21 March 1884, also describes the emerging suburb, and reports in *The Guardian*, 4 April 1884, and at the time of consecration in September, describe the project as it then appeared. Butterfield's drawings – in both the Victoria and Albert Museum and Drawing Matter Collections – suggest a project for which his ambitions were very high. The subsequent history, in which a chancel and south porch seem to have been added by other architects, is uncertain.

9. Anon. [Harrison Ainsworth], 'Suburban Babylon', *New Monthly Review*, new series, vol.2, 1872, pp 51–8.

10. The account is partly taken from news reports; A.P. Baggs, Diane K. Bolton, Eileen P. Scarff and G.C. Tyack, 'Enfield: Churches', in T.F.T. Baker and R.B. Pugh (eds), *A History of the County of Middlesex, Volume 5: Hendon, Kingsbury, Great Stanmore, Little Stanmore, Edmonton Enfield, Monken Hadley, South Mimms, Tottenham*, Victoria County History, London, 1976, pp 245–9, transcribed in British History Online: www.british-history.ac.uk/vch/middx/vol5/pp245-249; W.C. Ingram, *A Memoir of the Rev. Henry Twells*, Wells Gardner & Co., London, 1901; and T. Francis Bumpus, *London Churches, Ancient and Modern*, T.W. Laurie, London, 1907, p.273.

11. Francis William Adams, 'At The India Docks . . . August 1883', *Songs of the Army of the Night*, Federal Steam and Binding Works, Sydney, 1887; English editions starting in 1894.

12. Edward Josselyn Beck, *Memorials to Serve for a History of the Parish of St Mary, Rotherhithe*, Cambridge University Press, Cambridge, 1907.

13. Among the sources cited or consulted for the history of the Portsmouth church were *Hampshire Telegraph and Naval Chronicle*, 12 October 1872; *Church Builder*, no.69, 1879; Reginald Shutte, printed appeal 'The Mission of St Michael & All Angels, Portsmouth', June 1876, in University of Southampton Hartley Library; and, on the condition of life in which the missions intervened, the wonderful memoir of Robert R. Dolling, *Ten Years in a Portsmouth Slum*, Swan Sonnenschein & Co., London, 1896.

14. The project history relies largely on Andrew Saint's account in Peter Guillery (ed.), *Survey of London, Volume 48: Woolwich*, Yale University Press, New Haven, Connecticut, 2012, pp 298–9, which includes the full quoted text on the building's situation.

15. There is a full account and description of the Caterham chapel in *Surrey Mirror*, 19 February 1887.

16. For St Mary's, Dover Castle, see *The Builder*, 12 December 1863, and *The Guardian*, 16 January 1889. A remarkable set of drawings by Butterfield for the project, filed with the War Office, is in the archives of Historic England.

VI CHARACTER BUILDING

Walter · Trevelyan ·
Colonel · Coldstream · Gvards ·
Died · of · Cholera · at · Varna ·
21ˢᵗ · Avgvst · 1854 ·
aged · 36 · years ·

Robert · Edward · Boyle · M·P ·
Son · of · Edmvnd · Earl · of · Cork · and · Orrery ·
Lievt · Colonel · Coldstream · Gvards ·
Died · of · Fever · at · Varna · 3ᵈ · Sept · 1854 ·
aged · 44 · years ·

Henry · Thomas · Bvtler ·
Captain · 55ᵗʰ · Regiment · of · Foot ·
Depvty · Assistant · Adjvtant · General ·
Killed · at · the · Battle · of · Inkerman ·
5ᵗʰ · November · 1854 · aged · 41 · years ·

THIS · PORCH ·
Has · been · prepared ·
and · beavtified ·
By · WILLIAM · of · WYKEHAMS · SONS ·
as · a · sacred · shrine ·
In · which · the · memories · of · their · thirteen · brethren ·
who · died · in · the · war · of · the · Crimea · A·D · 1854-5 ·
may · be · preserved · for · an · example ·
to · fvtvre · generations ·
Think · vpon · them · thov · who · art · passing · by · to-day ·
Child · of · the · same · family · bovght · by · the · same · Lord ·
Keep · thy · foot · when · thov · gvest · into · this · hovse · of · God ·
There · watch · thine · armovr · and · make · thyself · ready · by · prayer ·
To · fight · and · to · die ·
The · faithfvl · Soldier · and · Servant · of · Christ ·
And · of · thy · Covntry ·

OF · THE · DEAD · BVT · OF · THE · LIVIN

CHAPTER 16

LIBERAL EDUCATION: RUGBY, 1867–85

'QUIT YE LIKE MEN'

'FAITH, VIRTUE, knowledge, temperance, patience, charity': these were the six words of the biblical virtues that Butterfield inscribed in 1858 above the tablets of his memorial for students of Winchester College lost in the Crimea, each cradled in the hands of an angel hanging there to guard their memory; and on the central panel he calls upon the generations living in their shade to awaken daily to their fellows' sacrifice and school their own conscience to duty. Likewise, under the Crimea window at Rugby School, he honoured those lost 'for Christian service and true chivalry' by writing a call to follow their example, and around the rim of his tower at Rugby Chapel were the words 'Quit ye like men'.

It was the growing idea of the age that the character of a child, as 'father of the man', could be guided through education towards 'an inward purity and moral purpose' without which no 'inherent nobleness of disposition' could resist the blandishments of a world intent on carelessness, frivolity and vice.[1] The words are those used by Frederick W. Farrar to introduce the fourth edition of his *Eric, or Little by Little* (first published in 1858), the most popular children's novel of the era, in which a 'noble soul' is led, little by little, astray, as the character building and call to duty of his schooling weakens in the dishonest face of 'the way we live now'. The notion is expanded to embrace the duty to civilisation as a whole in the plea that Matthew Arnold uttered at his father's grave in the old chapel of Rugby, when he cried: 'Order, courage, return'.[2] It was put most plainly by 'the greatest schoolmaster of the age', Frederick Temple, when he announced that 'the purpose of a school,

and a loyal following of old boys grew up to support the institution, with his memory at its core. In 1857, the legend of Arnold grew to international proportions with the publication of *Tom Brown's School Days*, and it was in the full flurry of this recognition that Butterfield, who counted Arnold's poet son, Matthew, among his friends, began his association with the school.

At that time the main school consisted of a single quadrangle, with a headmaster's house attached, a small chapel adjacent to the west, and a single playing field. Most of the work was a generation old, using the pale brick of the town as its basis with a sort of manorial or fortified Gothic as its theme. The first formal boarding house had just been completed by Gilbert Scott on the far corner of the open fields behind the playing ground. Butterfield was engaged first for memorials to Rugbeians lost in the Crimea – with a window of the Centurion at the Cross – and then for those lost during the rebellion in India – with an Entombment and Resurrection; the long lists of names gave a clear prediction of the paths into military and colonial life that, along with the Church, many of the pupils at mid-century were to follow. A drawing suggests that he partially raised its roof at this time and proposed a number of other interventions. He then built a first set of racquets and fives courts for a subscription raised by the pupils and old boys in 1860, and followed them with a cricket pavilion, erected in a long process ending in 1869, and including extensive grading and terracing of the rough land on the southern perimeter of the school grounds. Meanwhile, he had built a private house for one of the masters, and then extended it to accommodate a preparatory boarding school, completed in 1867.[4]

Frederick Temple arrived as headmaster in 1858, and immediately began a programme of reform and expansion that culminated in a 300th-anniversary campaign to add an ambitious set of 'New Schools' to form a quadrangle with the chapel extending to the crossroads to the west, and to rebuild the chapel itself for a population now comprising almost 500 pupils. The choice of Butterfield, whom he knew well, to undertake this work was entirely his, and the shaping and functioning of the first major works at

above everything else was . . . to make duty the one supreme consideration of his life'.[3] It was a terrible charge, and perhaps a terrible crime, to lay upon the youth of Victorian England the burden of learning the means and passing the tests of honour at every pass in life. But of such were citizenship and a faithful life at the time (and for long after) conceived.

THE NEW SCHOOLS

Rugby School, typical of a Tudor-era foundation, had been established and endowed by a local merchant as a grammar school for his townsmen and evolved by the late eighteenth century into one of the handful of England's 'great public schools', educating the sons of gentry from throughout the country. It had established a reputation for educational progress through the reforms of Thomas Arnold in the 1830s, converting a riotous playground of youth into something like a modern school, governed as much by Arnold's moral instruction in the nature and necessity of duty, honour and leadership – and by his readiness to expel the disruptive – as by his structural changes in the working of the school. A cult of respect had grown up around Arnold since his death in 1842,

Rugby were developed together. Neither quadrangle nor chapel could be entirely completed in the first campaign, for want both of funds and of the right to a portion of the land, but Butterfield would return from 1882 to 1886 to add the last section of the quad to a new design, finish the cap of the chapel tower, and bring the western portion of the chapel into better scale and conformity with the rest.

ENQUIRY: SCIENCE EDUCATION AND THE 'MODERN SIDE'

The first view of the New Schools, as completed in 1869, glimpses it as a frieze of startling animation and modernity behind the plain surfaces of the old school and chapel, the latter still intact, with sheds and stables in the centre of the quadrangle, which Butterfield would remove as work on the new chapel began less than two years later. Temple had introduced a revolutionary 'modern side', in which foreign languages, English literature and language, modern history and the sciences could be studied as an alternative, or in addition, to the Oxford curriculum of classical mathematics, Greek and Latin. Instruction in natural science had been introduced to Rugby eight years before, but Temple now engaged two accomplished lecturers in chemistry and physics, and built a small yellow-brick annexe, to Gilbert Scott's design, with a natural science lecture room on the ground floor, a small fireproofed lean-to laboratory, and an upper floor as a senior common room to encourage a collegiate approach to the educational mission. By 1864, science at Rugby was a compulsory subject of study, with over 350 boys starting the course in botany and studying geology in Rugby's Lias quarries. As plans for the New Schools developed in 1867, Butterfield began working with the new science lecturers, T.N. Hutchinson and James M. Wilson, to develop the entire ground floor and basement of his new north wing as research labs and demonstration theatres, and to convert Scott's lecture room into a working laboratory in which tests and experiments could be conducted by thirty students simultaneously. Wilson travelled to Edinburgh to see the pioneering lecture rooms and labs of Lyon Playfair and brought Playfair's assistant down to help Butterfield with planning.

The ambitious scheme to build and equip such facilities, and to work out how a laboratory could be organised for large numbers to engage in, or observe, experiments, was unique for its time. There were articles in the daily press, discussions at learned societies and invitations to its teachers to lecture across the country. Butterfield's designs were discussed, even before fully completed in 1869, in the first issue of *Nature* magazine, the most widely circulated scientific journal of its time; and presented there more fully early in 1870, with two illustrations (fig.195). The General View shows Scott's slightly quaint Gothic lecture room (A) now fitted out to into a 'natural science' laboratory; independent worktables for each of thirty boys; a furnace, boiler, sand baths and drying ovens. The Ground Plan shows its place in a chain of laboratories, more than 140 feet long. Scott's little lab (B) has been converted for experimental research among teachers and advanced students. There are demonstration laboratories for chemistry (C) and physics (D), constructed like surgical theatres, descending well below ground level, and providing steeply raked desks (fifty for chemistry and sixty for physics). Dampered conduits bring in air, gas, water and hot air from the furnace in the natural science lab, with a complicated system of down draughts, waste disposal and exhausts, some of which can be seen in the sections that follow. A mechanical room (E) was equipped for the storage, repair and manufacture of tools and instruments and to prepare illustrations for instruction.

The teaching of sciences was fundamental to the idea of liberal education to which all Butterfield's works at Rugby School were dedicated. Thus, Hutchinson described experimental science as a vehicle for mental training through which to develop powers of observation and deduction that came from seeing and doing, so that the mind would be equipped to help boys think and discover for themselves. Since the days of Thomas Arnold in the 1830s, Rugby had built a reputation for free thinking that alarmed conservative thinkers. This

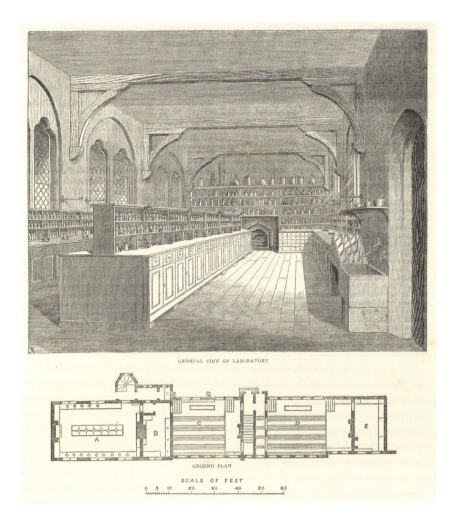

GENERAL VIEW OF LABORATORY

GROUND PLAN

SCALE OF FEET

194

194
Rugby School: general
view and ground plan
of laboratory, from
T.N. Hutchinson,
'The New Natural
Science Schools
at Rugby', *Nature*,
10 March 1870

which a central seated chamber predominates, was dedicated as much to moral instruction and common discourse as to worship. The light engineering workshop that soon followed under Butterfield's gymnasium introduced physical discipline and training into education on an unprecedented scale. The cricket pavilion, terraced close, heated swimming bath and racquets and fives courts brought a new civil order to sporting life, in place of the shooting, running, riding to hounds and river-dipping that had governed it for generations. With the provision of a library, art museum, observatory and performance hall to complete the scattered complex, we are left with something like an ideal city for the development of mind and body, individual and society.

Each element is given a markedly different shape to fit its functions, but there is, through twenty years of work on eight dispersed sites, a consistency of characteristics in townscaping and signposting between them all. Some of these rhymes are readily recognised – like a pattern of walls and railings that is repeated from one enclosure to the next, and lintels and doorways shaped to similar form. Some are subtler – like a skyline of echoing finials and gables. Others almost undefinably bring a sense of commonality to works of striking individuality: perhaps a metaphor for the moral intention of forging a common ethic among young people of disparate abilities, qualities and tempers.

Butterfield's two street elevations for the New Schools are presented on a single sheet to demonstrate the implicit symmetry between them (fig.196). Both show the use of the busy ground-floor street front at the corner to accommodate storage, services and toilets. Above, the west elevation towards Dunchurch Street carries a flap over the right quadrant to show the 1885 scheme for the southern stages, which had been left unbuilt in the first campaign and were dramatically revised as Butterfield reconsidered them when the opportunity to complete the quadrangle finally arrived. The flap includes a wonderful chiaroscuro outline of Butterfield's rebuilt chapel, in which the great extrusion of the two transepts that form the principal volume is very apparent. The recladding,

was the spirit in which Bishop Archibald Tait, celebrating the 1867 anniversary of Rugby, warned that 'of all the misfortunes which could befall the Church of England the worst would be the refusal to enquire . . . Rugby school was a protest against this error', producing 'a set of men who fully entering into the wants of the age, would at the same time show that they were devoted servants of the Church'.[5]

These were the principles on which all Butterfield's commissions at Rugby School were grounded. The New Schools provided sites of learning and enquiry that covered an exceptional variety of knowledge and culture, from rooms for drawing lessons and musical instruction, to an enormous and hazardous suite of rooms equipped for learning from the activity of things – mechanics, hydrostatics and magnetism. His new chapel, in

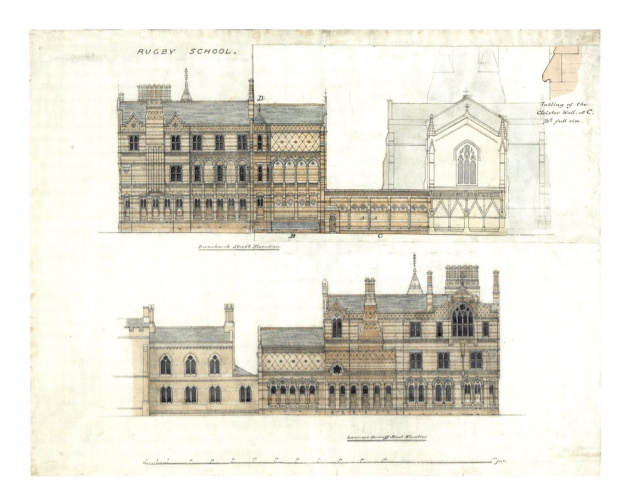

195
Rugby School,
Proposed New
Buildings: elevation,
1867, with flap
showing west range
as redesigned in 1885

cleansing and refinement of the chapel's old west
end and its carved memorial porch, which were
also undertaken at this time, are portrayed on the
front plane in the colour of their stone. The north
elevation below shows, to the east, the small Natural
Science Building by George Gilbert Scott of 1861,
which Butterfield reworks internally to house the
new student laboratory depicted in *Nature*, and
then the extraordinary system of window and funnel
venting for the two new scientific demonstration
lecture halls and experimental laboratories on the
ground floor. Both elevations show the adjustments
in scale and articulation with which Butterfield
manages to reconcile a startlingly adventurous new
scheme with the rather conventional historicism of
its neighbours, lowering the north range at its east
end to balance the roof with that of Scott's existing
building, and then brilliantly revising his original
plan for the southernmost classrooms to provide
blind arcades and a cloister that merge line and

rhythm with the older portions of the chapel and its
memorial porch.

The sections show the extraordinary extent of
glass fronting into the quadrangle, and the elaborate
and austerely beautiful systems of brick-lined
circulation, all bringing the chapel into view at every
stage of progress. For the first drawings, teachers,
who had contributed largely to the cost, specified
the character and arrangements for their own
rooms. The section of the north range (fig.197) offers
a detailed presentation of the complex organisation
of the laboratories on the ground floor at the north,
with theatre seating for demonstrations of electrical
and physical sciences, bare brick walls, secure
anterooms for storage and preparation of material,
and below-ground extraction and neutralisation
devices against hazardous fumes and currents. We
see some classrooms in exposed brick and others in
plaster for light, and a huge, vaulted space with a
north-light studio window for drawing instruction

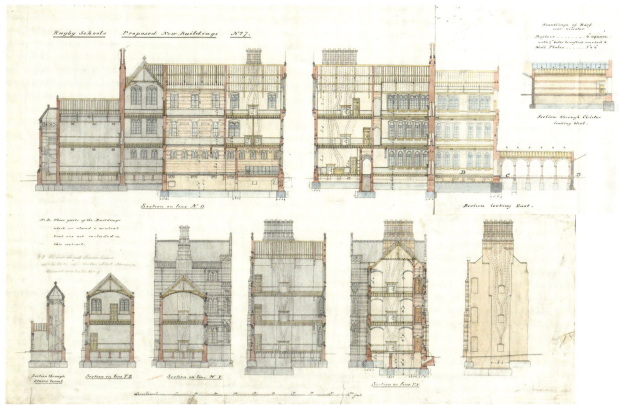

196

Rugby School, Proposed New Buildings: sections of the north range, 1867

197

Rugby School, Proposed New Buildings: sections of the west range, 1867, with flap showing portion redesigned in 1885

Rugby School: view
of new buildings
from the north-west
upon completion,
photograph attributed
to E.H. Speight, 1885

on the great top-floor corner. Smaller spaces include
music rooms and a cloak and common room for
town boys. The section of the west range (fig.198)
is shown with the original unbuilt scheme for the
southern extension of the schools on the left, and
the flap down on the right to show the revised
scheme of 1885. The first design, with its drop in
height and scale, would have balanced the two-
storey wing and stair tower that closed the north
range of the New School. The revised scheme has a
stack of three large classrooms continuing the wall
of windows that face the quadrangle, and adds a
cloister to the antechapel to complete the closure
of the quad, line up the pupils for orderly entrance
and provide a street door for visitors, now that the
growth of the organ has inhibited access through
the north-east door.

An image by the local photographer and
schoolmaster Edward Hall Speight (fig.199)
captures the extraordinary vigour and solidity of the
new schools as they anchor a vital corner of a busy
market town, butting tightly on to the intersection
of two thoroughfares but raising the classroom
windows well clear of the streets and using the
problematic low level of the corner itself for toilets
and storage rooms with mostly blind frontage to
the roads. The running of flues into consolidated
chimneys produces landmark stacks that thrust

the building out over the street, with their vertical
bracing ribs descending into the pattern of the
ground-floor arcade. The cut-off corner and setback
allow the drawing studio on the top floor with its
huge shallow bay window to overhang for better
light. The lighter tones, flatter façade, blind arcade
and brick and stonework in Butterfield's revised
south extension are very clearly seen, reflecting
the steps taken in many of his works at this time
towards more articulated, symmetrical and plastic
surface patterning, bearing floods of broken light
rather than a dappled plane. The pleasure he could
take in the blank and pierced wall was now replaced
by a fascination with the ways in which architectural
relief on blind walls can reflect or speak to the logic
of the interior. It reached an apogee here and in
the assembly hall known as the 'New Big School',
designed for Rugby at the same time, and that
we will visit in the next chapter, with even more
evident echoes of another ideal city of learning and
community – thirteenth-century Siena.

MORAL INSTRUCTION: THE CHAPEL

Butterfield's rebuilt chapel had to work around a
number of seemingly impossible constraints that
produced a design of astounding originality and
effectiveness. He was obliged to retain a portion of
the west end in order to preserve a closed western
passage at street-side, built not long before by
subscription of the old boys; to reinstall memorial
plaques and windows (including his own from the
1850s), as well as the early stained glass scavenged
in Europe by Thomas Arnold to adorn the old
chapel; to leave in place Arnold's tomb, which lay
in the floor of the nave; and to follow as much of
the old footprint as practical. At the same time the
chapel, visible on all four sides, was to be accorded
a prominence in the whole ensemble that indicated
its place as the physical conscience and moral heart
of the activities surrounding it. An early study at the
RIBA proposed a bell turret over a crossing at the
centre of the south transept that had recently been
added. For the time being any attempt to extend
to the west was scotched, so the short white-brick

199

Rugby School Chapel:
view from the east
on completion,
photograph by
J. Edmunds, 1872

quadrangles, and the street fronts to the south and east were carefully calibrated to admit a view even from the streets of the town running down towards the market.

A first attempt to extend eastwards to reach the desired expansion produced a narrow rectangular closing for an 'English' chancel; but the passage from Close to quadrangle could not be resolved, and Butterfield ended up shaping a five-sided, heavily buttressed chancel with a quasi-domed roof. It comes close to touching the corner of the old school building to its north-east, so that the meetings of the buttresses with the ground are pierced to suggest an ambulatory, cast shafts of light and make the passage feel broader. It creates the effect of the talons of an eagle touching the ground with its head erect and the wings of the transepts about to close.

The chapel is built in a mosaic of predominantly yellow brick, interfused with blue and red brick and stone trim that fuse into the eye as a burnt orange streaked with white. By buttressing the tower externally, Butterfield was able to organise the chapel into a sequence of distinct spaces moving eastwards that are divided by tall and delicate arched crossings, so that the eye is drawn deep into a progression of high chambers, each drawing in a different light, to end in a suffusion of the ineffable. A narthex within the western porch opened to the short nave of the old chapel, which he was able to modify into an uncrowded form in 1882. Then came the wide arcaded open crossing at the two high transepts, forming the principal space of assembly, flooded with the broken light of stained glass, new and old. A choir follows, with a second shorter transept to the south and a northern chamber stretching into the quad behind like a Renaissance treasury; then a void within the tower, flooded with light from enormously tall windows on either side; and finally the apse itself, a pentagonal gallery of light with the Flemish window from the old chapel at the east end and four very lightly coloured windows, almost in grisaille, on either side.

Stone bands, brick diapers and graphite runes anchor the progression and, like the simple roof beams, set up an equilibrium between vertical and horizontal, emphasising both the great width

nave of the old chapel was retained, and greater space obtained by expanding the south transept and adding a matching wing of equal strength to the north, so that pews faced across from one another like the chamber of the House of Commons – an apt arrangement for a chapel devoted more to disquisition than ceremony. The polygonal shape of the tower begins to emerge in a second scheme seen on a drawing in the same collection, and it is then raised in the final design – only the torn fragment of a section remains among Butterfield's drawings – so that it can be seen not only as a landmark from the Close to south and east, but as a peak to be viewed above the walls of both the old and the new

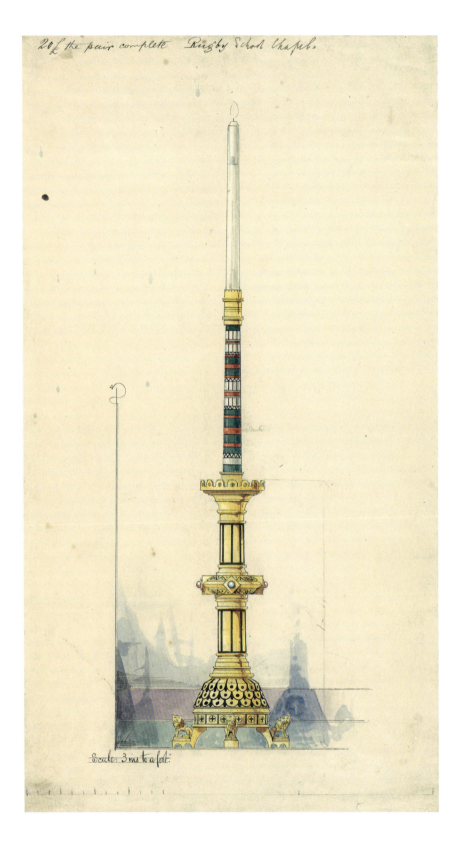

Scale: 3 ins to a foot.

200
Rugby School Chapel: design
for an altar candlestick, *c.*1872

between, and height of, shafts in the central arcades. Glass mosaics, designed by Butterfield after gilded manuscript illuminations and made by the Venetian firm of Antonio Salviati, form a frieze above the dado of the apse, and the Four Evangelists catch the light on the reredos, framing a great white cross among vines. The gigantic tile mosaic of the Majesty added into the dome was worked with Alexander Gibbs, and Butterfield's own wonderful but now long-gone painting on the pipes made a vivid pattern of the organ. Butterfield would return in 1878 to fill the matched pairs of three-light windows with Gibbs, as memorials in stained glass of exceptional beauty and instructive force, with the Fathers and Mothers of the Church to the north, and a Transfiguration and Glory to the south. Inside and out, the distinctive form of the chapel, illustrated by Muthesius as the essential example of the investment of architecture with 'character',[6] leaves an indelible impression. That ready recognition of its shape and persona was fundamental to its purpose, which was to inscribe a memory of its daily moral instruction and its gathering into a common fellowship that would last a lifetime.

NOTES

1.   Frederick W. Farrar, *Eric, or Little by Little*, fourth edition, Cassell & Co., London, 1889.

2.   Matthew Arnold in the elegy 'Rugby Chapel', written on an 'autumn evening' in 1857, first published in his *New Poems*, Macmillan, London, 1867, and appearing in almost all collections and anthologies of his works thereafter.

3.   Frederick Temple, address at Exeter on his taking up the bishopric of the diocese, January 1870, quoted in *Western Morning News*, 4 February 1870.

4.   Summary accounts of Butterfield's work at Rugby can be found in Paul Thompson, *William Butterfield*, Routledge & Kegan Paul, London, 1971, p.435, and in William Henry Denham Rouse, 'A Chronicle', chapter 14 in his *A History of Rugby School*, C. Scribner's Sons, New York, 1898, pp 296–311. See also John Barclay Hope Simpson, *Rugby Since Arnold: A History of Rugby School Since 1842*, Macmillan, London, 1967, and Francis Elliot Kitchener, *Rugby Memoir of Archbishop Temple*, Macmillan & Co., London, 1907. News accounts of new work at the school appear regularly and extensively in the Rugby, Nuneaton, Coventry and Leamington press of the time. For the sciences, I have relied upon Frederick W. Farrar (ed.), *Essays on a Liberal Education*, Macmillan, London, 1867, especially James M. Wilson, 'On Teaching Natural Science in Schools', pp 241–91; T.N. Hutchinson, *Science Work at Rugby School*, Billington, Rugby, 1870; and Anon., 'The New Natural Science Schools at Rugby', *Nature*, 10 March 1870.

5.   Quoted in *Birmingham Journal*, 29 July 1867.

6.   Hermann Muthesius, *Die neuere kirchliche Baukunst in England*, Ernst & Sohn, Berlin, 1901.

201

Rugby School Chapel: design for mosaic of Christ the King for the vault above the east window, *c.*1876

202

Rugby School Chapel: interior view looking east, photograph by E.H. Speight, *c.*1886

MODERNITY AND MOTION: RUGBY SCHOOL

Chapel from New Schools

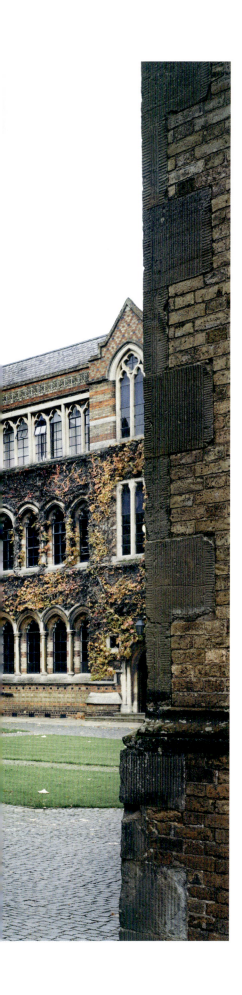

Apse of the chapel and new quadrangle
Overleaf: Chapel cloister and new quadrangle

New quadrangle: street fronts

CHAPTER 17

PHYSICAL DISCIPLINE *and* MENTAL CULTIVATION: RUGBY, 1865–85

'SELF-RESPECT': GAMES AND PHYSICAL TRAINING

'A BOY CANNOT SEE much difference between the nominative and the genitive cases,' wrote Arthur Helps in an essay on childhood recreation, 'but he is a good hand at some game or other; and he keeps up his self-respect, and the respect of others for him, upon his prowess in that game. He is better and happier on that account. And it is well, too, that the little world around him should know that excellence is not all of one form.'[1] Helps – a confidential friend of Prince Albert and Queen Victoria, and Butterfield's dinner and travelling companion – was an occasional writer whose essays on politics and progress addressed every area of social inequality and oppression, from the historical injustice of empire to the ruthless materialism of contemporary practices in employment, housing and public hygiene, while those on more general cultural questions, such as conformity and religious zeal, carried the open-minded and progressive tenor of Tennyson, F.D. Maurice, Charles Kingsley and the Cambridge Apostles, with whom he had been associated as a student. Implacably conservative as Butterfield was in so many matters of comportment, morality and religion, Helps was one among many personal friends of the most liberal stripe, and his conversation with them was wide and free. In the same spirit he seems not to have baulked at the invitation to develop building typologies to accommodate the progressive recreational reach of a modernising, rationalist public school – from an astronomical observatory to a mechanical workshop, and from a teaching gallery of art to a performance centre for music and the spoken word – but rather to delight in their possibilities. To look at his roofs

203
'Hillbrow'
Preparatory School,
Rugby: postcard
view from the south
by The Rugby Press,
c.1900

alone, there are great covers of glass for racquets courts, flapped closings for a giant swivelling telescope, and four different open-span systems: for a swimming bath, an art museum, a concert hall over 80 feet long and a gymnasium carrying a 40-foot climbing pole into an open cupola.

Kenneth Grahame, famed for his authorship of the children's classic *The Wind in the Willows* (1908), remembered his leisure time at a typical preparatory school of the 1860s as a matter of simply being let loose to wander the fields and town, or to find a game of scuttling – or mock battles – with his fellows in the woods.[2] The concept of 'organised games' as a part of education was only just emerging. The idea of a 'school yard' was not commonly defined until 1865 and generally became a requirement of school plans for local boards only in the 1870s, when physical drills and exercises in movement were introduced into the activities. The notion of the playing field as the centre of a school social life, of games with rules as a force for socialisation and self-discipline, and of physical development as part of educational growth was linked worldwide to the reorganisation of leisure at Rugby School, and especially as it was refined under Frederick Temple after 1858. Its passage into common culture was rapid, and its impact on the lives of working people immeasurable. We have seen how urban churches, beginning with cricket teams and then with what became association football, adopted sports for working youth; though the YMCA was originally established by London

drapery workers for Bible study and refreshment, it was quickly led by Christian Socialists with a Rugby School background towards activities centring on physical fitness, first with holiday camps in 1873, then with boxing and, by 1881, the first full gymnasiums. And by 1888, after his first visits to Rugby, the founder of the modern Olympics, Pierre de Coubertin, published his widely adopted educational thesis that it was from well-ordered competitive sport that 'moral and social strength' were best developed.[3]

Butterfield's first major work at Rugby came, alongside commissions for racquets and fives courts, in the form of a master's house for the family of Rugby's modern language teacher and for his preparatory school, where some thirty-five boys under fourteen were prepared for the life of a public school, with the playing fields, a physical regimen and separation from family life as a training ground in peer socialisation. It is one of the largest of Butterfield's domestic works, in which ideas from his brick parsonages are woven into the fabric of a household of more than fifty people, with extensive grounds falling south from a 'hill brow' terraced with Butterfield's customary geometrical rigour. It established a domestic language for the surroundings of Rugby that would reappear soon after in a now lost fever hospital, and in the curators' houses at Temple Reading Room and Observatory.

A view of the Rugby Close shows Butterfield's 1867 cricket pavilion (beneath the spire of the church and convent of St Marie – the work of A.W.N. Pugin and his son Edward Welby Pugin); his novel gymnasium of 1872, with running track and gallery, extensive floor equipment and the famous climbing pole, with an enormous metal and wood workshop beneath; the porch of one set of his fives courts; and the equally pioneering heated swimming bath of 1875. These activities were entirely voluntary at the time (though the workshop was supervised by an engineer from London), gradually entering an obligatory games and physical education curriculum as the century progressed. The principal courts for racquets and fives, some distance to the left of the pavilion, are not seen. Butterfield raised the cricket field, built long earth terraces in grass, dried

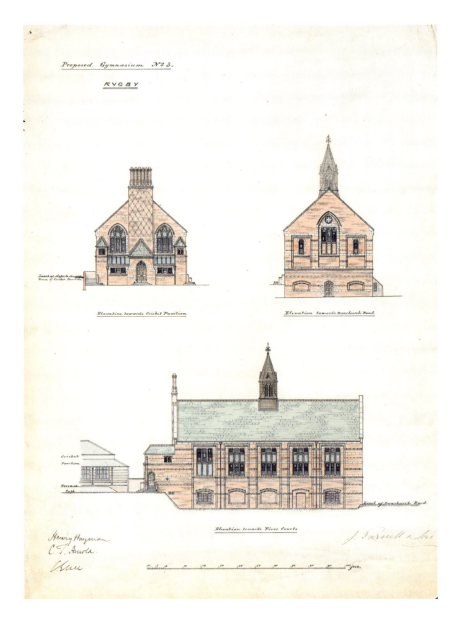

out the swampy ground to the right known as 'the Pontines', planted trees, levelled the football field in the foreground, and generally disciplined a Close that had held a legendary place in the culture of the school for 100 years. The scale of things is not modest – the gymnasium, with an interior over 90 feet long, is the size of a moderate village church. But they are sited to let the lovely sward and elm trees dominate the space.

'HIGH CULTURE OF THE MIND': READING ROOM AND ART MUSEUM

If Rugby was a pioneer in the culture of the body, it was unique, if less loudly sung, in its recreational encouragement for the arts, the observation of nature and the culture of mind. Ten years after the anniversary building campaign, land was acquired for a library and art museum bearing Temple's name, set back in a large grassy precinct to face the Close across the Barby Road. It was designed with the footprint of an adjoining 'New Big School', or assembly hall, in mind, which was planned but never built for the south side of its great stair. A library for students to enrich their leisure hours and expand on their study texts was not exceptional, but one of these dimensions, segmented into quiet, nearly private reading alcoves, was highly unusual; and the provision of what was essentially a visual library above was rarer still. The curator's house to the left was provided for the family of the principal art teacher, with a door both to the gallery on the top floor and the prints and books exhibition cases running through the reading room, so that he could serve on call as the students' guide, though a schedule of regular gallery talks was also provided. The library was quickly supplied with reference

204
Rugby School: elevations of the gymnasium, *c.*1871

205
Rugby School: view of the Close from the north, photographed *c.*1890

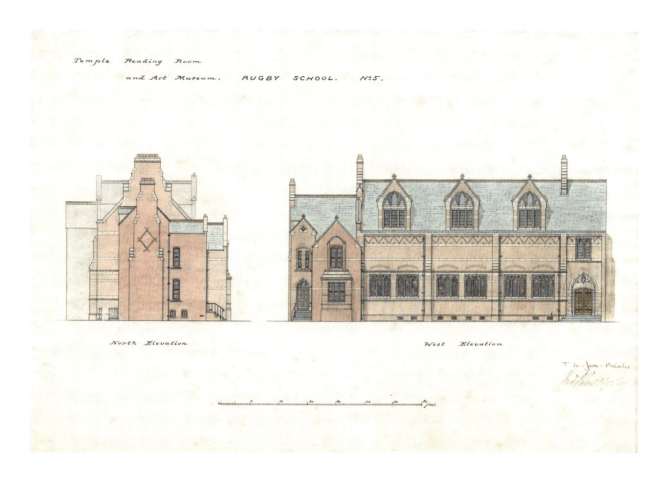

North Elevation

West Elevation

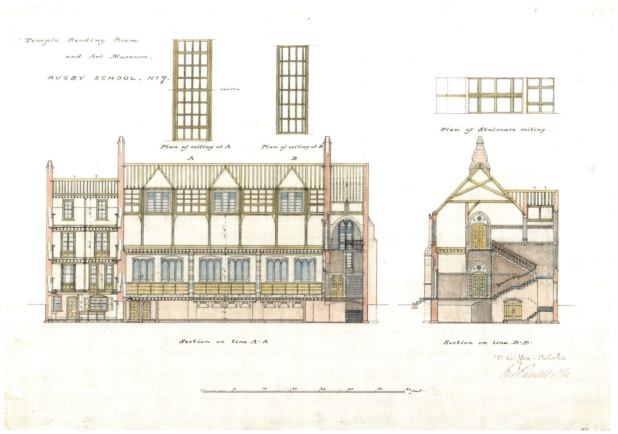

Plan of ceiling at A

Plan of ceiling at B

Plan of Staircase ceiling

Section on line A·A

Section on line B·B

206
Temple Reading
Room and Art
Museum, Rugby
School: north and
west elevations, 1877

207
Temple Reading
Room and Art
Museum, Rugby
School: sections
looking south and
east, 1877

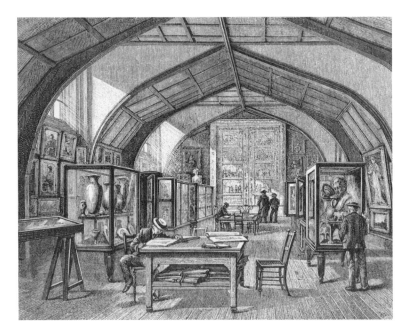

works and a remarkably uncensored collection of recent literature in English, open to all. The museum housed a substantial collection of original art, much of it deriving from the Rugby antiquarian Matthew Bloxam and the collection of the great painter Sir Thomas Lawrence, to whom he was related; many casts and copies of classical sculpture; a great cast of Ghiberti's bronze doors from Florence baptistery, which commanded the north end; and casts and examples of art from many epochs and cultures. For at least the first ten years, major loan exhibitions were installed each summer and open to the public. Within five years the programme of art observation and instruction at Rugby had attracted great attention, and an account of its objectives and means, with examples of drawing by both student and teacher, was presented in the most important art journal of its time (fig.210), by curator and master Thomas Lindsay. It is a remarkable building, with gables at an almost unprecedented scale, carrying slate panels above the windows to manage light, and a front façade, stood far back from its approaches, of stunning presence and severity. The bowing of the roof beams and marble banding in the reading room, with a little stained glass in the windows, lets structure account for every element of ornament, and the coved art gallery is completely unadorned. The enormous tiled staircase, designed to serve the great hall anticipated on its right as well, is a powerful social thoroughfare.

A natural history society, with a library and museum ranging in scope from fossils to antiquities,

208 (top)
Temple Reading Room and Art Museum, Rugby School: interior view of the library looking north, photographed c.1890

209 (middle)
Temple Reading Room and Art Museum, Rugby School: interior view of the museum, illustration by T.M. Lindsay published in *The Art Journal*, vol.47, 1885, p.52

210 (bottom)
Temple Observatory and Master's House for the astronomy curator, Rugby School: view from the south-west, engraved from a photograph at the school and published in Edward Crossley, Joseph Gledhill and James M. Wilson, *Handbook of Double Stars*, Macmillan, London, 1879

had been run by the students for some years, as a mode of recreational enquiry supported by the school but independent of its curriculum. With the reading room and museum, Butterfield was asked to design an observatory, placing it in the garden of a curator's house, which he built as a model town villa for households of the middling and professional class. J.M. Wilson had acquired a remarkably advanced telescope to share observations with the boys, arguing for the fundamental place of astronomy and natural history in the cultivation of mind through observation of 'common phenomena'. There was, he said, 'a real pleasure of the intellect, which boys attain when they first understand the causes of these great common phenomena [seasons, changes of the moon etc]. They stand thenceforward on a higher platform. The universe presents to them not a wonderland, but a reign of law. These are the *literae divinae* written in the universe by the finger of God.' This turned out to be much more than an elementary exercise in discernment and natural logic, with Rugby's students reporting significant astronomical discoveries in the 1870s.

PERFORMANCE AND COMPETITION: THE NEW BIG SCHOOL

The last of Butterfield's works at Rugby School was the realisation of his new assembly hall, now moved to a site standing alone across the main road from the entrance to the headmaster's house and raised above a suite of three classrooms. It was driven by the need for a dedicated venue for performance, general lectures and ceremonial events, and especially to host the remarkable competitive culture that had grown up around singing and playing music under long years of guidance from Otto Goldschmidt and Jenny Lind. Butterfield designed a single large hall, with an internal ridge line of 26 feet and great, deep-set windows placed high on the two longer sides above panelled dados 9 feet high. It is thickly walled, and virtually sealed east and west, both for acoustic qualities and to allow for temporary stages and movable ranks of choir and orchestra stands. There were unpolished marble floors for durability in heavy traffic, and two separate entries and flights of stairs – one to file a long line of boys in from the east, the other a more graceful ascent for dignitaries

211
New Big School, Rugby: view from the south-east, postcard by Stewart & Woolf, *c.*1895

212
New Big School,
Rugby: elevation of
principal front, c.1884

entering through the centre doors and turning left.
It is built on a very shallow foundation of concrete
slab and posts; rises from ground to roofbeam in
four stages, each of 13 feet, with the 'Big School'
open to double height; and its roof is domed on the
segment of a circle whose fulcrum, as Butterfield
shows the builder in the section (fig.213), is based
on the same half-measure – 6 ½ feet – below the
ground. It is a virtually symmetrical composition,
but as an early postcard shows, it is animated by
shadows and recessions and capped with stone and
metal pier caps, finials, turrets and gable crosses,
echoing those at the new quadrangle and chapel.
The boundary wall and rail matched those at Temple
Reading Room.

An anonymous writer in *The Leaflet*, an ephemeral
student literary magazine happily preserved in the
Rugby Town Library, described the New Big School
just before completion as 'a coloured haystack'

with 'windows from Venice, walls from Siena,
and twirligigs on the roof from heaven knows
where'. But it is a wonderful work from the same
family of idiosyncratic personalities as the one that
produced the chapel, echoes of which, especially the
apse and tower, are reintroduced here in a changed
and less solemn context. There are moments of great
delight – a dais set before a window of crystalline
animation; the glorious blind arcades at either
end that tell us a theatre is within, their dove-grey
marble shafts playing against the blank slate in their
oculi; and a grand portico of double doors. It was
an unusual instance of an urban work in a distinct
precinct whose entire form could be grasped in a
single view; early souvenir photograph and postcard
publishers seized on the prospect from the south-
east; and it became for the Edwardian era one of the
best-known monuments of the midlands.

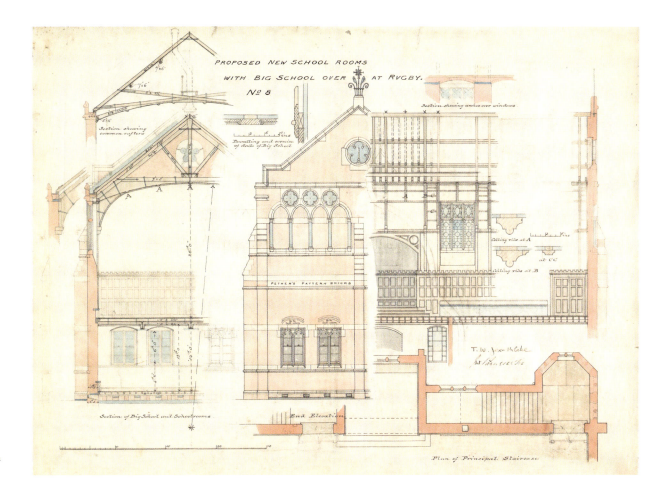

213
New Big School,
Rugby: end elevation
and sections, *c*.1884

NOTES

1. In addition to the sources cited for chapter 16, this chapter draws upon Arthur Helps, 'Recreation', in *Friends in Council*, a compendium of essays published in numerous series and editions starting in 1847; J. MacAloon, 'The Vision at Rugby Chapel', *The International Journal of the History of Sport*, vol.23, nos 3–4, May–June 2006, pp 393–445; James M. Wilson, *An Autobiography, 1836–1931*, Sidgwick & Jackson, London, 1932, p.64; Edward Crossley, Joseph Gledhill and James M. Wilson, *Handbook of Double Stars*, Macmillan, London, 1879; and Thomas M. Lindsay, 'Art Teaching at Rugby School', *The Art Journal*, vol.47, 1885, pp 49–52.

2. Grahame's recollections of his Oxford prep school are referred to in most biographical studies of his work – see, for example, Peter Green, *Kenneth Grahame, 1859–1932: A Study of His Life, Work, and Times*, John Murray, London, 1959, pp 40–49.

3. See MacAloon, 'The Vision at Rugby Chapel', op.cit., pp 393–445, on Pierre de Coubetin and the idea of sport as a source of moral and social education.

CHAPTER 18

THE EXPANSIVE SCHOOL, 1858–86

WINCHESTER COLLEGE

BUTTERFIELD'S WORKS within William of Wykeham's great fourteenth-century complex of Winchester College had begun – as at Rugby – with his memorial to the Crimean fallen in 1858, there in the form of a new cloister running between the chapel and hall, opening up a passage from one of the front courts to the cloisters behind, and providing a moment of reflection, entering and leaving the chapel as a body, to think on, and vow to emulate, the virtues of those who had gone before (p.247). Each of the biblical virtues is listed, and the names on the plaque below are sheltered by a seraph.[1] A second project was undertaken to rebuild, at his suggestion, a much-decayed and badly revised bell tower as a commemoration of two recent wardens of Wykeham's colleges at Oxford and Winchester, a meticulous archaeological reconstruction and

re-creation in which stones that could be were numbered, cleaned and re-laid in place.

His major intervention at the college answered an invitation to rationalise a set of much later buildings that had come together rather carelessly in 'Commoners', an adjacent site to the west of the original building, in order to provide more hygienic student lodgings, in place of the fatally unhealthy chambers that existed, along with lecture rooms and a library that would be open to all without cognisance of college hierarchy. Butterfield's solution was to sweep away what was there and begin again on some of the older footprint, with new brick buildings evocative of the better elements of late Perpendicular or seventeenth-century work on the site. The result was two open-sided quadrangles with a bridging structure carrying the library. A twentieth-century fire took down the

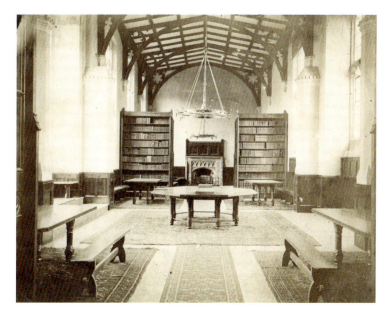

frontispiece, but the scheme remains essentially intact and sets up what amounts to a second college with a character as persuasive as Wykeham's and in sympathy with the patterns, scales and proportions of his original. For many decades, Flint and Moberly Courts perhaps accidentally held an essential place in a critical bird's-eye view in the Banister Fletcher's *History of Architecture*,[2] making it one of the most widely seen (and least-remarked) Victorian monuments in the study of historical buildings.

Butterfield was called on again in 1877 to work on the two chapels in the grounds, returning for junior chapel use a chantry that had been employed as a library and fellows' common room, and – to howls of protest – reseating the main chapel to accommodate a vastly expanded body of students and a much-diminished college of fellows. This had been dressed in the seventeenth century and after with wooden stalls and carved panels, obscuring the medieval stone tracery. By the time Butterfield intervened, the best of the woodwork had been removed by a patron in order to reveal old tracery and add new sculpture to the stonework at the east end. The remaining stalls were of no great significance but were remembered with some affection. Butterfield removed them, stripped the walls and placed low pews facing forward, while building new choir stalls of magnificent design and quality, entirely in scholarly sympathy with the fourteenth-century character the chapel now bore

214

Winchester College: view from the south-west showing Flint Court, the dining hall and Butterfield's Tower of Two Wardens, photograph by H.W. Salmon, published as 'The Moberly Library, College Chapel' [sic] in the portfolio *Views of Winchester College: A Collection of Permanent Photographs*, *c.*1890

215

Moberly Library, Winchester College: interior view as originally fitted by Butterfield, looking east from just west of the central bay windows, photographed 1880

216

Moberly Court, Winchester College: looking south to the windows of Moberly Library and the passage beneath to Flint Court, photograph by H.W. Salmon, *c.*1890

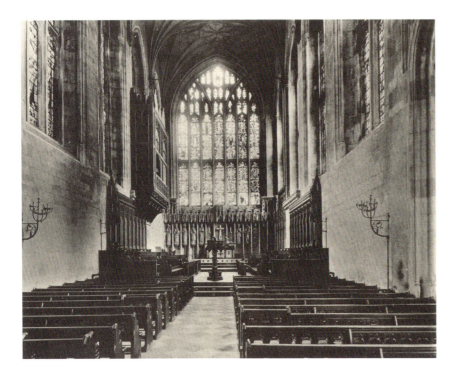

217
Winchester College
Chapel: interior
view looking east,
photograph by
H.W. Salmon,
published in the
portfolio *Views
of Winchester
College: A Collection
of Permanent
Photographs*, *c.*1890

again. He was condemned as a vandal, could find
no way to explain his course of action that would
not embarrass a generous trustee, and so kept
silent. A photograph taken about 1890 (fig.218)
shows the chapel during the very short life in which
Butterfield's conception remained intact. From
it one could suggest that the unacknowledged
objection was to Butterfield's reversion from a club-
like hall into the sacred space Wykeham intended,
communicating the humbling power of divine light
and its history of salvation that he allowed to pour
on to plain walls through its windows.

EXETER: THE MODEL GRAMMAR SCHOOL

There was an outcry when Gladstone appointed
Frederick Temple, a liberal thinker associated
with the rationalist wing in the English Church
and with positivism and scientism in educational
theory, as bishop of Exeter in 1869. He remained
close to Butterfield, who gifted the design of an
extraordinary episcopal staff in his honour and
undertook the refurbishment of the bishop's palace
and chapel, which Temple and his family – he
married at this time – were reoccupying. Temple's

appointment coincided with the re-evaluation of
the status of Exeter's tiny city grammar school,
an old foundation within the complex of a charity
hospital. Within days of his consecration, the
bishop, its principal trustee, was called to speak at
the school's anniversary, in January 1870. Reports
of his address on that occasion find him calling
on his audience to follow his vision of the role of
a school in the building of character: 'They were
bound, not only to see that their schools were places
where the understanding was to be cultivated, but
that they were places where, to a great degree, their
characters were to be formed, where principles,
which were to regulate their after-life, were to be
stamped upon the soul.'[3]

Over the next four years a movement to build
a new school to better answer the terms of its
foundation and the needs of the city and county's
middle class had begun.[4] There were long debates
first as to whether the school should remain a
Church of England establishment and maintain
its classical educational character or be a 'middle-
class school' geared to preparation for commercial
and managerial life; whether to include boarding
scholars or not; and then as to location, with some
anticipating the continued growth of the city and
proposing a suburban site, and others looking
to expand within the town. The consensus that
emerged by 1874 was a definition of the new 'first-
class school' – the origin of modern grammar and
high schools – as we find it in its ideal model at its
infancy. It should have low fees and attract mixed
social ranks of pupil; it should be sited to draw
both city and suburban families and to board a
proportion of country pupils from the county; and
its principal objective – with a number of endowed
university exhibitions already in hand – was to
open an opportunity to prepare for and enter the
universities for those who 'have not otherwise had
the means to do so'. The practical final choices,
driven by Temple, were to establish a course of
instruction equivalent to that of a public school;
to provide initially for up to fifty boarders and
150 day pupils; and to purchase a huge swathe
of meadowland on the eastern perimeter of the
urban area, where buildings could open on to

including, for the time being, the headmaster's lodgings. These opened on the dormitory and study floors for supervision. A temporary chapel seems to have been housed in a room below, with one classroom for a junior division. This, with an arched gateway and a temporary circulation system at the north end of the classrooms (less impressive than the grand staircase anticipated in the drawings), were all that was built in the first phase. The two north wings running east and west were planned as a second phase for a 'big school' and science lecture rooms and laboratories abutting the garden court. The unbuilt wing leading east from the hostel was barely defined, but intended for a third phase of construction, with a headmaster's house and a second section of classrooms on the same system as the principal range. Butterfield clearly planned for incremental realisation to produce a satisfying result, and – as a head at the turn of the century complained, when expansion finally became possible – laid things out in such a way that it was virtually impossible not to follow in outline the intention of his plan. The work is in the wonderful orange brick of south-eastern Devon with box stone deployed for trim and green slate roofing from Whitland Abbey. A bid of £15,000 from Stephens & Barstow of Bristol won the building contract, and after the addition of a temporary lab for chemistry and various improvements, including fire-suppressant tanks and piping from the hostel attic, it was brought in at £17,000. Here Butterfield presents the modern scale of a hugely expanded new institution by quite unapologetically presenting it, free of demonstrative self-importance, as an expression of usefulness, finding force, harmony and beauty through the simple clarity with which its separate functions are expressed. It is like a plan in profile. Temple declared in his widely reported address at the opening of the school that it stood in its simplicity and realism for a new aesthetic ideal and that, if not yet, 'posterity will see what for generations and generations' would be recognised as beautiful, with the rooms 'so very simple, so very unaffected, so perfectly true to their purpose, . . . simply what they professed to be and nothing else'.

playing fields, which, Temple insisted, were 'the most effective means of bringing a school together' when scholars came from different backgrounds, and the best instrument for bringing the moral influence of teachers into play. It was understood that Butterfield, 'the bishop's architect', would undertake the design. Removal to the new site was authorised in 1876, and the first students in the new model school began instruction in its old city site in 1877. The cornerstone of the new building was laid in July 1879, and the school had moved into its new quarters by the following autumn.

Butterfield's plan, developed through 1877 and completed in May 1878, was for a building of five wings on an H plan, lying on the slight downwards slope at the top of a hill looking west to Dartmoor, with playing fields and recreation fields, terraced and drained through a programme of earth-moving, staggered down the open slope. A long central bar of the H contained the five principal classrooms, with dormitories and studies for boarders above; the shorter western arm housed a high floor for a traditional college Hall, with kitchens and informal dining below, service areas and laundry opening to a terraced quadrangle of kitchen gardens, on to which the washroom facilities of the school faced. At the hinge was a six-to-seven-storey residential tower for five teachers and the serving staff,

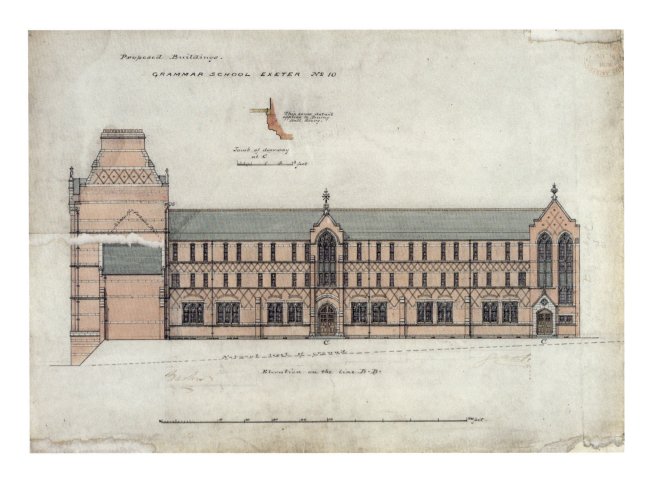

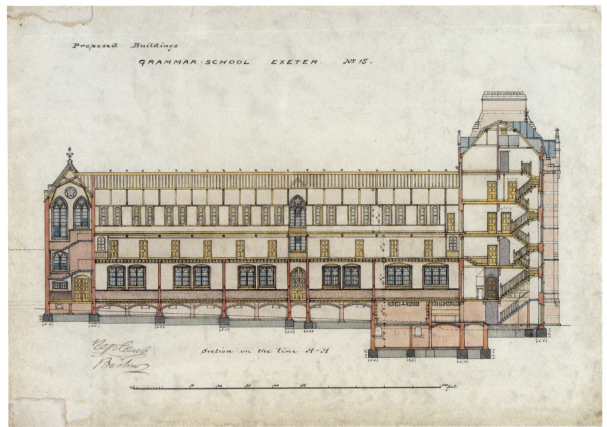

219

Exeter Grammar School: east elevation of classroom, study and dormitory wing, 1877

220

Exeter Grammar School: section of classroom, study and dormitory wing looking east, 1877

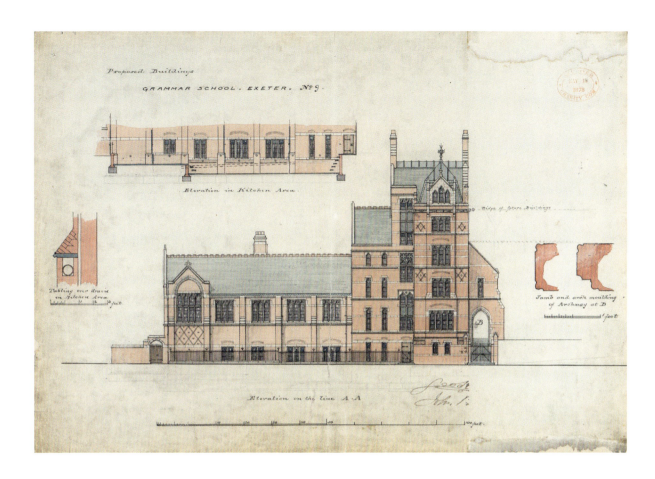

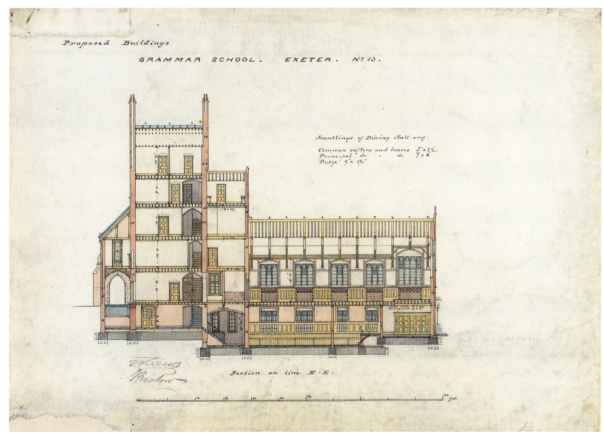

221
Exeter Grammar
School: south
elevation, 1877

222
Exeter Grammar
School: section of
south wing looking
south, 1877

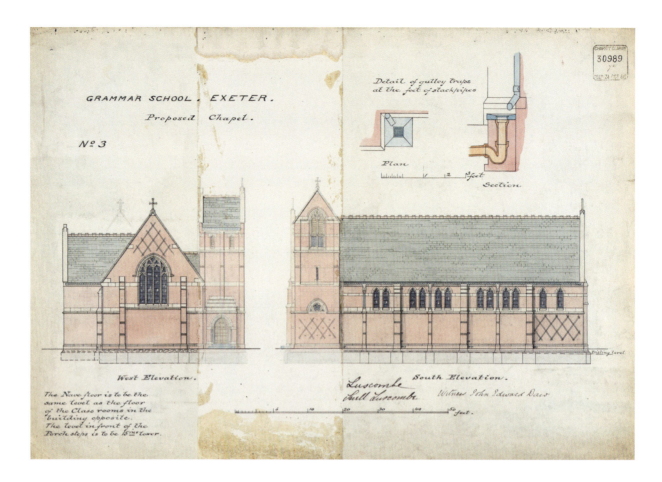

GRAMMAR SCHOOL . EXETER .

Proposed Chapel .

Nº 3

Detail of gulley traps
at the feet of stackpipes

30989

Plan

Section

West Elevation .

South Elevation .

The Nave floor is to be the
same level as the floor
of the Class rooms in the
building opposite.
The level in front of the
Porch steps is to be 15ᵗʰ Tower.

Luscombe

Witness John Edward Davis

223

Exeter Grammar
School: west and
south elevations of
chapel, *c.*1886

It was an extraordinarily democratic and modern system, with the community living and learning together as a corporate body. There was no central schoolroom for declamation; the five separate classrooms represented each of the five years, masters moving between them for different specialisms. There was equality between town and boarder; uniform study rooms, except for one or two larger ones for the tiny cadre of student captains. There was no distinction between scholar and commoner, on the grounds – strenuously presented by Temple – that cleverness displayed at a young age was no predictor of success, which came from diligence, regularity and attentiveness rather than native genius; and school captains were selected for their moral leadership rather than academic pretensions. Parents were encouraged to attend Sunday services in chapel. Funds were started soon after the opening in 1880, using the proceeds from sale of the old site, for a dedicated chapel, on which Butterfield laboured with great affection. The short

bell tower could not be completed on the funds available, but the refinement of a building in which Butterfield seems at first to offer next to nothing is extremely seductive. There is a simple perfection to the shifts in scale and rhythm, as in the insertion of tiny dove marble columns between the windows, in breaking the stringcourse of dark brick below, in the gentle collision of window tracery heads with the roof and the purposive thick drip moulds, corners and bands of stone.

Butterfield was involved with two other expressions of the reformed grammar-school movement that began with the studies of parliamentary commissions on endowed schools in the 1860s and bore fruit in the 1870s. He expanded the grammar school at Wantage, re-established in 1850, to accommodate a sudden growth up to 150 pupils, with two gabled pavilions of great domestic charm, and extended his own Sir Walter St John's School of the 1850s in Battersea, also growing at a rapid pace. In both instances, placement and

224
Exeter Grammar
School: view from
the south-east,
photographed *c*.1900

plan are designed to provide much more extensive common ground, both in outdoor open space and indoor gathering and circulation. This social space was now regarded as essential to the new scale of operation and to the mix of students, as educational theorists now proposed it was as critical for human animals to have room to manoeuvre in order to develop their social skills as for young cows and horses. For his pioneering Upper Class School for Girls in Wantage, built at this time for the preparation of young women to fill places just opening in the universities, Butterfield established lawns as social space, and crafted, over two phases, wings of domestic, dormitory, studio and classroom space that stretched into them. The contrast with the confines of an historical college is most strongly evident at Exeter, where the single wide passage beside the five classrooms gives an extraordinarily generous internal cursus, while on all sides Butterfield shaped and levelled the ground into a 'bigside' – the concept (and term) borrowed from Rugby's Close – of lawn and playing fields opening out to a view of Dartmoor; and for most old boys, coming from the town as day pupils, it was this common ground that encased their memories and earned their loyalty.

In Exeter itself, future business prospects were ruined by the Suez Canal, which changed the pattern of shipping routes and the business of its port; the population remained steady at about 45,000; the suburban community near the school remained largely a resort of retired military; and the school may perhaps have over-anticipated a need for advanced education on the modern model that neither the local middle class perceived, nor the universities could satisfy. Exeter Grammar for a long time struggled to maintain its numbers of senior students, let alone expand to fill Butterfield's full plan; but even in truncated form, only half realised, it is a magnificent rendering of efficiency.

SCHOOLS FOR A CHANGING SOCIETY: THE UPPER GRADES

Rugby did not become a borough until well into the twentieth century, so that the town parish retained full control of its schools (each linked to one of what would soon be numerous daughter churches), setting up by the 1880s different levels of education within the parish system. The reform of endowed schools had established a secular town

grammar school from the foundation that created
Rugby School, in order to meet the terms of its
charter without obliging the privileged public school
to admit more 'town boys' than it chose. But the
parish, under the rectorship of Moultrie's successor,
John Murray, took charge of most other schooling,
and began to extend the levels of education for an
urban parish numbering, by 1880, well over 12,000
inhabitants. Butterfield's Bath Street school, a
tempered economical variant of the grammar-school
model he had established for London at Sir Walter
St John's, Battersea, more than twenty years before,
was built at great speed in 1882. It was on a small
plot of open meadowlands facing a new district
of modest bow-fronted 'garden terrace' housing
between the town and the railway yards, where a
large centre of employment was developing, with
the famous cattle market moving there, along with
engineering and cement plants. It was a district of
the little-recorded but rapidly expanding new class
of town-dweller: skilled mechanics, builders and
craftspeople; schoolteachers; transport workers;
and postal, factory, bank, insurance and shop clerks.

The Bath Street school was designed to serve
the same class as the district in which it was built.
It began as a supplementary site for the parish's
school for higher grades, linked to Moultrie's
second subsidiary church of Holy Trinity, by George

Gilbert Scott, which had been built on the east end
of St Andrew's burial ground, but became rapidly
overcrowded and was reformed to become one of
Britain's first modern secondary schools, teaching 200
boys from the ages of ten or eleven to leaving age, and
providing a varied curriculum for different aptitudes
and interests, preparing pupils for apprenticeship,
training colleges or trade school. It was a remarkable
early acceptance of the fact that young people outside
the most privileged class might have the power to
choose a path of employment rather than follow that
of a parent. A separate girls' secondary school formed
at the same time, allowing Butterfield to improve
the entry, yard and services that had at first been
overcrowded by the need to segregate sexes.

Minutes of the building committee show
Butterfield deeply involved in the planning of a
hygienic and pleasant learning environment for
a new type of town school, working on a very
constrained budget but insisting on such features
as a bellcote, a huge gabled classroom window
facing the open fields to the east, and an assembly
room with semi-ecclesiastical dignity for morning
prayers.[5] The high-walled yard was used for choral,
orchestral and band practice, and for woodworking,
as well as games and physical training drills. A
photograph from the school's prize-giving day
in 1906 (fig.225) looks to the west from the gate
in a wall of the yard that opened to a substantial
school allotment of vegetable, nursery and fruit
gardens, with conservatory and potting sheds, all
maintained by the pupils as part of their curriculum.
Community allotments for townspeople to grow
their own food had begun to form at this time
and would become required municipal facilities
under the Local Government Acts of 1908. Garden
training not only prepared pupils for farm and
nursery employment, but taught principles for the
supplementation of household food supplies.

With pupils staying longer as the school-leaving
age rose, Butterfield's school – which was eventually
renamed the Murray Upper Grade School in honour
of its founder – built an extraordinarily potent and
enduring sense of belonging right until its final
years in the 1960s. It was only a single generation
since Butterfield's first town schools appeared, in

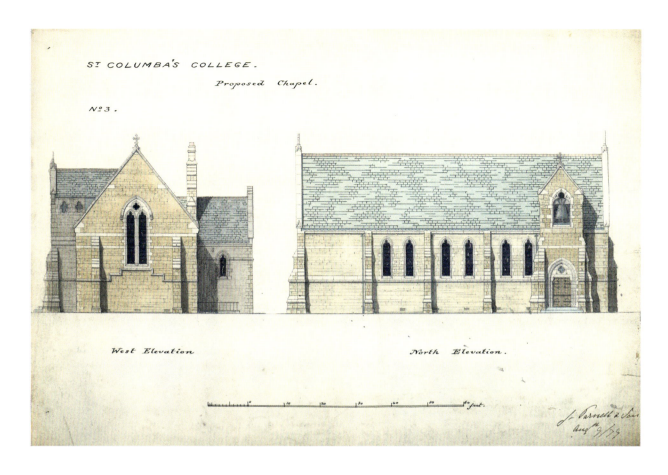

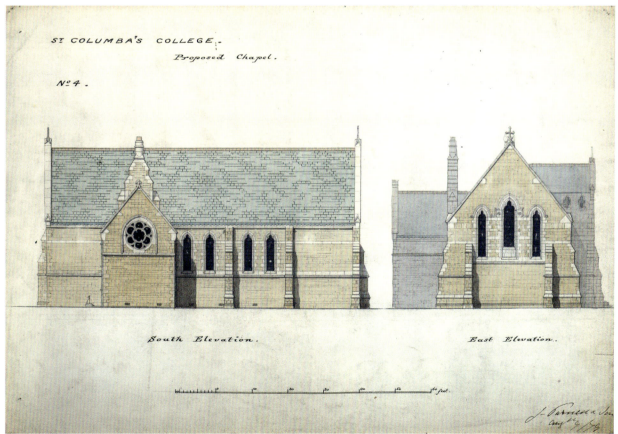

226
St Columba's College
Chapel, Dublin:
west and north
elevations, 1879

226B
St Columba's College
Chapel, Dublin:
south and east
elevations, 1879

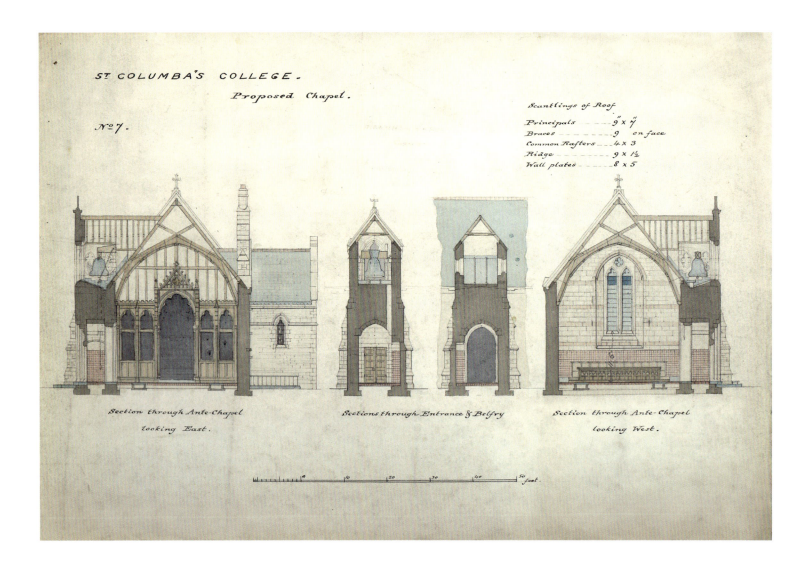

ST COLUMBA'S COLLEGE.

Proposed Chapel.

Nº 7.

Scantlings of Roof

Principals --------- 9" x 7"
Braces ----------- 9 on face
Common Rafters ---- 4 x 3
Ridge ------------ 9 x 1½
Wall plates ------- 8 x 5

Section through Ante-Chapel
looking East.

Sections through Entrance & Belfry

Section through Ante-Chapel
looking West.

227
St Columba's College
Chapel, Dublin:
sections through
antechapel, belfry
and organ transept,
1879

Jedburgh, Canterbury and Stoke Newington, and from a time when the very need and purpose of day schooling for the young was questioned to one in which attendance was legally compelled. Yet Butterfield's passionate commitment to providing uncommon new models of moral and functional aesthetics for such common places of improvement had not waned. It is hard to name another architect of such eminence with such dedication to making the extraordinary out of the ordinary.

ST COLUMBA'S COLLEGE, DUBLIN

St Columba's College was a brainchild of the eccentric high churchman William Sewell, conceived, and run by him for a while, as a school of rigorous classical teaching within an enveloping culture of prayer-book observance and piety, with a dedication to returning the Irish people to what he saw as their true religious and linguistic heritage, in the English Church that had descended from the Celtic, and in the Irish language spoken by its saints. This was a rather fanciful notion that did not quite survive the brutality of his regime. But in tempered form some of its spirit persisted as the college settled, after a difficult period, into the role of a public school with a pronounced religious life. It lay on a hillside country estate in Rathfarnham, south-east of Dublin, housed in a largely Georgian manor house, with rugged stone extensions in monastic Gothic added by Philip Charles Hardwick as part of an ambitious collegiate scheme, originally conceived with a central chapel and a large hall that were never built. By the early 1870s a temporary chapel was doing duty, furnished with donated stalls and carved pulpit, with an enormous bell housed in a frame and sounded not simply to call scholars to prayer but to be heard across the land below to awaken its people to what Sewell believed were the echoes of a long and neglected tradition of faith uncorrupted by the Tridentine practices of Rome.

The plan to build a new chapel emerged in 1869 but came to maturity only slowly during a period when the college was recovering from financial difficulties and reorganisation.[6] But with support from an Irish foundation related to the family of Alexander Beresford Hope, Butterfield was able to send preliminary plans to the warden in October 1878 and obtain Hope's consent in April 1879 to a finished plan for a chapel estimated at £5000. Butterfield took the radical step of setting the building apart from the body of the college on newly terraced and raised ground behind the old chapel, aligning his porch with that of the schools, and sweeping away what lay between to create a close. Joseph Parnell of Rugby was engaged to build, the old chapel cleared away, and a quarry opened just behind the site for the primary building material. Finished drawings were acknowledged by the builders in August and the chapel completed in October 1880. The pulpit and senior stalls of the old chapel were incorporated in the new one, and a gigantic belfry constructed above the porch to carry the great bell. There was a screened anteroom for household and visitors, and an arched transept for the organ. Neither figurative representation nor a cross could adorn the walls of the east end, given the severely Protestant taste of the newly disestablished Church of Ireland and the college community. Butterfield therefore resorted, with strikingly powerful effect, to an abstract pattern of tilework that constitutes, with a little tracery and the great screen, the entire extent of his ornament. His elevations suggest with some precision the cutting and laying of stones into heads, courses and corners in a pattern that gently underlines the structure, and Parnell's work in carving and laying blocks faithful to the rhythm of this quiet mosaic was extraordinary. What results is a chapel marvellously sited in a manner as firmly evocative of Irish antiquities as it is anticipatory of a new sobriety of ornament and efficient in lighting, opening and warming space: ancient and modern, structure within and structure without.

NOTES

1. This short account of the four complex interventions at Winchester College, one highly contentious, draws from many sources, but essential are Butterfield's letters in the college archives, many published in Sheila Himsworth (ed.), *Winchester College Muniments*, 3 vols, Phillimore, Winchester, 1976 and 1984; letter of Butterfield to John Duke, Lord Coleridge, 14 August 1877, Coleridge Papers, British Library; and C.A.E. Moberly, *Dulce Domum: George Moberly, His Family and Friends*, John Murray, London, 1911.

2. Banister Fletcher and Banister Flight Fletcher, *A History of Architecture on the Comparative Method*, first published 1896 (B.T. Batsford, London), with multiple subsequent editions.

3. Temple, address at Exeter quoted in *Western Morning News*, 4 February 1870.

4. The account of the Exeter Grammar School project has been traced largely through the extensive local newspaper reports accounting for its evolution, construction and subsequent institutional history, noting especially *Western Times*, 1 August 1879 and 15 January 1880; 30 July 1880, in which Temple's quoted remarks at the opening are recorded; and 18 May 1886, on laying the foundation stone of the chapel. See also *Building News*, 8 August 1879.

5. The minutes and other records are in the parish archives at Warwickshire Record Office.

6. The account of St Columba's College derives primarily from Butterfield's letters to the warden in the college archives and from newspaper and journal reports, notably *Building News*, 10 October 1879, *The Columban* (student newspaper retained in the college library) for April and September 1880, *Irish Times*, 2 October 1879, and *The Guardian*, 8 September 1880. See also Gregory K. White, *A History of St Columba's College, 1843–74*, published for the Old Columban Society, 1980, and the college guide to the chapel by Julian Girdham.

VII FELLOWSHIP, DISCIPLINE, DUTY

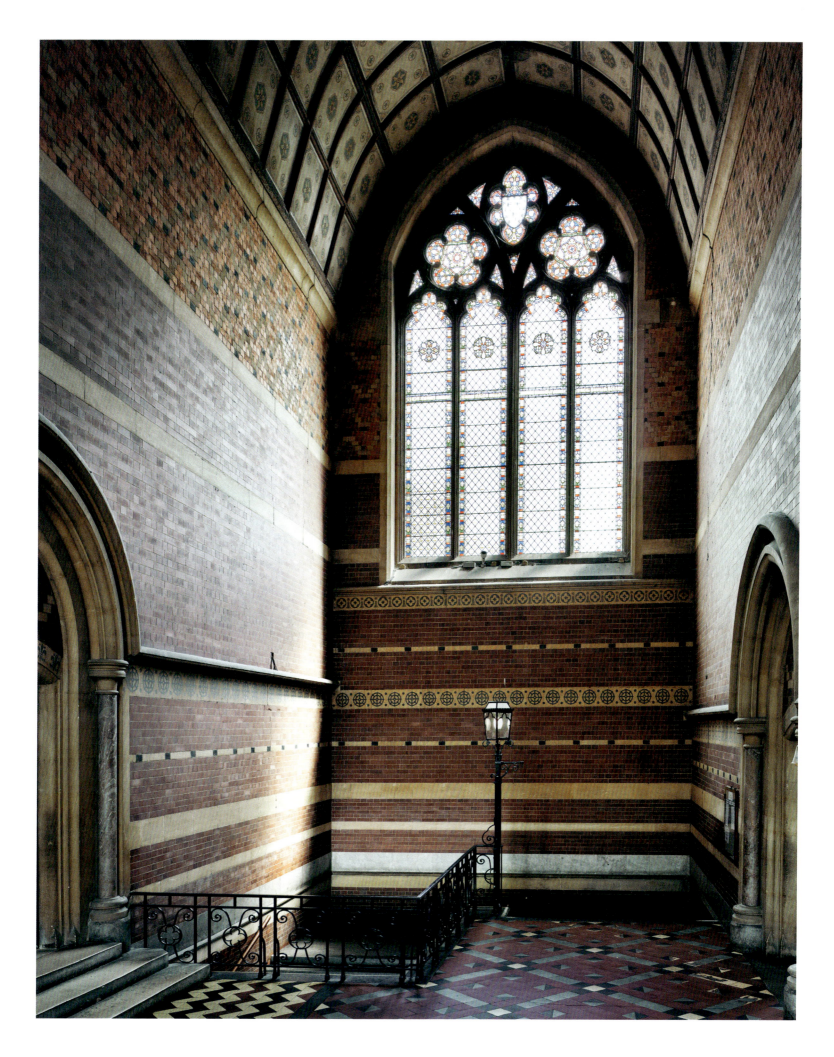

CHAPTER 19

SELF GOVERNMENT, 1874–92

ST AUGUSTINE'S COLLEGE AND THE IDEAL OF THE DOMUS

WE FIRST MET William Butterfield in the middle of the 1840s as we watched him bring into being a set of service and training institutions unprecedented in modern Britain, and develop an architectural language to express their character, principles and purpose. Most were experiments, dying soon or radically changing scope and purpose. But St Augustine's College, Canterbury, was remarkably sturdy, following the same general programme of training and the tradition it first established of austerity and self-denial,[1] maintaining a corpus of students and sending them out to service for nearly a hundred years before the Baedeker bombing of Canterbury on the last night of May 1942 shattered its windows and ended its life as a missionary college. The First World War disrupted the college, and the horrifying dearth of young men in its aftermath slowed down intake between the wars, but by 1914 more than 800 students had 'sailed' from its walls, armed with the skills of teacher, catechist, chanter, carpenter, medic, linguist, printer and clothier.

Though by statute scholars entered between the ages of seventeen and twenty-two, in practice admission ages ranged from nineteen to twenty-five, and many of the men whose fees were sponsored by a colonial diocese or a local congregation were entering from artisanal backgrounds rather than gentry, with mechanical schooling and apprenticeship in their experience rather than classics and mathematics, for which they were given an additional probationary term to catch up. With

a master craftsman among the teaching fellows and students brought together from across the usual barriers of age, class and manners, the challenge for the college was to create a common culture through patterns of living that would transcend habits and constraints of rank and background. William Hart Coleridge had been immensely careful to construct a communitarian framework for this. Intake began slowly so that students in the first two years could be guided towards setting a tone for the newcomers. The rigorous daily timetable involved community physical drills, gatherings for prayer and meals, and sessions of general instruction rather than tutorials. There was no Arnoldian talk of a leadership elite,

and sets and cliques were deliberately inhibited by focusing gathering space on the single open cloister and its terrace. The ruling ethos – exemplary of so many new and reformed institutions of training, education and learning in this era, but here fundamental to the survival of missionaries in remote, lonely and physically challenging circumstances – related first to 'self government', the building of a disciplined mental, moral and physical character to young men's lives, and secondly to establishing a fellowship of allegiance to a common purpose and code, the memory of which could sustain and restrain its members however far afield and long into the future.

The economy and lack of social hierarchy in student life at Canterbury would serve as a model for Keble College. But perhaps the construction of a collegiate memory was even more influential. To this end, the second warden, Henry Bailey, instituted a valedictory ceremony for those 'sailing', whose names, destination and dates were then inscribed on the cloister walls as a constant reminder; prolific

St Augustine's College, Canterbury: view of the warden's, fellows', and 'native' lodgings looking south-west from the library terrace, Judges postcard, *c*.1910 (reprinted in sepia at a later date)

St Augustine's College, Canterbury: detached room and Tudor wall, Judges postcard, *c*.1910 (reprinted in sepia at a later date)

carpentry; and – acutely sensitive to light, depth and scale – recording Butterfield's work on the ground. Her view of the cloister (fig.228) shows the wall of 'sailing' dates and the stone benches to prevent 'cliquing' that provided the major social space of the college; and the photograph of the upper passage (fig.229) shows Butterfield's, corridor lined with the wooden partition wall, that he conceived as a solitary ambulatory.

The original plan had been placed to allow for expansion. By 1860, workshops in the chapel crypt had moved to the land behind the library, and Butterfield converted the vaulted space into memorial walls for those lost in the missionary field. There were adjustments to the front of the warden's house as further workshops moved out of his cellars. And, extending south into the 'Tudor garden', a large new 'native' wing was attached to provide sleeping and common rooms for students from 'foreign parts'. Here Butterfield stepped the structure back to make a staggered line – as he would in his last 'New Buildings' at Keble – and found a third, stripped-down variant on the scheme of the lodgings to differentiate it. Ten years later a free-standing garden pavilion known as the 'Detached Room' was built for a student common room and recreational library, each of its four tall sides wonderfully and differently gabled and windowed. In this configuration the college remained, as something like an ideal townscape or cathedral close, with an emphatic sense not of an institution but of the collective 'domus' Beresford Hope evoked, bearing a character between the urban and domestic that would reappear most conspicuously for the 'Gordon Boys' nearly twenty years later.

Recreation grounds were added to the north in 1882; and the undercroft of the main library was reworked in 1883-4 as a museum in memory of Edward Coleridge, along with Butterfield's last major intervention, the memorial embellishment of the upper chapel. The shapes and incidents gained variety as the complex expanded, but the simple architectural character stayed true to that conveyed by Bishop Medley, who saw in the atmosphere Butterfield had constructed in the first college buildings a purposeful sincerity, restraint and

college publications, printed and edited by the students, were devoted to reports from graduates in the field; and there was an impressive annual anniversary assembly, at one of which Beresford Hope called for a new toast to replace the standard '*Floreat Collegium*' with '*Floreat Domus*', recognising that the habits and traditions of the community had become as close and lasting as the bonds of loyalty and affection in a model household. To another assembly, in July 1904, came the young Norfolk photographer Olive Edis, who made a remarkable record of the site at the height of its maturity, capturing the practical training of the students in darning, nursing, printing, weaving and

232
St Augustine's
College, Canterbury:
interior of the
Coleridge Museum,
photograph by Olive
Edis, July 1904

'material truthfulness' that was analogous to the character of the men the college sought its scholars to become and built to inculcate those virtues: 'severely simple but winningly attractive; frugal, yet not parsimonious; gentle, and yet firm'.[2]

CONVIVIUM: SEMINARIES IN SALISBURY AND MADAGASCAR

In 1877, 480 priests and deacons of the Anglican Church in England were ordained; 330 were university graduates and 120 came from theological colleges, with the long-established St Bees providing

as many as twenty-five, but the others came from the twelve small diocesan colleges. These had begun to form in 1838, some as a means of increasing the numbers of clergy by drawing in those from outside the universities, some to answer Pusey's call to reassert the place of the cathedral as a site of learning, and some to provide existing graduates of the universities with the formal theological training that had until then been thought an unnecessary qualification for an Anglican priest. The Salisbury college had begun modestly early in the 1860s in a seventeenth-century town house on the cathedral close. When Butterfield's friend George Moberly of Winchester College assumed the see in 1869, a plan evolved for its development into a fully residential fellowship of students, akin to a university college.[3]

Butterfield's work began in 1874 with an entirely new semi-quadrangle of flint, brick and cut stone, to the north of the existing house, with suites for sixteen students and an entry, dining and social space linking to the town house. He used a mix of flint, brick and cut stone common to the local vernacular and evident in an ancient boundary wall on the site. He added to it in 1876 with a house and garden for the resident subwarden, establishing its place in the hierarchy by standing it out from the terrace with a triple stack of bay windows and more generous ashlar trim. Five years later came a remarkable chapel, with bell tower, library, a small lecture hall and study room, built entirely in flint and stone like the church at Barnet, then in progress. The chapel's simple bell turret faced into the close, presenting to view a niche with a statue of the Virgin as patron saint of the diocese. Each sector of its plan is marked clearly by the way the distinct volumes are assembled and articulated, and rough walling lends the chapel a humility and structural clarity that seem to speak in reproachful contrast to the flying buttresses, crocketed pinnacles and flamboyantly irrational massing of the monument across the lawn. A very fine early colour-printed view (fig.233) looks from behind the complex towards the spire of the cathedral, with the subwarden's house and garden in the foreground, the chapel and library across the quadrangle, and a portion of the three-storey wings of student lodgings

this mother house . . . They point with great
pride to the peace and social harmony which
they sustained during the recent revolution and
invasion which had left the rest of the region
devastated.[4]

Gregory, one of the clerical sons of the Dean of
St Paul's, had arrived with the first Anglican bishop
of Madagascar in 1870 and moved inland not long
after to take up an infant training programme
for Malagasy missionaries, which he would then
lead for a quarter of a century. The church for
this college, at Ambatoharanana, was designed in
drawings and specifications gifted by Butterfield in
about 1874.[5] It was to be the chapel for the college
community and a mother parish church for the
missions and chapels in surrounding villages, and so
laid out to a full 110 feet, with a great organ transept
and an enormous porch. Construction work
was delayed for some years by a series of deadly
epidemics and disorders, and by the incompetence
of the first contractor. But by the time the church
opened, sixteen men were already in training for
teaching and the diaconate ministry, living in
cottages with their wives and children, for whom
a primary school was provided. At the same time,
eighteen boys from the higher classes of Malagasy
were receiving a general education in Gregory's
effort – supported by the Queen – to establish an
elite within the island's governing class sympathetic
to Christian ethics and traditions. It was the model
of a colonial programme of self-development not
unlike that Lyautey would later enunciate (and
implement brutally) for overseas France.

that complete it. The college quickly developed
within its new walls an ethos of quiet convivium
in which clergy would be steeled for service by
training in a collegial atmosphere aloof from the
world, there to lay the spiritual anchor that would
secure them when they came to work in it, an idea
of training for duty through fellowship and retreat
much influenced by the experience of the college at
Cumbrae, with which many of those most attached
to the Salisbury college had been long associated.

In 1897, soon after arriving in Madagascar with
the French occupying forces, General Louis-Hubert
Lyautey journeyed into the highlands, arriving after
nights sleeping *en bivouac* and days of dusty trails
to find himself taking tea, dressing for dinner and
sleeping in a comfortable bed as the guest of St
Paul's Missionary College and its founders, Francis
A. Gregory and his wife Ann Marie. Waking the next
morning to the sound of church bells and the view
from his window of trimmed hedges and flower
gardens, he imagined himself 'in the county of Kent'.
There were before him,

> in a great park, three schools, a large college,
> a hospital, a sanatorium, workshops, a farm, a
> Romanesque church in the best manner, and
> in the midst, the charming cottage they live in.
> From here, the work has spread throughout
> the neighbouring district, and many villages
> live, prosperous and happy, in the shadow of

The hope was for an eventual complement of
fifty men and 150 boys, and with the church in place
an annual building programme was undertaken to
gradually achieve this capacity. The most impressive
of the secondary buildings was a two-storey college
hall of lecture rooms and library, built for £2200
from 1887 to 1890 to Butterfield's design in a layer
of randomly cut and heavily mortared sandstone,
exposed inside and out. There was a verandah
on the east side and a beautifully bulky tower at
its western end, housing lecture hall and gallery
under a belfry, with a rigorous geometric pattern

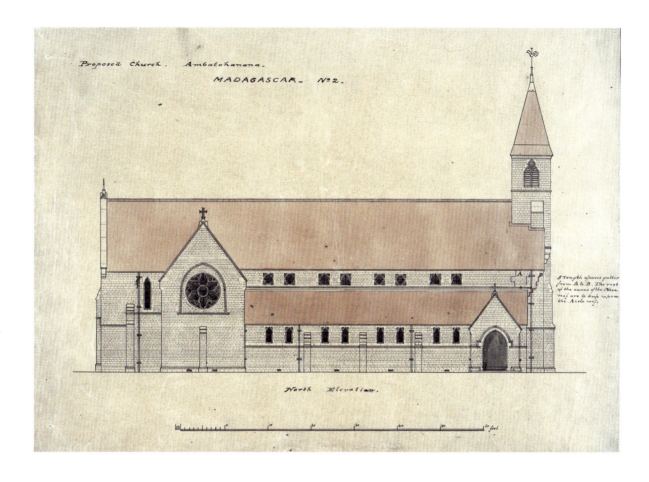

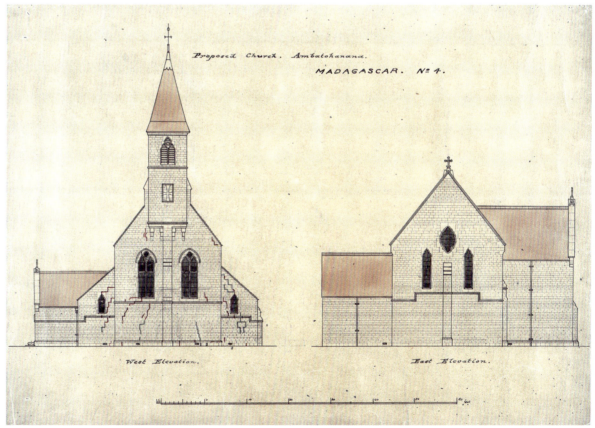

234
Church at
Ambatoharanana,
Madagascar: north
elevation, *c*.1874

235
Church at
Ambatoharanana,
Madagascar: west and
east elevations, *c*.1874

of slit openings. The former cook and porter who had taken over responsibility for construction, Rainatratra, was noted as a builder of genius both for his tailoring of stone into structure and for his extraordinary skill as a master carpenter. Captured into slavery as a boy in Mozambique, he had been a servant of the royal households until liberation, and would, when the Gregorys finally left the college, be granted a tract of land nearby where he established a settlement of his fellow Africans, leading the national community of these Zazamanga people until his death in the 1930s.[6]

The laying of stonework was as impeccably faithful to the laying patterns in Butterfield's drawings as Parnell's at St Columba's in Dublin. Interiors of both church and college were kept cool by exposing the thick stone, and by narrowing openings, most unglazed, to slits of light and air, notably in the hall and gallery set high within the college tower. Carved woodwork filled the college library under panel-coved ceilings and framed the bannisters and skirtings of the stairs, while the panelling, seating and cabinetry of the library in the warden's house took Lyautey's mind back to his own chateau in France. While the college, laid on to the same narrow terrace as the church, is severely and assertively enduring in character, the church itself has a wonderfully relaxed and delicate austerity, its side windows carefully oriented

to gather changing shafts of light, and its most visible northern aspect dominated by a great rose window in the transept in the inventive tracery of a six-petalled tropical flower, very like a *Mammea*, perhaps one of the new specimens gathered and forwarded to the Royal Botanic Gardens, Kew, by Ann Marie Gregory from her botanical excursions into the Madagascar highlands.

A 'LITTLE COLONY': THE GORDON BOYS' HOME

The unlikely and eccentric national hero and maverick military commander Charles George Gordon died in January 1885 after a year in the defence of Khartoum. He had dedicated his leisure to helping his 'kings' of the Gravesend docklands – one branch of the vast fleet of boys cut adrift that lived on their wits in the streets and waste ground of the port and garrison towns of England, and to whose rescue and reform he was devoted. It was Alfred Tennyson and his son Hallam, friends of Gordon, who first proposed as his national memorial a home to house, discipline and train these unlucky outcasts for useful lives. It became a project of the War Office, whose perilous naval training ships had rightly gone out of favour, but which had a growing need to find youth to fill the lower ranks of the forces, from bandsmen to machinists, tailors and orderlies. An enormous project of national fundraising was launched with the Prince of Wales in the lead; a temporary camp in Hampshire was opened; recruitment began through municipal authorities, police referrals, parishes, workhouses and the messenger corps of the Boys' Brigade; and a permanent site was found on the sand and scrub heaths of Surrey in West End, Chobham, near Woking.

Butterfield agreed, as honorary architect – which suggests a donation of his design services and perhaps a reduced role in supervising execution – to design a campus to house and train some 240 friendless and destitute boys between the ages of fourteen and sixteen.[7] The project was to proceed in stages, but Butterfield's plan for the whole and

236
Gordon Boys' Home, Chobham: view from the south, engraving by Waterlow & Sons after an illustration by Evelyn Stuart Hardy, from *Illustrated Naval & Military Magazine*, August 1890

Gordon Boys' Home, Woking.

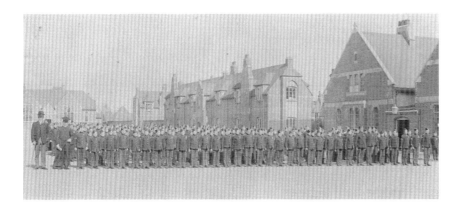

237
Gordon Boys' Home, Chobham: view of the north range from the south-west, Hood & Co. 'Sanbridge Series' postcard, *c*.1903

238
Gordon Boys' Home, Chobham: view of Parade Ground looking south-east, photographed *c*.1892

his approach to design seemed fixed by March 1887, when Joseph Norris received a contract for £19,000 to build the first two dormitories of eighty beds each, workshops, officers' quarters and a modest dining hall. A hospital came soon after in a second phase, along with a third dormitory, pool and gymnasium, and by 1891, with a full recreational hall and schoolrooms, all the essential facilities were in place. Here 'Gordon Boys' could be provided with 'a thorough general education, . . . carefully instructed in various trades according to their individual tastes. The choice of a career, whether

Naval, Military, or Civil, is left entirely to the boys; the object . . . being simply to qualify them to become good citizens.'

The project attracted press, subscribers and visitors from around the country, and 'Gordon Boys' had a very busy life in magazine literature and novels for young people. The children's book illustrator Evelyn Stuart Hardy was nineteen years old and at the start of a famous career when she visited the Home to sketch its activities in August 1890 for a popular boys' military magazine, just as the rapid sequence of Butterfield's works there were reaching completion. Her general view (fig.236) is taken from the narrow southern end of the 45-acre wedge of land in which the home was established. On the westerly perimeter is Butterfield's 1887 housing for commandant and senior officers. We then see behind and to the right of it his pool and gymnasium of 1890 in connected structures of brick and iron under high roofs suspended from a metal framework; these form the west side of the huge elongated quadrangle and parade ground on the northern perimeter of the site. Next we see the low double schoolroom of 1889, standing free at

239
Gordon Boys' Home, Chobham: west front of the Napier Memorial Hall, photographed *c.*1891

240
Gordon Boys' Home, Chobham: south front of the school, photographed *c.*1892

the far west end of the long north side of the quad. The museum pavilion and the tailor's shop are seen to the east of it at the end of the long north range of workshops. The principal face of the first free-standing dormitory, on the south side of the quad, then appears, with the assembly hall to the right and the second, matching dormitory to its east. Behind them, across the parade ground, further portions of the long range of workshops and housing for training sergeants are just visible.

Hood & Co.'s souvenir view (fig.237) shows the north side of the parade ground, formed up to the entry gate by Butterfield's street-long range of workshops and instructors' lodgings, with high gabled ventilating roofs and windows fit for task

lighting. To the east of the gatehouse is a two-storey brick, timber and stucco residence for officers, and then the Napier recreational and dining halls of 1891. A very early photograph (fig.238) carries the panorama to the south-east with the head schoolmaster and what seems to be the entire complement of 240 boys assembled at attention. To the far left is Napier Hall again, with the roofs of bakery, dairy and kitchen facilities visible behind it to the right. The north end of the third dormitory, which faces west, appears next, then one of the paired original dormitories that faced south, and half of the double-fronted assembly hall that sat between them. Behind, the roof and chimney of the three-winged hospital of 1888–9 is just visible, standing beside the playing field in hygienic isolation, open to the western breeze and planned for cross ventilation, with one wing segregated for fever. It was much admired by visitors as comforting and bright but failed so thoroughly to follow the severe hygienic specifications offered by Florence Nightingale that she asked for Butterfield 'to be *cashiered*'.[8] Together, the two views give a clear sense of Butterfield's plan, which was effectively to lay out a small town, its functions dispersed in discrete containers, and a distinctive expression afforded for each of the four main typologies: the boys' quarters all of plain red brick, with hipped dormers; social and assembly halls in red and blue patterned brick trimmed in stone, with emphatic gables; the workshop range arrayed like buildings at wharfside or a great farm yard, in a long low row of brick and glass with enormous peaked gables; and the officers' residences in brick with white stuccoed upper floors and a mix of peaked and half-hipped gables. The gym and baths were built of iron posts supporting glass roofs within a brick frame.

In 1889–91 Butterfield added the recreational and dining hall donated by the Royal Engineers and named after Lord Napier of India, chair of the trustees; a schoolroom for desk instruction; and the large double, glass-roofed pavilion for swimming pool and gymnasium, funded by supporters of the home, to redress the appalling physical condition in which some of these destitute children were found. The hall – of which a photograph was taken at the

241

Gordon Boys' Home,
Chobham:
the tailor's shop,
photographed *c*.1900

time of completion (fig.239), shortly before the installation of a front terrace on which an artillery piece was mounted – would be converted into sole use as a dining room in 1898. Set back from the workshop range at the north-west end of the paved parade ground, the new schoolrooms faced the forecourt of the swimming bath and gymnasium. The interior of the building was an open space with movable partitions in order to separate instruction for different classes. There were generally two divisions, with separate entrances for both. Subjects included report writing, bookkeeping, mapmaking, military history and topographical drawing. A small teaching museum was added just to its east, with artefacts related to General Gordon, memorials of the Home and 'curios being collected by the Head Schoolmaster' for visual instruction.

The tailors' workshop was at the western end of the northern range in one of the projecting wings running north to south, providing large windows along the end wall towards good light. Here, from their first day in residence, boys made their own boots and uniforms, learning enough of the tailor's and cobbler's art to serve in quartermaster divisions, as well as to be equipped for these trades

in civilian life. A view of the carpentry shop in the *Public School Magazine* of 1900 shows boys building dining and work tables for the Home, and reports from 1890 suggest that most of the furniture throughout the home was made in the shops. As with tailoring, metalwork, bakery, cobbling, saddlery, laundry, and band and kitchen duty, this was a trade useful to military support as well as civilian employment. A photograph of the smithy machine shop appears to show the boys also fabricating military and transport hardware. All the sergeant instructors were soldiers.

There were four sleeping wards of twenty beds each in what were by 1890 three matching dormitory buildings, with a common room and resident junior officer on each floor. Nightingale strenuously objected to Butterfield's initial plans for these quarters, as overcrowded, unhygienic in managing the separation of clothing, under-ventilated and psychologically redolent of a barracks rather than a home. It is likely that he modified the design, for the general aspect makes for something much more comfortable and domestic than a barracks. Gentle divisions are made by the cross-beams; windows suggest cottage dormers; there is a window niche

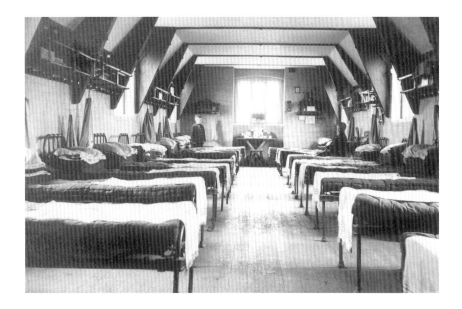

242
Gordon Boys' Home, Chobham:
room in one of the dormitories,
photographed *c*.1892

243
Gordon Boys' Home, Chobham:
Commandant and Senior Officer
quarters, photographed *c*.1900

for writing and displaying letters, high shelves for personal belongings, and no foot or floor lockers. Elements of 'military discipline', which, said Nightingale, equals '*in*discipline', were in force: punishment cells for miscreants and flogging for absconders. Nightingale was particularly disturbed by the confinement of the sister and matron to sick duty in the school hospital rather than providing a woman's presence in the course of daily activities, without which she felt no civilised man could be formed. But it was also in the ethos of the Home to build the self-confidence that comes from self-sufficiency and the social confidence that comes from teamwork, and a system of internal leadership and promotion constructed elements of peer monitoring and discipline within the boys' community.

By the summer of 1892, with Butterfield's scheme complete, the rate of intake and successful discharge accelerated. Ninety-five boys were successfully placed out in the following year: fifty-six in the army; nine to government service in the Cape and Canada; and thirty into civil employment. After ten years, in 1897, the home could report a total of 865 boys passing through, nearly 600 of whom could be accounted for – 344 in military service and 240 in civil employment. By 1900 it was estimated that 500 old Gordonians were then in active service, and with seventy already listed in arms in South Africa, the long roster of the Home's war dead would begin to be commemorated. By 1900 there was a commandant, a staff-officer and sixteen specialist sergeant-instructors, with a school headmaster, chaplain, matron and nursing sister. A farming operation had opened north of the schoolrooms. A bland non-denominational chapel, designed by Colonel Robert William Edis of the Artist Rifles, was added in 1897 to the space between the commandant's quarters and the gymnasium, which would be replaced a little later by a new library; and a second floor was added to the workshop wing in 1904. But the general integrity of the Butterfield plan was intact, and the character of what he was said to call a 'little colony', to whose design he was so devoted in his last years, remains.

NOTES

1. The continuing history of the college is largely drawn, like the discussion of its origins in chapter 1, from George Frederick Maclear, *St Augustine's, Canterbury: Its Rise, Ruin, and Restoration*, Wells Gardner, Darton & Co., London, 1888; Henry Bailey, 'Twenty-Five Years of St Augustine's College', 1873, in *Occasional Papers from St Augustine's College*, published by the college and assembled in a compendium of 1953; Robert Ewell, *Guide to St Augustine's Monastery and Missionary College*, Cross & Jackman, Canterbury, 1896 and 1902; and the annual reports, addresses and occasional papers of the college with other print ephemera, found in the digital library Project Canterbury (http://anglicanhistory.org/england/).

2. 'Farewell letter from the Bishop of Fredericton', *Colonial Church Chronicle and Missionary Journal*, September 1848, p.104.

3. Sources on the Salisbury Theological College project include a review of accounts in the records filed with Wiltshire and Swindon Archives; *Salisbury and Winchester Journal*, 1 July 1876 and 2 July 1881; *The Guardian*, 14 July 1875 and 16 October 1876; and *Bath Chronicle*, 7 July 1881.

4. Author's translation from Lyautey's letter to his sister, 25 November 1897, in *Lettres du Tonkin et de Madagascar, 1894–99*, Librairie Armand Colin, Paris, 1920, vol.2, pp 216–17.

5. The account of the project in Madagascar is drawn principally from published sources, including *The Guardian*, 12 July 1882, *John Bull*, 19 August 1882, and *The Net*, 1 June 1883.

6. Michel Razafiarivony, 'Les descendants des anciens esclaves importés d'Afrique à Madagascar: tradition et réalité', *Journal of Asian and African Studies*, no.70, 2005, pp 63–80.

7. The account of the Gordon Boys' Home project is taken principally from the plethora of press reports and pamphlets on its inception and progress, noting especially in the early years: the thoroughly researched young person's novel of Emily Brodie, *Right about Face; or, Ben The Gordon Boy*, John F. Shaw & Co., London, 1892; *Saturday Review*, 27 April 1889; Lieut.-Col. Arthur Collins, 'The Gordon Boys' Home', *Illustrated Naval and Military Magazine*, August 1890, pp 485–500; and *Daily News*, 12 March 1887. A portrait of the 'waifs' attended to by a central London mission in the year the Gordon Home opened is provided by one of the clergy at Butterfield's beautifully extended and modernised church of St Giles in the Fields: D. Rice Jones, 'St Giles in the Fields', *English Illustrated Magazine*, vol.4, October 1886 – September 1887. See also Lieut. Col. Derek Boyd, *The Gordon Heritage: The Story of General Charles Gordon and the Gordon Boys' School*, Robert Hale, London, 1985.

8. Nightingale's involvement and strictures appear, and are further discussed, in Lynn MacDonald, *Collected Works of Florence Nightingale*, vol.5, Wilfred Laurier University Press, Waterloo, Ontario, 2003.

COMMON GROUND

Winchester College, Flint Court

Exeter Grammar School and Chapel

Gordon Boys' Home, Chobham

St Columba's College Chapel, Dublin

St Columba's College Chapel, Dublin

CHAPTER 20

'TO OXFORD': UNIVERSITY EXPANSION *and* REFORM, 1857–64

BALLIOL COLLEGE CHAPEL, GROUNDS AND LIBRARY

LATE IN THE 1840s, Oxford colleges had begun to widen the number of their undergraduate admissions and to enhance services and encourage attendance at their chapels. Merton College, whose chapel also served as a parish church, introduced choral services and evening prayers and engaged Butterfield to undertake the extensive restoration work of 1849–51. Shortly after, he became the last in a line of architects, starting with A.W.N. Pugin in the late 1840s, invited to address the reordering of the Balliol College chapel. Discussions began in 1854, and Butterfield proceeded with proposals for rebuilding the chapel, together with modifications to the library and fellows' gardens, facing north towards stable-yards and carriage houses at the rear of the college grounds, that would bring the chapel on the garden side into harmony with its setting.[1]

On completion in 1857, the *Oxford Chronicle* told the story succinctly:

The old chapel, which has recently been destroyed, was effected in 1529, in the very indifferent Gothic of the time. The windows were round-headed and depressed, and yet were filled with tolerable tracery; but in the interior fittings the Gothic harness was altogether thrown off, and there was not the least pretence to appropriateness of style or beauty of form. The bell-turret only, in the whole edifice, was worthy of notice . . . indeed its pleasing aspect has become so familiar to the Balliol mind that the college seems not to have liked parting with their old friend . . . and Mr Butterfield has reproduced it, we might almost say, though, of course, he has improved the character of its detail and outline.

Fearful of Butterfield's frequent 'eccentricities of originality', the writer approached the new chapel with trepidation but was unhesitating in his praise of 'the beautifully chaste, and yet rich, tracery', comparing it to the 'preposterously heavy' Stoke Newington.

Butterfield's album includes a remarkable early photograph taken very soon after construction at Balliol was completed (fig.244). It stands a little back to show his revisions to the garden, whose boundaries he delineated with a long low wall and corner post of entirely original design, reordering its pathways on geometric lines. His work on the library adjoining, completed a short time after the chapel, included a wonderful new tall frontispiece of chimney, windows and portal, balancing the heights and openings with those of the newly ordered chapel and placing the larger library buttress at the same distance from the bell turret as that of the first

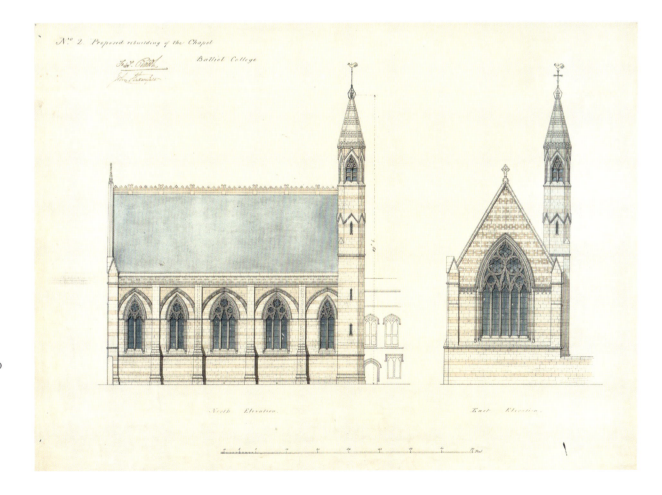

244
Balliol College,
Oxford: view of
chapel, library
and garden,
photographed *c*.1860

245
Balliol College
Chapel, Oxford:
rebuilding – north
and east elevations,
c.1856

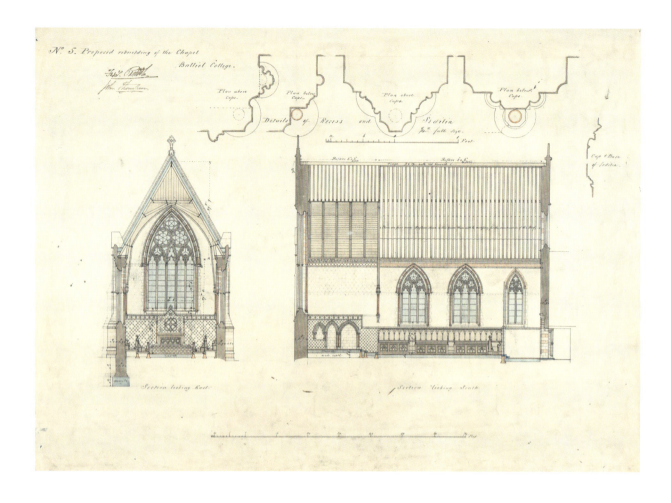

246

Balliol College Chapel, Oxford: rebuilding – sections looking east and south, *c.*1856

247

Balliol College Chapel, Oxford: interior view looking east, photograph by Henry W. Taunt, *c.*1870

buttress on the chapel side. A unity between two disparate elements is subtly created.

Butterfield followed most of the basic template of the old chapel, based on five bays separated by buttresses, with a corner bell turret anchoring the composition. This allowed him to keep the important fragments of early stained glass and to make use of the existing footprint on the south side. To the north, although deep concrete bearing shafts were sunk to carry taller windows and a weightier roof, the same line is followed. But there is a dramatic shift in volume and pitch, the chapel roof now rising to nearly twice the height of the library wing to its west, which the old chapel ridgeline had lain below, and though the octagonal profile of the turret remains, the change in height produces a complete transformation. The east front of the chapel, facing into Trinity College's front lawn, readily seen from foot traffic on Broad Street and engraved in a number of early views, bore a band of carved rosettes, and, as the pencil notes on the elevation suggest (fig.245), the corner buttresses were modified slightly to add caps in the shape of little Gothic tombs reminiscent of the Scaligeri tombs in Verona, which Butterfield visited in 1855 while the project was under way and recorded in his photograph album. Butterfield's drawings show an assiduous and very beautiful attention to the openings and sight lines that made crowding a large college into the footprint of a chapel for a tiny one comfortable; and there was an intimate grandeur to Butterfield's interior, beautifully caught in Henry W. Taunt's view some fifteen years later (fig.247).

The chapel was not at first well liked. Butterfield's crisp newness, meant to age, looked strident as it met the dusty dull monochrome of the crumbling quad beside it. After only two or three years maturing in the Oxford air, however, it proved less startling, and its critics generally relented. One of Butterfield's most discerning commentators, Arthur Rawson Ashwell, looked back at the changing reputation of Balliol when confronted two decades later by the originality of Keble Chapel.

248
Balliol College Chapel, Oxford: view from the front quadrangle, photograph by Henry W. Taunt, *c*.1865

Ashwell cautioned his readers that Butterfield built for posterity and in anticipation, knowing that his work would 'look more beautiful to our children than to us', citing Balliol Chapel as a prime example of the culture growing into the aesthetic condition that the building was designed to satisfy, so that the outrage had long passed and 'no one in his senses will deny now that, outside and inside, it is one of the most beautiful, as well as most strikingly original, of all small churches.'[2]

There was a sense of personal proprietorship over Oxford's landscapes that made it extraordinarily difficult to welcome any insertions or changes. Hopkins expressed the sense of the town as an embodiment of the personal within the public in his first fully crafted lines of verse: 'This is my park, my pleasaunce, this to me / As public is my greater privacy, / All mine, yet common to my every peer.'[3] A similar ideal is at work in the principle that buildings make up a *genius loci* not by deferring to a perceived generic quality of place but by holding true to their sense of themselves within it. Butterfield's Balliol is a model of such placemaking, by first attaching the new building to the memories and adjacencies of the old and then marking it out by a tone and character of its own. It is also a powerful instance of the notion of the building as 'commonplace', something seen daily from different viewpoints and absorbed into a personal geography, whose shape and sense must satisfy familiarity. Butterfield makes this memory of place within place by building at a height and scale of definition that produce a persistent changing prospect in the approach, the chapel shifting perspective and proportion in the gathering distance. This is captured with astonishing precision by Hopkins in the second of his two sonnets 'To Oxford', of 1865:

Thus, I come underneath this chapel-side
So that the mason's levels, courses, all
The vigorous horizontals, each way fall
In bows above my head, as falsified
By visual compulsion, till I hide
The steep-up roof at last behind the small
Eclipsing parapet; yet above the wall
The sumptuous ridge-crest leave to pose and ride.

very fond. The loss of these buildings was wrongly reported to journalists in 1861 as part of Butterfield's settled scheme and aroused a chorus of protest from the local and national press. Butterfield had in fact strenuously resisted the fellows' invitation to tear Mob Quad down entirely and made a perhaps overly ingenious plan to rearrange it, by flipping one wing of the library to run to the west. This was rejected; the proposition to sweep the quad away was repeated by the warden; and after many disagreements Butterfield settled on a site for an entirely new structure where a grove of trees stood on the south-west corner of the college grounds. His block faced east to establish a new three-sided court below Mob Quad, clearing and restoring the south side of the library, which had been long obscured by sheds and outbuildings, to form its north flank, and adding passages through its lower level to connect to Mob Quad. In Butterfield's final 'reduced plans' of May 1862 there were sixteen sets of rooms on four floors with a lower floor for services. It was clad in a durable Bath stone, rising to a height – and adopting a set of proportions and rhythm – that brought it into conversation with the seventeenth-century fellows' wing to its south. It opened in 1864.

Ten years before, Butterfield had worked through three summers on the rehabilitation of the great college chapel, and at the time the new residences for Merton were first under discussion in 1860, he returned to record in his sketchbooks window and door outlines from the medieval domestic buildings of the college: a triplet and a double lancet, both under light hood moulds, an untrimmed arched doorway and a single repeated narrow lancet. His variations on these unifying Merton themes are clearly seen in the new buildings at the Grove, bringing echoes of the ancient college into a decisively plain modern structure. Ruskin, said the Oxford Orientalist Max Müller, was deeply offended by the new buildings and compared their style to that of a London police station.[5] But that unsentimental west façade, where Butterfield emphasised the constructive efficiency of the building, with its windowed stairwell bays, displays the powerful functional logic behind a composition that stresses structure and varies the floor plans

249
Merton College, Oxford: view of Merton Field from the east, detail from Henry W. Taunt's workprint, 1865

250
Merton College, Oxford: view of new buildings from the south-west, photograph by Henry W. Taunt, 1870

MERTON GROVE: A COLLEGE EXTENSION

Shortly after the completion of Balliol, the fellows of Merton College came to Butterfield to ask for proposals for a 'college extension' of twenty suites of rooms to allow for a large increase in undergraduates.[4] There was much debate over its location, including the proposal made by the warden to replace the partially ancient, bitterly cold and inhospitable quadrangle of mixed date called Mob Quad, containing the tall twelfth-century treasury building and an L-shaped upper library – a sort of cloister south of the chapel of which many were

to maximise vista, producing a collision of layered symmetries in which no floor wraps around in quite the same fashion, but all hang together.

What was alarming to the dyspeptic and anti-modern culture of Oxford was appealing to the popular *Illustrated London News,* which showed a panorama of it that autumn, much admiring the manner in which it completed the townscape behind the ancient city walls, spoke in the local tones of stone and simple surfaces, and anchored the western perimeter of the college.[6] Souvenir prints and watercolours would quickly take it up as the centrepiece of views across the meadows. All seemed thoroughly sympathetic to Hopkins's well-known reflection on 'Duns Scotus's Oxford', a looking back on the Oxford of his youth, in which buildings find 'that neighbour-nature' their 'grey beauty is grounded in', so that masonry settles unmediated but belonging into the green meadows and woods about it.[7] It recognises, as the works of Butterfield so firmly express, that sense of containment and 'character' that John Duns Scotus – the fourteenth-century philosopher friar once resident in the college – defined as '*haeccitas*' or 'thisness': the nature of all beings to display their individuality, and, with such modern thinkers as Hopkins, to thereby establish such natural authenticity and integrity that, as Auden has it, 'shapes can so to their own edges keep' that, true to their own boundaries, they converse in confidence and sympathy with the place and substances about them.[8]

Oxford's discomfiture with the Merton College Grove building persisted. Twentieth-century 'improvements' disfigured it completely, and eradicated the discrete social courtyard that it once commanded by blocking up Butterfield's passages through to Mob Quad. But the brick-clad interiors with their high ceilings, ventilating windows and tall, wide, hygienic, well-lit stairwells remained, so that its rethinking of the shape of collective living, in which circulation and 'pleasaunce' unite, the staircase turning into a street and the court a *piazzetta*, is still evident. They were steps towards the democratic organisation of movement and congregation at a modern scale that would flower at Keble College, whose design began three years later.

THE FOUNDATION OF KEBLE COLLEGE

Broad measures of reform in the educational system at Oxford and Cambridge had been mooted for many years but progress towards widening the course of study beyond classics, ancient history and mathematics was slow; the system of private tuition used so much of the senior fellows' time that research was inhibited; college lectures were restricted to members and regarded as a rite of passage for young dons rather than a contribution to learning; fellows could not marry; college fees and charges for board – Oxford's 'battels' – were high; and there was little in undergraduate culture to discourage profligate and largely independent lives, dining in rooms, privately tutored and devoting social life to clubs and sports. At Oxford the rehabilitation of college halls and chapels and the extension and improvement of residences, which took Butterfield to Balliol, Merton and New College (where he also contributed improvements), were all part of an attempt to strengthen a collegiate way of life as the demand for university education increased, numbers of admissions grew and colleges began to require chapel attendance and dining from fellows. Modern studies began to be better recognised and served with the opening of the Taylor Institution for European languages, swiftly followed by examinations in modern history and the building of a museum of natural history, which was completed in 1860. But opportunities open to students of lesser means through scholarships and bursaries had dwindled in proportion to numbers, and most bursaries were still restricted to one or other of the great public schools.

John Keble had proposed as early as the 1830s the institution of a new college or hall on a principle of economy, with modest fees, an insistence on frugal habits and a collective life built around the chapel. And when his closest friends – Butterfield among them – gathered in April 1866 for his burial in the churchyard at Hursley in Hampshire, where he had been vicar for many years, the idea of founding a new Oxford college in his name was at once advanced as his memorial. A fundraising campaign was begun, the archbishop's sanction as

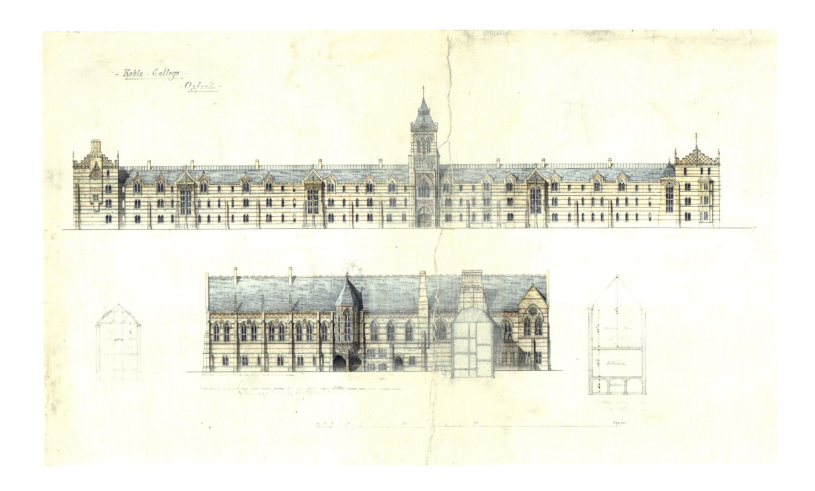

251

Keble College, Oxford: sketch presentations of the initial design, 1867, showing east elevation of gateway and living blocks and north elevation of hall and library

chancellor of the university was obtained, land was acquired to the north of the other colleges, across from the new museum, belonging to St John's College and then used as a market garden, and by the autumn of 1867 Butterfield, who had effectively been a part of the process from the inception, was at work on a proposed plan and buildings. His involvement had long been assumed, but not all donors were happy with the choice. A typical 'Oxford' response came from Archdeacon Edward Churton: 'With great respect for Butterfield, who has done well where he had to build in a plain field,' he wrote, in May 1867, 'but in his buildings at Balliol and Merton he has shown himself so incapable of entering into the genius of the place, that I should have the greatest fears of entrusting the work to him.'[9]

The dedication to an economy of life remained, encapsulated in the college motto, which takes a phrase from a familiar sonnet by Wordsworth lamenting the gaudy greed of the new century in which 'plain living and high thinking are no more'.[10]

There seem to be three surviving drawings from Butterfield's original concept, presented in December 1867 to the college building committee. There were funds to make only a beginning, but a general plan had already been prepared and approved for the entire project. On this sheet, Butterfield shows a large square to the north with buildings on its perimeter, a library and hall to the south and a second smaller quad as yet undefined on the narrower, triangular parcel below the proposed library. A second surviving drawing shows detail for an informal social space, designed as a cloister, within one of the anticipated building blocks. This, like the presentation sheet of elevations (fig.251), is in two tones of stone, one of red and the other a yellow-grey. The study of elevations shows ranges of living spaces on either side of the gateway as they would have looked from the east, using the materials

Butterfield first proposed: stone for most of the facing and construction, and roofing in a fine grey-blue Welsh slate, with masonry of different hues setting up the unified pattern of horizontal bands.

Except for the gateway, busier polychrome patterns are used more sparingly than in the final work, most of them with the distinct purpose of drawing the eye upwards to the gables that punctuate this continuous built landscape, 480 feet wide. A running skylight is suggested along the top-floor corridor – a modern idea not followed in the first three living blocks as built, but carried out in D Block, the third phase of expansion, which also raised the southern section of the scheme to four storeys. The dining hall and library, with common and lecture rooms below, remained an aspiration, but form an ensemble quite close to the design that would be realised over ten years later. A pencil section, at a different scale, of the dining hall and kitchen seems to have been added during discussion to demonstrate the width of the building for library and hall that he had in mind. Determined to lower costs for the project, the committee asked for estimates in brick with a cheaper roofing tile; and once it was received – although Butterfield protested that the difference from the cost in stone and slate was relatively minor – he was instructed to proceed in the brick and tile. Butterfield reconciled himself to the colour and quality of the inexpensive and largely unvaried brick stock the committee's budget demanded; but was never happy with the cheap slate he was obliged to deploy on the roofs of the first living blocks. Work went ahead on the first segment of the eastern range. Known as Block 1, it ran north from the gateway and porter's lodge, stopping short a few feet shy of the empty site for the chapel on the north-east of the site. A temporary dining hall, kitchen and chapel were put in place on the site of the future library and hall. J. Parnell & Sons of Rugby, Butterfield's builders at Rugby School, were contractors.

NOTES

1. From the many contemporary sources and commentaries on which I have drawn for the account of the Balliol College chapel project, note especially *Oxford Chronicle*, 27 January 1857, and Charles Locke Eastlake, *A History of the Gothic Revival*, Longmans, Green & Co., London, 1872, p.361; see also Peter Howell, 'Oxford Architecture, 1800–1914', in M.G. Brock and M.C. Curthoys (eds), *The History of the University of Oxford, Volume 7: Nineteenth-Century Oxford*, Oxford University Press, Oxford, 1984, Part 2, pp 728–77.

2. Arthur Rawson Ashwell, 'Classical and Byzantine – St Paul's and Keble Chapel', *Church Quarterly Review*, July 1876, pp 447–64.

3. 'Sonnet 1', from a manuscript of 1864–5, and 'Sonnet 2: To Oxford'. Hopkins scholars, among thousands of words of exegesis and speculation surrounding Sonnet 2, have somehow failed to notice how precise is the reference to Butterfield's Keble chapel. Readers can locate the full sonnet at www.poetrynook.com.

4. The short account of the Merton College Grove project is based primarily on the clippings file and records in the college archives, especially notes of meetings in the college Register, and upon reports and debate, principally during 1861, in the pages of *The Ecclesiologist*, the *Jackson's Oxford Journal* and *The Times* of London; accounts of construction in the *Reading Mercury*, 22 November 1862; and on the detailed description in *Illustrated London News*, 12 November 1864.

5. Max Müller, *My Autobiography: A Fragment*, C. Scribner's Sons, New York, 1901, p.225.

6. *Illustrated London News*, 12 November 1864.

7. Richard Cross, 'Medieval Theories of Haecceity', *Stanford Encyclopedia of Philosophy*, Winter 2022, plato.stanford.edu/entries/medieval-haecceity/.

8. W.H. Auden, 'Shapes', 1956; we will meet the same mutation of the Scotian idea in Arthur Hallam's 'secret truth of things', cited in the Epilogue.

9. Letter to the treasurer of the Keble fund, J.A. Shaw Stewart, in Keble College Archives Foundation files.

10. The phrase, from the sonnet known as 'Written in London, September 1802', was adopted as a title by the popular writer on character building and self-improvement W.H. Davenport Adams for a book of essays: *Plain Living and High Thinking; or Practical Self-Culture, Moral, Mental and Physical*, John Hogg, London, 1880.

'A COMMUNITY OF FEELING': KEBLE COLLEGE

Chapel from the Senior Common Room

North quadrangle and gateway;
south quadrangle and Servants' Building

North quadrangle and hall

Hall and Library Stair

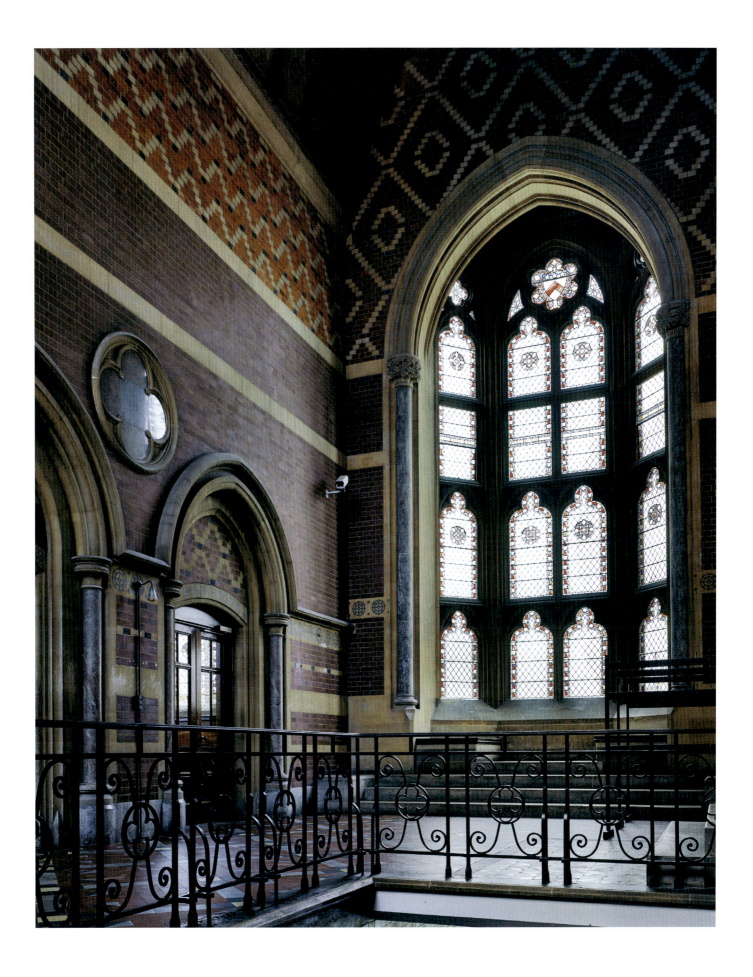

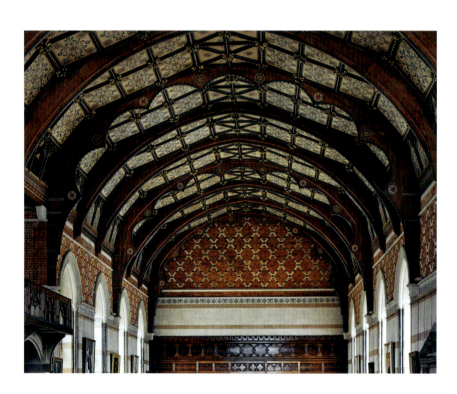

Library and dining hall

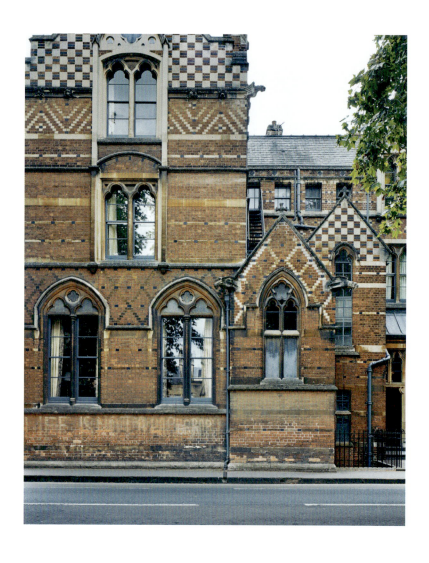

Warden's lodgings

CHAPTER 21

'PLAIN LIVING *and* HIGH THINKING': KEBLE COLLEGE, 1867–82

'THIS SCHOOL OF SIMPLICITY': LODGINGS

BY PLACING THE PRIMARY buildings of Keble College on the extreme perimeter of the site, Butterfeld gained the most ground possible for his main quadrangle; its walkways were seen as the principal social space of the college, and he sunk it a full seven steps from ground level, thereby setting off the buildings – again like Canterbury – to increase their presence. Simple brick staves capped with stone are the only decoration, and the changes in level and wide geometric voids are as essential to the composition of his townscape as the placement of the living blocks themselves.[1] Certain fundamentals were established from the start: the repetition of window forms and tracery, single or paired, with triplets on the street side; the projecting staircase bays which help to buttress the whole; and in defiance of the Oxford tradition

of a warren of short stairs, highly economical long corridors for an efficient, hygienic and convivial mode of circulation, like the student lodgings at St Augustine's Canterbury, though students paid the price of cold draughts for this convenience.

A low gatehouse was at first designed, in the hope of raising its height when funds allowed; but Butterfield and Edward Pusey, one of his firm allies on the committee, with whom he boarded at Christ Church when in Oxford, agreed that a more prominent feature was needed to announce the presence of the new reforming college; the full gateway tower and porter's lodge was designed and approved, with Pusey himself pledging a fund in instalments for its completion. By 1870 this first portion of the college opened with fifty students, a young warden, Edward Talbot, and a warden's wife, Lavinia, daughter of the building committee

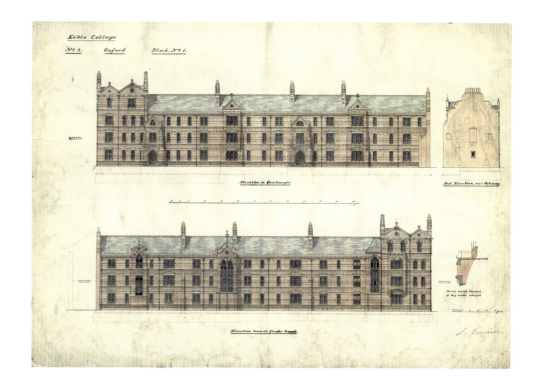

252
Keble College, Oxford:
elevations of Block 1 facing
west to main quadrangle and
east to Parks Road, *c.*1868

253
Keble College, Oxford:
elevations of gateway, *c.*1868

chair, Lord Lyttelton, and niece by marriage of
William Gladstone. The *Guardian* of 29 June
celebrated the event with a telling occasional verse,
which read in part:

> For here shall piety be nursed,
> Simplicity be shown,
> The chains of luxury be burst,
> And Study claim her own.
> . . .
> The spacious chamber's here curtailed,
> To modest cell's meet size.
> Here simple meals together shared
> Tutor to pupil bind.

The construction of the second and third blocks
of lodgings, completing three sides of the first
quadrangle, began soon after the 1870 inauguration.
The same pattern is followed in the long multi-
bayed ranges of both Block 1 and Block 2: the wide
staircase in a well-lighted projecting bay, the central
corridors and the simple room sets of small study
and connecting bedroom, with fireplaces lying back-
to-back and away from the outer walls at the point
the chimneys rise, and wainscoting beneath the
windows as a barrier against cold and damp. The
college provided each undergraduate sitting room
with a table, two straight and one 'elbow' chair, a
bookcase-dresser, carpet and fireplace equipment;
the bedroom was fitted with bed and bedding, a
washstand, looking glass, chest and chair. Much of
it seems to have been furnished by Parnell with the
larger items built or built-in to Butterfield's design.
Students provided their own towels and linen but
were not allowed, for quite some time, to improve
on this simple setting with cushions or comfortable
chairs of their own. The shorter wing of Block 3
on the north side was articulated more simply to
allow for the wide cloister at its eastern end. This
social space had at first been placed in the centre
of the wing, but Butterfield was now beginning to
formulate ideas for the chapel to which it would be
adjacent, imagining a cloister rising into it wide and
high. Between Blocks 2 and 3 can be seen the little
connecting house built to accommodate the warden
and his family until funds appeared for a full set
of lodgings and the status and configuration of the
awkward southern boundaries of the Keble land
could be resolved.

This uncertainty also affected the extension
of the buildings along Parks Road south of the
gateway – perhaps explaining the imbalance

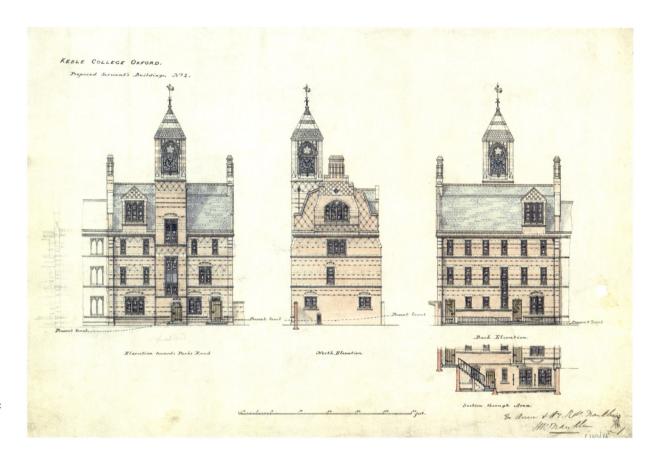

255
Keble College, Oxford:
elevations of Servants'
Building, c.1872–4

in the original elevation, where the southern
portion is considerably shorter than the northern
sections; and the entire configuration of the
second quadrangle remained unsettled until 1882,
when Butterfield's last set of 'New Buildings' was
constructed. Meanwhile, accommodation for college
servants was built in a tower behind the temporary
hall with, at Butterfield's insistence and finally
aided by a gift from the architect, a bell tower and
clock – both very great luxuries for a college whose
building funds were stretched to their narrow limits,
but in his view essential steps in setting the rhythm
of life that would bring a community together.
With dormitories, a staff common room and library
furnished by gift, and offices and bedroom for the
steward, this was an unusually civil revision of the
traditional Oxford system, which scattered 'scouts'
on call for tips among student lodgings and engaged
young men from large working households in the
town for the menial services, for whom sanitary
quarters would protect their own health and that of
the college as a whole.

An extension of the Parks Road front to the
south was completed as 'D Block' in 1874–5; and the
new warden's lodgings then began a long process
of construction on the south-east corner of the site
a little distant from it. D Block was denser than its
three companions, appearing to follow the pattern
of its neighbours to the north and west, but its
principal bays actually rise another floor into a
gabled set of rooms beneath the roof, which carries
an extraordinarily advanced running skylight.
Designs for a continuation of D Block that would
join the warden's house are drawn in light profile on
a number of sheets. This would have completed a
magnificent, barely interrupted line of building along
the entire eastern perimeter of the college, with the
chapel anchoring the north end and the warden's
house the south. It was never accomplished, and the
warden's lodgings retained the slightly odd blind
wall and temporary north porch that had been
designed to abut the extension of D Block.

In 1876 the chapel was completed, and two years
later the complex of library and hall that separated

the two quadrangles in lasting form, leaving a lovely passage between the library east wall and D Block – one of the incidents of changing voids and paths in an incipient urbanism that is among the great triumphs of Keble's architecture. That urbanity is the essential character of the warden's lodgings, which is an experimental model of a town house or parsonage. A little peak-roofed oratory faces Parks Road beside a public entry of great discretion. A separate portal with an entry hall windowed to the street brings fellows in from the south quadrangle before rising to a great corner dining room to the left and a reception room to the right looking over a sunken garden. The family drawing room was on the first floor. The foils and cornices carved into the woodwork match those of the hall and library, and there is throughout the varied works at Keble a pattern of repeated motifs that brings them subtly together. Here, as in the hall and library, the extraordinary restoration work of the college allows us to see Butterfield's interiors in the colours,

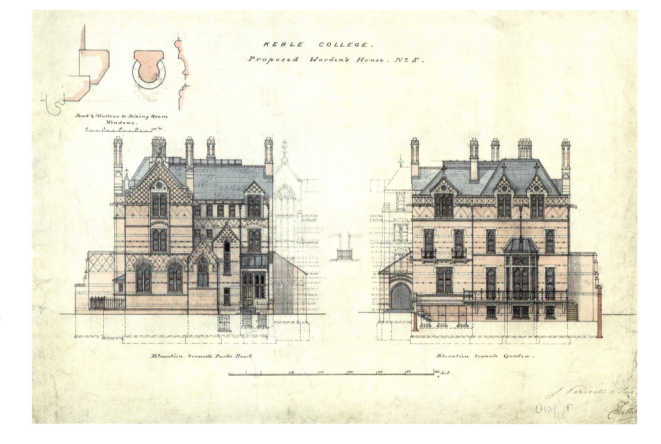

256
Keble College, Oxford: 'Pusey Quad', view looking north-east and showing the entire east range of living blocks and gateway, photographed *c.*1880

257
Keble College, Oxford: east and west elevations of warden's house, *c.*1874–5

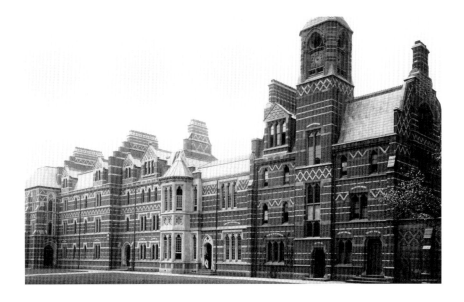

a stairwell and common rooms in a tower at the end of the terrace, and a wide course of skylights running through the roof. The boundary of the site narrows to the rear, allowing Butterfield to stagger his volumes like a city street, flatten the fronts in metropolitan fashion and top them with dormered gables that bring things into synchrony with their older neighbours. A photograph on completion (fig.258) shows in the adjacent Servants' Building how greatly the building darkened in eight years of exposure to the Oxford environment. The sense of an urban collage is now so strong that, once absorbed, the whole college within the walls begins to read as an ideal city behind its bastions, a built landscape in which the disparate and repeated, the gorgeous and simple, are brought into coherence, and vistas open at every turn, at once familiar and unexpected.

258

Keble College, Oxford: view of the new buildings upon completion, photograph by Francis Frith, 1882

259

Keble College Chapel, Oxford: view from the north, photograph by Henry W. Taunt, 1880

fabrics, wallpapers and carpeting reconstituted as he intended.

Butterfield's final addition to the Keble grounds was completed in 1882 in a mixed set of 'New Buildings' attached to the 'Servants' Building', and it closes the west side of the new or 'Pusey Quad', especially by means of a little apostrophe jutting a stair tower eastwards. It comprises offices for the bursar with a college lecture hall above; a bay-fronted set of bursar's lodgings; and two four-storey sets of student and tutors' lodgings, with

'THIS SCHOOL OF FAITH': CHAPEL

The full development plans presented by Butterfield from the start of the project left only a blank space at the north-east corner for the chapel, with no indication of its form or possible footprint. He had provided a scrupulously economical temporary hall and chapel (fig.265) on the footprint of the hall and library, careful to do nothing to compromise the site of the future chapel. For the permanent chapel, he was clear on four principles: it would stand free of the range of lodgings to the south, with a narrow dead space between them; there would be a ceremonial entry at the south-west corner in a high frontispiece that projected out from the body of the chapel; a second approach for members of the college would rise through a western cloister; and forms would rise into the sky above the college to mark the landscape, like the pinnacles of the cathedral in a distant city, with a spiritual vision that was open to all (fig.259).[2] The key, as a discerning critic noted, was to mark it out as 'a church of itself and by itself'.

Butterfield's old friend, and John Keble's closest friend, Sir John Taylor Coleridge had been quietly instrumental in the Keble college endeavour from the start, and now took it upon himself – surely with

New Chapel Keble College
N.º 4

East Elevation

260
Keble College
Chapel, Oxford:
east elevation,
c.1872

Butterfield's knowledge and encouragement – to locate a means of bringing the chapel to fruition. In the summer of 1872, he advised Butterfield that the retired banker William Gibbs of Tyntesfield, near Bristol, proposed to fund the chapel in its entirety. Butterfield promptly summarised for Coleridge and Gibbs the concept he had in mind: 'I planned rooms and a chapel for 250 students. At present we have built rooms for 100 only. This chapel as planned is 120 feet long by 32 feet wide . . . a stone staircase at its west end 45 feet long by 16 feet wide would lead up to the chapel' – the body of the chapel being raised high above the surroundings by a crypt

beneath it. Butterfield then worked with Gibbs's nephew Henry Hucks Gibbs to develop a rough plan and estimate costs, and met with the college to define them further.

By 9 December Butterfield could write to Gibbs enclosing drawings, emphasising the freedom of the building from those adjacent. Gibbs advised next day that he was 'much pleased' with the plans; design proceeded for a chapel at a cost approaching £50,000; and Butterfield joined the Gibbses at Christmas to cement an extraordinarily fruitful friendship with both William and his ethereal wife, Matilda Blanche. Many strenuous disagreements

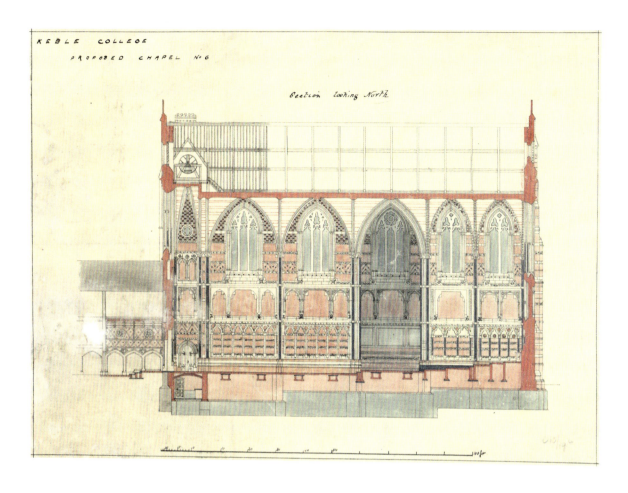

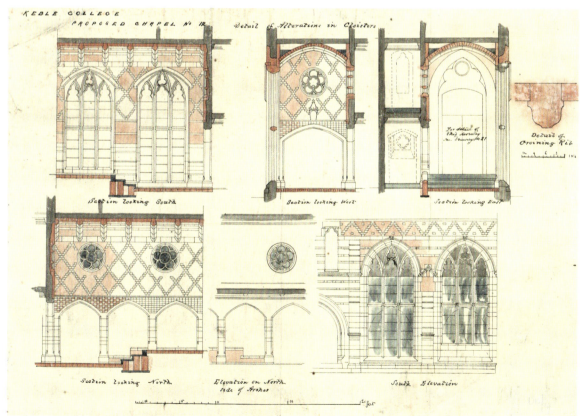

261
Keble College Chapel,
Oxford: section
looking north, *c.*1874

262
Keble College Chapel,
Oxford: detail of
alterations in cloisters,
*c.*1874

KEBLE COLLEGE
PROPOSED CHAPEL N° 8

263

Keble College Chapel, Oxford: sections looking east and into the south transept, with elevation and section of the sacristy, *c*.1874

followed among the trustees' building committee, especially between Butterfield and Henry Liddon, first over Butterfield's proposal to seat the college facing eastwards in congregational fashion, and then over his iconographic programme. Butterfield objected to a Crucifixion above the altar, arguing that the culmination of the spiritual narrative should end with Christ in Glory, which he proposed to render in pictorial tile mosaic after Dürer's apocalyptic vision of St John, in which Christ is seen with the seven candles of his churches. Butterfield also resisted a plan to install William Holman Hunt's *The Light of the World* in the chapel, a gift made to the college with the intention that it be hung there. In both cases Butterfield eventually made appeals of last resort to Gibbs, who came

down firmly and unhesitatingly on the architect's side. Butterfield had objected to the Hunt not only because it was an imagined scene without Biblical authority and infused with a dramatic narrative and palette contrary to his own chapel narrative, but because he predicted that this most famous picture of the age would become such an object of curiosity that the sanctity of the chapel would be disturbed by tourists. He designed a quieter home for it in a central niche of the large reading room in the Library, where for a number of years it anchored the vista to the east. Liddon persisted, and the painting eventually found its way into a side chapel in the south aisle of Butterfield's chapel, at which point the architect brought his association with the college sadly and abruptly to an end.

an uninterrupted open space of the dimensions Butterfield called for. The illusion of a lower chapel or crypt is created by a blind arcade on the south wall that suggests it. It is a delicate deception but such an uncharacteristic gesture in Butterfield's work that it feels uncomfortable. In the same way, stone bands attempt to reconcile the scale and lines of the chapel with the living blocks on either side, again perhaps uncomfortably, since the vast difference in proportion between chapel and college – so evident in the very beautiful drawing of the east elevation (fig.260) – seems best left in tension, unresolved, which is surely why Butterfield insisted on the reveal between them. The windows, all set to the same height, look not like a clerestory but like part of an edifice lifted up to float above the college – another illusionistic effect, but one that works with extraordinary power from the north, where the tree-lined boundary of the 'parks' conceals the base and sets the chapel above its ideal city. Critics of the time, so accustomed to questioning Butterfield's unornamented severity, were now troubled by the chapel's excessive animation – sculptured figures of chancellors set into buttresses, dentils and finials extending and decorating projections and cornices, a huge St Michael slaying his devil above the great porch and an Agnus Dei resting within it – which seemed to put the exterior of the chapel at odds with the economy and restraint of the college around it.

But step inside, and the experience is so transcendent that any stratagems used to achieve it seem justified. The patterns of the arcades and brickwork, the tiled floor, the ribbed and groined vaulting of the roof and the steady high line of vivid mosaics all seem to merge into a single glowing convergence of what Ashwell called 'soaring and horizontal lines, at one and in harmony'. He found at the dedication that this architectural transfiguration of varied colours, materials, structural and surface pattern and shafts of light into a cohesive whole had a profound psychological effect, performing the same unifying transformation on the disparate congregation, so that the churchmen and women there, of all stripes and tempers, 'suddenly found themselves as one united by the great work'. Ashwell saw both the root

Butterfield's initial plan was to ride the body of the chapel above a crypt to raise the ceremonial space above the quotidian movement of undergraduate life, and approach it through a long rising cloister. Both the approach and the rise were shortened as the design developed, though the abbreviated cloister, with great tracery windows to the south and a beautifully patterned and arcuate wall to the north, is marvellously effective (fig.262). Instead of a raised chapel, Butterfield achieved the same effect by organising the space as a basilica, like that of the upper church at Assisi, whose windows sit at an enormous height in the walls, which remain blank to the outer world and richly decorated within, all under a ribbed, groined and vaulted roof. A formidable set of buttresses was required to form

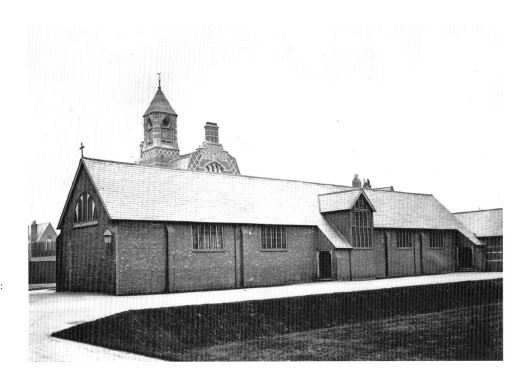

265
Keble College, Oxford:
view of temporary
chapel (left) and hall
(right), photograph
by Henry W. Taunt,
c.1870

sources and the comparable effect not in the Gothic, but in the Byzantine and its Italian expressions in the basilicas of Torcello, Ravenna and Santa Maria Maggiore, Rome. Looking at the chronicle of revelation in the band of murals, he called Keble Chapel, as Ruskin called St Mark's in Venice, 'an illuminated building', a 'book-temple', its narrative events composed with classical clarity and showing 'their power . . . in their severity and splendour': 'rich, genuine, imposing, and historic, intelligible to learned and unlearned; weighted with meaning and devotion; full of the grandeur of sacrifice'. In place, the central mosaic of the reredos, which discomfited so many when proposed, reads simply, as Butterfield himself pronounced it, as an assertion of Christ's majestic and suffusing presence; and the huge swathe of red in the robe at his feet seems to draw all the colours around the chapel to it, in an instant of absolute unification and acknowledgement.

At matins on the day of opening in April 1876, Pusey addressed his sermon to the undergraduates. 'You have come here', he said, 'to be developed in all the powers of mind and body, not in any stiff or constrained or narrow way, but in largeness of heart; . . . to this school of faith, in contrast with the world's faithlessness; . . . to this school of simplicity,

in contrast with the world's ever-degenerating, heartless, enervating self-indulgence'; and to 'this school of reality' in which everything, exemplified by its architecture, stands 'in contrast with the world's whited-sepulchre of unreality'. To the 350 guests at lunch in the temporary hall, it was Lord Beauchamp, who had stood by Butterfield on the college building committee from the start, who made the address. In it he recounted the history and purpose of the college, calling its main objects 'the principle of frugality and the . . . high culture of the mind', and dating its origins to an idea first mooted by Keble in 1846 to found 'an institution in which undergraduates should be able to live without being exposed to those temptations to extravagance and expense which undoubtedly exist in the older foundations' and, without the differentiation of cliques and clubs, to follow a pattern of 'corporate life'. The founders, Beauchamp said, had recognised from the start that the architecture itself should work towards this principle of 'Comune Magnum', not simply in its planning but by introducing 'the element of splendour which, infused into common actions, elevates the imagination and habits of thought by associating the constantly repeated acts of every-day life with beauty of form and of

266
Keble College,
Oxford: view of
library and hall
from the north-east,
photograph by Henry
W. Taunt, *c*.1878–80

colour', and he was astonished to find a chapel that so far surpassed those goals as to represent a work of architecture unequalled in his mind since King's College Chapel at Cambridge: 'so noble in its proportions, so perfect in its arrangement, so gorgeous in its details'.

'THIS SCHOOL OF REALITY': HALL AND LIBRARY

At the opening of the chapel, the announcement was made that anonymous donors had appeared to provide the entire funding for Butterfield's great hall and library.[3] This would be the heart of the 'corporate life' of a college that had already become one of the largest in the university, with a household of nearly 300, still growing, and an instance of higher education at a new scale. The donors would be revealed as the two sons of William

Gibbs, and Henry Hucks Gibbs was again the agent through whom the gift was sought and made. As work on these two great collegiate buildings moved forward, the warden's lodgings were also brought to completion. At the same time, Oxford college life was transformed by the removal of the university requirement of celibacy on the fellows. A new suburb began to emerge around and north of Keble for the family households of the academic community, and the architectural character of Butterfield's Keble and its warden's lodgings became a yardstick for the villas of north Oxford.

Two years later the new buildings opened. There were a junior common room and lecture halls beneath the library, which was for some time a dedicated study facility for the fellows, who had a suite of common rooms beneath the hall. But all came through a common portal, and the entire building thus became a forum, the centre of college social life, intellectual work and movement. The furnishings below were intimate, unpretending and domestic, while the great concourse and staircase that connected it all provided a common passage of extraordinary spaciousness, activity and grandeur, with a carefully calculated capacity to quiet the voice and slow the pace, the brick surfaces banded and patterned so that light would constantly change the character of the walls. The two great upper rooms of hall and library, richly coloured, were panelled and roofed in a way that broke up the vast spaces acoustically and psychically without ever diminishing the drama of their deep perspectives; and the library floor was raised to give the space more intimacy.

Outside, the most powerful effects come first from the gigantic bay window and gable of the central concourse, then from what are in effect two great arcades, two floors high, formed from buttresses and arched windows supporting the two huge open spans within. The five arches of the library are wider and more assertive than the rhythm of the dining hall to the right; the relationship is inverted on the interior; but the arc above the library windows is recollected in the roofs above both great halls. The building appeared at a moment in the discussion of architecture when attention to Butterfield, and much else, had taken second place to the proliferation of flamboyant public buildings and fashionable dwellings, so that this towering masterpiece, like the Cheddar Hospital opened in the same year, passed into use almost unnoticed.

By now the pattern of life at Keble and the character of college culture had been deeply imprinted by Talbot. His memoirs paint a wonderful portrait of the near-revolutionary system of life, comportment and restraint that he tried to achieve among his students. The great object was to ensure 'that men of small means should be as free of the whole life of the College as those who had more', and strict rules were applied to restrain any spending that might mark out any member of the college for vanity and display or for hosting private entertainments. Any additions of furnishing to the rooms had to fall within a very limited list – sofas, curtains and mirrors were forbidden; permissions,

both tutorial and parental, were required to bring in wines from the outside; there was a limit on personal spending each term and an annual prize to students spending the least. There was no signing out for meals without tutorial approval. And the nightly curfew fell at 9 o'clock. All were expected at early morning service, and no shouting or singing in the quadrangles was permitted. These were circumstances in which there could be no shame in poverty or pride in wealth, but they are austere terms, and one wonders if there was in fact much delight in them.

Fees were kept very much below the level of the traditional colleges, yet Keble undergraduates were perhaps offered more within the walls in terms of tutorial support, college lectures and access to a very carefully assembled staff of fellows with a wide range of knowledge, and – a mark of Talbot's philosophical ecumenism – an equally provocative range of opinion. Tutors lived among students in the bay-fronted towers of the Blocks, and, expected to monitor their adherence to rule, were close to their lives as a result. Talbot tells us in his memoirs that he was scrupulous in avoiding any indication of the high-church bias that had been feared by many in its founding years. Instead, he 'carefully tuned our religious life to embrace all within the church'. There was an unqualified welcome for science, encouragement of free enquiry, and an insistence on the benefits of conviviality. Keble was the first college with a natural-science tutor and laboratory. Talbot breakfasted in the lodgings with his fellows. And in the early years, unique among Oxford colleges, the whole student household was convened for evening prayers, including one calling for a blessing on their studies that they might be used to 'better the church and Commonwealth of this land'. This not only captured the ideal of Keble, as building knowledge as a means to fulfil duty, but the equally powerful reformist definition of that duty as working for the general improvement of society. Above all, Talbot's regime, like the disposition of Butterfield's buildings, was designed to generate not an ideology but what Arthur Stanley called 'a community of feeling' about which a disparate middle class could unite.

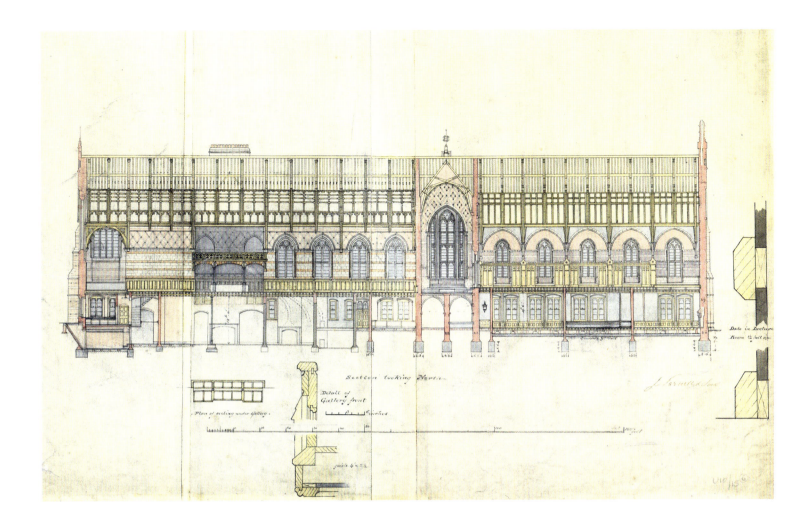

A section taken just short of the north wall
(fig.267) best shows the general configuration of
the building. Reading from west to east, Butterfield
details the north transept of the hall at the high
table, then the minstrel gallery built out from the
kitchen chimneypiece, and the remaining north wall
of the hall, with kitchens and the fellows' common
and writing rooms below. The great stair is shown
at the point of the hung bay on which the whole
composition hinged; and the library is seen with its
four facing bays, each housing a book-lined study
alcove, and an open reading and discussion room
closing the east end. Lecture and common rooms
for students are below. The window narratives in
the hall quote the Prayer Book canticles in praise of
the fruits of the earth and fellowship; and those in
the library, partly from the Book of Wisdom, relate
to knowledge, thought and revelation. Hunt's *The
Light of the World* was brought into the sequence by

taking its place on an entablature Butterfield built
for it at the east end of the Library.

Three sheets from a large and lovingly drawn
set of smaller contract drawings show the essential
elevations and sections looking east and west. The
first (fig.268) starts with the two elevations, showing
at the east end a lantern lighting the open walk
between the library and D Block and a connecting
wall between the library and the Servants' Building
to the south, which baffles the 'earth store' toilet
facilities for staff. The west elevation of the hall
faced the fellows' garden, which Butterfield asked
to design as a structured geometrical open court,
like that of the principal quadrangle, but the fellows
refused, preferring informality. The second drawing
(fig.269) shows sections of the library looking east
and west, and then the east and west walls of the
great stair. The library sections looking east show
the end walls of the junior common room below,

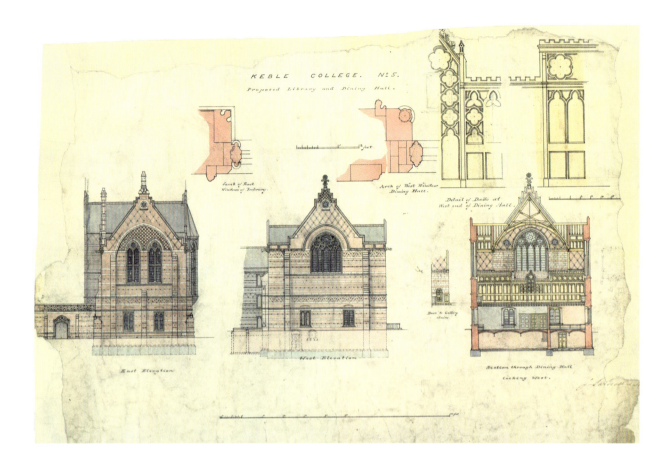

268
Keble College
Library and Dining
hall, Oxford: east
elevation (library),
west elevation (hall),
and section through
the west end of
the hall showing
treatment of the wall
and ceiling, 1876–7

269
Keble College
Library and Dining
Hall, Oxford:
sections through
the library looking
east and west, and
through the principal
staircase, showing
entry doors east to
the library, and west
to the hall, 1876–7

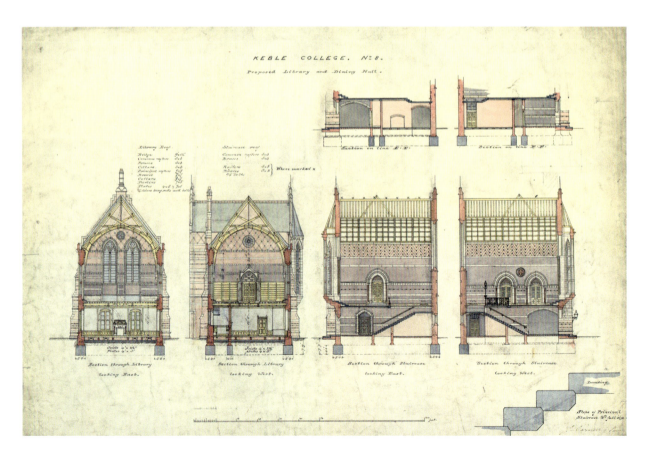

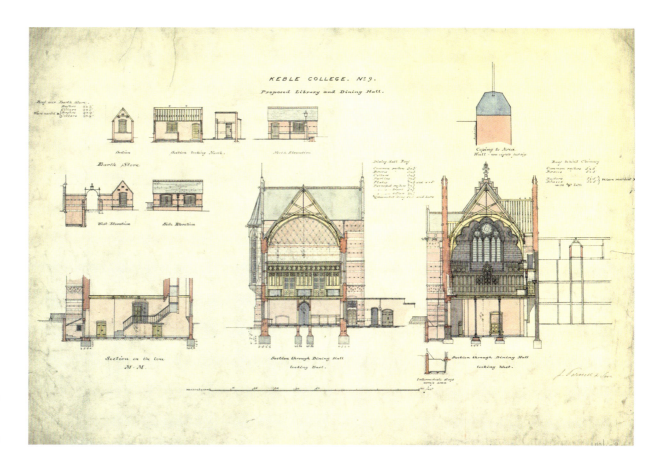

270

Keble College Library
and Dining Hall,
Oxford: sections
through the hall, 1877

while that looking west shows the entrance door
and the lecture hall beneath. The studies of the great
stair, detailing in semi-elevation the extraordinary
patterning of the side walls, show the single door to
the library and the double door entering the hall,
with its slate cartouche above. The third sheet of
sections (fig.270) is devoted to the hall and kitchen.
The first of the larger sections shows the doors
from the hall to the great stair, the panelling and
brickwork of the eastern wall, and the complex
curve of the rafters in the body of the hall, which
follow the same curve as those of the library but
are sculpted and alternated in a different pattern.
The second large section looks west across a line
between the hearth and the minstrel gallery, to
show a distanced view of the central portion of the
fellows' dais and the first of the scalloped timbers.
The sections cannot show the short transepts that
open out to the north and south from the high
table in two high-windowed bays, each framed by
a highly wrought wooden canopy (p.331). There
is a wonderful portrayal of the iron shafts

supporting the floor of the dais for high table
above the kitchen.

The great staircase was the passage where the
whole life of the college passed. It was clad, lit,
stepped, roofed and railed like the enclosure of a
great city court. It served the ideal of a sense of
community: an awareness of those passing by; the
civilising effect of forming an orderly queue where
dining companions choose to gather; steps into the
bay forming a meeting point; and, with all three
meals obligatory, a way of ensuring that no member
of the college could be hidden from view – passed
through thrice a day, with a sense of importance and
grace. The inside of the north bay, with its stepped
stone benches and sloped stone sill, required
extraordinary engineering to bear that added weight
and let the vast projection ride clear of the wall.
A large detail drawing was made to show each of the
primary elements of this complex structure (fig.271).
It shows the great bay partly supported on a central
post of stone blocks (seen on the bottom right of the
'outside elevation') that divides the entry into two

channels of circulation. This drawing of half details was evidently prepared to reassure the committee of its viability, as well as to direct the builders, but the hand, pens and brush linger, as they do in each of the section drawings for this amazing building, showing almost tactile delight in its coming fabrication and astonished wonder at the *ingenio* – not the designer's invention but the genius inherent in the work itself – from which it derived.

This central structure of the Keble campus is, perhaps, the surpassing work of Butterfield's maturity, in which he finds and controls a new freedom in the handling of tone, scale, light, proportion, weight and matter, all exactly evoked in the working drawings. It was said that he would be lost to himself at night on the drawing table, forgetting time and sleep out of sheer fascination for the exactitudes required of his pen to bring the shape and sense of an envisioned reality into being. While scrupulously efficient as reassurance to anyone questioning the engineering, and perfectly detailed to instruct the builder in their execution, these drawings are the dreamscapes of an architect with a passion for reality. With the opening of the hall and library, the significance of the ensemble could finally be fully understood, with Hucks Gibbs referring to the college, to cheers from the assembly, as a 'group of buildings, the like of which for beauty and originality of design has not been exceeded, if equaled, for nearly four hundred years'; and Gladstone declaring that 'it is no mere great revival; it is a great original work, and it carries upon it the stamp of genius'.

NOTES

1. The account of the origins and living quarters of the college is reconstructed from many sources, including most essentially the printed *Proceedings at the Laying of the First Stone of Keble College Oxford,* Rivingtons, London, 1868, in which Butterfield presents the plan and description of the proposed project; and the extensive building committee and fundraising files in the college's Foundation archives, including correspondence with Butterfield, much of it superbly calendared, along with extracts from the diaries of Lavinia Talbot and other sources, by Faye McLeod. See also local and national newspapers, weekly magazines, and especially Edward Stuart Talbot, *Memories of Early Life*, A.R. Mowbray & Co., London and Oxford, 1924, and architectural journal reports are extensive throughout the

building and fundraising campaigns of 1866 to 1870 and provide substantial coverage of the opening event of 1870, including the *Illustrated London News,* with sketches, 25 June 1870, and notably *The Guardian,* 29 June 1870, with the anonymous and telling doggerel quoted here. The subsequent additions are well reported in the Oxford city and county press. *The Church of England Magazine,* 4 April 1874, illustrated with a sketch of the gateway, on the laying of the foundation stone of the chapel, carries Warden Edward S. Talbot's extraordinarily frank statements on the character and life of the college in its first years; and see also, here and throughout this chapter, Averil Cameron and Ian Archer, *Keble Past and Present,* Oxford University Press, Oxford, 2008.

2. In addition to the sources cited above, specific sources primarily relied upon for the account of the chapel include *An Account of the Proceedings at Keble College on the Occasion of the Opening of the Chapel and the Laying of the Foundation-Stone of the Hall and Library,* John Parker, Oxford, 1876, which carries the sermons and addresses of Pusey and Earl Beauchamp; letters of Sir John Taylor Coleridge in the Coleridge Papers at the British Library; the *Morning Post,* 26 April 1873, and *Jackson's Oxford Journal* of the same date, both reporting on the laying of the chapel stone; the *Oxford Times,* 9 April 1876; *The Globe,* 26 April 1876; and *Illustrated London News,* 26 August 1876. *The Architect,* April 1876, carries in convenient form the report of the *Guardian,* much of the text deriving from notes by Butterfield. The commentary here and later is from Arthur Rawson Ashwell, 'Classical and Byzantine – St Paul's and Keble Chapel', *Church Quarterly Review,* July 1876, pp 446–64. See also Butterfield's *Correspondence Concerning the Mosaics in the Chapel of Keble College, Oxford, During the Year 1873,* privately printed by Butterfield in 1893, from which Peter Howell has included a carefully chosen, characteristic selection of excerpts in '"Our Very Quaint Old Architect": Some Letters of William Butterfield', *Architectural History,* vol.53, 2010, pp 217–43.

3. Among additional sources referred to for the account of the Keble College hall and library, note especially *Oxfordshire Weekly News,* 17 October 1877, on the progress of the works, and the account of proceedings and speeches at the opening – including the remarks of Henry Huck Gibbs and William Ewart Gladstone quoted later – in *The Standard* and *Manchester Guardian,* both for 26 April 1878. The *Illustrated London News,* 4 May 1878, recounts and illustrates the event, and details are provided by *Building World,* 14 May 1878.

KEBLE COLLEGE. Nº 17.

Proposed Library and Dining Hall.

Detail of Bay Window over Principal Entrance.

Outside Elevation.

Section

Inside Elevation

Plan

271

Keble College
Library and Dining
Hall, Oxford:
interior and exterior
details of the entry
bay window, 1877

VIII REFUGE, REFRESHMENT, REPOSE

CHAPTER 22

COTTAGE, LODGE *and* COUNTRY RETREAT, 1853–90

COUNTRY LIFE

Those who have gazed with admiration upon what Mr. Butterfield has achieved in ecclesiastical work, with costly materials and ample resources, may here see what the same master mind can produce with ordinary means for private accommodation and home comfort . . . for here is to be found . . . a correct and beautiful . . . example of the medieval domestic style, readily adapted to the taste and requirements of modern times.[1]

THUS READS THE WIDELY published report of a visit to Milton Ernest Hall by the Bedfordshire Architectural Society in June 1863, nearly ten years after it had been completed. Built for the London merchant Benjamin Starey, whom Butterfield's sister Anne had married, and with whose family he remained very close, Milton

Ernest Hall, in a small park on the River Stour, was a thoroughgoing replacement of a rather ordinary Bedfordshire manor house, which Butterfield almost entirely demolished, gathering the debris to raise a wide, well-drained platform upon which the new house could be supported.[2] Humble local materials and methods were employed in construction – simply cut limestone from the nearby Pavenham quarry and ready-made tiles from St Neots, with quoins and trim in Bath stone sparingly disposed. A simple, symmetrical front frames the principal living and sleeping rooms, where bays and French doors open to terraces and gardens. In contrast, Butterfield assembles at the entrance in the rear a wonderfully complicated but perfectly logical vista of rising rooflines, chimney stacks and staggered volumes. Grounds were structured in horizontal planes and geometric divisions, with avenues planted to grow to different heights,

PREVIOUS PAGE:
All Saints' Church,
Harrow Weald

taking advantage of the possibility for intensifying perspectives in this landscape of mead and river.

The building was part of an emerging domestic system in which train travel had made it possible for a large country house, if close enough to London, to be devoted to everyday family life throughout the year, rather than seasonal occupancy and holiday entertainment, or the full-time management and representation of a working estate. The arrangements, inside and out, are for the society,

leisure, comfort, pleasure and learning of a family, and eschew those statements of rank and authority once thought essential to the country house of the great landowner. Its greatest internal effects were reserved for the informal daily passage through the front hall, with great windows and arcaded landing, piers finished in Minton tiles, rails of painted iron scrollwork and walls in coverings derived from an ancient printing block. In the same spirit, the servants' hall and services are carefully segregated

but placed on the same floor as the three family rooms, and with ease of movement to and from them. Those rooms – dining room, library and drawing room – each face the gardens and are modestly proportioned. A 'private room' looking north with an upper sleeping chamber near the entry serves to seclude a working guest – perhaps Butterfield providing for his own long visits. The hall was designed at the same time as Sandford's rectory in Alvechurch and follows much the same pattern, which we will see enlarged at Heath's Court in Devon where the same emphasis is placed on circulation as a succession of informal internal vistas.

While Milton Ernest Hall eschewed the architectural pretensions of a great hall, it was still the hub of a substantial river-front agricultural estate, which Butterfield and Starey set out to modernise. They rebuilt the home farm; added a wooden boat barn with a Dutch-hipped roof; furnished a new three-bedroom brick cottage for the gardener in the grounds and another for the coachman on the principal street of the village; and went on to rebuild the old mill into a model granary, with a huge modern hydraulic plant, improved

bridge, pond and race to run it at higher capacity, and a substantial new dwelling for the miller – the most prosperous and important of Milton Ernest's tenants. Here, Butterfield's stripped-down variations on local building traditions produce a rustic severity animated by what reads as the near-random disposition of dormer, half-hipped gable and arch. In fact, they follow a rigorous functional logic: great height was needed to carry the modern mechanical system of cogs that drove the production rate from water-milling closer to meeting the extraordinary demand, and a sturdy and very graceful Gothic arch and buttresses are provided for a tower, capped with a half-hipped dormer attic, so that it can straddle the mill race and still bear that load.

MODEL COTTAGE HOUSING

Increasingly uncomfortable with his inheritance, the young positivist James Beaumont Winstanley (whom we met as patron of the school at Kirby Muxloe) appealed to his mentor Auguste Comte, shortly before Comte's death in 1857, to guide

274 (left)
Cressida Place,
Braunstone,
photographed *c*.1880

275 (right)
Main Street,
Braunstone,
photographed *c*.1880

him on how to dispose of his landed estate with the greatest benefit to society. Comte insisted that he retain his properties and devote the income to improving the physical well-being of those who worked on them, so that he could establish a prototype for the economically and socially balanced new social system they sought. Winstanley turned almost at once to Butterfield to design a sequence of hygienic, uncrowded and efficient housing as representative models for this new society, producing three astonishingly progressive groups of mixed managerial and labourers' housing – two in Braunstone, one in Kirby Muxloe. The plans of the three brick housing schemes, each for six households, are entirely different and quite unlike the carefully scattered plans with picturesque effect of the comparable group at Baldersby St James, which was taking shape at the same time. They are in general plan, in the shaping of the dwellings and in their simplicity of expression clearly as well suited to a suburban townscape as to a village, and perhaps, as the prototypical housing systems for Winstanley's vision of an egalitarian new society, so intended.

One is a terrace of six cottages on the far edge of estate land in Braunstone, which runs counter to the road at its west end and is fronted by linked gardens along a path leading towards the parish church, with a swathe of common open land beyond. The two end units for artisanal families are larger. The second is a row of three separate semi-detached units set on spacious plots, with large fruit and vegetable gardens, running along a portion of the village Main Street just beyond the bounds of the Winstanley estate. Each is configured and oriented differently, to obtain as much privacy as possible and avoid a relentless streetscape, both in the general plan and in the relation of each semi-detached unit to its adjacent neighbour. Scales differ slightly, with two of the units taking a smaller footprint to accommodate the elderly. The third set is at Kirby Muxloe, on an L-shaped plan of two adjoining short terraces, again with a 'common' approach to land, and now with a larger unit built into the terrace for the local estate manager.

Neither segregation nor any change in building material and expression distinguish between households of different means. The paired houses

on Main Street answer the low-slung, street-fronted, barely windowed traditional cottages across the road with a full dormered floor under the roof rather than an attic; rise at least 4 feet higher; are ventilated; consolidate chimneys and carry their smoke as high as practical; provide and project windows large enough to give light for school work, home crafts or industry; and extend into the orchard gardens at the rear to segregate outhouses, wood and coal storage and drained extensions from the scullery. Though the projects escaped wider architectural notice at the time, they became well known in the communities around – as early photographs make clear (figs 274 and 275) – so it may not be fanciful to see Winstanley's pragmatic idealism carried forward in the placement and shaping of the vast model suburb built just between Braunstone and Kirby for 'Homes for Heroes' in the 1920s. In July 1862, with these first plans for labourers' housing under way, Winstanley – on the cusp of assuming the dignity of high sheriff of the county – suddenly disappeared, perhaps having drowned in the river at Koblenz, though the fate of this rather extraordinary landed member of the British positivist movement, who had been drawn to Comte by his tutor at Rugby, has never been fully established.

We have already noted Butterfield's alms cottages for the aged at Baldersby St James, terraced one-storey garden dwellings made visible to the watchful eyes of the parish. A larger and more collegiate

version of the same system appeared at the same time for Lord Eversley in his village of Heckfield in Hampshire, where Butterfield built a set of brick and half-timbered terraced cottages ranged around an open roadside court, with a small common hall at its centre. A courtyard group very similar in shape and style came a little later through Frederick Moore Boultbee, who had retired in his forties from a lucrative naval career to a sporting life in the middle of the New Forest. The district did not provide an easy living for its villagers, and Boultbee devoted his means to their welfare, providing a school and schoolhouse, turning to Butterfield for a tiny brick parish church and then, in 1871, for a courtyard of five almshouses set around a well. With their courts and common gardens, Emery Down and Heckfield adopt the comforting and efficient lines of a restrained cottage architecture rather than the monastic manner that characterised so many Victorian charitable dwellings in the countryside.

THE CITY GOES TO THE COUNTRY: MODEL FARM AND PARK ESTATE

The country house, great park and estate buildings at Aldenham, near Elstree in Hertfordshire, had passed in 1850 to Butterfield's friend Henry Hucks Gibbs, by then managing partner of the Gibbs company and on his way to becoming the richest man in London. Gibbs rented Aldenham House out while establishing his extraordinary 'White House' in Regent's Park; but in 1869, as London became smokier and noisier, and country commutes more convenient, he followed the general movement among the well-to-do to set up a country retreat as a principal dwelling and began the restoration and expansion of the now dilapidated great house and its park for his own use. The extent of his work with Butterfield in and around the main house is still uncertain, but the development of the Home Farm into a hygienic farm, starting about 1878, is entirely his: a set of model labourers' cottages, the rebuilding of the bailiff's dwelling into a model farmhouse, and the addition to it of two cold zones – a bacon room and a dairy. Bovine tuberculosis and meat- and

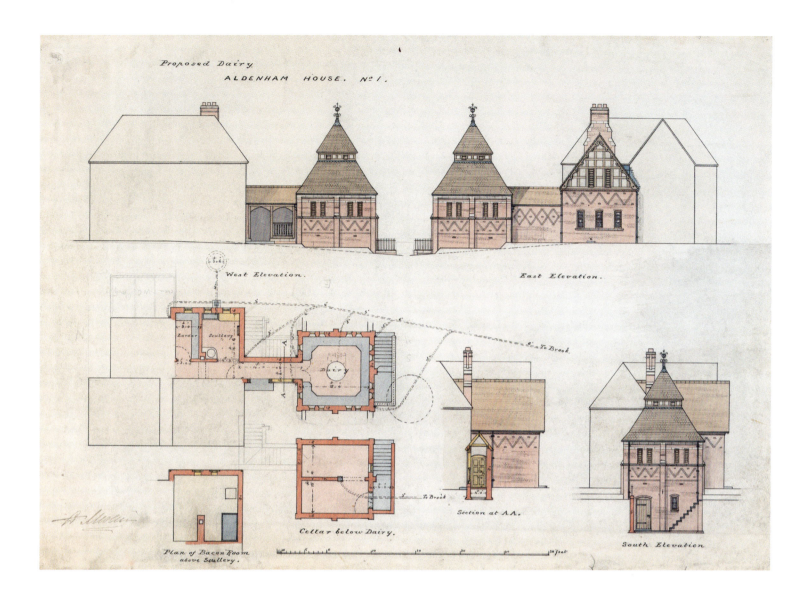

Proposed Dairy
ALDENHAM HOUSE. No 1.

West Elevation.

East Elevation.

Larder Scullery

Dairy

Cellar below Dairy.

Plan of Bacon Room
above Scullery.

Section at AA.

South Elevation

277

Aldenham House
Dairy: elevations
and plan, *c.*1880

dairy-borne early infant diseases were among the leading killers of London's children; and the tiled dairy, with its screened cupola, high louvres for ventilation, and separation by a vented passage from the pantries in which bacon and game were hung, was a model exercise in improving food hygiene to combat these plagues.

Gibbs was a man of great taste who had scrupulously assisted his uncle William in locating European master paintings for his house at Tyntesfield and whose Aldenham garden would become one of the finest landscape designs of the turn of the century; and the dairy for which Butterfield provided him with exquisite drawings was clearly one of his exercises in the aesthetic

imagination. The external profile of the extension is both the clearest evocation of medieval manorial architecture in Butterfield's oeuvre, with its echoes of fortified keep and dovecote, and astonishingly modern, a marvel of functional tile mosaic in the precise tones of aquamarine and carmine that Butterfield had first established long ago for colouring surfaces close to the fall of light in his restoration of Hellidon church. Shortly before the Aldenham dairy addition, Gibbs's cousin Henry Martin Gibbs – who had with his brother Antony funded the library and hall at Keble College – had engaged Butterfield for another model working farm, at Ardingly in Sussex. Here, Butterfield had deployed the same rustic but hygienic vocabulary

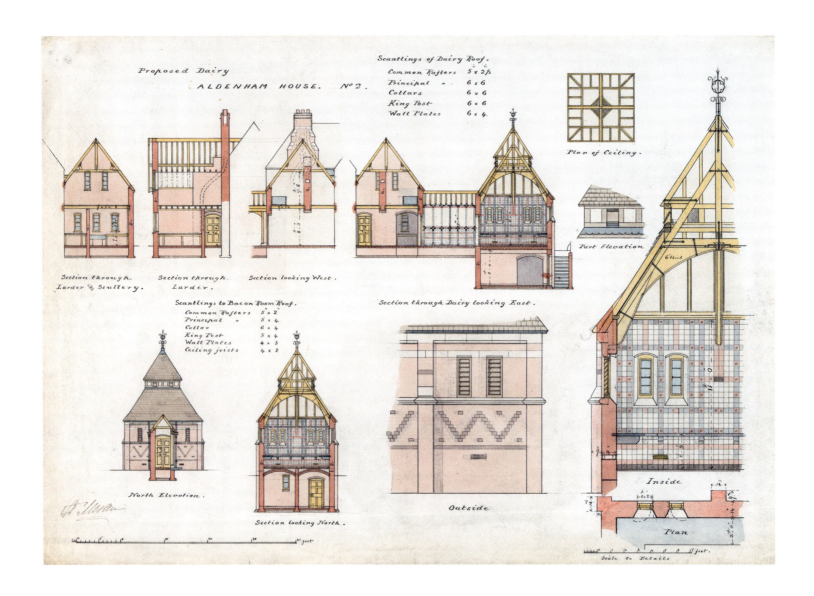

Scantlings of Dairy Roof.
Common Rafters   5 x 2½
Principal   „   6 x 6
Collars   6 x 6
King Post   6 x 6
Wall Plates   6 x 4

Proposed Dairy

ALDENHAM HOUSE. Nº 2.

Plan of Ceiling.

Part Elevation.

Section through
Larder & Scullery.

Section through
Larder.

Section looking West.

Section through Dairy looking East.

Scantlings to Bacon Room Roof.
Common Rafters   5 x 2
Principal   „   5 x 4
Collar   6 x 4
King Post   5 x 4
Wall Plates   4 x 3
Ceiling joists   4 x 2

North Elevation.

Section looking North.

Outside

Inside

Plan

Scale to Details

278

Aldenham House
Dairy: sections
and details, *c*.1880

of diapered brick with half-timbered and shingled gables, half-hipped tile roofs, lofty skylights and wide doorways, and provided a sanitary dairy – a windowless brick octagon with a clerestory of stone and a continuous high tapered roof broken only by lucarnes at the peak. It was an idea for ventilation that the Aldenham dairy develops more thoroughly, with its easily reached windows and staggered roof, drawing and circulating air in many directions.

The Whiteknights Park estate was originally a single neoclassical country villa within a mostly wild and woodland park in Berkshire, between Reading and Wokingham. It was occupied and ornamented extravagantly for many years by the profligate and dissolute Marquess of Blandford but, was divided in the 1860s, some time after his bankruptcy, into

40-acre lots for country residences for London merchants and professionals, partly as a speculation and prospective home by the Manchester architect Alfred Waterhouse. By 1887, when the estate had fallen into the new municipal boundaries of Reading, the boundaries were firmly marked and managed, with gate, watchmen's lodges, extensive walls, high railings and gated entry points installed by Butterfield. The two gate lodges – services for a community rather than ornaments to a great house – are fine and varied late examples of the half-timber-and-gable compositions that Butterfield had first introduced to his cottage architecture nearly forty years before, and the pattern in the open metal fences he placed to bound the roads sings very gracefully in the same key as the diapering on

tribute to his friends. Butterfield continued to work until the end of his career on dyking, landscaping and draining the many unsettled acres of the watery site, including the construction of a new coachman's lodge close to the western gate (pp 376–77)– perhaps the last of the long essay in compellingly sturdy rustic cottages that marked his career, and almost of a piece with the work for the 'Gordon Boys'. By the turn of the century, the 'Bishop's Park' for which Butterfield had laid this groundwork was a municipal resort for the working people of Fulham and Hammersmith, with walkways, a wading pond, a promenade, boating and the famous re-creation of 'Margate Sands'.

279

The Lodge, Whiteknights Park, Reading: view from the west, photograph by Philip Osborne Collier, *c*.1905

the walls. It marks the early suburbanisation of the country villa estate, the extension of public access to suburban parkland and the increasing level of control over open space that accompanied it.

Fulham Palace was the ancient home of the bishops of London, which lay in a vast swathe of gardens and parkland in a bend of the Thames. In 1857, Butterfield began to restore and reorganise the Tudor dwelling as a family home and diocesan centre for his friends Archibald and Catherine Spooner Tait.[3] The Taits were country people who had no love, and some fear, of the bishop's official 'London House', in a dangerously unsanitary and crowded part of town. Everything Butterfield did at Fulham, over ten years of new work and changes, reflected the Taits' love for family life, a free and easy home for the revitalisation of a family often in precarious health. The Taits happily shared the health-giving pleasures of their country park with the people of Fulham and Hammersmith, many of them country folk recently arrived in an area of extraordinary overcrowding and poverty, and to whose welfare both of the Taits were devoted. The most important work was a new chapel, free-standing in brick, finished in 1867. Its decoration was completed by Butterfield in Tait's memory in 1882, and, with testimonial funds to spare, he then added a commemorative fountain in the public western court, whose Tudor fronts he had restored. It was a wonderful low-lying brick and stone reduction of a classical cistern that stands as the architect's

RHAPSODY IN THE COUNTRY SUBURB: ALL SAINTS', HARROW WEALD

By the time of the Golden Jubilee year, the rural village of Harrow Weald was host to a large number of country-suburban villas for merchant and manufacturing families seeking fresh air and comfort. Notable among them were those of the preserved food suppliers Edmund Crosse and Thomas Blackwell, two humble city warehouse clerks who had made their fortune first in supplying dried foodstuffs to the ships of the naval and merchant fleet and then, as the world's first multinational purveyor of foodstuffs, producing pickles and sauces for the family tables of the new middle class. Their patronage permitted not only the completion of the rough pebble-dashed church that Butterfield had begun for Edward Monro in 1850, by the raising of a tower over the porch, but its expansion, with a spacious new north aisle for the growing population of what was now, in the new parlance, a 'flourishing suburban village' of over 1500 people. On completion in 1891, there were 420 sittings. Though the tower is taken to an urban scale, Butterfield chose a simplified approach to it, to its folded cap and to the shaping of the new north aisle and vestry, which take their cues from the row of sheds with which medieval halls like that at Stokesay in Shropshire were assembled. To the disappointment of a generally admiring press, Butterfield chose to mix his materials and leave them rugged and raw, rather

ALL SAINTS CHVRCH.

HARROW WEALD.   N°3.

North Elevation

280
All Saints' Church,
Harrow Weald:
north elevation, 1890

than cover and finish them into a consistent scheme. As a result, the whole ensemble, shrouded within a grove, shows the same sense of history, displayed through parts unselfconsciously accumulated over a long passage of time, as the legion of parish country churches assembled from the twelfth to fifteenth centuries that he had spent so much of his life bringing back to life.

Within this rustic ensemble Butterfield then installed wall decorations, in light, open and informal patterns of fruit, flower and vine, including two extraordinary tile mosaics – one covering the chancel arch and the other filling the east wall above the reredos. They carry into the sanctuary a rich harvest from nature, in abstract patterns of metropolitan subtlety, composed by exaggerating the scale of the abstracted forms of flowers, vines and fruits that he learned from medieval ironwork and that provided a vocabulary in brass for his altar rails for many years. They were now rendered in the

three distinctive tones of aquamarine, burnt gold and carmine first specified so precisely forty years before for the soffits of his first churches. In these three hues he saw the optical basis of all colour and of light itself, and with them he calibrated the tones of the fall of light within the structure.

In 1846, John Keble had invited Butterfield to Hursley church to work with him to devise and design a sequence of windows that – in the manner of the medieval windows at Fairford, Oxfordshire, that Keble had known as a boy – would recount a narrative of the progress of the Christian story from prophecy to sacrifice to triumph. And we have seen Butterfield since carrying the same broad narrative pattern into all the major works in which a pictorial element could be introduced. In his later works, the culmination of that symbolic parade is increasingly expressed through abstractions from forms of nature. Of this, Harrow Weald is an almost extravagantly dynamic example. The chancel arch

West Elevation

Joseph Morris

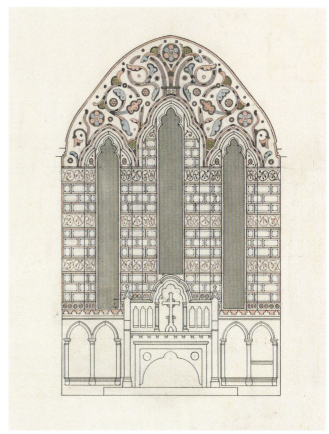

281 (left)
All Saints' Church,
Harrow Weald:
west elevation, 1890

282 (right)
All Saints' Church,
Harrow Weald:
design for the east
wall mosaic, c.1890

(p.353) carries a composition almost identical to that at All Saints' Margaret Street, but with curled tendrils as the alpha and the omega; while at the end wall four large sprouting vines, nearly 4 feet high and wide, dance like angels in the heavens above the windows, the same vision of the Majesty from the Book of Revelation that Butterfield and Morris used in the east window of St John's, Dalton, where the Evangelists gaze upon the Godhead seated in glory (p.117) – here represented by a five-petalled blossom nested between two branches at the point of the arch. There is rhetorical splendour in these signs, but it is the cleansing vision of the living countryside in bud, bloom and fruit that lends it life – an evocation of what Hopkins calls,

A strain of the earth's sweet being in the beginning
In Eden Garden . . .
Before it cloud . . . and sour with sinning.[4]

NOTES

1. *Bedford Times*, as cited in *Leicester Chronicle*, August 1863.
2. On this project, see Mark Girouard, 'Milton Ernest Hall, Bedfordshire', *Country Life*, 23 October 1969, pp 1042–6.
3. The account of the work at Fulham Palace is taken principally from *Illustrated Times*, May 1867; Randall Thomas Davidson and William Benham, *Life of Archibald Campbell Tait*, 2 vols, Macmillan, London, 1891; William Benham (ed.), *Catherine and Craufurd Tait, Wife and Son of Archibald Campbell, Archbishop of Canterbury: A Memoir*, London, Macmillan, 1879; *West London Observer*, 16 April 1892; Charles James Féret, *Fulham Old and New*, 3 vols, Leadenhall Press, London, 1900; and letters from Butterfield relating to the palace, chapel and grounds in the papers of the Bishops of London in Lambeth Palace Library.
4. Gerard Manley Hopkins, 'Spring', May 1877, unpublished manuscript in Harry Ransom Center, University of Texas.

ART AND CRAFT OF RURAL LIVING

Aldenham Home Farm: estate cottages

Kirby Muxloe: schoolhouse,
school; cottage group

Braunstone: terraced cottage
group and double dwellings

White Knights Estate: gate lodges

Aldenham Home Farm Dairy

Fulham Palace: restored west wing,
fountain, coachman's lodge

CHAPTER 23

'FOR THE SOLACE *of* HIS SICK POOR': CHEDDAR HOSPITAL, 1875–84

THE IDEA OF THE SANATORIUM

'**T**WO SONS AND two daughters . . . were taken successively to their rest. With the removal of the last of these, a beautiful girl who died in the spring of last year, a shadow seemed to settle down upon Tyntesfield, shutting out its inmates from much communion with the outer world.'[1] So wrote one who knew the family of William Gibbs well, in the weekly *Guardian* published a few days after his death on 3 April 1875. Charlotte Yonge, meeting Gibbs's widow Matilda Blanche at the Keble gate-lodge on 25 April the following year, as they both arrived early for the consecration of the chapel he had funded, found her pale, frail and still much saddened by her bereavements. But in the year since William died, with three of her children now lost to consumption in their young adulthood, she had not stood still,

launching an ambitious plan to establish a model home that would offer the poor the benefits – discovered by the German physician Hermann Brehmer and others, but hitherto only available to the wealthy – of a regime and environment conducive to respiratory health. Blanche explored a number of possible sites, before purchasing 6 acres of farmland on a south-west-facing, well-drained alluvial slope between Axbridge and Cheddar in the Mendip Hills. The site was sheltered from cold north and east winds but open to kinder breezes from the south and west, which were believed to gather health-giving ozone as they crossed the Bristol Channel and the Somerset Levels. It was prime land for raising food; gentle ground for light walking; sunny and warm enough to famously produce the first strawberries of the English season; with limestone water pure for drinking and rich in

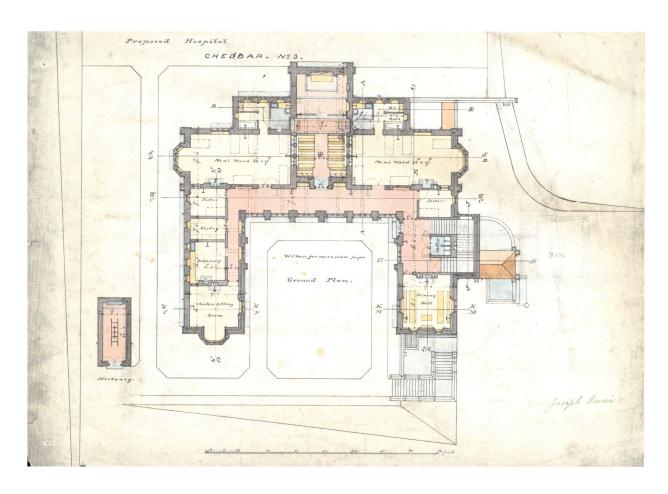

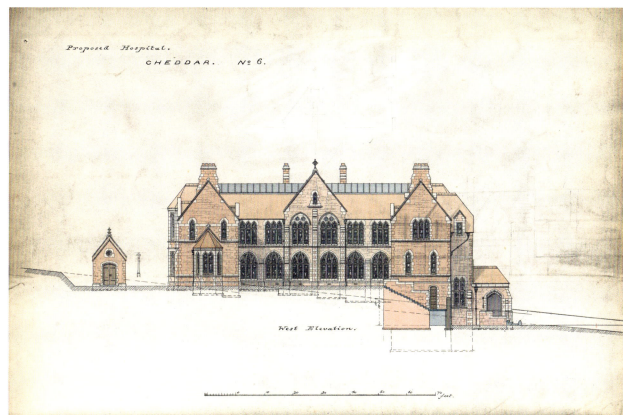

283
Cheddar Hospital:
ground plan, *c.*1876

284
Cheddar Hospital:
west elevation, *c.*1876

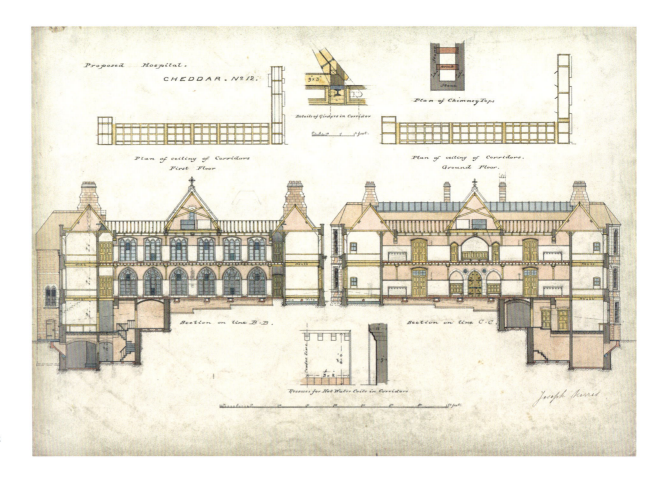

minerals for bathing therapies. It was within striking distance of the Gibbs home in Tyntesfield and of two of the most notorious vectors of tuberculosis in the land: the city of Bristol, where the incidence of the disease as it took hold in the first decades of the century had been the worst in England, and the dairy country of Somerset, where it was virulent and widespread among farmworkers.

The foundation stone for this 'Home', dedicated to St Michael, was laid in a quiet ceremony in October 1876, Blanche and Butterfield using the trowel with which Gibbs had laid that of Keble Chapel two years before.[2] The vast earthworks, deep foundations and elaborate system of hygienic drainage, in which run-offs were piped and scrupulously segregated, were already largely in place, and the lone press report provides such a detailed description of the work to be built that the principal drawings must have been completed. Butterfield set up the home on a huge terrace floating above the slope, as a two-storey pavilion opening to a garden court nearly 60

feet wide. A tower of circulation and services uses the incline to drop down four floors to a working entrance on its southern end. The lowest level was partially underground, allowing all sources of possible contamination, coming in or out, to be carried away, and keeping service visitors isolated from the patient community. Two dazzling flights of Portland stone, each of fifteen 6-foot-wide steps, brought visitors up to the garden court, where one path led directly to the mortuary for mourners and another turned right to the public entry and a great internal staircase in the south-east corner. The functional circulation system was carefully confined to a single great shaft with strictly separated service lifts for coal and food and wide stairs with shallow treads for the movement of patients.

Within the pavilion were two floors of continuous windowed promenade for exercise, air and delight in the views. Their gently arched ceilings rose from 10 to 12 feet high, and windows filled nearly the entire extent of the outer wall, with ventilating glass panels at different points that could be adjusted to winds and weather. Under-floor heating pipes and elaborate under-floor spacing, ventilation and buffering protected against two principal hazards for consumptives: dust and moisture. Behind the corridor sat the two storeys of wards with two on each floor, the upper for twelve women and the lower for twelve men. Each ward ended in an enormous projecting bay to north or south. The chapel, set in the centre between them, extended one bay to the east. The corridor continued into the two wings beside the garden court. That in the north housed the nursing sisters, and the south wing provided a main entry, a common dining room and access to services, with nursing staff above. Abutments on either side of the chapel in the rear housed bathing, toilet and scullery for each of the wards, open to the air, and confining water, waste and drainage related to patient care to easily maintained compact zones. Four separate and extended drainage systems were constructed for bath, soil, sink and rainwater. Segregation of anything carrying bodily effluents, especially those from the chest, would help avoid transmission to those at close quarters. Details on his drawings show Butterfield's elaborate trap and filtering systems for the cleansing process in these sculleries.

Though the discovery of the agent causing pulmonary tuberculosis did not come until 1882, the nature of consumptive conditions, as diseases spread through extended contact and poor hygiene, had been recognised since 1869. While no cure had been found, it was believed that fatal deterioration of the lungs might be slowed with ample fresh air and sunlight, free from dust and damp, and a regime where the lung inflammation and the wasting condition and weakening of other organs could be ameliorated with ample fresh food, bed rest, regular bathing in minerally rich water and gentle exercise. St Michael's was a pioneering instance, on an especially generous, life-affirming and comfortable model, of this first stage in the sanatorium movement, in which consumptives were placed in general health-giving and palliative conditions. As knowledge of the tubercular virus and its behaviour increased in the later 1880s and

1890s, regimes became more strenuous, leaving consumptives lying in crowded rows on open terraces, in effective permanent quarantine, blasted with breezes to take away the 'poison' believed to invade night air indoors, and subject to the torture of ice baths, lung deflation and rib removal.

SPIRITUAL AND TEMPORAL WELFARE

St Michael's would introduce a number of these treatments at the turn of the century, but the pattern of its life remained, as it began, a well-tended household with a focus on gentler means of succour, helping residents, in words used at the laying of the foundation stone, 'to end their days in comfort, with provision for their spiritual as well as their temporal welfare'. Four sisters of St Peter's Kilburn, a community founded by Susan Oldfield in Kilburn to care for the incurable, where the Gibbs' daughter had served and died, were engaged to nurse both body and spirit; and the chapel was fitted out for a resident chaplain and a daily cycle of prayer.

Butterfield adopted a plan that slotted the chapel like a jewelled cabinet between the wards. Within a mere 35 by 17 feet are high-backed stalls for six nursing sisters at the rear and three bays of bench pews for the men and women in care, set up on either side of a wide centre aisle along which a bath chair could easily be moved. A step upwards comes to a narrow choir with a small organ on the north and seating for the superior, chaplain and patron to the south. A compressed version of a full chancel then rises on three levels, with side windows and east window bathing it in light. Ornament works to a scale, chromaticism and simplicity that respect the domestic dimensions of the room. Patterns of red tile and white and red marble play against the tones of simply shaped wood and white walls, with repeated small diamond and rosette motifs leading east to a single point of modest grandeur where the canopy of the reredos, carrying a celestial ring of circling orbs, points to the Agnus Dei in the head of a great triple window showing Christ enthroned between Saints Peter and Paul. Light from the north and south windows allowed Butterfield and

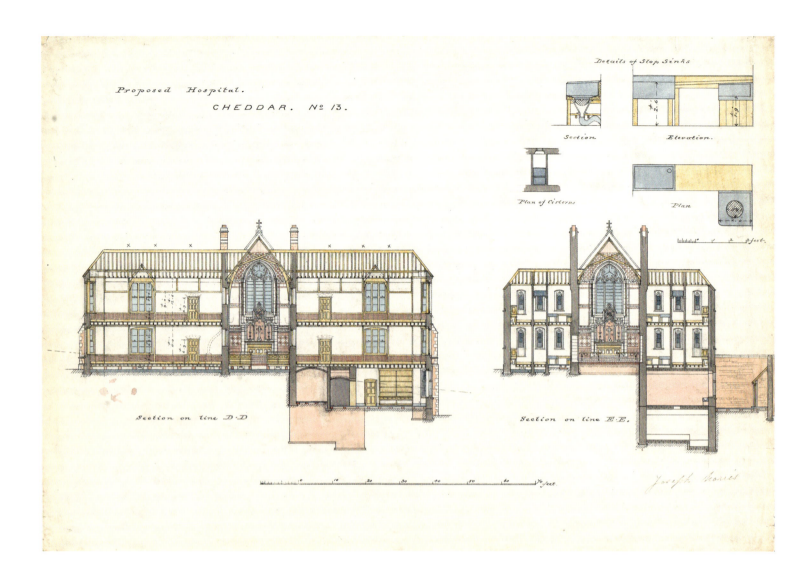

286

Cheddar Hospital: sections looking east through wards, sanitary facilities and chapel, *c.*1876

Gibbs to use deeper tones without darkening the space, and, as at Keble Chapel, allows the blood red of sacrifice and regeneration to predominate. Six wooden shutters are installed within the arches on either side of the nave, which can open as windows from the four wards, allowing bedridden patients to listen to the liturgy. On the west wall over the doorway is a large carved stone Crucifixion based on thirteenth-century manuscript illuminations, presented as a memorial to William Gibbs and carrying the motto 'For the Solace of His Sick Poor'; while facing the entry to the chapel on the outer wall of the corridor is a large relief of St Michael Slaying the Devil, probably a plaster model for the carving above the south door of Keble Chapel. The wards were enlivened by Blanche with a changing

display of works from her collection of Christian art. For many poorer inmates this was the first time religion and its visual narratives had approached them. As a result, the chaplain and bishop were kept as busy with baptisms and confirmations as with the sad duties of the mortuary, which sat to the north-west corner of the great terrace.

'A PATTERN OF LIFE FOR THE WORLD'

The second imperative was to comfort the eye and cheer the spirits through wide, handsome, high, bright and calm spaces, opening vistas both within and without, whether at rest or in movement. Gone were the discouraging 'gaunt brown walls . . . infinite

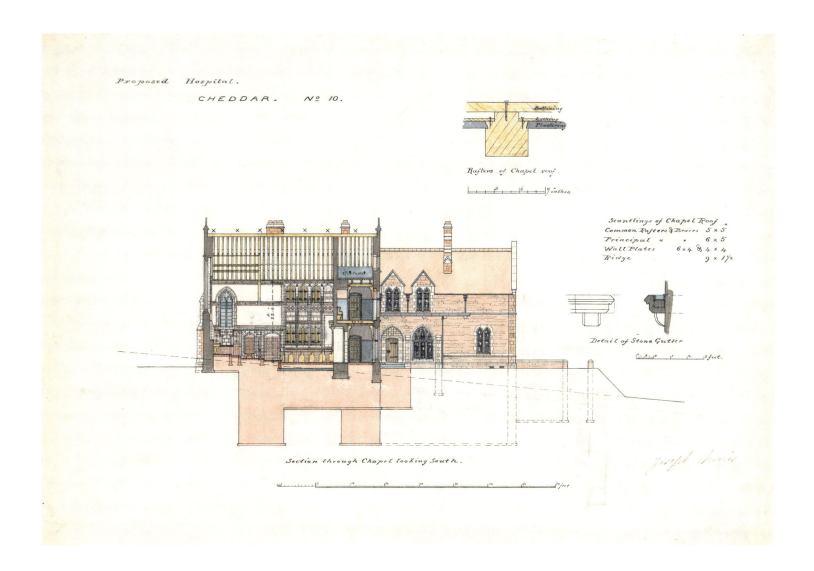

Proposed Hospital.

CHEDDAR. No. 10.

Rafters of Chapel roof.

Scantlings of Chapel Roof
Common Rafters & Braces   5 × 5
Principal   "   .   6 × 5
Wall Plates   6 × 4 & 4 × 4
Ridge   9 × 1½

Detail of Stone Gutter.

Section through Chapel looking South.

287

Cheddar Hospital:
section through
chapel looking south,
with the elevation of
the principal entry,
*c.*1876

in their decent meanness' recorded by the tubercular poet William Ernest Henley during his days of incarceration in a grimly economical Edinburgh hospital. In its place came an open, dignified country house, the sisters living alongside their patients, with a great sheltered promenade and a collegiate dining hall, views out to a beautiful but familiar landscape, planned with the efficiency and sanitary conditions of an infirmary, but expressed as a household for rest and refreshment, so that patients would not, like Henley's ward-mates in Edinburgh, 'lie as in training for shroud and coffin' but, as one of the sisters assured a patient, find a beauty in their surroundings that would nurture the beauty of their soul.

That beauty – social as well as aesthetic – came from many things: the high hygienic red-tiled

dados; the woodwork framing the bay windows; the placing and refinement of the enormous marble fireplaces in the wards; the coloured upper walls of the promenade; the division of the wards into large uncrowded chambers with a sense of balance between containment and community; and above all an absolute consistency of material, palette and scale. As increasing levels of outside exercise began to be prescribed for those who had gained weight and strength, the daily promenade would bring many out into the parkland, or to join in the work of the kitchen gardens and the Home Farm, where nearly all the basic foods of the hospital were produced, growing a community of activity close to nature.

On its opening in September 1878, one writer declared 'this *house*', as the Gibbs memorial so

288

Cheddar Hospital: group photograph at the upper entrance showing William Butterfield with Matilda Blanche Gibbs (seated right), the chaplain and the nursing sisters, *c*.1878

rightly called it, the 'most original and beautiful' of all Butterfield's works, noting the extraordinarily satisfying landscape of platforms 'set perfectly into the hills', the reminiscent quality of the rough local Draycott composite – the same rough-textured and warmly toned stone with which the local barns and farms were built – and the play against it of the smooth wide planes of Bath stone trim, conveying a sense of 'special dignity'. Others spoke of the 'wonderful simplicity' of the chapel; the vigour brought to both chapel and wards by the light-toned 'arcades' of wooden shutters; and a 'singular degree of warmth that characterizes the whole of the interior' and gives it the makings of a 'house itself'. The *Guardian* concluded that this was the work, along with the library and hall of Keble College, completed in the same year, in which the nineteenth century had finally found a 'genuine style of our own'.

Registers show admissions of farm labourers, domestic servants and rural artisans, all from hard

circumstances. Said one who knew it would be short, the time at St Michael's was still the happiest and most comfortable of his life. 'This', wrote another young patient, looking to a future he would not live to see, 'could be a pattern of life for the world.'

By 1882, greater skill in differentiating a patient's condition and mode of care was leading to a more varied range of requirements and accommodation. Plans for the first extension added another six patients in intensive or private wards, increased the nursing staff and added a men's smoking room and a larger refectory to replace the dining room and allow its conversion into a well-ventilated dormitory for staff. Along with this extension to the south came revisions to the entry sequence, including a new arched entry to the great stair and an almost Romanesque tower to cover the entrance – an evocation of those Norman models which had just begun to mark Butterfield's work, as at St Columba's College in Dublin, and would come into full flower at Ascot Chapel.

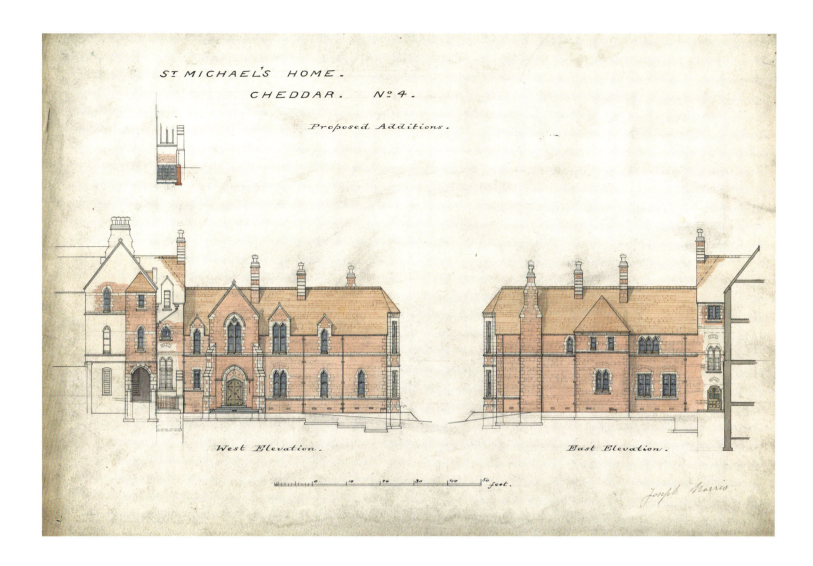

ST. MICHAEL'S HOME.

CHEDDAR. No. 4.

Proposed Additions.

West Elevation.

East Elevation.

Joseph Morris

289

Cheddar Hospital: additions – west and east elevations, 1882

TOWARDS THE IDEAL VILLA

Drawings for the gate lodge at the roadside, which fronted the hospital's stables, carriage house and yard (all kept at a hygienic distance from the patients), show a Draycott stone structure capped with gables in timber frame, sparingly placed but boldly scaled (fig.292). This was an approach Butterfield then applied even more boldly at the chaplain's house, marking the domestic character of both buildings out from the institutional with very powerful effect. At the time of the opening in September 1878 this 'parsonage house' was still in construction. The chaplain's post came with a curacy serving the remoter settlements in the parish, requiring an elaborate stable block and yard to work effectively. There is one large guest bedroom facing west that perhaps housed Blanche Gibbs on her frequent visits, and another on the top floor facing east, probably for the first chaplain's surgeon father, Thomas Hickes, who had retired from his practice among the poor in Bristol and come to live there and perhaps assist with the care of residents.

There are all kinds of freedoms here that Butterfield – unconstrained by an existing building, selecting his own site and working outside the constraints of Church Commissioners and diocesan grants – may not have been able to enjoy elsewhere: placing the largest window at the highest peak of the roof; setting gables within gables; laying half-timbering against stone to support an overhang above; and leaving windows relentlessly squared and plain. The house sits very simply on a levelled site at the edge of a long grassy slope, upon which

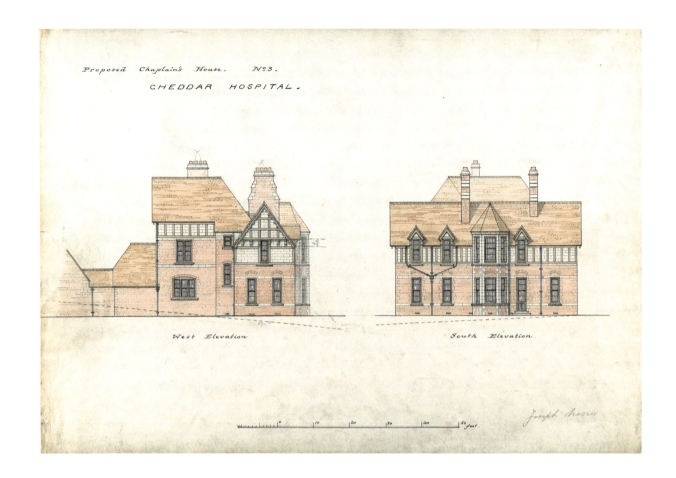

Proposed Chaplain's House.   No 3.

CHEDDAR HOSPITAL.

West Elevation.

South Elevation.

Proposed   Chaplain's   House.   No 4.

CHEDDAR HOSPITAL.

East Elevation.

North Elevation.

290

Cheddar Hospital
chaplain's house: west
and south elevations,
*c.*1878

291

Cheddar Hospital
chaplain's house: east
and north elevations,
*c.*1878

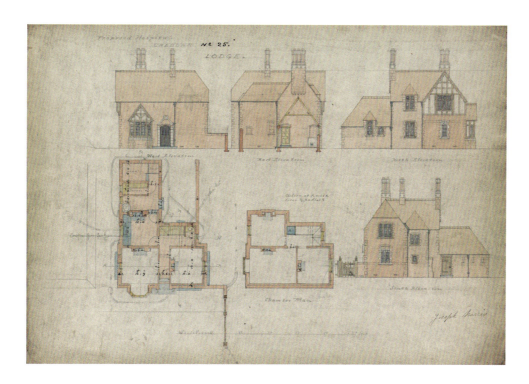

292
Cheddar Hospital:
lodge, elevations and
plans, *c*.1878–80

a wonderfully asymmetrical set of family rooms and chambers looks out where there is neither terrace nor garden, but graded meadow. The entry takes the least prominent place along the north–south axis, within a collage of varied recessive volumes for which it effectively works as the hinge. By following the logic of a tripartite plan in which services, servants and family are ingeniously linked for purpose but divided for hygiene and propriety, it produces one of those marvellous Butterfield collisions of apparently incompatible volumes that startle when seen compressed on the drawing sheet, but look perfectly at ease within a larger spatial frame upon the ground.

A single clerical gesture or 'remonstrance' lies at the entrance where the doorway opens, as in all Butterfield's later vicarages, into a short vestibule from which visitors can turn immediately and privately into the chaplain's study. Here, however, the entry establishes its parochial presence not from a diapered cross like Landford or a tracery window like Baldersby, but through a solitary buttress bearing the widest and most staggered of thick stone drip moulds. While undoubtedly doing duty in supporting and sheltering the portal, this single buttress – the only one in the house – joins the humble window of the maid's room above, which is

set like a sexton's parvis under a steep plain gable. It echoes the porch of an ancient abbey church, evoking the long succession from which Butterfield believed the authority of the priesthood derived. It takes a moment to recognise what Halsey Ricardo, so close to Butterfield for so long, said of his work: that there is often the greatest wit where the design has the greatest apparent gravity; and it is the comforting humour of such features throughout St Michael's Home, like the shutters of the chapel on the walls of the wards, that refuses to express seriousness through solemnity and turns the making of a place to gently succour the dying into a site of quiet gaiety.

NOTES

1. *The Guardian*, 7 April 1875.
2. The primary sources for a history of the Cheddar Hospital or St Michael's Home currently open to research are few, but the extent and detail of the drawings – only a selection of which are presented here – allows for a thorough reconstruction of the project. The essential references were to: *The Guardian*, 7 April 1875 and 2 October 1878; *Bristol Mercury*, 1 October 1878; *Western Gazette*, 4 October 1878; and David Hassell and Zera Wilson, *This Special Place: A History of St Michael's Home*, White Space Design, Axbridge, 2005. See also Henry C. Burdett, *Cottage Hospitals: General, Fever and Convalescent*, Scientific Press, London, 1896.

CHAPTER 24

RETREAT *and* COMMEMORATION: HEATH'S COURT, 1878–82

IN MEMORIAM

ON 1 FEBRUARY 1878 the artist Jane Fortescue Coleridge, wife of William Butterfield's great friend John Duke Coleridge, 'drove out' from their house at Sussex Square in Paddington, then a country suburb of London, to visit the first winter exhibition of the vast new Grosvenor Galleries in Bond Street. While looking at the finest array of Italian Old Master drawings ever assembled in England, Lady Coleridge began to feel unwell and went home nursing an 'ordinary cold'.[1] This took a turn for the worse the next afternoon, and a few days later she died from an infection of the lungs. She was taken to Heath's Court, the Coleridge family home at Ottery St Mary, and buried in the great churchyard it stood beside, whose restoration Butterfield and the Coleridges had famously undertaken some thirty years before.

There, two years before, had been laid Butterfield's friend's father – and his own once 'inseparable companion' – Judge Sir John Taylor Coleridge, and John Duke then took on the south transept, long blocked up, for Butterfield to restore and 'beautify' as a memorial chapel to his parents.[2] The great clock would be restored, the walls cleared and decorated, and the windows revealed, with open pews for fifty. Butterfield's plans were moving forward at the time Jane died, and they were quickly adapted so that it could be dedicated to her memory, too, with a marble recumbent effigy commissioned from Frederick Thrupp, in which angels guard her head and an otter her feet. Nothing quite like Butterfield's decoration had yet been seen: vivid, patterned walls in squares of simple geometric tiling inset with panels in tessera mosaic, like the floors of Murano and Torcello, carrying sinuous lines of blossom, leaf, tendril and stamen. All – including the tiny heads and quarries in the window lancets – were rendered in the same palette of gold, maroon and aquamarine, except for two columns of cobalt marble, amid a huge neutral field of alabaster white. A ferny Syrian cross was the only patent Christian symbol in this panoply of abstractions from nature.

'A LIFE DESIGN'D': THE PLAN

From mid-August to October for many years the Coleridges had stayed at Buckland in the Moor, where John Duke spoke of a landscape, sweeping and sublime, that he often wished for as '*a lovelier* home than Ottery'. But, he writes in 1870, 'I have made up my mind to stay where my father and grandfather stayed', and he began to discuss with Jane and Butterfield an expansion of that modest house to serve a long prospect of retirement, to welcome friends to lazy days and to stand – beside the church whose restoration the family had taken in hand – as a landmark to the growing dignity of the 'house' of Coleridge.[3] Diffident, solitary, never at home in the city, and uncomfortable with the burden of precedence attendant on her high rank in society, Jane had what was in the town mason's opinion the remarkable quality of being 'a lady one could talk to', and looked forward to living there with nothing but a dog, a vista of skies, her collection of Old Master prints, her sketchbook, the working people of the village around her, and the 'hilly field' of Samuel Taylor Coleridge's 1797 poem 'The Lime Tree Bower' for company. She engaged so fully in the first discussions of extension that the new house was, with her sudden loss, accorded another sorrowful memorial duty: to provide, as Coleridge wrote to his friend the theologian John Henry Newman, a residence for her spirit, where he hoped to live out his years in '*her* house' under '*her* roof'.

Coleridge had met Jane in 1842, and they married in 1846, when Coleridge was called to the bar. Living with his father near Regent's Park and supporting his family in great part by writing

criticism and short essays for weekly journals, he eventually established a lucrative practice in the western circuit. In 1861, he became a Liberal MP for Exeter, then served as Attorney General in Gladstone's first government, was created Baron Coleridge in 1873 when he became Chief Justice of the Common Pleas, and finally rose to become the country's first Lord Chief Justice in 1880. As John Duke, Lord Coleridge's income grew, and with his father's retirement to the country, he and Jane moved to Paddington, eventually acquiring the place in Sussex Square which Butterfield then refined for them, working through the summer of 1868 to fabricate a large library for their vast collection of books and prints, an unaccustomedly spacious study, an entry and principal staircase to carry Jane's life-size studies after Michelangelo, and a famous dining room where fashionable London dined under Butterfield's infamous wallpaper of 'seaworms, slugs, and seaweed'.

The house in Ottery had originally been tied to the clerical college at St Mary's Church as the chanter's home, and was bought by Colonel James Coleridge on his retirement in 1796 to provide the 'roof-tree' under which his progeny would be reared, close to the school which his father had led, and among the meadows where he and his brother, the poet, had wandered in their youth. It had a famous moment in its history, when Oliver Cromwell and Thomas Fairfax met there in a panelled room in 1645 to sign the Convention that effectively commenced the Civil War. The house seems to have changed little before 1836, when Sir John Taylor Coleridge inherited it, but in time for his retirement in 1858 he extended service areas to the rear and converted a little garden room to the west, added earlier, into a drawing room. Coleridge was wedded from the start to retaining this original 'Chanters' House', with its echoes of great events in the Civil War, of a father with whom he had been as confidential and intimate as a friend, and of a wife whose loss could be partly recovered by suffusing it with her memory. There would be no great halls, grand avenues, splendid carriageways, ascending entries or fine ballrooms. He was looking for a home which could furnish his retirement with 'lettered ease', welcome his

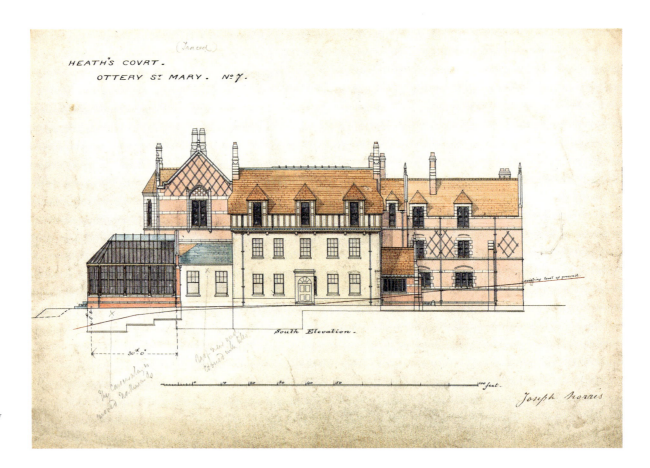

many friends to an atmosphere of 'stillness, quiet, and delicious idleness', fit the figure of a man who stood 6 foot 3, and accommodate one of the largest private libraries in England, all the while leaving its principal rooms from the seventeenth century intact. But Coleridge asked that it also represent the particular '*aesthetics*' of its history, proprietors, site and setting. This was the term his great-uncle Samuel Taylor Coleridge had been first to use in discussing the fabrication of beauty, demanding that art seek 'unity in variety' and express an innate truth to itself, an intuitive aesthetic that we might call 'character'. The sense of how this aesthetic richness might emerge from the comforts of 'a life design'd' was strikingly imagined in Tennyson's 'The Palace of Art', a popular poetic fantasy of the ideal 'English home' whose adornment would recount 'cycles of the human tale' and whose Socratic 'sounding corridors' would echo with the discourse of the learned.[4]

Client and architect were so close that we must imagine them virtually working together. Contract drawings were mostly completed by late summer of 1880. Butterfield and Coleridge were looking at wood samples in the beginning of October, and later that month Joseph Norris costed the project and supplied a timetable, based on commencing groundwork in January, with occupancy in August 1882. In the New Year holiday of 1881, Coleridge moved into his sister's house at the Manor behind the church; books, art and furniture went into sealed storage in the front rooms of the old house; and the extensive outbuildings, kitchen, offices and other rooms erected in 1849 were demolished. The task of levelling the ground and managing its landscape was enormous: drawings show a 14-foot drop from east to west under the built footprint and 15 feet falling from north to south. A vast system of terraced landscape to the west of the house was needed to accommodate excavation and fill, laid down in Butterfield's familiar pattern of precise parallel lines, with trees scrupulously protected. Work slowed in the first summer campaign of

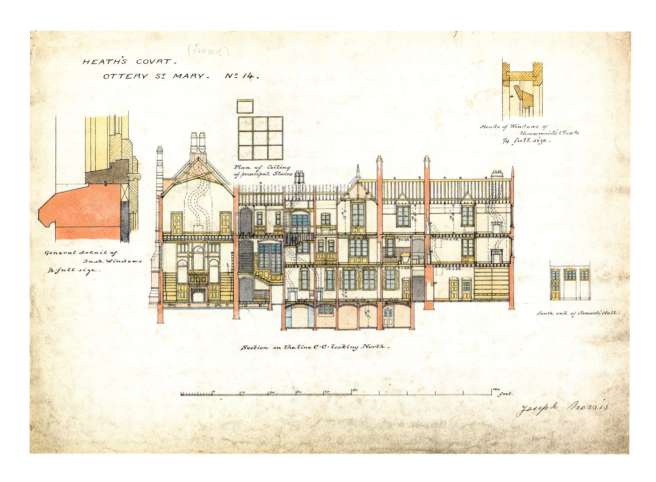

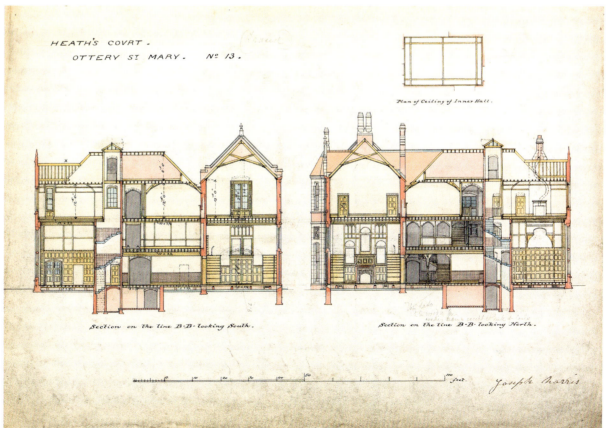

294
Heath's Court, Ottery
St Mary: section
looking north, 1880

295
Heath's Court, Ottery
St Mary: sections
looking south and
north, 1880

1881, as the conservatory was entirely rethought, and again in the following year when Coleridge had a long period of painful illness. But reports in November 1882 say the house was then almost completed, and a grand ball for 150 was held in the library to welcome the New Year of 1883. Gates and walls continued to be built until August that year, when Butterfield submitted a final bill. The total cost was just under £17,000.

The great entry porch at the centre with the massive east window of the hall beside it indicates very clearly where the central two-storey circulation path runs behind it. A new north block of kitchen, services and staff bedrooms lies on the right, continuing to the west for some distance behind the old house to enclose the passages through the inner core; an arched entry separates it from a long low L of sheds and other 'offices' forming the north-east corner of a service court. The small dining, drawing and private rooms of the old house to the left face south with a passage and door to a sitting garden; the original visitor and family chambers above are left intact; but an entirely new bedroom floor at quite a different scale rides over it, marked out from the generations of building beneath by an assertive end gable and continuous timber framing. There were ten bedrooms in addition to the manservants' suite on the second floor and another six on the first.

Nothing in either approach to the house, from the north courtyard or west gardens, reveals the other element of this scrupulously divided building, in which the separate parts are folded into a single cube. This is a tall symmetrical pavilion on two floors, running south to north on a newly graded platform above the meadows to the west, with a range of high wide windows, the most important of them set around two projecting bays. Within is a galleried library, the length and width of a nave – 70 feet long, 22 feet high and 25–30 feet wide – with two huge principal bedrooms above, lying under 20-foot coved ceilings. Here, pattern, scale and proportion, echoed precisely in the courtyard entrance façade, have a life and character entirely unrelated to the original house, luxuriating in the burnt-orange clay brick of the district.

The general plan ensured that servers and served, the workings of the household and its pleasures, were scrupulously kept apart, yet the overlapping of the volumes makes for extraordinary efficiency. There is only one moment on each floor where the two lives intersect, seen in the 10-foot-square shaft that breaks the inner from the outer hall, where the service stairs and lift appear, and where what Butterfield calls the kitchen corridor is carried out to the east. It is a system that allows food to flow into living and entertaining with a minimum of visible traffic; but it also permits Butterfield to provide staff with the extraordinary comfort of a 30-by-40-foot kitchen, scullery and pantry, at the cool north-east boundary of the home. The first plan was for a conservatory on the south-west corner, entered from the simple drawing room that had been added by Coleridge's father in the 1840s; but by August 1881 the conservatory was expanded, with an aviary and promenade, and moved north to an outlying site, 54 feet long, that required excavating a much larger level platform for the house. Most of the drawings where the amendments were minor were simply left in the previous configuration; but east and west elevations were revised to convey the profile of the new long cloister with its aviary, and the winter garden turned to face back as an apostrophe at its furthest end. Approaches and perimeter walls were not fully defined until February 1882, with steps, gates and walls to the churchyard, a diapered high brick fence between carriageway and gardens, and a resplendent brick gate at the entrance from the college road.

'CYCLES OF THE HUMAN TALE': THE LIBRARY

The elevation of the library's north wall, as we see it in the general sections (figs 294 and 295), would be modified in details to admit a door on the north-west corner leading to the new conservatory (fig.296). At that point the carved overmantel would be replaced by a Thrupp frieze, after Flaxman, showing Athena's dismissal of the Furies, from Aeschylus's *Eumenides*, with an

296
Heath's Court,
Ottery St Mary:
west elevation,
1880, redrawn
after conservatory
moves, 1881–2

inscription – 'They say that Justice is the child of God and that she dwells hard by the sin of man', and the word 'Andromeda' placed above it – all reflections on crime, punishment, sacrifice and the foundation of civil society. Above are frames for three of Jane Coleridge's full-scale drawings after two Sistine Chapel sibyls and the prophet Jeremiah, brought from Sussex Place. Two frames at the south end carry more Michelangelo studies by Jane, one after the Bruges Madonna and the other from the sketch published in William Young Ottley's *The Italian School of Design* of 1823 as a study for his Sistine Isaiah. To the left and right the panelling would soon after be modified to hang two enormous cartoons, rejected long ago for Old Testament frescoes at Wyatt & Brandon's Italianate church in Wilton, near Salisbury, by Sir William Boxall, Butterfield's friend and travelling companion and Jane Coleridge's teacher: these recount the expulsion of Ishmael and Hagar and the Prodigal Son. A second Thrupp bas-relief above

the fireplace in the east wall is taken from William Blake's 1817 vision of Hesiod's 'Golden Age', in which mankind was imagined dwelling under the shelter of a first perfect rule of law.[5] This whole elaborate iconographic scheme contemplates the prevision of civil and divine justice, the founding of nations and the construction of a peaceable society. Busts of John Milton and other writers stood on the library bookshelves. Carved wood fragments salvaged from the Ottery church during the 1849 restoration appear as end panels in the shelving.

Coleridge's private collection of books was one of the largest in the land, rich in print folios and illustrated books, from the late fifteenth-century *Nuremberg Chronicle* onwards, which only a setting at the scale and openness of the Heath's Court library could make comfortably accessible. A sequence of 12-foot bays allowed discrete study alcoves, with moving steps, stairs and tables making the maximum use of available space, and a full-length gallery of shelves along the east wall. A small door off the gallery leads

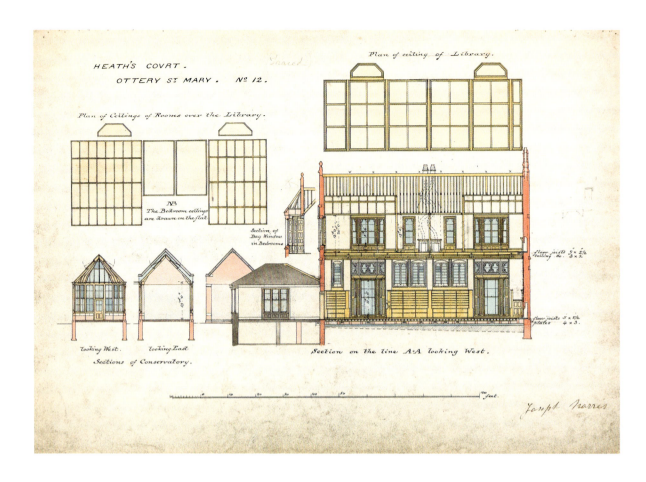

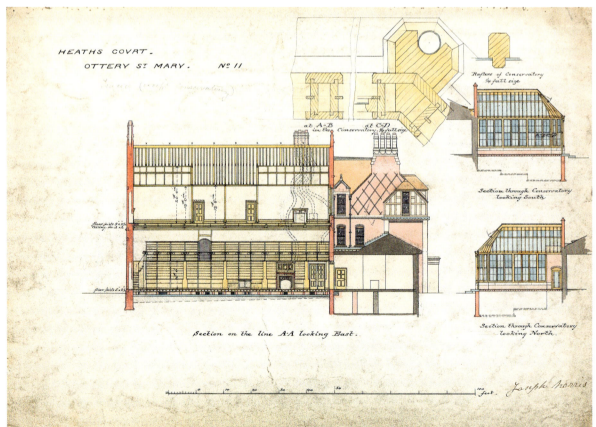

297
Heath's Court, Ottery
St Mary: section looking
west through the library
and principal bedrooms,
including sections for
the first scheme of the
conservatory, 1880

298
Heath's Court, Ottery
St Mary: section looking
east through the library
and principal bedrooms,
including sections for
the first scheme of the
conservatory, 1880

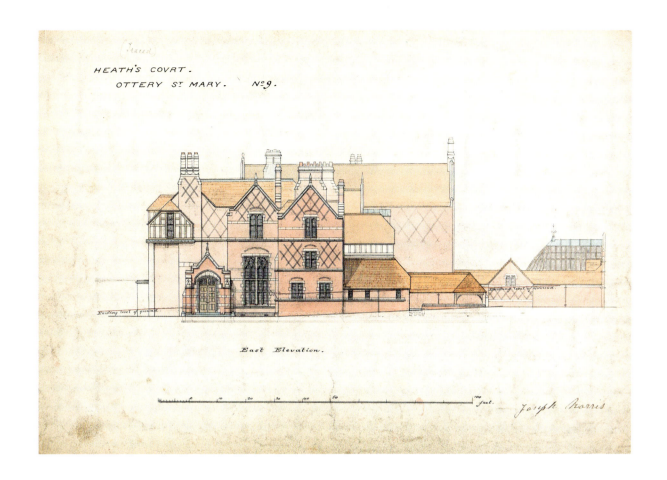

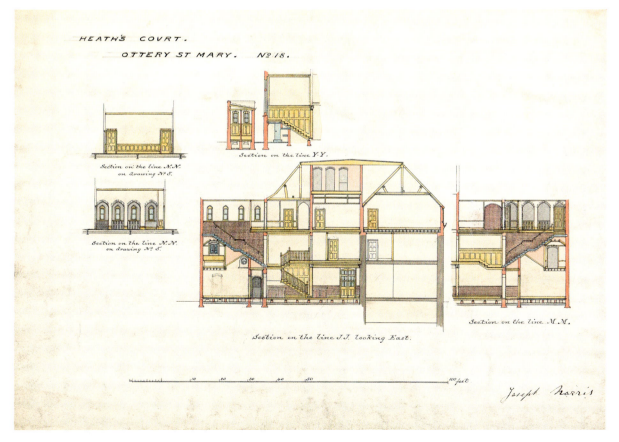

299
Heath's Court, Ottery
St Mary: east elevation,
1880, with additions
1881, 1882

300
Heath's Court,
Ottery St Mary: sections
looking east and west
detailing passages to
chamber floors and
showing the library
study room, 1880

to what was at first intended as a *studiolo* but then redesigned to house the cast of Thrupp's effigy of Jane. She was laid beneath a stained-glass window based on her study of a Virgin and Child after Dürer, and the ceiling coved to suggest the vaulted roof of a tomb. Beneath it is the full text of Wordsworth's sonnet ending: 'A lovely beauty in a summer grave'.[6]

'SOUNDING CORRIDORS': ENTRY AND SEQUENCE

The driveway brings us into a courtyard fit for carriages where the windows of the kitchen and its corridor lie straight ahead. The entry porch stands to the left, and the entrance takes us immediately through a small efficient portico, turning us right into a reception hall bearing an enormous representation of the Coleridge arms in a cartouche, with a magnificent wall of glass on our right through which can be seen the towers of the church to the east. Though used for household prayers, it is a transitional zone, turning us once again, through a third door, into a short passage, before the last door opens to the inner hall and an almost unexpected vista opens as we enter an atrium, from which the whole of the life within branches up and around in a mingling of stair, door, gallery, little window arcades and hidden alcoves, whose shadows and recessions we have already seen beautifully described in the first great section looking north (fig.295). Nothing could speak more clearly of a house to move about in than this collision and cascade of public routes. Doors were not sentried by a footman; and guests might wander at will. The detailing of the cascade of minor stairs and corridors is unified by red tiles and consistent light-wood simple cabinetry, so that even incidental passages are both animated and coherent.

The service areas traditionally buried in a basement were firmly placed above ground and treated with real care. But the serving hierarchy is strictly maintained, with butler and housekeeper housed on the ground floor, their rooms and service staircase seen in the general northward-looking section (fig.294), while three manservants

are housed in a dormitory duplex in an attic above the scullery. The kitchen carries shuttered sash windows placed above head height to allow ventilation without bringing in contaminants; lamps are specially designed to hang high up the kitchen walls and project nearly 4 feet into the room for task lighting. Oriented and windowed to prevent the build-up of heat, the kitchen is a mark of the house's generous provision of pleasure and comfort to those working in it. The attached larder, in which meats might be hung, takes a high-gabled shape of its own with stone cold counters and a set of narrow screened and louvred windows 10 feet high.

'AN ENGLISH HOME': NATURE AND LANDSCAPE

There is a curious effect of assemblage and passage at Heath's Court, in which, within a single enclosed volume, the eye catches a variety of spatial transitions and changes in character, as old meets new and one scale meets another, the direction of movement shifts and diverges, alcoves and dead ends appear, public corridors and stairs adopt different dados, railings, woods and turnings, and lamps and lanterns are encountered, hung like those on a city street, like the convergence of a townscape. At its culminating point at the north end of the library, the journey passes through a near-secret door to leave the world of human society behind and enter a long promenade with a city of birds singing on its eastern side and a vista to hilly fields on its west. Butterfield designed for the comfort of the birds in his aviary scooped hollows for nesting and a stream to drink and bathe. This ambulatory turns at the end into a glasshouse, filled with a fountain, and perched like a turret above falling ground to look away upon the land. Progress ends with 'The Walk', nearly half a mile long, that Butterfield wound round the meadow below, past rows of oak planted to mark the birth of sons, among pines sent from cherished friends, to the poet Coleridge's 'hilly field', so loved by Jane that winter grasses and flowers had been cut from it and rushed to London to be beside

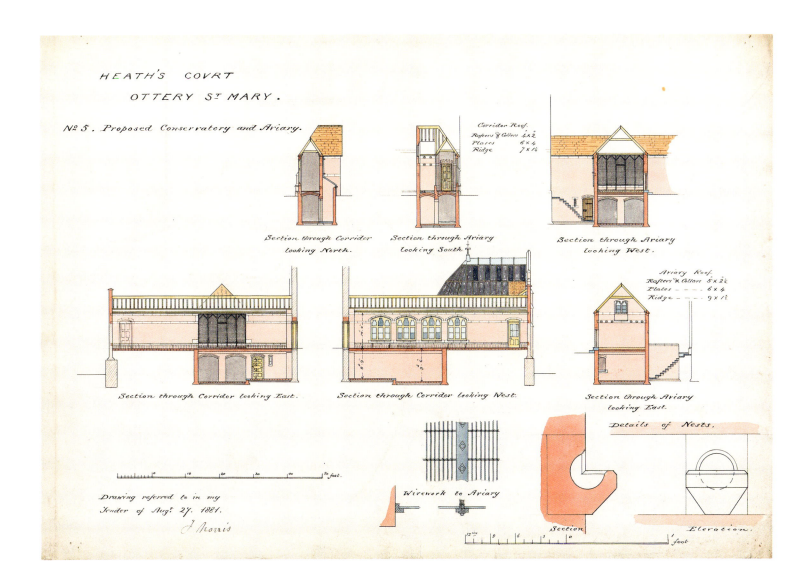

301

Heath's Court, Ottery
St Mary: sections and
details of conservatory
corridor and aviary,
August 1881

her in her few last days. These are the grounds
of an 'English home',[7] replete with memory, and
Butterfield calibrated the banks and paths closest
to the house to let their canopies spread and their
roots flourish.

'Would you be surprised to hear . . . ?' This was
the phrase with which Coleridge opened each new
tale from his inexhaustible storehouse of anecdote.
In summer 1883, Coleridge left on a speaking tour
of America, returning in October in the company
of Amy Lawford, a young woman with a rather
uncertain history. London society in August 1885
was 'surprised to hear' that Coleridge, whose
libellous dispute with his daughter's lover had
already crowded the columns of the yellow press,
had suddenly shocked his family by marrying.

Nevertheless, Amy, 'pretty, graceful affectionate
and devoted . . . made the last years of his life
extraordinarily happy'.[8] Smoking and billiard rooms
were quickly and rather crudely added to Heath's
Court; and though the new Lady Coleridge told
the press that she spent her days lazing in a bay
window of the great library, Coleridge was the first
to say that she was too young to settle in the country
and give up London. So that is where they stayed,
with short holidays in a Heath's Court filled with
friends. The long-awaited retirement never came,
and he died in office at Sussex Square in June 1894.
The house did not go to Amy, but the chattels were
hers, and most of its astonishing collection of books
was quickly sold. In the long lists of mourners and
friends at the funeral in Westminster Abbey and the

302
Heath's Court, Ottery
St Mary: view from
the south-west,
photograph by
'Miss Walsingham',
publisher and
bookseller, 1890

burial in Ottery the name of William Butterfield is not found. He had been too ill that winter to attend Butler's funeral in Lincoln, though he had written the eulogy and made its arrangements, and he seems to have begun periods of seclusion in Bedford Square that would increase into the isolation of his three final years, when his capacities were evidently diminished. But one wonders if, in the wake of the marriage and scandals, into which Butterfield had been unwillingly drawn, the paths of these two great friends had diverged. But the mentions of Heath's Court in the memoirs of that time are fond and legion, as the luxurious freedom of the house is celebrated by Thomas Hardy, Benjamin Jowett and, among many American guests, James Russell Lowell and Henry James (who famously cites 'the clustered charms of Ottery', where Butterfield had made such a strong sense of Scotus's 'thisness' that the house itself generated a pervasive sense of ease, happiness and pleasure).[9]

With the house nearing completion, Coleridge had begun to assume the role his father had played in the life of the nearby hamlet of Alfington, working with Butterfield on sealing the little church of St James and St Anne that Butterfield and his father had built for the poor farm people of the place over thirty years before, adding a burial ground, vestry, organ chamber, new belfry, and stained glass in one of the southern lancets in his father's memory, in which Butterfield and Gibbs show Moses bearing the tablets of the Law, with the towers of the Temple of Solomon, the great judge of the Hebrews, rising behind him. Yet none of its characteristic rugged simplicity was lost, and the little church remained reminiscent of a time when, impatient to test new ways of doing good, the judge's haste to rescue the souls and welfare of his tenantry had left no room for refinement. With its elevation to a full parish in 1882, the boundaries were carefully drawn to bring Heath's Court into its district. Hence, for all Coleridge's wit and vanity, sarcasm and pride, and in spite of the splendid representations of his dignity and cultivation at Heath's Court, this simplest of all Butterfield's country churches – where his cousins had preached to the poor and where his father lived on in a simple window testifying to the birth of justice – became his spiritual and parish home, and it does this contradictory figure best justice to find his own memorial there, remembered among the labourers of his parish for his piety rather than his vivacity, and for his humane passions rather than his judicial wit.

NOTES

1. The obituary by Dean Richard Church of Jane Fortescue Coleridge is in *The Guardian*, 13 February 1878, and notices of the funeral proceedings in the *Western Times*, 15 February 1878.

2. The chapel is described at its opening in the *Exeter and Plymouth Gazette*, 16 September 1878, *The Guardian*, 18 September 1878, and *Building News*, 20 September 1878.

3. The project history of Heath's Court is drawn principally from biographical sources and recollections, especially volume 2 of Ernest Hartley Coleridge, *Life and Correspondence of John Duke Lord Coleridge Lord Chief Justice of England*, William Heinemann, London, 1904; Lord [Bernard] Coleridge, *The Story of A Devonshire House*, T. Fisher Unwin, London, 1905; and from newspaper reports, notably *Western Times*, 31 January 1881, as work commenced, and *Exeter and Plymouth Gazette*, 30 November 1882, as it reached completion. Butterfield's letters to Coleridge on the project – in the Coleridge Family Papers, British Library – date mostly from the initiation of tender in autumn 1880 to his final accounts in spring 1883, including letters relating to the work at Alfington church in 1882. Of the many memoirs, exchanges of letters and recollections describing the house and its proprietor, those drawn upon the most extensively are William Pinckney Fishback, *Recollections of Lord Coleridge*, Bowen-Merrill, Indianapolis, 1895, and Charlton Yarnall (ed.), *Forty Years of Friendship as Recorded in the Correspondence of John Duke, Lord Coleridge, and Ellis Yarnall During the Years 1856 to 1895*, Macmillan & Co., London, 1911.

4. Alfred Tennyson, 'The Palace of Art', 1832, revised 1842.

5. William Blake, 'Golden Age', one of his engravings after John Flaxman's illustrations to *Compositions from the Works, Days, and Theogony of Hesiod*, Longman, Hurst, Rees, Orme & Brown, London, 1817.

6. William Wordsworth, 'Methought I Saw the Footsteps of a Throne', 1806.

7. Tennyson, 'The Palace of Art', op.cit.

8. Lady St Helier, *Memories of Fifty Years*, Edward Arnold, London, 1909, p.299.

9. See Henry James on James Russell Lowell at Ottery in *Atlantic Monthly*, January 1892, p.50.

REPOSE: OTTERY ST MARY

St Mary's Parish Church: Coleridge
memorial chapel

THIS · TOWER · IS · BEAVTIFIED · IN · PIOVS · MEMORY · OF · THE · RIGHT · HONOVRABLE · SIR · JOHN · TAYLOR · COLERIDGE
AND · MARY · HIS · WIFE · AS · A · THANKOFFERING · TO · GOD · FROM · THEIR · REVERENT · AND · GRATEFVL · SON

TO · THE · FAIR · AND · HOLY · MEMORY · OF · JANE · FORTESCVE · BARONESS · COLERIDGE · HER · HVSBAND · DEDICATES · THIS · MARBLE
THANKFVL · FOR · HIS · HAPPINESS · SORROWING · FOR · HIS · LOSS · HOPING · STEDFASTLY · THROVGH · GOD'S · MERCY
TO · MEET · HER · WHEN · THE · NIGHT · IS · PAST · IN · THE · PERFECT · AND · VNENDING · DAY
1878

Heath's Court: entry court

Heath's Court: service courts; library

Heath's Court: library

St James and St Anne's Church, Alfington

EPILOGUE: REGENERATION, 1884–94

A TESTAMENT: THE CHAPEL AT ASCOT PRIORY

Ascot priory had been established in 1861 on Lydia Sellon's initiative for the orders of sisters at St Dunstan's, Plymouth, at St Saviour's, Osnaburgh Street, and in the convents and homes of St Mary's, Wantage, as a place of contemplation and refreshment and as a centre from which to disperse in response to outbreaks of disease or conditions of unusual social distress.[1] With their work taking them increasingly to attend to the health and welfare of young women in the east end and docklands of London, the cycle in which their charges were constantly returned to the same conditions that had led to their sickness – often before regaining strength – became a major concern, and the priory began to serve as a convalescent home, both for the recoverable and the incurable, with acres of heath and pine to help cure or comfort.

The first buildings were built to designs by George Gilbert Scott, though largely effected by Charles Buckeridge, with financial backing from Pusey. They were a simple but slightly picturesque translation of a Norman theme, with a small oratory added by Sellon in 1870 at the eastern end, with the twelfth-century circles, sawtooths and triple arches of St Mary's, Iffley, as her model. When Mother Sellon died in 1876, her associate Bertha Turnbull returned from St Dunstan's mission in Hawaii to serve as mother superior, and Pusey began to assume the character of a warden, spending much of his time at the 'hermitage' in the grounds that he had built there for himself. Butterfield and Pusey, now affectionate friends for thirty-five years, would meet there often as the latter's health declined, wandering among the pines and talking about the character of a chapel they might add to the priory.

Funds had not been found to build it when Pusey
died in 1882. But in 1884 one who had tried to
join the first sisterhood in Regent's Park in 1845,
but whose family duties then prevented her, now
joined the community, bringing with her funds 'to
complete the buildings', beginning with Butterfield's
chapel and the conversion of space adjacent into a
substantial new ward to his design, which brought
the number of convalescent beds to thirty-three.
Butterfield also installed a great cross in Pusey's
memory at the spot where he would read, write and
pray among the pines; and took on the quarters for
novices and guests envisaged in the original plan,
rendering them in his now familiar domestic style,
breaking stone walls with gables and half-hipped
dormers under soft red roofs.

The chapel was built out over sloping ground
from the little two-bay Norman oratory which
established the stylistic starting point. Butterfield
retained the two original bays with their low aisles,
ridged arches, clustered piers and deep-set oculi, the
first with high stalls and the other as the beginning
of the nave. He then built a wide crossing into
which he extended the nave, with short transepts on
either side; a choir with twenty stalls for the sisters,

set up as in a college chapel, with a north sacristy
to the side; and then a chancel, now far extended
above the ground plane to accommodate a vaulted
mortuary beneath. At first sight the finished work
seems reminiscent of the twelfth-century St Cross
(fig.12), or of the French abbeys of Fontevraud or
Sénanque, but nothing in fact matches a definite
precedent, as if Butterfield had somehow invented
a whole phase of the Romanesque to suit his time
and taste. The interior effect comes from the
extraordinary shaping of space, with empty aisles
recalling cloisters, arcades of choir and sanctuary
forming a single procession, shifts in height and
light marking the progress eastwards, a collision
of arches of different scale and character, repeated
convex circles playing against concave, and dark
polished pipe-thin columns, some rising and some
falling. Every feature reflects another.

The sisterhood and chapel were both dedicated
to the Virgin. Pattern and colour in the east wall
are restrained in order to focus on two arched
niches bearing the figures of the Annunciation
between which the Cross rises on its blood-red
background into an arch and battlemented canopy.
It is the most architectural of all Butterfield's east

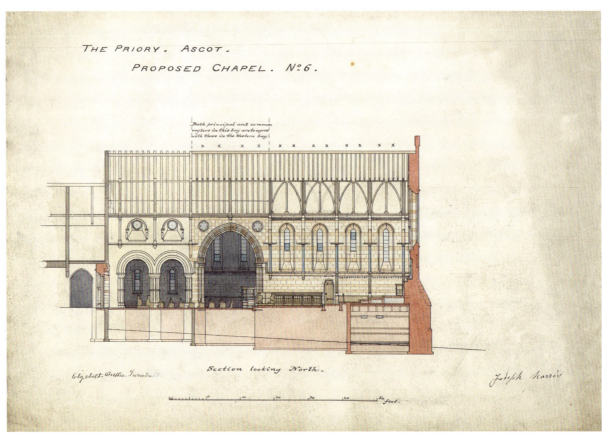

304
Ascot Priory Chapel:
south elevation, 1884

305
Ascot Priory Chapel:
section looking
north, 1884

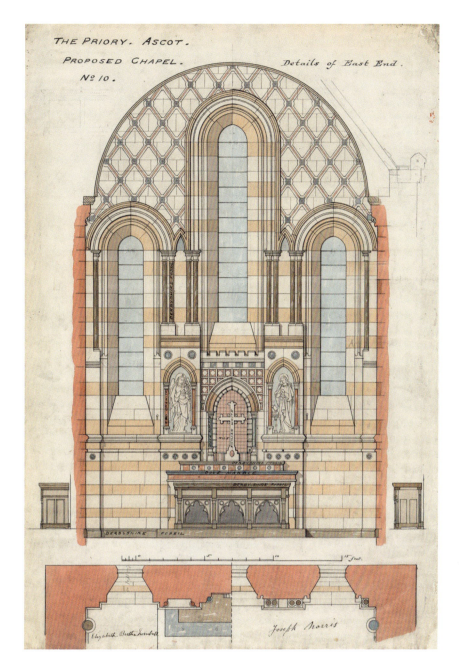

306
Ascot Priory Chapel:
details of east end, 1884

ends, with the pattern of blocks of construction
stone inscribed on the wall, and with arches based
on five different radii, the sharpest squeezed
between dark columns of Derbyshire fossil marble
and the most open marking the line of the internal
roof. The same point of focus is shown by a Maltese
cross in a circle on the outside wall, a stringcourse
carried above to shelter it, a great buttress beneath
to tell us of the true foundation, a celestial mosaic
of stone flanking the central lancet as it reaches
for the stars, and the two crosses in their cusped

rings of window as tombstones beneath the
true level of the ground, offering consolation to
the mortuary that sat beneath. It was a symbolic
end wall of staggering logic, wisdom and beauty,
exemplifying Ricardo's observation that 'the
resolution to be true and faithful to the uttermost
burns through every line that Mr. Butterfield
fashions – it charges his forms with grave steadfastness, the passion of it endues them with
romance, with poetry, and the mystery that
comes from high aspirations.'[2]

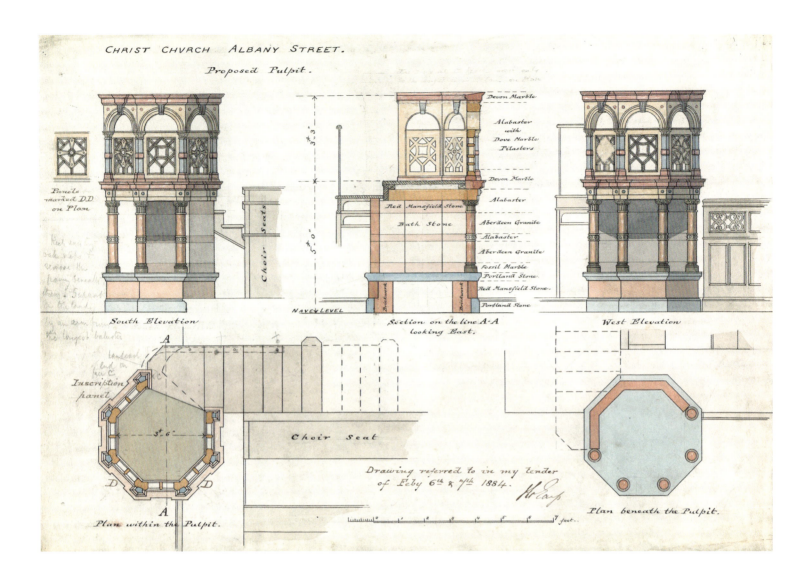

CHRIST CHVRCH ALBANY STREET.

Proposed Pulpit.

Panels marked DD on Plan

South Elevation

Inscription panel

Plan within the Pulpit.

Choir Seats

Section on the line A·A looking East.

NAVE LEVEL

Choir Seat

Drawing referred to in my tender of Feby 6th & 11th 1884.

Devon Marble

Alabaster with Dove Marble Pilasters

Devon Marble

Alabaster

Aberdeen Granite

Alabaster

Aberdeen Granite

Fossil Marble

Portland Stone

Red Mansfield Stone

Portland Stone

Red Mansfield Stone

Bath Stone

West Elevation

Plan beneath the Pulpit.

307
Christ Church,
Albany Street:
design for pulpit,
1884

'THE SECRET TRUTH OF THINGS'

Much small-scale and decorative work dominated Butterfield's later years, partly as so many of his circle departed and had to be memorialised, and partly as churches which had deferred their programme of symbolic adornment found the means and will to enhance their fittings, walls, altars, windows and instruments. Meanwhile, Butterfield's very small remaining office and sometimes weakened condition reduced his capacity to supervise major constructions: at Leeds and Dundela, he relied upon associated local architects to see the addition of the chancels through. Perhaps it was now more satisfying to seek and effect commissions – from murals to chalices, and lighting to reredoses – that could be completed on the drawing board and then contracted to master craftsmen with whom he had worked for so long: there was now a growing delight and patience shown in the drawings themselves. But there were two other causes for this increased attention to object and ornament. One, he said, was to leave a repertory behind for the Church Commissioners in the next century to deploy, a sort of *Instrumenta Ecclesiastica* for the coming Edwardian age. The other, less tangible but surely more powerful, was the impulse of an old man now 'watching and waiting' to explore more widely and deeply the character and mysteries of sacred symbols. Stylistic preferences and inhibitions of all sorts were now abandoned. He was happy, in his extraordinarily discreet intervention and extension

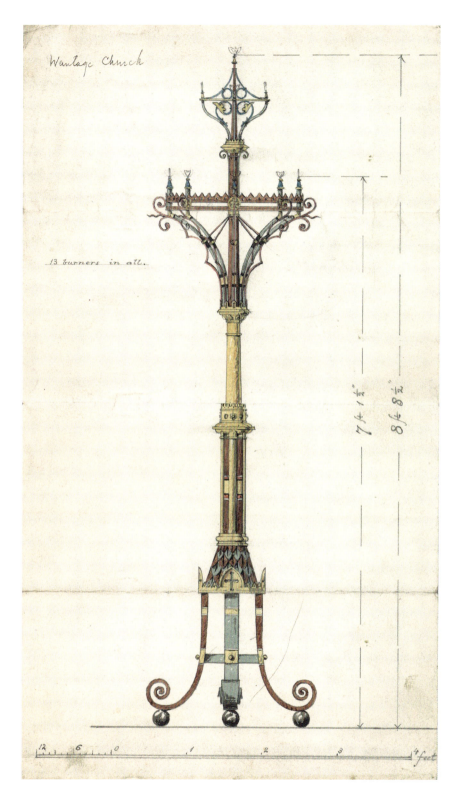

Wantage Church

13 burners in all.

308
Wantage Parish Church:
design for standard gas
lights *c.*1885

at London's St Giles-in-the-Fields, to turn to the symbolic vocabulary of the neoclassical in order to complement the work of the building's original architect, the brilliant Henry Flitcroft; to make metal pieces that now bore only the remotest relation to precedents for scrollwork; to honour his friend Bishop Robert Gray with a column assembling, in shades of Roman red, elements of the Ionic order as they appear in Vincenzo Scamozzi's 1615 treatise *L'Idea della Architettura Universale*; and then to discover an entirely new order of proportion, scale and pattern as he traced and pressed flowers, stalks and leaves from the natural world.

Among the last of the works, done over thirty-five years, by which Butterfield turned the rather sombre late neoclassical Christ Church, Albany Street, into a vivid home for worship, was a pulpit in memory of Mrs Fox, who had been a leading light in the advancement of the Church schools. It uses eight different coloured and textured stones, deploying geometric patterns for the pierced panels that draw upon Italian early Renaissance pavements, closing columns and shafts with Ionic and Corinthian capitals, and carving cornices and dropped corbels according to the formal rules of the classical tradition in which every architect of his time had been schooled, but which Butterfield had studied most closely and affectionately in its late Byzantine expressions at Venice and Ravenna.

Stone was the first among the many minerals that Butterfield, apprenticed at fourteen to a mason's yard, derived an almost mystic satisfaction from selecting and handling. Metalwork, metal tracery and the turning of metal into scrollwork was his second great fascination, and his late work delights in vivid metal polychrome. In working on the parish church of Wantage, which he began to extend, heat, rearrange and ornament shortly before his great friend William Butler left it for Lincoln in 1880, he brought eight 9-foot-high gas standards into the sides of the nave, each with thirteen small burners; the effect of these 104 sharp points of white flame overhead on a winter evening was reported to be scintillating.

From the 1870s onwards, designing tombs and memorials for his friends had become a sadly frequent task. The work he did for Robert Scott,

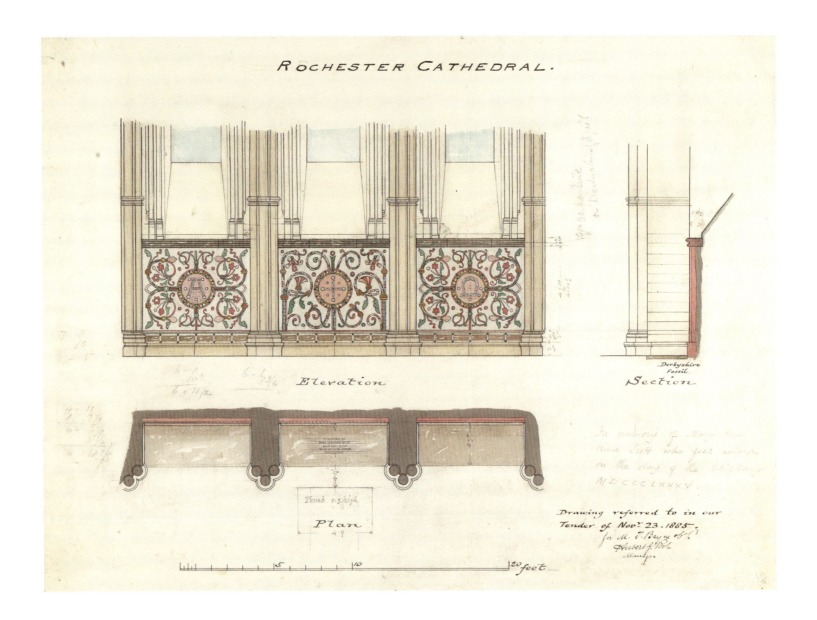

309

Rochester Cathedral:
design for tombs for
the family of Robert
Scott, 1885

who had engaged him at Balliol and was now
dean of Rochester, took the unusual form of three
memorial panels above the spaces of entombment
in the floor under the east or presbytery window of
Rochester cathedral; one was for his wife, who died
in 1885, when the drawing was made, and one of
the others was waiting for Scott himself, who died
two years later. The sprays of vegetation are more
conventionalised, especially in the central panel,
than many of Butterfield's other treatments of flower,
lily and vine; but the colours chosen lend them a
contradictory hint of realism, and the end result –
arising from the play between a natural palette and
abstracted forms – is an extraordinary vitality.

The turning, inlaying and chasing of silver
and gold plate for church instruments had
engaged Butterfield since his first agency with the
Ecclesiological Society in 1843; and new designs for
altar plate poured from his studio throughout his
career. A chased, engraved, pierced and enamelled
chalice for Butler's Lincoln Cathedral in 1887, with
fluid rivers raised on its bowl symbolic of the flow of
blood and wine, is exceptionally rich in contrasting
the dense surface of stem and foot with the smooth
sheen of its cup and the raised discs of coloured
enamel, on which the communicant's eyes will
focus to find, in Tennyson's words, 'hollow'd moons
of gems to mimic heaven'.[3] Here, as in so much of

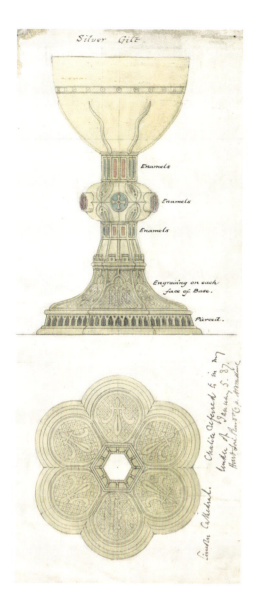

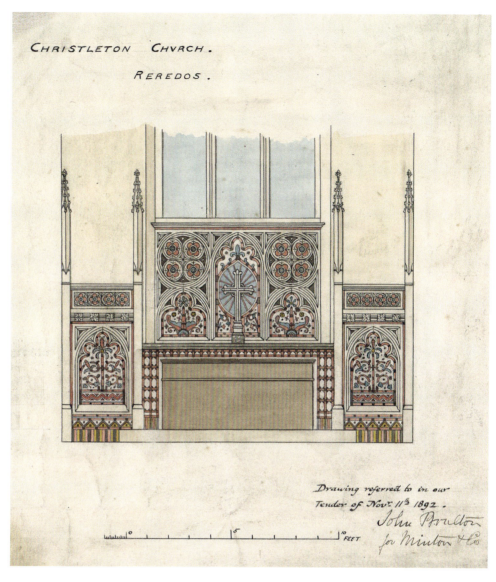

310 (left)
Lincoln Cathedral:
design for a chalice,
1887

311 (right)
Christleton Parish
Church: design for
reredos, 1892

his symbolic figuration and colour, we can sense
his debt to the work of Benjamin Webb and John
Mason Neale who, in introducing their translation
of the thirteenth-century work of Durandus on
the symbolism of churches,[4] developed theories of
archetype, analogy and derivation from nature that
relate quite precisely to the elements of a church
and to the forms and palette of decoration. It was
a work they were completing at the same time
Butterfield joined them as agent and at the height of
his own field investigations into the characteristics
of medieval form.

There are a host of large and splendid
decorations of the east end of church and chapel

in Butterfield's later corpus, from those added to
his earliest works at Canterbury, Harrow Weald
and Perth to some of the last in the chancels of
Leeds, Ascot and Harrow Weald. But the small-
scale reredoses and murals for country churches
that appeared at this nearly final moment in his
career are an especially eloquent testament to the
irrepressible gaiety in the order of nature. There are
notable examples at Milton Ernest, West Lavington
and Great Bookham, and perhaps the finest is at
Christleton, near Chester, where Butterfield had
rebuilt the ancient but degraded parish church
almost in its entirety. There, the stone tracery for
the east wall frames one of his last exercises in

rendering splendour from humble Minton tile, with palm trees and water lotus now invited to anchor the dance of lily, rose and daisy, in a pattern and palette so carefully balanced that the whole mural, though set into the stonework on a single flat plane, is discerned as relief, and the white canopy above the cross and aura reads as a glowing void.

SHELTER

There is less fancy but equal wisdom in another small-scale work of Butterfield's last years, at Romsey Abbey. This is a simple cover built to protect a late tenth-century effigy of Christ on the Cross, which 100 years after its probable making had found its way on to the wall of the nuns' cloister that stood alongside the church. The rood, perhaps unique in England, had then been preserved for some centuries by the accident of having a mason's shed built around it. With the Hand of God descending from a cloud, it is an evocation of triumph over death. A niche for a taper made it clear that this was once an object of great veneration, a status that Butterfield quietly restored with his oak canopy. The cover is 6 feet wide, carved in a progression of three different scales of circle (like those above the cross in the reredos at Leeds) that can still read as symmetry. Sheets of 5 lb milled lead line the roof and provide a plate at its juncture with the wall. It is braced with an invisible wooden collar and shanks and secured by a concealed iron bar driven deep into the wall upon which the structure hangs. There is a perfectly unapologetic drip pipe on either side, so that while the anchoring is concealed, the purpose of shedding rainwater

is made plain. This efficient and deferential cover – seeming to float on the wall yet showing plainly how it is anchored – draws us in with recognition, stands us back with awe, and lets us then see what this master builder has shown in all his works: that within all evident matter and intelligible form rightly made lies, in the poet Arthur Hallam's words, a 'secret truth of things'[5] from which a benign force can be summoned to shield, shelter and bless with regeneration. To quote Hopkins, from the sonnet written in Spring 1877:

> There lives the dearest freshness deep down things;
> And though the last lights off the black West went
> Oh, morning, at the brown brink eastward, springs –
> Because the Holy Ghost over the bent
> World broods with warm breast and with ah!
>   bright wings.[6]

NOTES

1. For the account of Ascot Priory I have drawn principally on sheets from a printed pamphlet *The History of Ascot Priory*, with a detailed description of the fabric after Butterfield's interventions, written about 1904, in the archive of the Society of the Most Holy Trinity, Royal Berkshire Archives; *The Churchman*, 1 April 1899; and Henry Parry Liddon, *Life of Edward Bouverie Pusey*, vol.4, Longmans, Green & Co., London, 1894.
2. Halsey Ricardo, 'William Butterfield', *Architectural Review*, August 1900, p.23.
3. Alfred Tennyson, 'The Palace of Art', 1832, revised 1842.
4. John Mason Neale and Benjamin Webb, *The Symbolism of Churches and Church Ornaments: A Translation of the First Book of . . . Durandus*, T.W. Green, Leeds, 1843.
5. Arthur Hallam, 'Meditative Fragments: II', *Remains in Verse and Prose*, W. Nicol, London, 1834, p.4.
6. Gerard Manley Hopkins, 'God's Grandeur', 1877, published posthumously by Robert Bridges under this unfortunate title.

Dedicated to the memory of my much-loved friend Måns Holst-Ekstrom, 1963–2023.

312
Romsey Abbey: cover for
the medieval rood, 1894

READINGS

WILLIAM BUTTERFIELD AND HIS WORKS

CHARLES LOCKE EASTLAKE, *A History of the Gothic Revival: An Attempt to Show How the Taste for Mediaeval Architecture which Lingered in England During the Two Last Centuries Has Since Been Encouraged and Developed*, Longmans, Green & Co., London, 1872. In this wonderfully sharp, beautifully written and pointedly illustrated account, Eastlake offers an acute appraisal of St Augustine's College, Canterbury; All Saints' Margaret Street; St Dunstan's (Abbey Mere), Plymouth; Balliol College Chapel; and St Alban's Holborn. There are briefer mentions of the first works at Keble College and the new buildings at Merton, both characterised as exercises in 'intense' or 'studied' simplicity.

THOMAS FRANCIS BUMPUS, *London Churches, Ancient and Modern*, T.B. Bumpus, London, 1881, and subsequently in continuing revisions and expansions in London and New York editions up to 1910.

HALSEY RICARDO, 'William Butterfield', *Architectural Review*, July 1900, pp 259–63, and August 1900, pp 15–23. The essential reflection on Butterfield's works, illustrated with photographs that he and Butterfield, drawing on the architect's own collection, selected together. The works most thoroughly addressed are All Saints' Margaret Street; St Alban's, Holborn; All Saints', Babbacombe; Royal Hampshire County Hospital; Rugby School new quadrangle and chapel; Keble College chapel; Rugby parish church; and Heath's Court: perhaps Butterfield's testamentary shortlist of his masterworks.

WILLIAM LOWDER, 'In Memoriam William Butterfield', *The Guardian*, 7 March 1900. A measured obituary with an indispensable reminiscence of Lowder's time as studio assistant at the start of Butterfield's career.

ARTHUR BERESFORD PITE, 'The Late William Butterfield, FSA', *Journal of the RIBA*, 24 March 1900, pp 240–48, illustrated; and 'A Review of the Tendencies of the Modern School of Architecture: The Influence of William Butterfield and Mr. Philip Webb', *Journal of the RIBA*, 22 December 1900, pp 89–90. Memorial essays from an adventurous designer of the generation emerging at the turn of the century.

P.W. [PAUL WATERHOUSE], *Dictionary of National Biography*, Smith, Elder & Co., London, 1901, pp 360–63. A contribution from the son and partner of Alfred Waterhouse, listing works at some length; noting the extraordinary sincerity of the work and austerity of the life; subscribing to the common opinion of the day that neither his use of colour nor his approach to restoration could be approved; and importantly describing how the drawings were generated and corrected so that 'all he sent out from his office may be looked upon as emphatically his own'.
E. SWINFEN HARRIS, 'The Life and Work of William Butterfield', *The Architect*, vol.83, 1910, pp 129–30 and 145–7, illustrated. The first major attempt to revisit and reassess the works, in a lecture presented with an exhibition of drawings by Butterfield on the tenth anniversary of his death, by an architect whose own work is steeped in the domestic language of Butterfield and whose knowledge of the catalogue of Butterfield's work shows that he must have known him well.

KENNETH CLARK, *The Gothic Revival: An Essay in the History of Taste*, Constable, London, 1928. The book which inscribed for a generation the notion that Butterfield's work was sadistic.

HARRY REDFERN, 'Some Recollections of William Butterfield and Henry Woodyer', *Architect and Building News*, 14, 21 and 28 April 1944.

JOHN SUMMERSON, 'William Butterfield, or the Glory of Ugliness', *Architectural Review*, December 1945, pp 166–75, based on a talk from 1938 and reappearing in his collection of *Heavenly Mansions and Other Essays in Architecture*, in many editions, starting 1949.

HENRY-RUSSELL HITCHCOCK, *Early Victorian Architecture in Britain*, Yale University Press, New Haven, Connecticut, 1954. A wide-ranging and wide-thinking survey of architecture in the era of the Great Exhibition, including an extended essay on Butterfield's early work, especially at All Saints' Margaret Street and Stoke Newington.

J.P.H. HOUSE, 'The Architecture of William Butterfield', *Transactions of the Ancient Monuments Society*, vol.2, 1963, pp 217–43. This first modern monograph includes an extensive catalogue of built works and a remarkable photograph of the gutted interior of St Alban's Holborn after bomb damage.

PAUL THOMPSON, *William Butterfield*, Routledge & Kegan Paul, London, 1971. A comprehensive monograph based on years of research in original and printed sources and drawing archives, some of it no longer accessible, and very fully illustrated in all media, including site photographs from the 1960s by the author of reference value, copies of which were placed with the RIBA Library. The work is organised by topic, so that projects may reappear in many places. 'Catalogue of Architectural Works', pp 428–52, and 'Other Designs', pp 469–73 and 503–5, constitute an exhaustive register of work with essential references indicated.

STEFAN MUTHESIUS, *The High Victorian Movement in Architecture, 1850–1870*, Routledge & Kegan Paul, London, 1972. The sections of this survey devoted to Butterfield, pp 59–76, follows convention in examining the constructional polychromy of All Saints' Margaret Street, but then branches away from the canon to show the work on village schools and churches and the projects for Viscount Downe.

GEORGE L. HERSEY, *High Victorian Gothic: A Study in Associationism*, Johns Hopkins University Press, Baltimore, 1972. An analytical study of form and source in Butterfield's work at All Saints' Margaret Street, St Matthias's Stoke Newington, St Alban's Holborn and St Augustine's Queen's Gate, with a shrewd riposte to the 'sadomasochistic' approach circulated by Pevsner and Clark in interpreting his architecture.

TYRONE LANDAU, *William Butterfield, 1814–1900, Pioneer of High Victorian Gothic Revival Architecture: Drawing and Metalwork*, Fischer Fine Art, London, 1982.

CHRIS BROOKS, *Signs for the Times: Symbolic Realism in the Mid-Victorian World*, Allen & Unwin, London, 1984, Part 3. A short book of sweeping scope, that culminates in a long concluding chapter on the 'architectural semantic' of Butterfield and looks in detail at All Saints' Margaret Street and Babbacombe.

ELAIN HARWOOD, 'Butterfield and Brutalism', *AAFiles*, Summer 1994, pp 39–46.

PETER HOWELL AND ANDREW SAINT (EDS), *Butterfield Revisited*, vol.6 of *Studies in Victorian Architecture and Design*, Victorian Society, London, 2017. A set of ten essays, looking afresh at Butterfield, largely uncluttered by the prior history of reception, and giving detailed examinations of a number of the works on which this book focuses: Hunstanton new town; the cathedral and college of the Isles; the works in Oxford; and All Saints' Margaret Street.

TIMOTHY ROHAN, 'Instrumentalizing Ugliness: Parallels between High Victorian and Brutalist Architecture', in Wouter Van Acker and Thomas Mical (eds), *Architecture and Ugliness: Anti Aesthetics and the Ugly in Postmodern Architecture*, Bloomsbury, London, 2020, pp 59–76.

PLACES AND POPULATIONS

Among the encyclopaedic resources that have proved most useful are:

Online Historical Population Reports (www.histpop.org), especially for the 1851 Census of Religious Worship in England and Wales.

British History Online (www.british-history.ac.uk), published by the Institute of Historical Research, especially for the indispensable accounts of place in the Victoria County Histories, and for the older (forty-seven) volumes of the *Survey of London*, continued on a dedicated site of the Bartlett School of Architecture.

A Vision of Britain Through Time, 1801–2001 (https://www.visionofbritain.org.uk), especially for the principal Gazetteers, with capsule descriptions of place, including census data.

The Historic England Archive for listings of built works, including references to the *Buildings of England*, and for an extraordinary photographic corpus, historical and modern, including the archives of the nineteenth-century Oxford

photographer Henry W. Taunt who photographed Butterfield buildings in a large area surrounding Oxford.

Nineteenth-century county and regional guidebooks, especially John Murray's *Handbooks for Travellers*, notably for *Yorkshire* (1867).

For Greater London, James Thorne, *Handbook to the Environs of London*, 2 vols, John Murray, London, 1876, and, in its many continuing, often undated editions, Walter Thornbury and Edward Walford, *Old and New London: A Narrative of its History, its People, and its Places*, 6 vols, Cassell & Company, London, 1873–95, are rich resources in which modern buildings are addressed with discrimination.

Stanford's Library Maps of London and its Suburbs, 1862 and 1878, in which detail to the level of a building footprint can be seen.

Charles Booth's London Poverty Maps (https://booth.lse.ac.uk), based on surveys from 1886–1903.

The Religious Census of London, Hodder and Stoughton, London, 1888, from a survey conducted on a single Sunday in the autumn of 1886, with commentary from interviews, by the *British Weekly*.

WRITINGS OF WILLIAM BUTTERFIELD

Butterfield's occasional letters to editors on matters of technical and liturgical detail first appear in February 1842 in the *Ecclesiologist* and continue with some regularity until the close of his life. It seems very possible that he contributed to unsigned editorial essays in the *Ecclesiologist* when first engaged as the architect of the society, in one of which, 'On Simplicity of Composition, Especially in Churches of the Early English Style' (April 1843, pp 118–21), his favourite principles and pet peeves are all very plainly enunciated. John Duke Coleridge's notes to his essay on 'The Necessity of Modernism', much cited in the text, indicate that its architectural theses derive from discussions with Butterfield. And Paul Thompson established from clippings that Butterfield probably contributed anonymously and regularly to high-church organs.

The only books in which Butterfield chose to leave his thinking behind under his own name are a pamphlet of 1886 on his system of church seats and kneeling boards, and the private publication twenty years after the fact of his *Correspondence Concerning the Mosaics in the Chapel of Keble College, Oxford, During the Year 1873*.

The most engaging and revealing of his scarce writings are the obituaries of his closest friends, 'Robert Brett', *The Guardian*, 11 February 1874, and 'William John Butler', *The Guardian*, 14 January 1894 – two superb examples of the Victorian memorial essay. Both were central figures of the Church revival and in the progress of Butterfield's career, and their thinking – which he scrupulously summarised – was almost indistinguishable from his own.

SELECTED MEMOIRS AND BIOGRAPHIES OF FRIENDS AND CLIENTS

Henry William Burrows, *The Half-Century of Christ Church, Albany Street*, Skeffington, London, 1887.

Randall Thomas Davidson and William Benham, *Life of Archibald Campbell Tait*, 2 vols, Macmillan, London, 1891.

Henry Parry Liddon, *Life of Edward Bouverie Pusey*, vol.4, Longmans, Green & Co., London, 1894.

Arthur John Butler, *Life and Letters of William John Butler*, Macmillan, London, 1897.

Ernest Hartley Coleridge, *Life and Correspondence of John Duke Lord Coleridge Lord Chief Justice of England*, 2 vols, William Heinemann, London, 1904.

Eleanor A. Towle (ed.), *John Mason Neale, D.D.: A Memoir and Letters*, 2 vols, Longmans, Green & Co., London, 1906 and 1907.

E.G. Sandford (ed.), *Memoirs of Archbishop Temple by Seven Friends*, Macmillan, London, 1906.

C.A.E. Moberly, *Dulce Domum: George Moberly, His Family and Friends*, John Murray, London, 1911.

Edward Stuart Talbot, *Memories of Early Life*, A.R. Mowbray & Co., London, 1924, pp 53–79: 'The Beginnings of Keble'.

THE PARISH, THE POOR AND THE SCHOOL

John Sandford, *Parochialia; or, Church, School, and Parish: The Church System, and Services, Practically Considered*, Longman, Brown, London, 1845, and his *Social Reforms; Or, the Habits, Dwellings, and Education of Our People*, Longmans, London, 1867.

Reports of the Royal Commission on the Employment of Children, Young Persons and Women in Agriculture, H.M. Stationery Office, London, 1867, extending to the three volumes of inquiry, 1868–70, published in *Parliamentary Papers*. One fine example can be found in the *Kidderminster Times* of 18 December 1869, providing testimony from the small town of Alvechurch, in which Butterfield had recently completed, school, rectory and rebuilt church.

Thomas Mozley, *Reminiscences, Chiefly of Towns, Villages, and Schools*, Longmans, Green & Co., London, 1885. A famous high-church theologian's witty recollection of the state of his country parishes.

Church of England school registers, logbooks, letters and reports appear frequently though not consistently in county archives, sometimes with diocesan inspector's reports. I drew especially on those for Butterfield's Poulton school, in Gloucestershire Archives, and his St Cross school in Clayton, in Manchester Archives and Local Studies.

Annual Reports of the National Society for Promoting the Education of the Poor in the Principles of the Established Church throughout England and Wales (from 1811) become especially informative as the diocesan inspection system strengthens from 1857 onwards.

H. Rider Haggard, *Colonel Quaritch, VC: A Tale of Country Life*, Longmans, Green & Co., London, 1889, revised 1906. Paints an extraordinary picture of rural life in the depth of depopulation and distress from the long depression.

Jerome K. Jerome, *My Life and Times*, Harper & Bros, London and New York, 1926. The author of *Three Men in a Boat* recalls a childhood in the 1860s in the rural perimeter of a London where 'town and country were struggling for supremacy'.

Ruth Jennings, *Lofty Aims and Lowly Duties: Three Victorian Schoolmasters*, Sheffield Academic Press, Sheffield, 1994.

IMAGE CREDITS

INDEX

NOTE: italic page numbers indicate illustrations; page numbers followed by 'n' refer to notes; William Butterfield is abbreviated to WB in headings and subheadings.

abbey churches 61, 125, 385
abbeys 14, 25, 26, 29, 39, 61, 120
    Amesbury 121
    Romsey 416, *417*
    St Dunstan's 20–21, *20*
    Tintern 151, 222
Adam Street, London, offices of WB in 23, 143
Adams, William 241
Adelaide Cathedral (Australia) 202, 222, 230, 231, *231*, 232n10
Aesthetic Movement 151–2
Ainsworth, William Harrison 121, 238
Aire and Don canal 60, 61
Albert, Prince 202, 268
Aldbourne (Wiltshire) *84*, 85
Aldenham Home Farm (Hertfordshire) 358–360
    dairy 358, 359, *359*, 360, *360*, *372–3*
    estate cottages *365–6*
Alexander Gibbs & Co see Gibbs, Alexander
Alfington (Devon) 396, *406–7*
All Hallows' Church, Tottenham (London) 236, *236*
All Saints', Babbacombe (Devon) *180*, 181–5, *181*, *182*, *183*, *184*
    fossils/minerals in decoration of 183–5
All Saints', Harrow Weald (Greater London) *353*, 361–3, *362*, *363*, 415
All Saints', Margaret Street (London) *6*, 8, 142–8, *143*, *145*, *146*, *147*, *148*, *149*, 157, 202, 363
    clergy house/choir school 148, *158–61*
    innovations in 147, 148
    public interest in 144
All Saints' National School, Margaret Street (London) *141*, 148–51, *150*, *163*
All Saints', Whiteparish (Wiltshire) 130–132, *131*, *132*
All Saints', Wykeham (Yorkshire) *64*, *64*, *74–5*
    parsonage 61

Allegheny County Courthouse (Pennsylvania, US) 206
almshouses 21, 88, 95, 203, *358*
altars 24, 96, 107
Altars, Hearths and Graves (Moultrie) 96
Alvechurch (Worcestershire) 98–101
    National School 100, 101
    rectory 98–101, *99*, *100*, 356
    St Lawrence's church 101, 199
Ambatoharanana (Madagascar) 294–6, *295*
Ambler, J. (photographer) *199*
Amesbury parish church (Wiltshire) 121–3
Angle, S.B. (& Co.) (photographer) *139*
Anglican Church
    in Canada 28–9
    in Ireland 286
    and poor relief 194–5
    revival movement see Church revival movement
    and science 251
    in Scotland 32
    and training of clergy 293
    in Wales 104–5
Antrobus, Edmund 121, 123
Architect, The 172
architectural style of WB
    and brickwork see brickwork
    and continental architecture 25–6
    and country schools 51–2, 82, 85
    criticisms of 125, 151–2, 173–5, 244, 278, 317, 318, 319, 320, 343
    and domestic architecture 53, 59–60
    economy/simplicity 23, 34, 52, 59, 61, 82, 145–6, 343
    flowers in decorations 106, 296, 362, 413, 414, 416
    furnishings/instruments 24–5, *24*, *30*, 31, 37–8, *38*
    geometric features 16, 25, 26, 57, 95, 135, 144–5, 183–5, 386–7
    hierarchies of space/function 57, 96, 97, 102
    lack of sentimentality 45, 48, 129, 318
    and local building materials/traditions 50, 53, 59, 87–8, 354, 356
    and medieval architecture 13, 23, 59
    mingling of ancient/modern 225
    and narrative elements 95, 143, 147, 153, 181, 205, 240, 342, 344, 362–3
    poetry analogy for 8, 31, 51–2

    polychrome features 106, 134, 144, 171, 243, 321, 413
    and Pugin, compared 17, 22, 151
    Realist 16, 22
    spatial freedom 58
    stonework of varied widths/lines 21
Ardleigh parish church (Essex) 135–9, *137*, *138*, *139*
Arnold, Matthew 7, 96, 248, 249
Arnold, Thomas 52, 249, 250, 254
Arts and Crafts movement 25, 85, 88
Ascot Priory/Chapel (Berkshire) 21, 382, 408–11, *409*, *410*, *411*, 415
Ashford (Surrey) 68, *69*
Ashwell, Arthur Rawson 317, 343–4
Ashwell (Rutland) 21, 59, 60, 98
Assisi (Italy) 25
Aston Cantlow village school (Warwickshire) 51
Atkinson, John 59, 98

Babbacombe (Devon) 179–86
    parish church see All Saints' Church, Babbacombe
Bailey, Henry 291
Baldersby (Yorkshire) 21, 60, 82, 94–6, 98, *109–11*
    cottages 95–6
    landscape of 96
    parish church see St James's, Baldersby
    school/schoolhouse 95
Balliol College Chapel, Oxford 314–17, *315*, *316*, *317*, 319
    and gardens/library 314, 315–16, *315*
Bamford, Hathersage (Derbyshire) 101–2
    rectory 102, *102*
    schoolroom 101–2
Banham, Reyner 9
Baring-Gould, Sabine 98
Barnet see Chipping Barnet
Bartholomew, Alfred 54
Bath stone 68, 136, 149, 222, 225, 318, 354, 382
Battersea (London)
    Sir Walter St John's School 282–3, *284*
    teacher training college 87
Beauchamp, Lord 344
Beech Hill (Berkshire) 104, 106–7, *107*
Belfast (Ireland) 21, 202, 221–2, 227–9, *227*, *228*, 412
Belmont (Durham) 68, 102

Bennett, W.J.E. 206

Bermondsey (London) 17

Betjeman, John 9

Birkby, Huddersfield (Yorkshire)
168–71, *169*, *170*, *171*

Birmingham 17

Bishop's Park, Fulham (London) 361

Blackwell, Thomas 361

Blake, William 391

Bliss, James 24, 52

Bloxam, Matthew 272

Bont Goch (Wales) *43*, 104–5, *105*

Booth, Charles 235

Boultbee almshouses, Emery Down
(Hampshire) 21, 358, *358*

Bournemouth (Dorset) 189–190, *190*

Boxall, William 391

Boyle, George Frederick 32, 34, 35, 41,
41nn1,2

Braishfield (Hampshire) 68, 102

Braunstone (Leicestershire) *356*, 357–8,
357, *368–9*
Braunstone Hall 87

Brehmer, Hermann 376

Brett, Robert 13, 235–6

brickwork 8, 21, 22, 45, 46, 57, 101, 107,
149, 175
exposed 52
WB's specifications for 54

Bridges, Robert 185

Brigham (Cumbria) 127–8, *128*

Bristol 14, 383
Congregational Chapel, Highbury 57
see also St Saviour's Church, Coalpit
Heath

British Empire 28–9, 52, 294

Brookfield (London) 233–4, *234*

Buckeridge, Charles 408

building manuals 54

building materials 14, 54
Bath stone 68, 136, 149, 222, 225,
318, 354, 382
concrete 48, 52, 54, 61
Draycott stone 382, 383
Huddleston stone 95, 105
limestone 21, 68, 87, 105, 180, 354
local 21, 33, 53, 57, 59, 87–8, 354, 356
Mansfield stone 145, 225
Portland stone/cement 136, 378
rag-stone 14, 68, 239
sandstone 33, 57, 64, 128, 132, 294
see also brickwork; marble; slate

Bumpus, Thomas Francis *173*, 175, 206,
234

Bunyan, John (horse) 55

Burges, William 206

Burne-Jones, Edward 105–6

Burrows, Henry William 237

Bursea (Yorkshire) 102–4

Busteed Ashley, Francis (artist) *125*, 127

Butler, William John 52, 396, 413, 414

Butterfield, Anne (later Starey, WB's
sister) 236, 354

Butterfield, William *8*
Adam Street offices of (London) 23, 143
Bristol connections of 55–7
and Clifton Bridge competition 23,
55–7
death/burial of (1900) 236
drawings of 7, 9, 22, 23, 24, 82, 138,
143–4, 151
early life 22–3
and Engagement pledge 13, 14
European travels of 25–6, 102
field studies of 23, 24
legacy of 9, 26
reputation of 8
restorations of *see* restorations of WB
style of *see* architectural style of WB
and theory of national Church 51

Byzantine style 25, 202, 244, 344, 413

Cambridge 9, 14

Cambridge Apostles 268

Cambridge Camden Society
see Ecclesiological Society

Cambridge University 319
King's College Chapel 345

Campbell, Colen 94

Canada 28–9, 300
see also Christ Church, Fredericton

Canterbury (Kent) 12, 13, 286, 415
see also St Augustine's College

Carlyle, Thomas 21

Castle Hill (Devon) *86*, 87

Caterham Guards Chapel (Surrey)
243–4, *243*

Cathedral or Abbey Church of Iona
(Ewing) 35–6, *36*, *37*, *38*

Cathedral of the Isles *see* College of the
Holy Spirit

Catholic Church *see* Roman Catholic
Church

Cautley (Yorkshire) 68, 102

cement 61, 136

chalices 412, 414, *415*

chancel screens 34, 57, 96, *106*, *126*,
135, 136

chapel-schools 52

Charlton-by-Wantage (Oxfordshire) 52

Chartist movement 12–13, 58

Cheddar Hospital (Somerset) 202, 346,
376–85, *377*, *385*
aesthetics of 380–382
chapel 379–380, *380*
chaplain's house 383–5, *384*
Gibbs memorial 380, 381–2
layout of 378–9
and poor inmates 380, 382
site of 376–8

and tuberculosis 376, 378, 379,
382

Chelsea Barracks (London) 243

Chipping Barnet (London) 202, 221,
224–7, *225*, *226*, 293

Chobham (Surrey) *see* Gordon Boys'
Home

cholera 17, 19

Chope, Richard Robert 202, 205

Christ Church, Albany Street (London)
17, *412*, 413

Christ Church Cathedral, Fredericton
(Canada) 14, 27–31, *28*, *29*, *30*, *31*,
231, 232n10

Christleton parish church (Cheshire)
415

Church Builder 135

Church of St Cross (Winchester)
25, *25*

church furnishings/instruments 24–5,
24, *30*, *31*, 95, 105–6, *122*, *123*, 128,
135, 143
chalices *412*, *414*, *415*
fonts 57, 66, 132, 145, *145*, *181*, 182
lecterns 45, 146, *146*, 183
metalwork 38, 95, 138, 146, 355,
362, 413, 414
quoins/trim 14, 57, 68, 354
roods 52, 416, *417*
and WB's inscription 95
see also mosaics; reredos; screens;
stained glass

Church revival movement 12–26
in countryside 44, 45, 51
and ecclesiology 22–6
and Lincoln Bedehouse Chapel 21–2,
22
and sisterhoods *see* sisterhoods

church-schools 50, 173, 413

churchyard crosses 45, 59, 97, 98

churchyards 45, 59, 64, 96–8, 139
and lychgates 45, 59, 64, 97, 98

Churton, Edward 320

Clarke, Gillian 200

Clayton (Manchester) *193*, 198–9, *199*,
213–19

Clevedon (Somerset) 188–9, *189*

Clifton Bridge 23, 55–7

coal industry 57, 60, 127, 199

Coalpit Heath, Westerleigh (Bristol)
55–7, *56*, 58, 98, 170, 415

Cobden, Richard 58, *58*

Cockermouth (Cumbria) 127

Colchester (Essex) 135, 138

Coleridge, Edward 13, 14, 292

Coleridge, Jane Fortescue (artist) *8*,
386, 387, 391, 394–5

Coleridge, John Duke (1st Baron) 22,
26n13, 61, 95, 386, 387, 388, 390,
395–6

Coleridge, John Taylor 17, 52, 339–340, 386, 391
Coleridge, Samuel Taylor 387, 388, 394
Coleridge, William Hart 14, 291
College of the Holy Spirit (Great Cumbrae, Scotland) 14, 35–41, 294
   canons'/choristers' houses 39–40, *39, 40*
   Church of 36–8, *37*
   parish church/primary school 41
   vista of 40–41, *41*
Collier, Philip Osborne (photographer) *107, 361*
Columba, Saint 35, 36, 41
compact churches 64–8, 102–7
Compton, Berdmore 147
Comte, Auguste 87, 356–7, 358
concrete 48, 52, 54, 61
convents 17
Cooke, Albert C. (artist) *231*
Cooke, George Theophilus 88
Coubertin, Pierre de 269
country schools 45–7, 48–51, 61, 64, 82–91
   Aston Cantlow (Warwickshire) 51
   Baldersby (Yorkshire) 95
   Castle Hill (Devon) *86*, 87
   and chapel-schools 52
   Dinton (Wiltshire) 89, *90*
   Dunchurch, Thurlaston (Warwickshire) 52, *52*
   East Farleigh (Kent) 49–51, *50, 51, 59*
   Hellidon and Catesby (Northamptonshire) 48–9, *48, 49*, 82
   Horton-cum-Studley (Oxfordshire) 88–9, *89*
   Kirby Muxloe (Leicester) 87–8, *88*
   moral imperative for 82
   moveable furniture in 89
   Sessay (Yorkshire) 59
   Tattershall (Lincolnshire) 85–7, *85*
   and universal education 82–3
   and WB's aesthetic grammar 51–2
country towns 34, 49, 94, 98, 120–121, 123, 194
country villas 88, 94, 186, 188, 189, 190, 360, 361
Cowick (Yorkshire) 58–64, 82, 195
   East Cowick 22, 61, *76–7, 79, 80*
   Hensall 22, 61, *63*, 66, *78, 81*, 190
   Pollington 22, 61, *62*, 66, *78, 80*
   Sessay *see* Sessay
Cowick Manor (Yorkshire) 60–61
cricket clubs 46, 198, 199, 269
Crimea Memorial Cloister, Winchester College *247*, 248
Crimean War 17, 20, 239, *247*, 248, 249, 276

Cromwell, Oliver 387
Crook, William (builder) 66, 132
Crosse, Edmund 361

Daily News 142
Dalton (Yorkshire) *see* St John the Evangelist
Davis, William Henry (photographer) 145, *145*
Dawnay, William Henry (7th Viscount Downe) 58–9, 60, 61, 64, 88, 94–5, 96, 168
   memorial church (St John the Evangelist) 104, 105–6, *106*, 107
Debenham & Gould (photographer) *190*
Delaroche, Paul 121
Dickens, Charles 206
Dinton (Wiltshire) 89, *90*
disease 89, 127, 171, 222, 237, 243, 358–9
   cholera 17, 19
   see also tuberculosis
Disraeli, Benjamin 153
domestic architecture 20, 53, 178, 179, 354–6
   almshouses 21, 88, 95, 203, *358*
   and country estates 203, 227, 360–361
   country villas 88, 94, 186, 188, 189, 190, 360, 361
   rural housing 59–60, *60*, 64, 94, 95–6, 356–8, *367, 368–9*
Dorchester Abbey (Oxfordshire) 25
Downe, Viscount *see* Dawnay, William Henry
Draycott stone 382, 383
Drayton Wyatt, J. (artist) *153*
drinking fountains 151, *242*, 243
Dropmore (Buckinghamshire) 104, *104*
Dublin (Ireland) *see* St Columba's College Chapel
Duncombe, Octavius 64
Duns Scotus, John 319, *396*
Durandus, William 415
Dyce, William 144, 145

East Cowick (Yorkshire) 22, 61, *76–7, 79, 80*
East Farleigh (Kent) 49–51
   village school 49–51, *50, 51, 59*
Eastlake, Charles Locke 16–17, 20–21, 151, *152*, 175
Ecclesiological Society 14, 23–4, 57, 414
Ecclesiologist, The 23–4, 29, 34n2, 47, 120, 126, 132, 171
   and country schools 82, 87
   critiques of WB in 34, 50, 58
ecclesiology 23–6
Edinburgh 250, 381

Edis, Olive (photographer) *291*, 292, *293*
Edis, Robert William 300
Edmonton (London) 9, 235, 236–8, *237*, 245n8
Edmunds, J. (photographers) *249, 255*
education 9, 45, 248–9
   and altruism 87
   and cathedrals 293
   and chapel-schools 52
   middle-class 33, 34, 49, 85
   military *see* Gordon Boy's Home
   moral 17, 58, 251, 254–6, 279
   and parish system 283
   physical 268–270
   and the poor 17, 44
   prep schools 269, *269*, 275n2
   science 250–251, 278
   universal 82–3
   university, modern studies in 319
   see also country schools; grammar schools; National schools
Eginton, Harvey 23
Elerch (Wales) *see* Bont Goch
Elford, Percy (photographer) *89*
Elton, Arthur 188
Emery Down (Hampshire) 21, 102, 358, *358*
Enfield (London) 233, 235, 236, 238–41, *239, 240*
'Engagement, The' 13, 14
English Civil War 387
Episcopalians 32, 34, 35
Etal (Northumberland) 68
Everett, Henry, & Son (builders) 138
Eversley, Lord 358
Ewart, William 227
Ewing, Alexander 35–6, *36, 37, 38*
Exeter Grammar School (Devon) 202, 278–83, *279, 280, 281, 282, 283, 304–5*
Eyre family 65, 66

Fairfax, Thomas 387
famine 17, 28, 58
Farrar, Frederick W. 248
Filleigh (Devon) 87
financial crisis (1873) 18
Finsbury (London) 235, *235*
Fletcher, Banister 277
Fletcher, Isaac 127, 128
flint 14, 85, 104, 132, 136, 293
Flitcroft, Henry 413
Florence (Italy) 272
Florey Building (Oxford) 9
fonts 57, 66, 132, 145, *145, 181*, 182
Forbes, Horace Courtney Gammell 32, 34
Ford, William 234
Fortescue family 85–7, 104
fountains 151, *242*, 243, 361, *374*, 394

France 185, 294, 296, 409
   Paris 12, 26, 143
Fredericton (Canada) 14, 27–31, *28*, *29*, *30*, *31*, 231, 232n10
Freeman, E.A. 175
frescoes 143, 144
Frith, Francis (photographer) 7, *69*, *180*, 186, *200*, 243, *339*
Fulham Palace (London) 361, *374–5*

Gaer Hill (Somerset) 68, 102
Gale & Porter (photographers) *244*
Galton, Douglas Strutt 201
Garrett, A.E. (artist) *22*
garrison towns 21, 33, 242–3, 296
Gaskell, Elizabeth 168
Gay, John (builder) 57
Gérente, Alfred 144, 146
Germany 26, 231
Gibbs, Alexander 135, 146, 147, 205, 256
Gibbs, Antony 359
Gibbs, Matilda Blanche 340, 376, 378, 380, *382*, 383
Gibbs, Henry Hucks 340, 345, 350, 358, 359
Gibbs, Henry Martin 359
Gibbs, William 340, 342, 345, 359, 376, 378, 396
      memorial to 380, *381–2*
Gilbertson, Lewis 104
Giotto 144, 146
Gissing, George 8, 189, 200
Gladstone, Stephen 40–41
Gladstone, William Ewart 13, 45, 202, 278, 336, 350, 387
Glynne, Stephen 120
Godwin, Edward William 151–2
Goldschmidt, Otto 273
Goodhard-Rendel, H.S. (photographer) *60*
Gordon Boys' Home, Chobham (Surrey) 292, 296–300, *296*, *306–7*, 361
      dormitories 299–300, *300*
         Napier Memorial Hall 298–9, *298*
         parade ground 297, *297*, 298
         schoolroom 297–8, *298*
         tailors' workshop 299, *299*
Gordon, Charles George 296, 299
Gothic revival 16, 18, 21, 25, 147, 152, 206
Gothic style 59, 125, 135, 171, 249, 250, 286, 314, 356
         High 26, 244, 245
Grahame, Kenneth 269
grammar schools 282–6
   see also Exeter Grammar School; Sir Walter St John's
graveyards *see* churchyards
Gray, Robert 413
Gray, Thomas 96

Great Bookham (Surrey) 60, 88, 415
Great Cumbrae (Scotland) *see* College of the Holy Spirit
Great Exhibition (1851) 24, 202
Great Mongeham parish church (Kent) 123–5, *124*
Gregory, Robert 237
Gregory, Francis A./Gregory, Ann Marie 294, 296
Guardian, The 46, 105, 336, 382

Hall, Radclyffe 190
Hallam, Arthur 188, 416
Hammersmith (London) 195, 197, *198*
Hanbury, Sampson 182, 185
Hardwick, Philip Charles 286
Hardy, Evelyn Stuart 297
Hardy, Thomas 396
Harrison, James Park 45, 46
Harrow Weald (Greater London)
   All Saints' *353*, 361–3, *362*, *363*, 415
   and Monro's funeral 46–7
   see also St Andrew's College
Hart, Son & Peard (metalworkers) 138
Head, Anna Maria (artist) *28*, 31
Heathcote, William 200
Heath's Court, Ottery St Mary (Devon) 356, *386–96*, *388*, *389*, *393*
      aviary 390, 394, *395*
      conservatory 390, *392*, *395*
      entrance/sequence 394, *400–401*
      gardens/promenade 394–5, *395*
      history of 387
      levelling/landscaping 388
      library 388, 390–394, *402–5*
      pavilion 390
      plan of 387–90
      servants' quarters/kitchen 394
      service court 390, *402*
Heath's Court library 388, 390–394, *392*, 395, *403–5*
      decorations in 390–391
Heaton & Butler (builders) 225
Heckfield (Hampshire) 21, 358
heliotypes 35, 36
Hellidon and Catesby
   (Northamptonshire) 47–9, 96
      cottage hospital 49
      St John the Baptist 47, *47*, 49, 359
      school 48–9, *48*, *49*, 82
      vicarage 48, *48*
Helmore, Thomas 46, 105, 173
Helps, Arthur 26, 268
Henley, William Ernest 8, 381
Hensall (Yorkshire) 22, 61, *63*, 66, *78*, *81*, 190
Hewett, John 181
Heytesbury, Lord 132–4
Heytesbury parish church (Wiltshire) 132–5, *133*, *134*

Hickes, Thomas 383
hierarchies of space/function 57, 96, 97, 102
High Barnet *see* Chipping Barnet
Highgate (London) 233
Hitchcock, Henry-Russell 9
Hitchin (Hertfordshire) 101, 198, *198*
Hoare, Peter Richard 198
Hobhouse, Edward 106–7
Holborn (London) 98
   see also St Alban the Martyr
Holthouse, Charles Scrafton 47–9, 96
Holy Saviour's, Hitchin (Hertfordshire) 101, 198, *198*
Holy Trinity, East Cowick (Yorkshire) 22, 61, *76–7*, *79*, *80*
Holy Trinity (Stratford-upon-Avon) 23
Hood & Co. *297*
Hook, Walter 172
Hope, Alexander Beresford 14, 135, 143, 287, 292
Hopkins, Gerard Manley 8, 146, 185, 191n5, 317, 319, 321n3, 363, 416
Horton-cum-Studley (Oxfordshire) 88–9, *89*
      church 88, 104
      school 88–9, *89*
hospitals 21, 25, 49, 200–202, *201*, 409
   see also Cheddar Hospital; Royal Hampshire County Hospital
houses of rest 21–2
Hubbard, John Gellibrand 57, 151, 153, 195, 202
Huddersfield (Yorkshire) 14, 168–71, *169*, *170*, *171*
Huddleston stone 95, 105
Hudson, George 94
Hunstanton (Norfolk) 177–9, *178*
      housing 178, 179
         New Inn/Golden Lion 178, 179, *179*
      and railways 179
      village green 178, *179*
Hunt, William Holman 342, 347
Hursley (Hampshire) 319, 362
Hutchinson, T.N. 250, *251*

Iffley (Oxfordshire) 408
Illustrated London News 14, *15*, 319
Instrumenta Ecclesiastica 24–5, 97, 412
Iona (Scotland) 35, 36
Ireland *see* Belfast; St Columba's College Chapel
Ireland, Church of 221, 222, 229
Italy 26, 144, 146, 254, 272, 274, 317
   see also Ravenna; Venice

Jackson, Magnus (photographer) *32*, *33*
Jackson, T. and M. (photographers) *230*

Jackson's Oxford Journal 68
James, Henry 396
Jedburgh (Scotland) 13, 26, 98, 286
Jewitt, Orlando (artist) *152*
Jews 172
John Bull (magazine) 45
Jowett, Benjamin 396

Kallmann, Gerhard 9
Kaye, Joseph (builder) 169, 170
Keats, John 21
Keble College, Oxford 16, 88, 291,
   319–21, *320, 322–33,* 334–51, *339*
      gateway/gatehouse *324,* 334, *335*
      lodgings 334–9, *336*
      'New Buildings' 292, 337, 339, *339*
      Parks Road extension *335,* 336–7
      quadrangles 202, *324–7,* 338, *338*
      and science teaching 346
      servants' building *324–5, 337*
      student life in 346
      suburb surrounding 345
      urbanism of 338, 339
      walkways/paths 334, 337
      warden (Edward Talbot) 334–6, 346
      warden's house *331–3,* 336, 338–9,
        338, 345
Keble College Chapel 205, 234, 317,
   323, 336, 337, 339–45, *339, 342,*
   343, 378, 380
      alterations in cloisters *341,* 343
      and building committee, WB's
        disagreements with 340–342
      and college buildings *340,* 343
      four principles for 339
      opening day service 344
      temporary building *344*
Keble College Hall and Library *289,*
   320, 320, 321, *326–330,* 337, 338,
   345–350, *347, 348, 349,* 359
      entry bay 349–350, *351*
      great staircase 346, 349
      as pinnacle of WB's work 350
      wooden canopy *331,* 347
Keble, John 13, 40–41, 45, 54, 96, 142,
   189, 195, 319, 339, 362
Kensington (London) 195
   see also South Kensington
King's College Chapel, Cambridge 345
Kingsbury (London) 235
Kingsley, Charles 268
Kirby Muxloe (Leicestershire) 358
   cottages 356–7, *367*
   school/schoolhouse 87–8, *88, 366, 367*

Lamplugh parish church (Cumbria)
   128–9, *129*
Landford parish church (Wiltshire)
   65–6, *67,* 235, 385
      rectory 102, *103*

Laprimaudaye, Charles 57
Latchmore, Thomas B. (photographer)
   198
Latimer, John 189
Lawford, Amy (Lady Coleridge) 395
Lawrence, Thomas 272
Le Strange, Henry Styleman 151, 177, 179
lecterns 45, 146, *146,* 183
Leech, Joseph 55, 57
Leeds (Yorkshire) 8, 14, 46, 412, 415
   poverty/slums in 171, 172
   St Thomas's, Leylands 171–2, *172,* 416
Leicester 9, 60, 87
Leigh, Lord 151
Lewis, A.J. (photographer) *105*
Liddon, Henry 342
Light of the World, The (Hunt) 342, 347
limestone 21, 68, 87, 105, 180, 354
Lincoln Bedehouse Chapel 21–2, *22*
Lincoln Cathedral 414–15, *415*
Lind, Jenny 273
Lindsay, Thomas 272, *272*
London 142–55, *157–67,* 233–44
   Adam Street offices of WB in 23, 143
   docklands of 241
   housing in 233–4
   population growth in 220, 237
   poverty/disease in 151, 152, 153, 154,
      233, 234, 235, 358, 361
   social progress in 220–221
   suburbs/commuting towns of 14, 47,
      355, 358
   see also specific boroughs/churches
Lowell, James Russell 396
Lyautey, Louis-Hubert 294, 296
lychgates 45, 59, 64, 97, 98
Lyttleton, Lord 336

Mackonochie, Alexander 151, 152, 153
Madagascar 237, 294–6, *295*
Manchester 7, 198–9, *199*
Manning, Henry 57
Mansfield stone 145, 225
marble 34, 95, 105, 132, 134–5, 144,
   145, 181–2, 183, 200
      Derbyshire fossil 411
Margaret Street Chapel, Fitzrovia
   (London) 13, 14, 17, 57, 142–3, 205
Martin, Charles (photographer) *236*
Maryport (Cumbria) 127
Maurice, F.D. 268
medieval architecture 13, 20, 24,
   120–121, 224
      continental 25–6
      domestic 359
   see also restorations of WB
medievalism 22, 121
Medley, John 16, 27–8, 29, 31, 34n2,
   292–3
Melbourne Cathedral (Australia) 202,

222, 230–232, *231,* 232n10
memorial chapels 227, 386, *398–9*
memorials 64, 66, 146, 243, 254, 380,
   381–2, 396, 413–14
      for the Crimean War dead 247,
        249, 276
      for Gordon of Khartoum
        see Gordon Boys' Home
      for missionaries 292
      windows 130, 248, 256
Merton College, Oxford 25, 314, 318–19,
   318
      Chapel 169–170, 318
      criticisms of 318, 319
      Mob Quad 318
metalwork 38, *95,* 138, 146, 355, 362,
   413, 414
Methodists 105, 172
middle class
      and education 33, 34, 49, 85, 278,
        283, 346
      and housing 168–9, 186, 235
mills/mill communities 101, 102
Milton Ernest Hall (Bedfordshire)
   354–6, *355,* 415
Milton (Oxfordshire) 66–8, *67,* 98,
   102
mining industry 13, 101, 127, 128
mission chapels 45, 197
missionary colleges 237, 290, 294
missionary societies *125,* 155
missionary work 19, 36, 41, 155, 172,
   181, 290, 291–2
Moberly, George 293
model farms 358–360
model housing 64, 94, 177, 356–8
Monro, Edward 45–7, 361
Moore, William Cameron 101
Moorhouse, James 222
morality and architecture 7, 82, 96, 101
Morris, James 7
Morris, William 88, 105, 106, 107n12,
   363
mosaics 136, 143, 144, 146, 188, 227,
   244, 287
      Salviati glass 183, 256
Moultrie, John 96, 222, 284
Müller, Max 318
murals 143, 144, 146, *146,* 147, 151, 205,
   344, 415, 416
Murray, John 284
Murray Upper Grade School, Rugby
   (Warwickshire) 284–5, *285*
Muthesius, Hermann 147, 148, *149,*
   256

Nairn, Ian 8
National schools 65, 85–7, 89, 100, 101,
   173
   see also All Saints' National School

Neale, John Mason 21, 23, 34, 96, 415
'Necessity of Modernism, The'
    (Coleridge) 26n13, 61, 95
Nelson, Earl 45, 65
Nelson, Lady 65, 66
New Brunswick (Canada) *see* Christ
    Church, Fredericton
New South Wales (Australia) 24
new towns 52, 98, 186, 233–4, 235, 237
New Zealand 24
Newbury (Berkshire) *see* St John the
    Evangelist
Newman, John Henry 387
Newton, Alfred (photographer) *49*
Nightingale, Florence 20, 200, 298,
    299, 300
Norman architecture 25, 66, 123, 128,
    382, 408, 409
Norris, Joseph (builder) 68, 297, 388

Ogbourne St Andrew (Wiltshire) 52–4
    parsonage 53–4, *53*
Otley, William Young 391
Otmoor (Oxfordshire) 104
Ottery St Mary (Devon) 25, 52, *398–407*
    Coleridge memorial chapel *398–9*
    parish church 386, 387, 391, *398–9*
    see also Heath's Court
Oxford 8, 345
    Florey Building 9
Oxford Architectural Society 23, 25
Oxford University 47, 276, 314
    and modern studies 319
    see also Balliol College Chapel; Keble
        College; Merton College

Paddington (London) 386, 387
pagan traditions 98
Paris (France) 12, 26, 143
Parnell, Joseph (builder) 222, 287, 296,
    321, 336
Parochialia (Sandford) 52
parsonages *see* vicarages/parsonages
Patteson, John Coleridge 180–181
Pearson, John Loughborough 195, 230
Peel, Robert 59
Pembroke College, Cambridge 64
Penarth (Wales) 101, 199–200, *200,
    209–12*
Penny, Edward 123
Perpendicular style 121, 135, 224, 276
Perry, Thomas Walter 135
Perth (Scotland) 33, 229–230
    see also St Ninian's
Pevsner, Nikolaus 9
Phillpotts, Henry 181, 182
Pickering, Vale of (Yorkshire) 58, 61
Piero della Francesca 146
Playfair, Lyon 250
plumbing 54, 202

Plymouth (Devon) 14, 408
Poe, Edgar Allan 173
poetry 96, 121
Pollington (Yorkshire) 22, 61, *62*, 66,
    78, 80
Poole & Sons (tilers) 146
Portland stone/cement 136, 378
Portsmouth (Hampshire) 9, 242
positivist movement 87, 278, 356–7, 358
Poulton (Wiltshire) 89–91
    St Michael's Church 89–91
    school 89, 91, *91*
poverty 19, 20, 21, 28, 33, 34, 89, 200
    and churches 106–7, 130, 151, 152,
        153, 171, 203, 233, 234, 396
    and education 17, 44
    and relief 194–5
    and slums 171, 172
    see also under London
Preedy, Frederick 151, 179
Pugin, Augustus Welby Northmore 17,
    21, 22, 52, 151, 269, 314, 408, 409
Pugin, Edward Welby 269
Pusey, Edward Bouverie 17, 142, 143,
    172, 293, 334, 344, 408

quarries 35, 57, 59, 127, 169, 180, 185,
    227, 354
    Lias (Rugby) 250
Queen's Gate, South Kensington
    (London) 203, 206, *207*, 234, 242

Radical movement 58, 152–3
rag-stone 14, 68, 239
railways 59, 60, 68, 121, 233, 235, 241,
    355
    and leisure resorts 179, 180, 186, 188
Rainatratra (builder) 296
Ramsden family 168
Ramsden, Isabella 168–9
Ramsden, John William 168, 170
rationalism 198, 268, 278
Ravenna (Italy) 25, 205, 344, 413
Ravenswood (Berkshire) 102
rectories 47, 98–102, 176
    Alvechurch (Worcestershire) 98–101,
        99
    Bamford (Derbyshire) 102, *102*
    Beckley (Sussex) 88
    Landford (Wiltshire) 102, *103*
    Ogbourne St Andrew (Wiltshire)
        53–4, *53*
    Sessay (Yorkshire) 59
    see also vicarages
Regent's Park (London) 9, 358, 387
    St Saviour's Home, Osnaburgh Street
        17–19, *18*, 408, 409
Reid, John 54
reredos 66, 95, 105, 106, 136, 138, 172,
    187, 230, 234, 344, 412, 415, *415*

Restall, William (builder) 91
restorations of WB 9, 23, 25, 47, 59, 66,
    101, 180, 244, 358
    All Saints', Whiteparish (Wiltshire)
        130–132, *131, 132*
    Great Mongeham parish church
        (Kent) 123–5, *124*
    Heytesbury parish church
        (Wiltshire) 132–5, *133, 134*
    Keble College, Oxford 338–9
    Merton College chapel, Oxford
        169–170, 314, 318
    opposition to 125
    Ottery St Mary's (Devon) 386, 387,
        391, *398–9*
    parish churches 121–8, 130–139
    St Bega's, Brigham (Cumbria)
        127–8, *128*
    St John the Baptist, Hellidon
        (Northamptonshire) 47, *47*, *49*,
        359
    St Mary the Virgin, Ardleigh
        (Essex) 135–9, *137, 138, 139*
    St Michael's, Lamplugh (Cumbria)
        128–9, *129*
    Wavendon parish church
        (Buckinghamshire) 120
Rhodes, Matthew 171
RIBA (Royal Institute of British
    Architects) 8, 26, 201, 224, 254
Ricardo, Halsey 8, 25, 129, 385, 411
Richards, William Upton 142, 146
Richardson, Henry Hobson 25, 206,
    207n15
Rievaulx (Yorkshire) 26, 222
Rochester Cathedral (Kent) 414, *414*
Roman Catholic Church 13, 171
Romanesque style 189, 294, 382, 409
Rome (Italy) 344
Romsey Abbey (Hampshire) 416, *417*
roods 52, 416, *417*
Rotherhithe (London) 9, 234, 241–2, *241*
Royal Albert Hall (London) 203
Royal Hampshire County Hospital,
    Winchester 16, 200–202, *201*
Rugby (Warwickshire)
    Murray Upper Grade School 284–5,
        285
    parish church 8, 221, 222–4, *223,
        224*, 225, 234
Rugby School 7, 8, 202, 222, 248–56,
    252, 253, 254, 259–67
    chapel 147, 248, 250, 251–2,
        254–6, *255, 256, 259–63*
    cricket pavilion 251, 259, 269
    Crimea window 248, 249
    New Big School 254, 270, 273–5,
        274, 275
    New Schools/science buildings
        250–254, *251, 259, 266–7*

preparatory school 269, *269*
quadrangle 249–250, *249, 251, 252, 260–265*
sports facilities 249, 268–270, *270*
telescope 269, 273
Temple Reading Room/Art Museum 270–273, *271, 272*
and town parish 283
rural life 44–54
and Church revival movement 44, 45, 51
and neglect of countryside 44, 49, 53
and revolts/riots 44, 52, 58
and village greens 68, 98, 179
and WB's housing *see under* domestic architecture
and WB's theory of national Church 51
see also country schools
Ruskin, John 9, 14, 146, 318, 344
Ruston (Yorkshire) 60

St Alban the Martyr, Holborn (London) 8, 57, 151–4, *152, 153, 164, 166–7,* 175, 195, 202
clergy house 154, *154, 165*
St Andrew's College, Harrow Weald (Greater London) 14, 45–7
conversion to housing 47
and Monro's funeral 46–7
Nursery 46
St Anne Bedehouses (Lincoln) *11,* 21–2, *22*
St Anne's, Dropmore (Buckinghamshire) 104, *104*
St Augustine's College (Canterbury) 12, 13, 14–17, *15,* 290–293, 334, 415
Coleridge Museum 292, *293*
expansion of 292–3
library 16, *16*
and missionaries 291–2
missionaries from 291–2
student lodgings *291,* 292, 334
students of 290–291
warden's house 292, *292*
St Augustine's, Penarth (Vale of Glamorgan) 101, 199–200, *200, 209–12*
St Augustine's, South Kensington (London) 202–6, *203, 204, 205, 206, 207*
site of 203–5, 207n13
St Augustin's, Bournemouth (Dorset) 189–190, *190*
St Barnabas, Rotherhithe (London) 9, 234, 241–2, *241*
St Bees Priory (Cumbria) 125–7, *126,* 293
New College Hall 126–7
St Bega's, Brigham (Cumbria) 127–8, *128*
St Clement's, Finsbury (London) 235, *235*

St Columba's College Chapel, Dublin (Ireland) *285,* 286–7, 296, *310–13,* 382
St Cross Church, Clayton (Manchester) *193,* 198–9, *199, 213–19*
St Cross Hospital (Winchester) 21, 25, 409
St Cuthbert's, Sessay (Yorkshire) 59, *71–3*
St David's Cathedral (Pembrokeshire) 25
St Dunstan's Abbey, Plymouth (Devon) 19–21, *20,* 408
St Edmund in Dunchurch, Thurlaston (Warwickshire) 52, *52*
St Giles-in-the-Fields (London) 413
St Helen's Tower, Wykeham (Yorkshire) 64, *64*
St James the Great, Waresley (Cambridgeshire) 64–5, *65, 66, 97,* 98
St James and St Anne, Alfington (Devon) 396, *406–7*
St James's, Baldersby (Yorkshire) *93,* 94–5, *97,* 105, *109–13,* 357, 358, 385
St John the Baptist, Chipping Barnet (London) 202, 221, 224–7, *225, 226,* 293
St John the Baptist, Hellidon (Northamptonshire) 47, *47, 49,* 359
St John the Baptist, Shottesbrooke (Berkshire) *23*
St John the Baptist's, Pollington (Yorkshire) 22, 61, *62, 78, 80*
St John the Evangelist, Clevedon (Somerset) 91, 188–9, *189*
St John the Evangelist, Dalton (Yorkshire) 98, 104, 105–6, *106,* 107, 107n12, *114–19,* 363
churchyard 96
St John the Evangelist, Hammersmith (London) 195, 197, *198*
St John the Evangelist, Newbury (Berkshire) 57, 195–7, *196, 197,* 202
Sunday school 195
St John's, Birkby (Yorkshire) 168–71, *169, 170, 171*
St Lawrence's, Alvechurch (Worcestershire) 101, 199
St Mark's, Dundela, Belfast 21, 202, 221–2, 227–9, *227, 228,* 412
St Mary Magdalene's, Enfield (London) 233, 238–41, *239, 240*
St Mary the Virgin, Ardleigh (Essex) 135–9, *137, 138, 139*
St Marychurch (Devon) 180
St Mary's, Beech Hill (Berkshire) 104, 106–7, *107*
St Mary's, Dartmouth Park (London) 234–5, *235*
St Mary's, Dover Castle (Kent) 244, *244*
St Mary's, Edmonton (London) 9, 235, 236–8, *237,* 245n8

St Mary's, Iffley (Oxfordshire) 408
St Mary's, Ottery St Mary (Devon) 391, *398–9*
St Mary's Snettisham (Norfolk) 28
St Matthew's, Ashford (Surrey) 68, *69*
St Matthias's, Stoke Newington (London) 173–6, *174,* 197, 235, 315
parsonage 175, 176, *176*
school 173, 175–6
St Michael's clergy house, Burleigh Street, Covent Garden (London) 154–5, *162*
St Michael's Home (Somerset) *see* Cheddar Hospital
St Michael's, Lamplugh (Cumbria) 128–9, *129*
St Michael's, Poulton (Wiltshire) 89–91
St Michael's, Weybridge (Surrey) 186–8, *187,* 190
St Michael's, Woolwich (Kent) 242–3, *242*
St Ninian's, Perth (Scotland) 14, 32–4, *32, 33,* 202, 231, 415
completion of 222, 229–230, *229*
St Paul's Cathedral (London) 237
St Paul's Cathedral, Melbourne (Australia) 202, 222, 230–232, *231,* 232n10
St Paul's, Hensall (Yorkshire) 22, 61, *63,* 66, *78, 81,* 190
St Paul's Missionary College (Madagascar) 294–6, *295*
St Peter's, Bont Goch (Wales) *43,* 104–5, *105*
St Peter's Cathedral, Adelaide (Australia) 202, 222, 230, 231, *231,* 232n10
St Saviour's, Coalpit Heath (Bristol) *55–7, 56,* 58, 98, 170, 415
St Saviour's Home, Regent's Park (London) 17–19, *18,* 57, 408, 409
St Thomas's, Leylands, Leeds (Yorkshire) 171–2, *172*
Saint-Pierre de Caen (France) 185
Salisbury Theological College (Wiltshire) 293–4, *294, 308–9*
Salmon, H.W. (photographer) *277, 278*
Salviati, Antonio 183, 256
Sandford, John 8, 52, 98–100, 101, 130, 144, 356
sandstone 33, 57, 64, 128, 132, 294
sanitary systems 18, 54, *242,* 243
see also toilets
Saturday Review 120, 224
Savage, William (photographer) *201*
Scamozzi, Vincenzo 413
schoolhouses 45, 51, 59, 64, 83–5, *83,* 88, 95
Bont Goch (Wales) 104–5

Tattershall (Lincolnshire) 85–7
Trumpington (Cambridgeshire) 83–5, *83*
schools *see* country schools; grammar schools; National schools; *and see specific schools*
Scotland 13, 26, 32, 98, 250, 286, 381
   see also College of the Holy Spirit; St Ninian's, Perth
Scott, George Gilbert 244, 249, 250, 252, 284, 408
   tomb of 413–14, *414*
Scott, John Haigh 87
Scott, Walter 121
screens 25, 37
   chancel 34, 57, 96, *106*
seaside resorts 177–86
   Bournemouth (Dorset) 189–190, *190*
   Clevedon (Somerset) 188–9, *189*
   see also Babbacombe; Hunstanton
Selby Abbey (Yorkshire) 29
Sellon, Priscilla Lydia 19, 21, 408
Sessay (Yorkshire) 59–60, 168
   cottages 59–60, *60*, 96
   St Cuthbert's church 59, *71–3*
   school/schoolhouse 59
Sewell, William 286, 287
Shaw Stewart, John Archibald 202
Shepherd, Thomas Hosmer (artist) 18, *18*
Shottesbrooke (Berkshire) *23*, 24, 28
Sibthorp, Richard Waldo 21
Siena (Italy) 254, 274
Sir Walter St John's School, Battersea (London) 282–3, 284
sisterhoods 17–21
   Plymouth 19–21, *20*, 408
   Regent's Park (London) 17–19, *18*
Sistine Chapel (Rome) 391
slate 21, 59, 105, 121, 134, 188–9, 195, 205, 272, 274, 279, 349
   Welsh 61, 321
slum churches 98, 171–2
Smith Carter (photographer) *171*
Smith, Samuel (photographer) *179*
social hygiene 82
socialist movement 152–3
Solomon, Temple of 182, 396
South Kensington (London) 202–6, *203*, *204*, *205*, *206*
   housing in 203–5
   Queen's Gate 203, 206, *207*, 234, 242
   see also St Augustine's
Southey, Robert 17
Southwell Minster (Nottinghamshire) 58
Speight, Edward Hall (photographer) *224*, 254, *254*, *257*
sports 46, 198, 199, 269–270

stained glass 16, 47, 125, 170, 225, 254, 255, 256, 316
Standidge & Co. (lithographer) *173*
Stanley, Arthur 346
Stanton, Arthur 153
Starey, Benjamin Helps 236, 356
Stephens & Barstow (builders) 279
Stewart & Woolf (photographers) *273*
Stoke Newington (London) 151, 197, 286
   see also St Matthias's
Stone, E.H. (photographer) *134*
Stratford-upon-Avon (Warwickshire) 23
Stuart, F.G.O. (photographer) *294*
Stuart Hardy, Evelyn (artist) *296*
suburbs 14, 47, 57, 94, 98, 221, 227, 239, 241, 358
   and country estates 361
Summerson, John 9
Swing Riots (1830) 44
Sydenham (Belfast) 227

Tait, Archibald 8, 151, 194, 203, 251, 361
Talbot, Edward 334–6, 346, 350n1
Tattershall (Lincolnshire) 85–7, *85*
Taunt, Henry William (photographer) 7, 195, *197*, *316*, 317, *317*, *318*, 339, *339*, *343*, *344*, *345*
Taylor, George Thomas (photographer) *31*
Temple, Frederick 8, 248–9, 250, 269, 278–9, 282
Temple Reading Room, Rugby 7
Tennyson, Alfred 44, 188, 268, 296, 388
Teversham (Cambridgeshire) 24, 225
Thompson, Paul 9
Thornburn, Dr (of Tadcastle) (photographer) *127*
Thorne, James 197
Thrupp, Frederick 386, 390–391
Thurlaston (Warwickshire) 52, *52*
tiles 14, 22, 23, 25, 57, 240, 244, 354, 386–7
   Minton 136, 355, 416
   mosaic 144, 146, 147, 188, 256, 287, 342, 359, 362
Tintern Abbey 151, 222
toilets 54, 251, 254, 347, 379
tombs 96, 97, 254, 317, 413–14, *414*
Topcliffe (Yorkshire) 94, 96, 105
Torcello (Italy) 25, 344, 386
Torry, Bishop 230
Tottenham (London) 233, 235–6, *236*
Tractarian movement 17, 32, 45
Treylan, John Charles 227
Trinity Church, Boston (Massachusetts, US) 206
Tritton, Henry 143
Trollope, Anthony 8, 195, 201, 232n2
Trumpington (Cambridgeshire), master's house at 83–5, *83*

tuberculosis 17, 376, 378
   treatment of *see* Cheddar Hospital
Tudor style 20, 225, 249, 292, *292*, 361
Turnbull, Elizabeth (Bertha) 408
Twells, Henry 189–190
Twells, Philip 239
Tyntesfield (Somerset) 340, 359, 376, 378

Upper Class School for Girls, Wantage (Oxfordshire) 283
urbanisation 19, 45, 194, 222

Valentine, James (photographer) 7, *25*, 40, *41*, *125*, 127, *189*, *197*
Valentine & Sons *see* Valentine, James
Varty, T. (artist) *29*
Veale, Henry (builder) 20
Venice (Italy) 144, 189, 205, 274, 413
   Torcello 25, 344, 386
Verona (Italy) 317
vicarages/parsonages 14, 45, 64, 95
   All Saint's, Wykeham (Yorkshire) 61, *74–5*
   'English House' style 176
   Hellidon and Catesby (Northamptonshire) 48, *48*
   Ogbourne St Andrew (Wiltshire) 53–4, *53*
   St Anne's, Dropmore (Buckinghamshire) 104, *104*
   St Matthias's, Stoke Newington (London) *175*, 176, *176*
   see also rectories
Victoria, Queen 220, 268
Victorian society
   and altruism/benevolent capital 87
   and Church revival 12–13
   countryside in *see* rural life
   and financial crisis (1873) 18
   and health/disease *see* disease
   middle class in *see* middle class
   poverty in *see* poverty
   rioting/violence in 44, 52, 58, 173, 235
   social change in 220–221
   urbanisation in 19, 45, 194, 222
   women in 17
   working-class movements in 12–13, 58, 152
village greens 68, 98, 179
village schools *see* country schools
Viollet-le-Duc, Eugène 26, 155

Walcot, William (artist) *154*
Wales *43*, 44, 101, 104–5, 199–200, *200*, *209–12*
Walford, Edward 151

Walsingham ('Miss') (photographer)
  396
Walter, J.W. 242–3
Wantage (Oxfordshire) 21, 52, 151, 282,
  283, 408
    grammar schools 282, 283
    parish church 413, *413*
War Office 243, 244, 296
Waresley (Cambridgeshire) 64–5, *65*,
  66, *97*, 98
water pumps *97*, 98, 151
Waterhouse, Alfred 360
Wavendon (Buckinghamshire) 120
Way We Live Now, The (Trollope) 195,
  221, 232n2
Webb, Benjamin 23, 25, 415
Webb, Philip 88, 106
Welch, Robert John (photographer)
  227
Welsh School (Ashford, Surrey) 68
Wesleyan chapels 29, 105
West Lavington (Sussex) 57–8, *58*, 82,
  415
West London District School (Ashford,
  Surrey) 68
West Pinchbeck (Lincolnshire) 61, 82
Weybridge (Surrey) 9, 186–8, *187*, 190
Whitehaven (Cumbria) 125–6
Whiteknights Park (Berkshire)
  360–361, *361*
    gate lodges 360, *370–371*
Whiteparish (Wiltshire) 130–132, *131*,
  132
Wills, Frank 28, 29
Wilmcote (Warwickshire) 14, 23
Wilson, Alexander 235, 236
Wilson, James M. 250
Wilson, James M. 273
Winchester (Hampshire) 200–202, *201*
  Church of the Cross 25, *25*
  Royal Hampshire County Hospital
    16, 200–202, *201*
  St Cross Hospital 21, 25
Winchester College 20, 276–8, *277*, 293
  Chapel 277–8, *278*
  Crimea Memorial Cloister *247*, 248,
    276
  Flint Court *303*
  Moberly Court/Library 277, *277*
  and William of Wykeham 276, 277,
    278
Windsor, Baroness 100, 101, 199
Winstanley, James Beaumont 60, 87,
  356–7, *358*
Woolston (Buckinghamshire) 54
Woolwich (Kent) 242–3, *242*
Wordsworth, John 127
Wordsworth, William 320, 394
working-class movements 12–13, 58, 152
Wyatt & Brandon 132, 391
Wykeham, William of 276, 277, 278

Wykeham (Yorkshire) 61–4, *64*, *74–5*, 82
  school/schoolhouse 64, 82

YMCA (Young Men's Christian
  Association) 220, 269
Yonge, Charlotte M. 8, 13, 376

First published in 2024 by Lund Humphries

Lund Humphries
Huckletree Shoreditch
Alphabeta Building
18 Finsbury Square
London EC2A 1AH
UK
www.lundhumphries.com

ISBN: 978-1-84822-371-4

A Cataloguing-in-Publication record for this book is available from the British Library

Unless stated otherwise, all illustrated buildings and drawings are by William Butterfield, the drawings being in ink and wash on paper.

Copy edited by Abigail Grater
Designed by Adrian Hunt
Set in Miller
Printed in Estonia

FRONTISPIECE:
All Saints' Church, Harrow Weald:
west elevation, 1890

FRONT COVER:
Temple Reading Room and Art Museum, Rugby School: north and west elevations, 1877 (detail)

BACK COVER:
Balliol College Chapel, Oxford: rebuilding – north and east elevations, *c*.1856 (detail)